TRUST-BASED LEADERSHIP™

MARINE CORPS LEADERSHIP CONCEPTS FOR TODAY'S BUSINESS LEADERS

Fidelis Leadership Group

Developing World Class Leaders

TRUST-BASED
LEADERSHIP™

Marine Corps Leadership Concepts
For Today's Business Leaders
Mike Ettore

Paperback ISBN: 978-0-9898229-4-7
Hardcover ISBN: 978-0-9898229-8-5
Ebook ISBN: 978-0-9898229-5-4

CONTENTS

Preface **11**
   Marine Corps Leadership Concepts. 12
   The Goal: World-Class Leader 15
   My Story. 18
   My Purpose 23
   Leadership Expert or Expert Leader? 25
   How to Use This Book 27

Section I: Marine Corps Leadership **31**
   Introduction: Marine Corps Leadership 32

Culture, Concepts, and Philosophies. **33**
   Chapter 1: Leadership is a Choice 34
   Chapter 2: Character 36
   Chapter 3: Accountability 38
   Chapter 4: Leadership by Example. 40
   Chapter 5: Servant Leadership 42
   Chapter 6: Self-Leadership 44
   Chapter 7: Zero Tolerance. 46
   Chapter 8: The Core Values. 48
   Chapter 9: Standards and Discipline 53
   Chapter 10: The Marine Mindset 57
   Chapter 11: Every Marine a Rifleman 68
   Chapter 12: Special Trust and Confidence 74
   Chapter 13: Teacher-Scholar 360°. 86
   Chapter 14: Speaking Truth to Power 97
   Chapter 15: Tribal Knowledge. 99
   Chapter 16: Defenders of the Culture 103
   Chapter 17: Leaders Eat Last. 105

Fundamentals and Techniques **107**
   Chapter 18: The 5 Laws of Leadership. 108
   Chapter 19: The 3 Main Responsibilities of a Leader. 110
   Chapter 20: The 5 Pillars of Leadership 120

Chapter 21: Leadership Traits 131
Chapter 22: Leadership Principles 143
Chapter 23: Delegation. 153
Chapter 24: Supervision. 159
Chapter 25: The 4 Indicators of Leadership 173
Chapter 26: Professional Reputation 177
Section I: Summary 186

Section II: Trust-Based Leadership™ **189**
Introduction: Trust-Based Leadership™. 190
Chapter 27: Trust 195
Chapter 28: Mission Tactics. 201
Chapter 29: Decentralized Command & Control 209
Chapter 30: Priority of Effort. 218
Chapter 31: Simplicity 221
Chapter 32: Standard Operating Procedures 227
Chapter 33: Common Operating Language 233
Chapter 34: Friction 235
Chapter 35: Detachment 243
Chapter 36: The Force Multiplier 249
Section II Summary 254

Section III: The Trust-Based Leader **257**
Introduction: The Trust-Based Leader. 258
Chapter 37: Character 263
Chapter 38: Accountability 270
Chapter 39: Courage. 276
Chapter 40: Bias for Action 283
Chapter 41: Thriving in Chaos 290
Chapter 42: Resilience 298
Chapter 43: Team Player 301
Chapter 44: Developing Leaders. 309
Chapter 45: Sharing Hardship. 319
Chapter 46: Lifelong Learner. 329
Chapter 47: Adaptability: Leadership Styles 337
Section III Summary 347

Section IV: Lessons Learned **385**
Introduction: Lessons Learned 386
Chapter 48: Leadership Development 388

Chapter 49: Leadership Tactics and Techniques. 393
Chapter 50: The Top 10 Reasons Leaders Succeed. 402
Chapter 51: The Top 10 Reasons Leaders Fail. 409
Chapter 52: Haters, Helpers, Critics, and Cowards 425

Section V: Leadership Articles **431**
Introduction: Leadership Articles 432
Chapter 53: On Self-Leadership 433
Chapter 54: On Servant Leadership. 440
Chapter 55: On Accountability. 447
Chapter 56: On Humility. 449
Chapter 57: I Had 3 Fathers. 453
Chapter 58: Ettore's Rules. 461
Chapter 59: Listen to Your Lance Corporals! 468
Chapter 60: Do Your Teammates Make Their Beds? 476
Chapter 61: The Marine Corps Trusted Me 485
Chapter 62: I Failed Twice That Day: Lessons for Leaders 489
Chapter 63: We've Always Done It This Way! 497
Chapter 64: Let Your Leaders Lead! 502
Chapter 65: 5 Leadership "Blind Spots". 506
Chapter 66: Having Tough Conversations. 512
Chapter 67: The Pursuit of Relevant Knowledge 519
Chapter 68: Taking Care of What's Precious. 524
Chapter 69: "The Voice". 528
Chapter 70: The Rolex Moment 531
Conclusion. 536
Acknowledgments 539
Notes and Sources
Endnotes. 550

This book is dedicated to leaders—the men and women
in the arena who strive valiantly to teach, train,
and inspire others to achieve great things.

THE MAN IN THE ARENA

"IT IS NOT THE CRITIC WHO COUNTS; NOT THE MAN WHO POINTS OUT HOW THE STRONG MAN STUMBLES, OR WHERE THE DOER OF DEEDS COULD HAVE DONE THEM BETTER. THE CREDIT BELONGS TO THE MAN WHO IS ACTUALLY IN THE ARENA, WHOSE FACE IS MARRED BY DUST AND SWEAT AND BLOOD; WHO STRIVES VALIANTLY; WHO ERRS, WHO COMES SHORT AGAIN AND AGAIN, BECAUSE THERE IS NO EFFORT WITHOUT ERROR AND SHORTCOMING; BUT WHO DOES ACTUALLY STRIVE TO DO THE DEEDS; WHO KNOWS GREAT ENTHUSIASMS, THE GREAT DEVOTIONS; WHO SPENDS HIMSELF IN A WORTHY CAUSE; WHO AT THE BEST KNOWS IN THE END THE TRIUMPH OF HIGH ACHIEVEMENT, AND WHO AT THE WORST, IF HE FAILS, AT LEAST FAILS WHILE DARING GREATLY, SO THAT HIS PLACE SHALL NEVER BE WITH THOSE COLD AND TIMID SOULS WHO NEITHER KNOW VICTORY NOR DEFEAT."

THEODORE ROOSEVELT

PREFACE

MARINE CORPS LEADERSHIP CONCEPTS

Can Marine Corps leadership concepts and techniques be used effectively by business leaders?

Yes, they can!

Now, I am quite sure that some people will be skeptical about the viability and applicability of Marine Corps leadership concepts in the business world. During the 20+ years that I've applied and taught these leadership lessons while serving as a business leader, there have always been some skeptics, on both the military and civilian sides of the equation.

Many civilians assume that the military, and the Marine Corps specifically, is strictly a rigid hierarchy and that its way of doing things cannot be effectively applied in business. In truth, the average Marine leader is much more flexible, agile-minded, and "business-ready" than the stereotypes promoted by Hollywood movies or the individuals who harbor (even if subconsciously) anti-military bias would have you believe.

I often explain to civilians that there is far more pushback among the leaders within Marine units than they might imagine. Marine leaders are trained to routinely solicit input and debate from trusted subordinates prior to making important decisions. And often, this leads to rather spirited and contentious debates among leaders with a wide-range of experience, rank, and responsibility. Commanders of highly-effective Marine units realize that the whole is greater than the sum of its parts. And, while there are exceptions, this type of collaboration is how the Marine Corps works in its purest sense.

For their part, many of my fellow Marines have privately expressed some concerns while contemplating retirement from the Corps, wondering how they would fit into the business world and whether they could apply the leadership skills they learned on active duty. My response is always to assure them that they'll do fine. "I lead civilians in the same way that I led Marines," I tell them. And when this statement elicits a doubtful look, I explain:

"Civilians are human beings, just like we are. And they will react to good or bad leadership just as Marines do. If you put a bad leader in front of them, they're going to underperform, shrivel up, mutiny, whatever. If you provide them with effective leadership, they will respond to it and excel. In this aspect, leading Marines and leading people in the business world are identical."

This is the key to understanding the leadership lessons I gained from my service in the Marine Corps that are contained in this book. In any environment, people are people and human nature reigns supreme. And good leadership is universally recognized as being good leadership.

While there are certainly some aspects of the Marine Corps that don't necessarily apply to the business world—such as very high standards of physical and mental toughness, the fact that Marines can't simply quit the Corps whenever they'd like to or jump ship to take a raise at another "company," and the fact that military decisions can often have life-or-death consequences—the leadership lessons featured in this book (and the leadership training and coaching that I conduct) aren't all that different from the curricula of many highly-respected institutions.

Whether a student trains at Harvard's Leadership Institute or one of the many other highly credible leadership schools, academies, courses, or seminars—and yes, even the Marine Corps' leadership program—many of the *fundamental* leadership concepts that are taught are nearly identical. All of these institutions or programs have evolved to identify a very similar core suite of concepts, principles, behaviors, and qualities that can enable leaders to effectively inspire, direct, and supervise their teams.

Beyond choosing a quality leadership curriculum, the key ingredient to becoming a World Class Leader is simply deciding to do it. Individuals must choose to begin their studies and follow through with commitment. I always emphasize to the men and women I coach that the onus is on them to take charge of their leadership journey. They need to expose themselves to environments and individuals that can help them achieve their goals, and they need to dedicate themselves to becoming an excellent leader.

I often tell them, "If you want to become a world-class athlete, choose parents with great genetics. If you want to become a world-class leader, commit to doing it and choose great role models, mentors, and coaches!"

"For the untrained, leadership is a school in which the tests are given before the lessons."

—Mike Ettore

THE GOAL: WORLD-CLASS LEADER

Before we go any further, I want to emphasize that my life's purpose is to help inspire people to become World-Class Leaders. And, because we'll be using the term "World Class" throughout this book, I want to ensure that everyone has a common interpretation of it:

"World Class: being of the highest caliber in the world…'She is a world–class athlete.'"—*The Merriam-Webster Dictionary*

I first became aware of this term in 1975, as I was reading an article that examined the results of a study of Olympic athletes. The research looked at competitors from various sports and dozens of countries around the world.

Among the many traits shared by these athletes, the vast majority of them had unsurprisingly inherited crucial physical attributes from their parents. It was common for endurance athletes to come from a bloodline that contained other endurance athletes, and the same results were found in gymnasts, weight-lifters, swimmers, and competitors from many of the Olympic sports.

The author acknowledged that resilience, training, and experience usually played a huge part in an individual attaining world-class status in his or her chosen sport. However, for sports which rewarded certain physical attributes—such as height for basketball players—he concluded that the vast majority of the very best athletes had won the "Genetic Lottery." The author more or less said, "If you want to be a world-class athlete, choose parents with great genetics."

As I was reading this article, I also happened to come across an article about leadership in a business magazine. The writer listed institutions and organizations that he believed had attained a world-class level in the sustained creation and development of leaders. Included in the list was the US Marine Corps. I was a young Marine corporal at the time and seeing the Corps mentioned in this article certainly got my attention, as did the piece's implication. While the research on Olympic athletes told me that I was never going to be a world-class runner because of my genetics, this article was telling me that world-class leadership was a skill that could be learned!

I reflected on my current status as a novice leader within an institution known for developing extraordinary leaders, and contemplated what I might achieve if I became a serious student of leadership. I realized that I was blessed to be living in an environment in which sound leadership was demonstrated by my leaders and more senior colleagues on a daily basis. I was surrounded by individuals who could help me become the type of leader my Marines deserved.

The immensity of this opportunity was humbling and exciting. It led to my resolution to learn everything I could about leadership and, hopefully, become a leader who met the high expectations of the Marine Corps.

I like to think that I achieved success as a leader in both the Marine Corps and my business career. But what I am most proud of are the leaders whom I've helped have their own "awakening" to become lifelong students of "The Art."

While teaching and mentoring these men and women, I always refer back to the term "world class" and what it means in relation to leadership. I assure them that whatever their specific situations may be in terms of their educational background, experience, the culture of the company they are working in, or the type of boss they are working for, they can become a good leader if they are willing to seek knowledge and resolve to lead their people well.

I also tell them that they can go well beyond what most people would deem to be a "good leader" and become a "World-Class Leader"—one admired and respected by the members of their team, department, company, and even across their entire profession and industry.

My experience is that once an individual truly believes this and decides to pursue leadership excellence, he or she usually begins to acquire these skills at an exponential rate. Even better, leadership is an art in which the artist can continue to improve for his or her entire life. With over forty years of leadership experience, my journey as a lifelong learner traveling along the path of leadership continues. At the age of 63, I'm still learning and consider myself a better leader than I was just a few years ago!

I believe that anyone with the desire to do so can become a World-Class Leader. I hope that this is—or will become—your goal, and I am committed to helping you achieve it!

"Business success is attained by decisive leadership demonstrated by men and women who are agile-minded, resilient, and able to adapt last week's plans to today's reality."

—Mike Ettore

My Story

Who is Mike Ettore and what makes him qualified to teach me about leadership?

This is a fair question, and as a way of answering it and other questions that readers may have, I have decided to include some information about my background, experience, and philosophies related to leadership at the beginning of this book.

I think it's best if readers learn a bit about me from both a personal and a professional perspective, and the biography page of my website gets it done efficiently. This is a high-level summary of my professional life, starting with my service in the Marine Corps and transitioning into my experience as a senior executive in Kforce and my current role as an executive leadership coach and developer of World-Class Leaders:

US Marine Corps

Mike enlisted in the US Marine Corps in 1974 and after completing boot camp and follow-on training, was assigned duties in infantry and associated units. He quickly demonstrated an aptitude for leadership and was promoted meritoriously (ahead of his peer group) on several occasions, which enabled him to be assigned to roles of greater scope and responsibility. In 1976, he volunteered for service as a Drill Instructor and upon successfully completing the rigorous training, Mike became the youngest Drill Instructor in the Marine Corps at the age of 20. He excelled in this role and helped lead and train several recruit platoons during the assignment.

In 1978, Mike decided to leave active duty and attend college, with the intention of returning to the Marine Corps as a commissioned officer upon graduation. He attended East Stroudsburg University, where he was also a member of the varsity wrestling team.

During the summer between his junior and senior years of college, Mike successfully completed Officer Candidates School, and upon obtaining his bachelor's degree in May of 1982, he was commissioned as a Second Lieutenant of Marines. He reported to The Basic School at Quantico, Virginia, and remained there until February of 1983, when he graduated from the Infantry Officer Course.

Mike served primarily in Infantry and associated units throughout his career as a commissioned officer. He served as a commander during several combat operations and developed a reputation as a decisive and highly effective combat leader. Mike received numerous awards and decorations during his career, including the Bronze Star Medal for Valor (with Gold Star denoting 2nd award) and the Combat Action Ribbon (with two Gold Stars denoting 2nd and 3rd awards).

Mike is also the 1992 recipient of the Leftwich Trophy, which is awarded annually to recognize one Marine Corps Captain who "... *best exemplifies outstanding leadership within the Ground Combat Arms community... is recognized by his seniors, contemporaries, and subordinates, as the officer who most exemplifies outstanding leadership... demonstrates the ideals of courage, resourcefulness, perseverance, and concern for the well-being of our Corps and his enlisted Marines... made an outstanding contribution to the development of esprit de corps and loyalty within the unit in which he serves and through personal example, set the standards that all other officers seek to emulate."*

During his military career, Mike continued to pursue educational opportunities and earned Master's degrees in Business Administration and Management.

In 1998, after 24 years of honorable service, Mike retired from the Marine Corps.

Kforce

Mike joined Kforce (NASDAQ:KFRC) in 1999 and initially served as the Director of Leadership Development. In this capacity, he designed and implemented a six-month Leadership Development Program (LDP) that identified, selected and trained high-potential internal and external leadership candidates for eventual assignment to leadership roles within the company. Many of the external LDP candidates had recently completed their service in various branches of the armed forces, which ultimately resulted in several dozen military veterans serving in key leadership roles in the company's field offices and in various corporate support organizations.

Several months after the LDP became fully operational, Mike was promoted to the role of Vice President of Operations. Retaining responsibility for the LDP, he was also charged with organizing and synchronizing the company-wide effort to streamline and standardize various field and corporate operational and technical policies, procedures, and systems. During this period of time, he was also responsible for creating the Training Department and a Knowledge Management cell—a function that was relatively new to the business world at that time—which captured, organized, and disseminated the company's intellectual capital and "best practices" throughout the sales force and various corporate support functions.

In 2001, despite having no formal education or previous experience in information technology, Mike was assigned duties as the Chief Information Officer. In addition to the other departments and functions mentioned previously, he was now responsible for the company's internal Information Technology (IT) department and its entire technology infrastructure. The IT department had, for various reasons, struggled during the previous several years, which resulted in technical platform unreliability and inefficiency. These shortcomings negatively affected revenue generation as well as team and company morale.

As Mike and his team members began making progress toward improving the operational effectiveness of the IT department, it became obvious that the company lacked a cohesive method of establishing, prioritizing, coordinating, and implementing enterprise-level initiatives. To remedy this, Mike sought and was granted permission by the Chief Executive Officer to establish a Program Management Office (PMO) that would be charged with standardizing and implementing program and project management policies, processes, and methodologies.

Over time, the PMO became the source for guidance, documentation, and metrics related to the practices involved in managing and implementing various strategic-level projects within Kforce, including the rapid and complete integration of several staffing companies that had been acquired. The PMO quickly became an effective strategic management tool that kept senior executives and other leaders informed of the status of the company's suite of enterprise-level programs and projects and enabled the effective synchronization of resources toward achieving the company's stated objectives.

Mike was promoted to Chief Services Officer and became one of Kforce's named executive officers in 2004. While serving as one of the company's most senior executives, he was responsible for the majority of its corporate support departments and functions, including Human Resources, Information Technology, the Program Management Office, Marketing and Internet Operations/Social Media, Procurement, Corporate Real Estate, and Kforce's domestic and Manila-based Financial Shared Services teams. He also served as the executive sponsor for strategic planning and most of the logistical activities associated with the integration of acquired companies and the divestiture of organic business units.

Mike retired from Kforce on November 1st, 2013 after nearly 15 years of service with the company.

Fidelis Leadership Group

Throughout his military and business careers, Mike was consistently recognized for his ability to assemble, train, and lead teams that consistently produced outstanding results in dynamic and challenging environments. Much of his success in the Marine Corps and at Kforce was the result of his willingness to invest a great amount of time and energy in the mentoring and development of other leaders.

After he retired from Kforce, Mike decided to continue his lifelong passion for the pursuit of leadership excellence and helping others maximize their leadership potential. He founded Fidelis Leadership Group for the sole purpose of sharing his leadership experiences and helping other executives reflect on the challenges facing them, learn new skills, and develop into World-Class Leaders.

Mike brings a wealth of practical, real-life leadership expertise and presence to every coaching engagement. His coaching perspective is highly informed and business-oriented, meshing more than 40 years of first-hand leadership experience with a pragmatic, down-to-earth philosophy that helps senior leaders become more effective by developing and refining their leadership skills. Individual executives, teams, and organizations turn to Mike to serve as a catalyst that accelerates change and achieves positive results.

MY PURPOSE

I wrote the words on the "My Purpose" page of my website in the hope that others will be able to quickly understand that leadership is the love of my life—and that I have a true passion for helping others develop and prosper as leaders.

From my website:

"To earn immortality, a man should...

- Have a child

- Plant a tree

- Build a house

- Write a book."

Variations of this quote have been attributed to various individuals such as Pythagoras, Picasso, Jose Marti, and the Talmud.

I love this quote and all that it implies. I have modified it for personal use by adding an additional bullet point:

- Develop exceptional leaders who can develop the next generation of exceptional leaders.

At this point in my life, my sole purpose is to pass on the leadership lessons I've learned on the battlefield and in the boardroom to those who will lead others long after my time on this earth has passed.

On the back of my business card is a quote from a prominent Greek statesman:

'What you leave behind is not what is engraved in stone monuments, but what is woven into the lives of others.'—Pericles, 450 B.C.

I will leave behind exceptional leaders!"

These words come from my heart and may help you understand why I have dedicated my life to teaching, training, and developing World-Class Leaders!

"Being a leader is not something you do, <u>it is who you are</u>."

—Mike Ettore

LEADERSHIP EXPERT OR EXPERT LEADER?

I am not a *"Leadership Expert."*

I respectfully reserve this title for those who've spent many years formally studying, researching, and writing on the topic. In my opinion, the majority of today's more well-known *leadership thought leaders* fit into this category—they have often spent decades in academic and scientific environments, conducting research, and, quite often, writing books or producing new leadership philosophies and methods. I've read and studied much of their work and I think most of it is excellent and can help people become better leaders.

That said, I've noticed that some of today's premier leadership authorities—the "gurus," if you will—lack significant (or any) time actually serving as leaders, especially in the senior leadership roles they tend to focus on.

I'm not dismissing or demeaning these leadership experts or their work in any way. I think many of them add tremendous value to the body of knowledge associated with leadership, and I know that I am a better leader for having studied their work. I'm simply pointing out that a surprisingly large number of experts apparently have very limited experience actually serving as leaders—and I think this is something others should keep in mind.

I am an *"Expert Leader."*

While I have earned graduate degrees in business administration and management, I have not earned a doctoral degree as have many well-known *leadership experts*. What I do possess is over 40 years of practical "hands-on, in-the-trenches" experience in leadership roles of increasing scope and responsibility in a wide range of environments.

My Marine Corps leadership experience ranges from being an 18-year-old corporal in charge of a squad of 12 Marines—including several "salty" combat veterans of the Vietnam conflict, many of whom were as much as ten years older than I was—to being a 20-year-old Marine drill instructor charged with training new recruits, and, ultimately, service as a commissioned officer with extensive experience organizing, training, and leading infantry units in both peacetime and combat environments. I also had the good fortune to serve as a leadership instructor at The Basic School, which is located at Quantico, Virginia and where all newly commissioned Marine Corps officers are trained prior to entering their respective occupational specialties and units.

My experience as a business leader ranges from initially serving at the Director level, then quickly being promoted to several roles at the Vice President level, and ultimately, appointment as a C-level executive and Named Executive Officer for a large publicly-traded company. In these roles, especially at the C-level, I was often the senior leader in charge of critical operations and functions that supported the company's field offices and revenue-generating activities.

Simply stated, while I do not consider myself a *leadership expert*, I do consider myself to be an *expert leader*. Even better, I have a passion for and long history of success at helping others become expert leaders!

If asked to boil it all down to a single sentence for a prospective client, I'd say:

"I'm a very good leader, but I'm an *exceptional* developer of leaders!"

"There's no expiration date
on a leader's duty to learn."

—Mike Ettore

HOW TO USE THIS BOOK

The lessons in this book reflect how, while serving as an executive leadership coach, I teach, train, and coach business leaders in the effective application of what I refer to as the Trust-Based Leadership™ model.

The leadership model is based on my experience studying, practicing, and teaching the science and art of leadership in both the Marine Corps and the corporate arena. While I achieved significant success as a senior executive in Corporate America, there can be no doubt that much of this success is rooted in my Marine Corps background.

As such, this book is based upon the fundamental philosophies, concepts, principles, and techniques of Marine Corps leadership training and development—and how I effectively adapted and applied them while serving in business leadership roles.

The book is structured in five sections, as shown below:

- Section I - Marine Corps Leadership

- Section II - Trust-Based Leadership™

- Section III - The Trust-Based Leader

- Section IV - Lessons Learned

- Section V - Leadership Articles

This book is a training manual. I want to *teach* you how to become a World-Class Leader, not merely present information for you to consider, forget, and move on with your life. As such, I often repeat elements to emphasize the importance of fundamental leadership concepts and ensure that readers learn and remember them. Some chapters are short and quickly explain key concepts. Others are long, featuring practical examples and additional context from the business and military worlds. This repetition and variation are used to drive the lessons home and make them stick.

Section I – Marine Corps Leadership:

This section explains the major philosophies, concepts, and principles associated with Marine Corps leadership. There is a heavy emphasis on the fundamental and time-tested aspects of the *Science of Leadership* taught to all aspiring Marine leaders. This approach must be fully understood and acted upon if one aspires to become effective at utilizing the many tactics and techniques associated with the *Art of Leadership.*

Section II – Trust-Based Leadership™:

Since I retired from the Marine Corps in 1998, I've effectively adapted and employed Marine Corps leadership concepts in the business world, and I've helped many other business leaders do the same. This experience has resulted in the *Trust-Based Leadership™* model. It is the foundation of all of the leadership training, coaching, speaking, and writing that I do under the auspices of my company, Fidelis Leadership Group. Topics covered in this section include the major *enabling philosophies and operating concepts* associated with the Trust-Based Leadership™ model.

Section III – The Trust-Based Leader:

In addition to relying heavily on several bedrock philosophies and operating concepts, the Trust-Based Leadership™ model requires a certain *type* of leader for it to be successfully implemented and sustained. Some of the individual leadership qualities and traits covered in previous sections will be discussed in greater detail, along with additional elements that are essential to effectively training and developing *Trust-Based Leaders.*

Section IV – Lessons Learned:

This section contains select stories and anecdotes that will convey some of the major leadership lessons I have learned over decades of practicing, teaching and coaching various elements of the *Science* and *Art of Leadership.* All of the content in this section builds upon and reinforces the lessons that are taught in previous sections.

Section V – Leadership Articles:

The articles in this section provide real-world examples of how various aspects of Trust-Based Leadership™ have been applied in the business world. Based upon my personal experiences and written in a style that business leaders at all levels will be able to relate to, the pieces enable readers to better understand how they can adopt and effectively utilize the Trust-Based Leadership™ model in their unique environments.

I always tell my clients, "I don't claim to have the answers to all of your leadership issues, but I'm sure that I have some of them. Many of these lessons were expensive, painful and embarrassing while I learned them."

—Mike Ettore

MARINE CORPS RANK STRUCTURE

Enlisted

E-1 Private	E-2 Private First Class	E-3 Lance Corporal	E-4 Corporal	E-5 Sergeant	E-6 Staff Sergeant

E-7 Gunnery Sergeant	E-8 Master Sergeant	E-8 First Sergeant	E-9 Master Gunnery Sergeant	E-9 Sergeant Major	E-9 Sergeant Major of the Marine Corps

Warrant Officers

WO1 Warrant Officer 1	CWO2 Chief Warrant Officer 2	CWO3 Chief Warrant Officer 3	CWO4 Chief Warrant Officer 4	CWO5 Chief Warrant Officer 5	CWO2-5 Marine Gunner

Commissioned Officers

O-1 Second Lieutenant	O-2 First Lieutenant	O-3 Captain	O-4 Major	O-5 Lieutenant Colonel

O-6 Colonel	O-7 Brigadier General	O-8 Major General	O-9 Lieutenant General	O-10 General

Section I:

MARINE CORPS LEADERSHIP

Introduction:

MARINE CORPS LEADERSHIP

The intent of this section is to provide readers with a thorough, albeit high-level, understanding of the Marine Corps, and how Marines think about the Corps as a whole, leadership, and the development of leaders. It will enable readers to better understand some of the tangible and intangible concepts covered in subsequent sections of this book.

To that end, this section explains the major philosophies, concepts, and principles associated with Marine Corps leadership. There is a heavy emphasis on the fundamental and time-tested aspects of the *Science of Leadership* taught to all aspiring Marine leaders. This approach must be fully understood and acted upon if one aspires to become effective at utilizing the many tactics and techniques associated with the *Art of Leadership.*

CULTURE, CONCEPTS, AND PHILOSOPHIES

Chapter 1

LEADERSHIP IS A CHOICE

Leadership, in its purest and noblest form, is always associated with an individual choosing to be responsible for the successful accomplishment of an organization's mission and the welfare of its people and their personal and professional aspirations. Simply put, there's a huge difference between being in a leadership role and actually being a leader.

Despite the Marine Corps' high standards and appropriate checks and balances, there are still instances in which individuals are granted promotions, given authority, and are assigned to prestigious roles and assignments even though they do not deserve them—and in some cases, when they don't even desire them! The business world is no different, with the exception being that in certain situations—such as in a family-owned business—individuals often inherit leadership roles.

The weight of leadership can sometimes feel like a crushing burden. But it can also be one of the most rewarding things a person can do during his or her life. Leading others is an incredible privilege and one that I believe is very much like the responsibility of parents entrusted with the safety, nurturing, and development of their children into moral, ethical, and productive adults.

Personally, I have found the great responsibilities and expectations associated with serving as a leader to be an almost indescribable honor; one that I can honestly say is not only something that I am passionate about, it is my very reason for being!

I made the choice in 1975, as a young Marine Corps corporal. I wanted to become the very best leader possible and I was willing to commit to doing whatever necessary, for as long as necessary, to achieve this goal. If you've also decided to become the best leader that you can possibly be, I applaud your choice. And I am committed to doing everything I can to help you achieve your goal!

"I'm a Marine. I'll always be one. I joined the U.S. Marine Corps during the Vietnam War, where I received the Combat Action Ribbon, Vietnamese Cross of Gallantry, and a Purple Heart Medal. Thanks to the Marines, I was able to enroll at the University of Baltimore where I received my BS in accounting. Every day I use the lessons and discipline I learned in the Marine Corps. I absolutely would not be where I am today without the experiences I had in the Marine Corps."

—Bob Parsons, Founder of GoDaddy, PXG, and the Bob & Renee Parsons Foundation

Chapter 2

CHARACTER

Leadership by example is one of the fundamental tenets of Marine Corp leadership doctrine. Marine leaders are taught that they are expected to lead by example in all that they say and do.

No aspect of this is more important than a leader's *individual character*. Marines are taught that for any individual of any rank to be worthy of being respected enough to be emulated and followed by others, he or she must first and foremost be a *"Person of Character."*

Marine leaders, because of the ethos by which they live, are trusted by *their* leaders to make sound, ethical decisions—even in the absence of orders or guidance. It is this absolute, unspoken *special trust and confidence* in each other that defines the ideal character of Marine leaders.

The rigorous training of Marine-officer candidates and young, enlisted leaders is the first step in developing and harnessing this character, with great emphasis placed on the Core Values: Honor, Courage, and Commitment. Marine leaders are taught that they must commit to constantly seek self-improvement and strive to achieve excellence in all aspects of their role as leaders. They must also be dedicated to the team and do everything possible to make their unit successful. This means caring for their teammates as much if not more than they care about themselves.

In the Marine Corps, everyone is of value regardless of race, national origin, religion, or gender. Leaders are expected to uphold this critical element of the Marine Corps' culture and also work to improve the character, intellectual development, combat readiness, and quality of life for the Marines whom they are privileged to lead.

Application to Business

History is full of examples in which companies helmed by leaders who possess impeccable character consistently achieve success in environments and conditions that seem insurmountable to many of their competitors. Likewise, there are countless examples of situations in which companies have failed—many to the point of having to close their doors and cease business operations—due to leadership failures stemming from the flawed character of one or more leaders.

Even if a company manages to weather a catastrophic event or somehow survive despite poor business results, its failures are often broadcast for all to see on various news shows and social media platforms. It seems that rarely a day passes without a story conveying gaudy details about the failures of well-known business leaders; failures that are clearly linked to flaws in their character, associated indiscretions, and poor judgement.

Because the stakes are so high, I have found that the development of leaders of character is a major priority within companies that have been exceptionally successful over the long haul. The senior executives in these organizations enthusiastically commit significant resources toward the selection, training, and continuous development of principled, ethical leaders who are, first and foremost, men and women of character. In this regard, there is much that leaders in all types of companies can learn from how the Marine Corps nurtures and develops leaders.

Its staunch emphasis on character as the fundamental component of effective leadership may seem quaint or unrealistic to those outside the the Marine Corps, but this fundamental philosophy has also proven to be quite effective in the business world. *A company's success or failure is always determined by the quality of its leadership team*. And it's an unassailable fact that the quality of the individual leaders on that team is always determined by their individual character.

Chapter 3

ACCOUNTABILITY

Accountability is the cornerstone of Marine Corps leadership. It is the reckoning wherein a leader answers for his actions and those of his unit and accepts the consequences, good or bad. One of the first lessons that Marine leaders are taught is that *a leader is responsible for everything his or her unit does or fails to do*.

President Harry S. Truman had a sign on his desk that read: "The Buck Stops Here." This simple statement affirmed that he accepted accountability for everything that happened or failed to happen while he served as our nation's leader. I've actually heard Marine leadership instructors cite Truman's quote while teaching new Marine leaders about the critical concept of accountability. Without question, Marine leaders at all levels know that "The Buck Stops Here" approach to accountability is an *institutional standard* that they will be held to every day and in every way.

Marines are taught two different variants of the term accountability: one deals with the physical responsibility for various types of assets (facilities, equipment, funds, etc.) and the other, as emphasized in the formal definition, is specific to one's actions and behaviors. In addition to being responsible for their own actions, Marine leaders are held accountable for the actions of all Marines within their chain of command; they are responsible for everything that does or does not happen within their units. The Trust-Based Leadership™ model that I have developed applies the same two variants of accountability to business leaders.

Application to Business

To be successful over the long-term, companies must have leaders who hold themselves and those they lead accountable. Accountability is an exceptionally important trait in the Trust-Based Leadership™ model; and without it, leaders who possess all of the other desired traits such as character, integrity, a bias for action, etc., will eventually fall short. In this model, a leader's long-term success relies on the willingness to take complete ownership of everything, good and bad, that happens within the organization he or she is privileged to lead.

I've found that Marine-like accountability does exist in some companies today, but, unfortunately, as the exception rather than the rule. This is problematic because even the most intelligent, innovative, hard-working, and well-intentioned leaders will ultimately fail to meet their assigned objectives in a company that lacks a culture of accountability. They will also fail at other aspects of leadership such as developing their teams, attracting and retaining top talent, optimizing operational effectiveness and efficiency, and more.

When business leaders are taught that they will be held accountable for all that their teams do or fail to do, they typically rise to this high standard and willingly take responsibility for the consequences of their decisions. Unsurprisingly, good things seem to happen in and for teams led by leaders who hold themselves and others to this high standard!

"Accountable leaders" do not make excuses, nor do they blame others when things go wrong. Rather, they focus on getting things back on track—they're problem solvers, first and foremost. And even better, they strive to develop other leaders who are capable of doing the same!

During my extensive business career, I have found that accountable leaders tend to create and sustain a *culture* of accountability that helps their companies and teams excel in every way. Leaders like this are very often the driving force in these companies, and they typically are the deciding factor in whether an organization succeeds or fails. Again, there can be no long-term success for leaders or their teams without a high standard of accountability.

Chapter 4

LEADERSHIP BY EXAMPLE

The Marine Corps' approach to leadership rests on the simple premise that leaders will serve as role models for all other Marines; <u>they will lead by example in all they say and do</u>. This requires leaders to consistently demonstrate the character, core values, attitude, work ethic, resilience, and other traits they desire in and from their Marines.

This concept—*leadership by example*—is a time-tested, exceptionally important aspect of Marine leadership, to the point that it is firmly and irrevocably "embedded into the DNA" of the Corps. It is passed on from one generation of Marines to another, in the same manner as parents pass their genetics to their offspring, albeit by education, training, mentoring, and, of course, through the example set by leaders.

Marines are taught from their first day as recruits that they are expected to strive for excellence in all they do. They are constantly told by their leaders, *"Follow my example—observe what I say and do and use this to guide your own behavior."* Leaders are trained to reinforce statements such as these by ensuring they are visibly adhering to the same standards, exerting the same level of effort, and making the same sacrifices they are asking of their Marines.

This willingness to lead by example—to perform above and beyond the call of duty and share hardship, no matter how miserable or inconsequential the task—has a positive and contagious effect throughout all levels of Marine units. It inspires individual Marines to strive for excellence, and it creates undeniable credibility and respect for the leader—through his or her actions, not merely words.

As Goes the Leader, So Goes the Team—*Always!*

In addition to the constant emphasis on personal character, integrity, and other leadership traits and principles, Marine leaders are taught that their success as a leader really depends on their willingness to take the following three actions on a daily basis:

- Set the standards.

- Live the standards.

- Enforce the standards.

Great emphasis is placed upon the idea that they cannot be effective Marine leaders unless they approach each of these actions with equal vigor and apply them in an unquestionably fair manner toward every member of their team, regardless of title, tenure, or past accomplishments. Simply stated, individuals are taught that the only way to be successful and live up to the high expectations of a leader of Marines is to *Lead by Example—Always!*

"My four years in the Marine Corps left me with an indelible understanding of the value of leadership skills.

I do not believe I could have built FedEx without the skills I learned from the Marine Corps."

—Frederick W. Smith, Founder, Chairman, President, and CEO of FedEx

Chapter 5

SERVANT LEADERSHIP

The phrase "Servant Leadership" was coined by Robert K. Greenleaf. In his 1970 essay *"The Servant as Leader,"* Greenleaf explains how and why he came up with the idea of Servant Leadership, as well as what a Servant Leader should be. While I want to ensure that Mr. Greenleaf receives credit for coining the term, I also want readers to know that Marine leaders were practicing the concepts associated with *Servant Leadership* for many decades prior to him doing so![1]

Servant Leadership

Many people associate the term "World-Class Leader" with people who possess impressive titles like "president," "ambassador," "senator," "CEO," or "general." These people are serving in positions of significance and power, so they must be the "World-Class Leaders" we've been referring to, right?

Not necessarily.

In fact, the very best leaders are not always those serving in such roles, nor others who constantly try to catch everyone's attention with their skill or bravado. In many instances, the true leaders within an organization are the ones away from the spotlight and not residing in the executive suite. They are the leaders and influencers working doggedly to help their teams meet objectives and quietly finding ways to pitch in to accomplish the mission. These individuals exhibit the characteristics and traits associated with being a servant leader: they are more concerned with ensuring that everyone else is empowered and enabled to perform than worrying about whether they'll be personally recognized.

This is never more evident than in the Marine Corps, which explicitly teaches its leaders the importance of being a servant leader and how they can become one. That may sound a bit backwards to some people. There remains a common perception that leaders have earned the right to be served by others with lesser title or authority.

This is simply not true in any well-led organization. And it's certainly not true in the Marine Corps, where Marines learn that _leaders serve those being led, not vice-versa_. This concept is a key element of the Trust-Based Leadership™ model that you will learn about in subsequent chapters of this book. Leaders exist solely to serve and enable those whom they are privileged to lead.

Application to Business

Many of the best companies in the business world share the Marine Corps' emphasis on servant leadership. _Fortune_ magazine's annual list of the "100 Best Companies to Work For" is chock-full of companies that practice servant leadership. A 2011 review done by _Modern Servant Leader_ found that five of the top 10 companies on that year's list were identified as organizations that practice servant leadership.[2]

In all, the 17 servant-led companies in the top 100 had anywhere from 1,200 to 167,000 employees with revenues in the billions. I suspect that many of the other 83 companies also practice much of what's known as servant leadership, but simply don't formally recognize or state this in various documents that convey their company's vision, mission, culture, and leadership philosophies.

Contrary to popular belief, being a leader does not mean you have earned the right to simply boss people around and have them do things to make your life better. Being a leader isn't about prestige or controlling others, it's about supporting your teammates in any way possible. It is about providing the leadership, guidance, and resources to enable those who work with you to do the best job possible. It's about serving your team so that they can perform at their very best.

Leadership is always about service. Remember it and practice it.

Always!

Chapter 6

SELF-LEADERSHIP

Marine Corps leaders are taught that before they can lead others well by becoming servant leaders, they must learn how to lead themselves; they must practice the concept of *self-leadership*.

Self-leadership essentially equates to the leader practicing self-discipline in every aspect of his or her life. This includes taking care of one's health, seeking education and professional development, and maintaining personal and professional relationships. Self-leadership is what inspires individuals to take purposeful action to acquire, enhance, and sustain the character and inner-strength that are necessary for servant leadership. And that's essential to the Trust-Based Leadership™ model.

Self-leadership involves continuous reflection on and development of three aspects: *self-awareness, self-confidence*, and *self-belief*.

- **Self-awareness** is about defining and remaining true to your personal core values, and being vigilant about identifying anything that could potentially derail you from adhering to them.

- **Self-confidence** comes from understanding your strengths and weaknesses and how they can help or hinder your success—first, as an individual, and second, as a leader.

- **Self-belief** is knowing that your personal core values are sound and that you are following them, that your self-confidence is based on substance vs. image, and that you can effectively handle any challenge that may come your way.

First, Lead Yourself!

Leading yourself before you lead others might sound simple, but few people are able to hold themselves to this basic principle on a daily basis. In general, society does not nurture self-leadership. We are inhabitants of a world where pride and divisiveness have become common in the workplace as people fight for status. It has almost become second nature for people to be overly willful, arrogant, intolerant, and rigid in order to establish dominance within the pecking order. However, leaders with these traits are trouble, for they erode the spirit of the organization by reducing staff resolve and creating chaos.

The opposite is true of self-leaders. Self-leadership is a form of self-discipline and psychological development that relies upon humility, compassion, acceptance, and emotional intelligence when reacting to circumstances. To become a Trust-Based Leader, you must genuinely have the *heart of a servant*—but even this noble attribute will be rendered useless if you are unable or unwilling to first lead yourself!

"Self-Discipline > Imposed Discipline"

—Mike Ettore

Chapter 7

ZERO TOLERANCE

Marine leaders are taught to routinely delegate authority to other leaders and certain individuals within their teams. While doing so, they are encouraged to selectively delegate "stretch" missions and tasks that will challenge their teammates' leadership capability and capacity by requiring them to step out of their comfort zones in pursuit of success.

Marine leaders are also taught that they should expect that those being delegated to will make mistakes. Leaders must be patient as they teach and mentor their teammates, enabling them to learn from these mistakes as well as the things they've done well.

That said, there are some things that a Marine leader simply cannot tolerate. Marines must enforce consequences if they discover that one of their leaders or any Marine has done or said something that is among what I refer to as the *"Zero-Tolerance"* behaviors.

When I teach this concept to a company's leadership team, I typically convey it on a graphic that uses the names of the client company and the leaders of the company who are in the audience. In this example, I would be teaching the leadership team of Acme, Inc:

An Acme, Inc. leader will not tolerate:

- *Illegal, unethical, or unprofessional behavior*

- *Breaches of Acme's Core Values and Culture*

- *Racism, sexism, or other types of discrimination*

- *Sexual harassment and sexual assault*

- *Inappropriate behavior, jokes, or comments*

I literally replace "Marine Corps" with "Acme, Inc." when creating this slide for various presentations; such is the strong alignment between what are considered *Zero-Tolerance* behaviors in the Marine Corps and those in well-led companies.

When showing this particular slide to a group of business leaders, the ensuing discussion is always interesting to observe. The leaders discuss each of the behaviors listed on the graphic and typically come to a realization: they will need to have additional discussions to ensure that everyone is operating within a common understanding of what constitutes *Zero-Tolerance* behavior in their company.

This common framework is essential, given the severity of the consequences. What behaviors will be deemed to be so serious that a person committing them will be immediately terminated, and which of them may be appropriately handled with counseling and perhaps some lesser form of disciplinary action?

As you read this book, you will encounter many instances in which you, as a Trust-Based Leader, will be encouraged to be patient, understanding, and adopt a Teacher-Scholar 360° relationship with your teammates. All of these tools are important in the successful implementation of the Trust-Based Leadership™ model. But equally important is the complete understanding by everyone that there are some *"Zero-Tolerance"* behaviors that simply cannot be fixed, overlooked, or otherwise rationalized as being acceptable. Doing so will only serve to undermine the credibility of the leaders—and the organizations—who lack this moral courage.

Chapter 8

THE CORE VALUES

Semper Fidelis is a Latin phrase that means "always faithful." This phrase has been the official motto of the United States Marine Corps since 1883, and it (and all that it implies) plays a special role in the sustainment of the culture of the institution. From the very moment young recruits arrive at boot camp or Officer Candidates School, they are taught that being a Marine means being faithful to the Nation, the Corps, and to each other.

This fundamental lesson is continuously imparted to every Marine throughout their entry-level training, and it is solidified by exposure to the Core Values of the Marine Corps:

- Honor

- Courage

- Commitment

These Core Values serve as the basis of all Marine Corps leadership training and education.

Marines undergoing initial training are introduced to various concepts which influence their definition of character, their understanding of the Core Values, and their determination to embody them. Daily emphasis is placed on principles such as integrity, discipline, teamwork, duty, and *esprit de corps.*

They are taught that adherence to the Core Values means doing the right thing in the face of overwhelming adversity.

These Core Values and associated traits distinguish Marines as a special breed of warrior. This uniqueness is due in part to the pride and the fervor with which Marines adhere to them. Individuals are taught to be men and women of honor, following in the footsteps of many others who have gone before them. They are courageous people who look to the Core Values as a source of fortitude when it is needed, and are committed to behavior worthy of the hard-earned title "Marine." This is a very powerful force that unifies all Marines and imbues them with the confidence to face any obstacle or foe.

This ethos endures far beyond an individual's time in service to the nation. "Once a Marine, Always a Marine" means that even when they are no longer serving, Marines are expected to continue to uphold and live by these values.

The Core Values Defined

Various Marine Corps leadership training manuals contain this explanation of the Core Values, outlining their importance to the individual Marine and the continued success of the institution:

> *"Honor ... Courage ... Commitment ... Core Values instilled in every Marine. Instilling values is an integral part of making Marines and, as a component of readiness, is essential to winning battles. Our Core Values inculcation begins with the first contact a potential Marine has with a recruiter, is driven home from the very first eyeball-to-eyeball experience with a Drill Instructor at ... Recruit Training, and continues throughout the course of a Marine's career—be it 3 or 30 years. Semper Fidelis ... the Marines pledge to be always faithful to these values and to God, family, country, Corps. Our Core Values remain the very soul of our institution, underlying all that is best in Marines, and must continue to frame the way we live and act as Marines."*[3]

MCWP [Marine Corps Warfighting Publication] *6-11: Leading Marines* explains the Core Values, which were codified by General Carl E. Mundy Jr., the 30th Commandant of the Marine Corps: [4]

> Generation after generation of American men and women have given special meaning to the term United States Ma-

rine. They have done so by their performance on and off the battlefield. Feared by enemies, respected by allies, and loved by the American people, Marines are a "special breed." This reputation was gained and is maintained by a set of enduring Core Values. These values form the cornerstone, the bedrock, and the heart of our character. They are the guiding beliefs and principles that give us strength, influence our attitudes, and regulate our behavior. They bond our Marine Family into a total force that can meet any challenge.

HONOR: The bedrock of our character. The quality that guides Marines to exemplify the ultimate in ethical and moral behavior; never to lie, cheat, or steal; to abide by an uncompromising code of integrity; to respect human dignity; to have respect and concern for each other. The quality of maturity, dedication, trust, and dependability that commits Marines to act responsibly; to be accountable for actions; to fulfill obligations; and to hold others accountable for their actions.

COURAGE: The heart of our Core Values, courage is the mental, moral, and physical strength ingrained in Marines to carry them through the challenges of combat and the mastery of fear; to do what is right; to adhere to a higher standard of personal conduct; to lead by example, and to make tough decisions under stress and pressure. It is the inner strength that enables a Marine to take that extra step.

COMMITMENT: The spirit of determination and dedication within members of a force of arms that leads to professionalism and mastery of the art of war. It leads to the highest order of discipline for unit and self; it is the ingredient that enables 24-hour a day dedication to Corps and Country; pride; concern for others; and an unrelenting determination to achieve a standard of excellence in every endeavor. Commitment is the value that establishes the Marine as the warrior and citizen others strive to emulate.

Reaffirm these Core Values and ensure they guide your performance, behavior, and conduct every minute of every day.[5]

Why They Are Effective

Many Marines, including me, feel that the Core Values Program is very effective for two reasons. First, Core Values training begins on the first day of a recruit's entry-level training and it is fully integrated in various events, curricula, and discussions between recruits and their leaders. One of the major objectives of boot camp or Officer Candidates School (OCS) is to rapidly transform young, impressionable, diverse, and often self-centered individuals into team players who are part of an institution that is much more important than any one person.

The second reason the Core Values Program has been so effective is that real-life examples are used in formal and informal discussions during various phases of the training program. I've read several post-training surveys that indicate that the recruits and officer candidates do not feel that they are being brainwashed by this inculcation; they believe that they are learning how to accomplish missions or solve problems they will likely face after recruit training—by leveraging the combined effort and shared purpose of their fellow Marines.

Many readers will undoubtedly think to themselves, "This is not a new or novel concept. The creation of a list of values or guiding principles for an organization is common."

They are correct in this observation, of course. But unlike many other organizations, the Marine Corps is relentless in taking steps to ensure that every Marine knows, understands, and attempts to demonstrate its Core Values in all they say and do. Emphasis on these values is not simply lip-service. Marines really are taught that they will be expected to live them—not only during their time on active duty but for the rest of their lives!

In several of the following chapters, I will outline how the "Marine Mindset," the ethos of the institution, and other factors influence and guide everything that a Marine does throughout his or her career. It's important to understand, however, that the Core Values remain the basis of these additional elements. Honor, Courage, and Commitment are the foundation on which other values are placed.

When asked about the importance of the Core Values to the success of the individual Marine, General James T. Conway, the 34th Commandant of the Marine Corps, said this:

"The values of Honor, Courage, and Commitment—imprinted on their souls during recruit training and strengthened thereafter—mark a Marine's character for a lifetime." [6]

"In my last visit to the business school at Columbia University in New York, a member of the class asked me if I could tell them the class that I took in business school that best equipped me for the leadership responsibilities in a Fortune 100 company. And like you, I've learned that there are not many ways to give people bad news so I gave it to them directly just like you would, when I said that I did not learn about leadership in business school.

I learned about leadership when I was 18 years-old and first introduced to the United States Marine Corps, where leadership is not taught by a favored professor in a three-credit hour course. It is taught by every officer and every NCO in every minute and every hour of every day, in every action, every word, every deed, and every circumstance. And, in that experience, you are immersed in a culture of excellence that is built on a foundation of virtue and value."

—Robert J. Stevens, Chief Executive Officer of Lockheed Martin, and Marine Corps Veteran

Chapter 9

STANDARDS AND DISCIPLINE

Before he became America's first president, George Washington served as "General and Commander-in-Chief" of the nation's armed forces. While serving in this role, he once said, "Discipline is the soul of an Army. It makes small numbers formidable; procures success of the weak and esteem to all." [7]

Along a similar line of thinking, the ancient philosopher, Aristotle once wrote "We are what we repeatedly do. Excellence then is not an act but a habit... so then if we repeatedly practice high standards and discipline, and it is the creation of those habits that enable us to defeat a determined and audacious enemy." [8]

The traditions and culture of the Marine Corps are very much aligned with the statements made by General Washington and Aristotle; the Corps is an institution that has exacting standards, a high level of organizational discipline and a relentless pursuit of excellence.

Standards and discipline are typically referenced together because when applied in concert with one another, they have a significant impact on the success of both individual Marines and the Corps as a whole.

Marine Corps standards are the formal and detailed regulations, policies, and instructions that are taught, trained, enforced, and supervised by the leaders at all levels of the institution. These standards are the benchmark by which individual Marines and units are evaluated.

At the highest level, the concept of discipline is associated with the Marine Corps' Core Values and guiding philosophies; it is the state of good order, respect for authority, and obedience that is woven into the fabric of the institution.

At the individual level, discipline is characterized as a Marine's prompt, willing, and enthusiastic response to orders and compliance with established standards. At this level, the trait of self-discipline is the driving force behind the competence and success of individual Marines. It is this trait that enables a Marine to willingly do the right thing in a wide range of environments and situations.

The Marine Corps has existed for more than 244 years. The institution's collective experiences during this time have shown time and again that high standards and uncompromising discipline are the difference between success and defeat in battle, and the deciding factors in whether an individual Marine or unit is average or exceptional. Simply put, seasoned Marine leaders know that the units that are highly successful in combat are those that meet high standards and have strong enforcement of discipline at every level of the chain of command.

Enforcing standards and appropriate levels of discipline are key to *any* organization's success. Although this concept may seem simple, it is actually quite difficult to achieve on a consistent basis across a large, geographically dispersed organization like the Marine Corps. As always, the execution and supervision of this task is the responsibility of Marine leaders, especially the small-unit leaders of the Corps—the non-commissioned officers (NCOs), staff non-commissioned officers (SNCOs), and junior officers.

As previously mentioned, Marine leaders are taught that much of their success depends on their willingness to take the following three actions on a daily basis:
- Set the standards.
- Live the standards.
- Enforce the standards.

Maintaining high standards through rigorous personal and professional discipline is essential to creating an organization that performs consistently and in the most difficult of situations. It is the linchpin of the Marine Corps' record of battlefield success.

WHAT MAKES A MARINE?

Expert instruction. Hard work. Discipline. Practice. Pride. Competition. Teamwork. And the will to *be* a Marine. At boot camp, the will to *make* a Marine comes in the person of the Drill Instructor. Carefully selected and schooled by the Marine Corps, he is the man in charge of the project— and the project is in very good hands. The DI molds a group of about 75 assorted individuals into a platoon of Marines. As far as he is concerned it will be the best platoon at the recruit depot. And the 75 begin to work together for that goal. They pull, push, march together. Lift, run, shout together. Study, shoot, climb together. They silently pray together that they will be everything the Corps wants them to be—for that is what *they* want, and that is what they will achieve. After boot camp comes individual combat training, where basics skills are polished and Marine weaponry and tactics mastered. Future infantrymen become familiar with the artilleryman's job, and vice versa. And because every Marine is first a rifleman, even those who will go on to such specialties as aircraft mainte-nance or communications perfect their marksmanship and learn the basics of infantry combat. The United States Marine is schooled by the best trainers. Built into a complete man in body, mind and spirit. Trained how to assault an enemy. Trained to hold his ground against any odds. Trained to be a winner—in combat, and in life.

Marine Corps Recruiting Brochure - 1974

"Once a Marine, always a Marine."

Being a Marine is a state of mind.
It is an experience some have likened more
to a calling than a profession.

Being a Marine is not a job—not a pay check;
it is not an occupational specialty.
It is not male or female, majority or minority;
nor is it a rank insignia. Stars, bars, or chevrons
are only indicators of the responsibility
or authority we hold at a given time.

Rather, being a Marine comes from the eagle,
globe, and anchor that is tattooed on the soul
of every one of us who wears the Marine Corps
uniform. It is a searing mark in our innermost
being which comes after the rite of passage
through boot camp or Officer Candidates School
when a young man or woman is allowed for the
first time to say, "I'm a United States Marine."

And unlike physical or psychological scars, which,
over time, tend to heal and fade in intensity,
the eagle, globe, and anchor only grow more
defined—more intense—the longer
you are a Marine.

Source: Leading Marines – Marine Corps Warfighting Publication 6-11

Chapter 10

THE MARINE MINDSET

The science of Marine Corps leadership is comprised of many ingredients, but a key element is the Corps' universal culture and the mindset that this fosters in Marines. There are challenges to replicating an incredibly strong culture like this in the business world, as most companies simply don't have the benefits of history, lore, patriotism, and, in some instances, successive generations of family service that define and motivate Marines. While many recruits grow up wanting to be a Marine and even more come to revere the institution, there are few private sector employees that feel the same magnetic pull to work for a specific organization.

Nevertheless, some businesses can and do design strong cultures—and use them to develop leaders with an intense drive to succeed. Let's take a look at how the Marines create this mindset, while applying these lessons to the business world.

Although being a Marine means something different to each man or woman who has worn the uniform, those who serve believe that it's a *privilege*—not a *right*—to earn the title of Marine. This mindset doesn't happen by accident. It is the outcome of carefully-designed training and cultural immersion that achieve what very few other organizations can: A lifelong bond with comrades and the institution itself.

From the initial encounter with drill instructors at boot camp or Officer Candidates School until graduation and the bestowment of the hard-earned title, it is made clear that the long and arduous weeks of training and selection serve as a chance for young men and women to *prove* that they deserve the *opportunity* to join the ranks of the Marine Corps.

This simple concept sets the tone and expectations. It challenges the prospect to see how he or she compares to those who came before and it effectively shifts the focus from simply "having to pass" to "wanting to excel." Initial training instills in each recruit a sense of individual and collective pride, a deep work ethic, and a *can-do* attitude. These traits are the building blocks of the Marine Mindset.

The Marine Corps sets very high standards of integrity, discipline, and resilience for those who accept this challenge. Prior to entering boot camp, many young recruits have never been in an environment where accountability is a daily reality. Those who don't adapt and meet the standards wash out and are unceremoniously returned to civilian life. Others rise to the challenge and thrive. This form of social Darwinism has a cold, calculated purpose: It makes men and women into Marines who strengthen the institution and the nation it serves.

Another purpose of these high standards and the penalty for failing to meet them is that they establish the value of becoming a Marine. Just as currency backed by a bankrupt government is worthless, so is simply telling a recruit that it's a privilege to join an elite organization and then letting anyone in. Marines who pass this difficult test and earn the title leave their training with a sense of accomplishment, unshakable confidence, and a strong work ethic and devotion to duty, and these qualities are reinforced and continue to shape their performance throughout their careers.

And while all Marines learn that they belong to something that is much more important than any individual, Marine leaders (enlisted and officer alike) are taught that they have a special, hallowed responsibility. They are the stewards of the history, traditions, standards, and ultimately the health and survival of the Marine Corps. In order to consistently maintain the quality of those who serve in the Corps, Marine leaders must continuously and unapologetically enforce the high standards they have sworn to uphold.

These are the basic steps taken by the Marines Corps to ensure that young men and women from all walks of life are effectively transitioned from recruits into Marines:

- Instilling Core Values

- Setting Clear Standards

- Requiring the Pursuit of Excellence

- Pushing Beyond Limits

- Creating Team Players

- History, Traditions, and Mystique

1. Instilling Core Values: All Marines are quickly introduced to the Core Values of the Marine Corps: Honor, Courage, and Commitment.

In order for any organization to excel, it must have a set of values that it and its people stand for and strive to meet every day. These values are the glue that unifies individuals from various backgrounds and belief systems into working together for a common cause. They create a camaraderie that conquers obstacles and informs a strong culture.

The business world is not all that different from the Marine Corps in this regard. A company's core values must be clearly defined and introduced to new employees from day one. New hires may be expected to learn the nuances of the company to various degrees over time, but leaders must get them onboard with the company's culture and core values immediately.

For example, a newly hired sales rep might learn that there is zero tolerance for cutting corners, falsifying reports, or any breach of integrity, and those guilty of doing so will be terminated immediately. This sends a very strong message about the company's core values and ethical standards, and immediately shapes the performance of new hires. My advice to business leaders is to establish (or review and refine) your company's core values and communicate them clearly and continuously, along with the definitions of Zero-Tolerance Behaviors.

The reality is that *every* company establishes a set of core values ... whether it's done officially or not. Senior leaders either create them formally or they are implied via their own words and actions, and the latter values will simply reflect the behavior that an employee witnesses and emulates. A fundamental axiom of Marine leadership is that *"As go the leaders, so goes the unit."*

This is why organizations must explicitly define and enforce core values that put leaders on the right path.

2. Setting Clear Standards: How can we judge if the Core Values of an organization are being adhered to? Leaders must outline specific standards that define the behavior and performance expected of all team members. The Marine Corps sets very high standards that all Marines must meet. Some of the written standards have to do with character, ethics, personal appearance, physical fitness, technical and tactical proficiency, and more. Other standards that Marines are expected to live by are unwritten, yet they are based on the Core Values and a far-reaching ethical and moral code:

- Always do the right thing.

- Mission accomplishment is paramount.

- Always strive for excellence.

- Always be prepared.

- Never give up.

- Never leave a Marine behind.

In a more specific and practical sense, a Marine must intimately know and perform his or her direct responsibilities. An infantry corporal knows exactly what his role is within his fire team, squad, and platoon, as well as what he will be expected to do if his platoon sergeant or platoon commander is killed or incapacitated in a combat situation. Individuals have to know both what they're supposed to do and to what standard they're supposed to accomplish these tasks.

This may seem like a commonsense principle, but, surprisingly, many companies do not define clear roles and standards. Job descriptions are often overly broad and malleable, as are the company's culture and core values. And while some adaptability can be a great thing, a failure to communicate clear standards often leads to poor performance, impaired teamwork, poor morale, and behavioral issues.

It's important to understand that setting clear standards applies to most aspects of any job or role, from how many and what type of widgets a manufacturer produces, a sales rep's expected productivity, what the acceptable dress code is, and whether any degree of racist or sexist behavior will be tolerated in the work place. If you don't set these standards, it becomes difficult to measure performance or create a positive environment—as people will simply do what they've learned they can get away with in present circumstances or while serving in previous jobs.

3. Requiring the Pursuit of Excellence: The written standards that Marines must meet are often graded events that become part of an individual's military record. Although there are usually *minimum* grades that will qualify as meeting a standard, most Marines always strive for the highest grade—they want to "max-out" on any task given. This pursuit of excellence is a mindset that all Marines are instilled with in their initial training—and they carry it with them throughout their time in the Corps and beyond.

In the case of the Marines Corps, the primary incentive for pursuing excellence is earning and maintaining one's self-respect and gaining the respect of fellow Marines.

The Guts Test

Consider this: Though I spent 24 years in the Marine Corps, I'm still not really sure what the exact minimum passing time is for the three-mile run that is conducted during a physical fitness test (PFT). I never wanted to know what the minimum standard was, as my personal standard (and the standard of most of my fellow Marines) was *expending maximum effort* during the PFT run.

Doing so meant running as fast as I could for the entire three miles and this level of effort meant that I would quickly experience a very high level of pain. For me, it was the challenge of facing and conquering this self-imposed pain and mental discomfort that was the real test: no matter what the stopwatch said when I crossed the finish line, only I knew if I'd really passed what I call *"The Guts Test"* and motored on when my inner voice was encouraging me to ease up.

I was not alone in thinking like this. Throughout my career in the Corps, I repeatedly observed that a Marine who collapsed in exhaustion as he finished his PFT run in 23 minutes achieved far more respect from fellow Marines than a naturally gifted runner who casually jogged across the line in 18 minutes or less.

Marines respect those who go "all-in" on any task and they frown at those who are content to coast and achieve minimum standards. In the running example, the peers of a gifted athlete who takes it easy know that if he expended the same effort as the slower Marine who gave all, he'd have turned in a much faster time; instead, he chose to avoid challenging himself. This has some *very practical* implications for how this person will perform in other, more vital tasks. And because of the Marine Corps Mindset, his standing among other Marines will suffer.

This is an important concept that I want to emphasize to you, so I'll repeat it: The Marine Corps does not teach new recruits to simply *pass* the PFT or any other test or event; the culture of the Corps teaches that *the minimum standard is to expend maximum effort at all times!*

In the corporate world, a company can create a similar environment by promoting the pursuit of excellence and, crucially, backing it up with rewards for those who demonstrate this behavior. Marine Corps training ingrains the drive for excellence so successfully that respect becomes its own reward, in addition to any recognition by senior leaders or positive implications for a Marine's career. In the business world, challenges must usually be more clearly tied to rewards, whether they are competitive compensation and benefits, flexible work arrangements, or an active culture of recognition and support.

In the private sector, employees who are regularly pushed to excel and "go the extra mile" without the realistic opportunity for tangible rewards will eventually burn out and feel taken advantage of, which often results in poor results and attrition rather than success. Thus, business leaders have more of a practical duty to make this standard directly reciprocal: "We expect you to give this job your all, and we will take care of you in return."

4. Pushing Beyond Limits: We all have certain limits that we believe we can't surpass. During initial training, young Marine recruits are put through some of the most physically, mentally, and emotionally intense challenges that many of them have ever experienced. They are often pushed to the limits of their endurance—or at least what these individuals *think of* as their limits. Those who hit these barriers and quit wash out. Those with courage and determination push forward. They emerge from the experience knowing that what they once thought they couldn't do, they did; what they thought was too hard was achievable.

The confidence created by doing what a recruit previously thought was impossible sets the stage for the challenges and adaptations that are required of Marines throughout their careers. The Corps routinely puts promising young leaders in difficult positions that, on paper, exceed their rank and experience, and each Marine is expected to rise to the challenge.

The reasons for this are practical and simple: These tests both assess and develop an individual's capabilities; and quick adaptation to rapidly changing situations and new responsibilities can be essential in a combat environment. It's a given that the Marine Corps expects you to do your best. But it also expects you to do your best in a job that you don't necessarily want to do, don't enjoy doing, and didn't ask to do...but guess what? You're doing it. And the expectation is that you will do it well!

This principle directly applies to the business world. While the employees of a company may never be required to do intense physical training or conduct cross-country marches while carrying heavy loads after several days of minimal sleep and during all types of weather, they should be expected to push beyond their individual and team *comfort zones* and meet new challenges.

This might mean burning the midnight oil on a crucial project, taking the time to help a colleague who is struggling with a task, or filling in on someone else's job in a pinch. In addition, promising teammates should be routinely tested with assignments and positions that challenge and expand their capabilities.

5. Creating Team Players: A new Marine's training and education involves learning how to function as part of a small team, which is part of a bigger team, which is part of an even bigger team, and so on. In order for the Marine Corps to succeed, it needs each smaller unit to succeed. The inverse is also true; to succeed as an individual, the entire team needs to succeed. Marines learn that success depends on accomplishing the mission, and in order to accomplish the mission, you need to work effectively with your teammates. This training shapes Marines into capable, independent, and trustworthy members of a team.

Teamwork has immense value in any human endeavor, but it is absolutely essential in warfare. Those who fail to work as a team in combat *will inevitably lose to opponents who do*. The high stakes involved in combat operations help form exceptionally strong teams in the Corps, as does the shared duress that Marines experience during routine training and deployments.

Once again, people in the business world don't have the threat of mortal combat or the shared hardship of a deployment to shape them into teams. But the motivations for working together are stronger than many people might realize. As an executive leadership coach helping companies build or enhance teams, I always gather the various individuals together and explain to them why working as a team is essential:

- We will get far more done as a team. The whole of a highly-functioning team is much greater than the sum of its parts, and group success translates into individual success.

- Everyone needs help at some point. Great teams consist of teammates who support each other to mitigate individual weaknesses, and they know their colleagues can help each of them become stronger.

- Finally, I tell individuals to look around the room at fellow team members and ask themselves: "Do you trust your fate or the fate of your family to these people?" I then say, "I hope so, because in some ways, you are. If everyone pulls together and works well as a team and achieves our goals, we'll all have a chance at getting a bonus at the end of the year. If we don't, you won't. Essentially, if the person to the left or right of you refuses to work as part of a team, they are taking money from you and your family—just as you are harming them, if you refuse to be a team player."

6. History, Traditions, and Mystique: The Marine Corps has distinguished itself through success on some of history's toughest battlefields and its unwavering commitment to defend our nation. Marines of previous eras have created a long legacy of proud and honorable service, exemplified by their character and courage on and off the battlefield.

The best Marines have always held themselves to these high standards: they have led by example, and they have always been faithful to the nation, to the Corps, and to their fellow Marines. This deep and reverent institutional history is inculcated in all Marines, and its effect is often transcendental. Many Marines view this history as a yardstick against which to measure themselves and their actions. They feel an obligation to maintain this legacy and excel. In essence, history creates the future.

Of all the ingredients that make Marines, this is perhaps the most difficult one to replicate in the private sector—at least to the extent that the Corps leverages it. Individuals may take pride in their work and company, but few organizations can match the history, traditions and mystique of the Marine Corps, and how that legacy translates into pride, loyalty, and motivation for members of the organization.

That said, instilling a strong culture by using the other ingredients that make up the Marine Mindset—establishing core values, setting clear standards, inspiring the pursuit of excellence, pushing beyond limits, and fostering teamwork—can make up some of this natural gap by *building* a shared history. And some civilian organizations do indeed have inspiring histories and missions, and almost all have the potential to create them.

Many older companies and family-owned businesses have long-held traditions that form part of a positive, strong culture. Less-mature organizations without much history, or companies that have tarnished reputations or a negative culture, do not. Whatever the case, the formula for building traditions that create a great culture is fairly simple: If there's any history out there that informs a negative culture, change the environment. If there are good elements, promote and amplify them. And if your organization needs to develop great history and traditions, start creating and recognizing them!

Whether it's introducing an annual awards dinner, the CEO personally handing out awards for performance, entering and winning industry competitions, or holding celebrations for achieving important business milestones, leaders can build traditions that inspire a sense of purpose and loyalty among employees.

The Best of the Best: A Self-Fulfilling Prophecy

Not every Marine will agree with or admit to this, but I'll let you in on a secret: Perhaps the biggest reason that Marines are considered "elite" is because they consider themselves elite. And Marines consider themselves elite because generations of them *are simply told by their trainers, leaders, and colleagues that they are elite.*

Often, what makes Marines special is the way we view ourselves, and setting this intention works in many walks of life beyond the Corps. If you are told you belong to an elite organization and that you will be held to high standards, and you believe this to be true, you will likely train a little longer, fight a little harder, and expect a little more from your comrades.

This sense of excellence is reinforced over and over through the Corps' training and culture, and it has shaped the perception of the organization among both Marines and observers. Imagine, for a minute, if your business inspired the following quotes, and these sentiments were proudly repeated by your colleagues throughout your career:

"The United States Marine Corps, with its fiercely proud tradition of excellence in combat, its hallowed rituals, and its unbending code of honor, is part of the fabric of American myth."

— Journalist Thomas E. Ricks; *Making the Corps*, 1997 [9]

"I love the Corps for those intangible possessions that cannot be issued: pride, honor, integrity, and being able to carry on the traditions for generations of warriors past."

— Cpl. Jeff Sornig, USMC; in *Navy Times*, November 1994 [10]

"Among Marines there is a fierce loyalty to the Corps that persists long after the uniform is in mothballs...Woven through that sense of belonging, like a steel thread, is an elitist spirit. Marines are convinced that, being few in number, they are selective, better, and, above all, different."

— Lieutenant General Victor H. Krulak [11]

"You cannot exaggerate about the Marines. They are convinced, to the point of arrogance, that they are the most ferocious fighters on earth—and the amusing thing about it is that they are."

— Father Kevin Keaney, 1st Marine Division Chaplain, Korean War [12]

Quotes and anecdotes like these are the tip of the iceberg of Marine Corps lore, and young Marines are steeped in them from the day they set foot in boot camp. The Corps has been highly successful at creating and burnishing its image for military prowess and patriotic duty—while backing up the boast when it comes time to fight.

The Marine Corps excels at this, but it is certainly not the only institution or community that has succeeded in developing individuals and teams who truly believe they are exceptional in some way. The Naval Academy, West Point, and the other service academies, paratroopers, submariners, fighter pilots, the special operations community, and many other military organizations have cultures that tell their members they are elite, better, or special in some way. The leaders of these organizations expect more from their teammates, and they typically receive it, in spades, in some of the most challenging environments imaginable.

The business world isn't terribly different. Google prides itself on hiring innovative thinkers and some of the world's best technology experts, and potential employees flock to the company for its perks, pay, and other rewards. It also has one of the most difficult application and interview processes in the business world.

For young college graduates seeking a career on Wall Street in finance, investment banking, or trading equities, getting a job at Goldman Sachs is akin to gaining admission to an Ivy league school, although it's actually harder. In 2013, only "about 4%" of 43,000 applicants were hired by the company, which is a lower acceptance rate than those of numerous Ivy League institutions. Goldman Sachs promotes the fact that it only takes the best and the brightest, and the individuals who work for the company tend to believe it. [13] [14]

Are *all* the employees at Goldman Sachs really superior to their counterparts at a lesser-known firm? No. Similarly, is a Marine's training *that* much better than that of *every* soldier, airman, or sailor? Not necessarily. However, high standards, an incredibly strong culture, and the fact that both Marines and Goldman employees are *told* that they are better creates the perception that they are better, and if managed well, this perception influences reality. The Goldman mystique—much like the mystique of the Marine Corps—drives the performance of its team members.

I think all companies seeking to establish a culture of excellence should, in some way, emulate this self-fulfilling prophecy. And all companies who are interested in developing a tradition of creating exceptional leaders can learn a great deal from studying the methods that help create the *Marine Mindset* and the "corporate culture" of the Corps.

Chapter 11

EVERY MARINE A RIFLEMAN

The strong culture of the Marine Corps can be attributed to various elements, but one of the most powerful is the institution's focus on instilling two beliefs in every person who begins training:

- Being a Marine transcends any other form of identity, including gender, race, religion, or ethnicity.

- "Every Marine is a Rifleman."

Once new recruits or officer candidates set foot on a training facility, these Marine hopefuls immediately learn that they are now equal in the eyes of the drill instructors. Regardless of their goals, identities, or previous qualifications, they are all starting from zero. And as training continues, they are taught and constantly reminded that they aren't there to be pilots, logisticians, supply clerks, or mechanics; they are, first and foremost, *Marine Riflemen*—and they will all be expected to fight as such if the tactical situation requires it.

Every Marine, regardless of his or her military occupational specialty (MOS), learns to proficiently operate all basic infantry weapons systems, beginning with the standard service rifle and including heavy machine guns. Every Marine is instructed in hand-to-hand combat and basic first-aid procedures. Additionally, *all* Marine Corps officers are trained to effectively lead an infantry rifle platoon in combat.

In order to develop and solidify this integral nature in all Marines, the introductory training pipeline for the Corps is by far the longest and the most demanding of the nation's service branches. All enlisted Marines attend 13 weeks of recruit training followed by several weeks of Marine Combat Training prior to attending their MOS school. Likewise, every newly commissioned Marine Officer attends six months at The Basic School prior to moving on to MOS training. These extended, physically and mentally challenging experiences prior to specialized training serve as the foundation for a shared, multi-dimensional mindset throughout a Marine's career. [15]

The Marine Corps also focuses its training methodology on the warfighting skills of the individual Marine rather than on mastering the equipment he or she carries into battle. Despite the fact that modern weapons and combat systems are critical in present-day warfare, the Marine Corps has, from its inception, focused on *"equipping the man"* rather than the *"manning the equipment"* philosophy followed by many other military organizations.

This is an important concept that you must understand: <u>The Marine Corps maintains that its principal weapons system has been and always will be the individual Marine.</u>

The common responsibility and identity that are instilled in every Marine in turn drive the organization's singular focus. Every component of the Marine Corps, from recruiting to training to aviation to motor transport, shares one overall purpose: to enable infantry Marines to defeat the enemy. This philosophy has driven success spanning centuries and diverse battlefields, from Belleau Wood and Iwo Jima to Inchon, Hue City, and Fallujah.

"People First" in Business

The Marine Corps' generations-long focus, consistency, and institutional success set an example for many organizations, regardless of their mission. There are many corporations that proclaim *"people are our most important asset"* in various vision statements or sets of core values. Nevertheless, I firmly believe that very few organizations actually foster and execute this concept as well as the Marine Corps has been able to do it for 244 years.

That said, some companies come pretty close—and those that do reap consistent rewards.

Take the Ritz-Carlton Hotel Company. Every guest or visitor who walks into one of its properties receives a "warm and sincere greeting," with an emphasis on "sincere." This is step one of the company's "Three Steps of Service," which make up one portion of Ritz Carlton's "Gold Standards." This comprehensive philosophy and set of values are designed to achieve a singular purpose—providing exceptional guest service—and the essential element of achieving this goal is the company's investment in its employees. "At the Ritz-Carlton, our Ladies and Gentlemen are the most important resource in our service commitment to our guests" begins the luxury hotel chain's "Employee Promise." [16] [17]

Crucially, this core philosophy and the methods to achieve it are not empty words. The Ritz-Carlton "hires for culture first, job knowledge second," and then puts new employees through "a lengthy orientation and training, during which they emphasize eye contact, smiling, remembering guests' names, and providing consistently exceptional service." [18]

And just as the Marines create an incredibly strong, sustained culture and identity to win battles, the Ritz does it for equally practical reasons: A study by the American Quality Association found that 68 percent of a business's customers are "turned away by the indifferent attitude of a company employee," making it the most important factor in customer retention, ahead of "dissatisfaction with the product/service (14 percent)," being "lured away by competition "(9 percent)," and all other reasons. It's not hard to see why this has even greater importance in the luxury hospitality business. [19]

"Regardless of whether you're spending $24.5 million to live with us in New York's Central Park, or $199 to stay with us for one evening at The Ritz-Carlton in Cleveland, we have one opportunity to wow you. And that 'wow,' if you would, or the mystique of our organization, comes hands-down from two places: our culture and our people," says Joe Quitoni, corporate director of culture transformation with The Ritz-Carlton Leadership Center. "I can train you to do anything I would like you to do... but I cannot train you how to deliver service from the heart. You've either got it or you don't—it's an innate behavioral ability. And in service, you've got to have it." [20]

The Ritz-Carlton has become so well-known for its ability to deliver great customer service that Apple benchmarked the service standard of its Apple Stores against the Ritz and adopted its own variation of the "Three Steps of Service:"

Employees at an Apple Store are also taught to own the experience. If you approach an Apple Store employee with a problem of any sort, that person "owns" the relationship. The employee can direct you to another part of the store (and they will often escort you to the appropriate product table) or might introduce you to another salesperson more specialized in the product you're interested in. But even if they hand you off, they will often introduce you to the other employee by name and even check back to see if you got your questions answered. The employee owns the relationship and must do everything in his or her power to make it right. [21]

There are numerous other companies that instill a guiding ethos and singular focus to some degree of success, from Wal-Mart with its four core "values in action," to Southwest Airlines' employee-centered culture, which has enabled the airline to vastly differentiate itself by providing excellent customer service in an industry known for doing, sadly, the opposite. But it's perhaps more instructive to look at companies that fail to prioritize hiring and developing the right people, nor training them in a shared culture that drives a positive goal. [22] [23] [24]

In 1999, banking giant Wells Fargo boasted that its customers held an average of three different types of accounts with the institution, and began an employee initiative to boost that number to eight accounts; this was dubbed the "Going for Gr-Eight" cross-selling program. Bank branch employees were incentivized and pressured to hit cross-selling targets, and within a few years, many of them began using incredibly aggressive sales tactics and even illegal practices to hit these goals. [25]

These methods ranged from pressuring "family members and friends to open unnecessary accounts" to "'pinning,' where the bank issued ATM cards and assigned PIN numbers without customer authorization." Many employees also input fake contact information for these accounts to prevent their discovery. One branch's workers even "talked a homeless woman into opening six checking and savings accounts with fees totaling $39 a month." [26]

Eventually, Wells Fargo's corporate leadership discovered something was amiss after reading the negative results from an employee survey, in which many respondents said that they were "not comfortable with what managers asked them to do." The media became involved when the *Los Angeles Times* published an expose about the company's aggressive sales practices in 2013, and soon the government stepped in. The US Treasury pushed Wells Fargo to conduct an internal investigation in 2013, and the City of Los Angeles filed a lawsuit against the company in 2015. [27]

This scrutiny culminated in a fine of $185 million from the Consumer Financial Protection Bureau, Senate hearings on the fraud, and a range of other penalties. Wells Fargo CEO John Stumpf was forced to resign in 2016, and the company fired over 5,000 employees (about one percent of its workforce), paid $110 million to settle a class action suit filed on behalf of its customers, took massive hits to its value and reputation, and was forced to overhaul its entire sales culture. [28] [29]

There are many cautionary lessons to draw from the Wells Fargo example, but one of the most crucial is the bank's failure to create a positive, top-down, corporate-integrity-based ethos shared by all employees. If the company had successfully instituted core values that put employees and/or customers first—and backed it up with real training and accountability—it's far less likely that a legitimate cross-selling strategy would have warped into a fraudulent sales culture and incentives plan. After all, it's basically impossible to deliver exceptional customer service when you're opening up fake accounts that bilk money from and hurt the credit scores of your customers.

By failing to clearly set the tone from the top and imbuing all employees with a singular, positive focus, Wells Fargo executives effectively created this poisonous culture among many mid- and lower-level leaders. The lawsuit filed by the City of Los Angeles stated that "Wells Fargo's district managers discussed daily sales for each branch and employee 'four times a day, at 11 am, 1 pm, 3 pm and 5 pm.'" [30]

You can bet your bottom dollar that few (if any) customer service or ethics discussions took place during these sales meetings. And as I've written earlier in this book (and will write again), *every* company creates a corporate culture and basic ethos–*whether they actively create one or not.* As goes the leadership, so goes the organization. Unfortunately, an ethos of sales at any cost led Wells Fargo to commit fraud—and suffer severe consequences.

Creating a positive culture and ethos is the stepping stone to a positive organizational mission—whether that mission revolves around winning battles, delivering exceptional service to retain customers, or hitting sales targets and revenue numbers in a way that strengthens an organization, rather than ultimately damaging it. All companies should consider what their own version of *"Every Marine a Rifleman"* is and take steps to define, create, and continuously reinforce this critical aspect of culture among teammates at every level.

I've been fortunate to serve in leadership roles for more than 40 years. My experience has taught me that leadership is always the critical factor in the success or failure of any organization.

Several years ago, while attending an executive summit, I was asked to summarize what I've learned about leadership into a single statement. This was my response:

Leadership > Culture > Strategy > Tactics

—Mike Ettore

Chapter 12

SPECIAL TRUST AND CONFIDENCE

The importance of impeccable integrity, character, and ethical behavior are at the center of all instruction that Marine leaders receive. It is continuously emphasized to them that these concepts should be the driving force that guides their actions and decisions as leaders.

As a second lieutenant, I attended The Basic School (TBS), the Marine Corps' training program for all newly commissioned officers at Camp Barrett in Quantico, Virginia. TBS teaches *"Five Horizontal Themes of Officership,"* the first of which develops "A Man or Woman of Exemplary Character." An individual who meets this standard:

- "Has a clear understanding that a Marine commission brings with it 'special trust and confidence' and the highest expectations of the American people."

- "[Is] devoted to our Core Values of Honor, Courage and Commitment."

- "Possesses a moral compass that unerringly points to 'do the right thing'—an ethical warrior." [31]

Special Trust and Confidence

One of the first classes was dedicated to the concept of *"Special Trust and Confidence,"* words which have been used for centuries in the commissioning documents of officers in both the US and British militaries.

This phrase expresses faith and confers authority in a commissioned officer, as well as conveys the responsibility to earn the privilege of being a leader through exemplary conduct. The Marine Corps places extraordinary emphasis on special trust and confidence and works hard to ensure that all of its leaders take this mandate seriously.

This seriousness was underscored by a class taught to my training company on the very first day of our time at The Basic School. The class was taught by the school's commanding officer. Needless to say, newly commissioned lieutenants sit up and take extra notice when lessons are delivered by a full-bird colonel; he certainly had our full attention!

The colonel began by explaining what Special Trust and Confidence was and went through some examples of how some officers had breached this sacred trust in the past. He made it very clear that any violation of Special Trust and Confidence—no matter how slight—was grounds for dismissal from the Marine Corps.

Noting that we were new officers just in from the civilian world—the college fraternity house or other environments where cutting corners and minor forms of dishonesty are often tolerated—he emphasized that we were now in the Marine Corps and were expected to live up to the high standards of conduct associated with being an officer of Marines.

"The Marine Corps takes this very seriously, gentlemen," he said. "Marine officers do not lie, cheat, or steal or tolerate those who do. An officer caught doing so will be removed from this training company class that same day, and will find himself drummed out of the Marine Corps and back out on the street soon afterward."

The colonel then gave us an illuminating example. He mentioned a new lieutenant who, several months prior, reserved a hotel room on base while his fiancé was visiting. The couple stayed there for a few days and ate several meals at the Officers Club restaurant. The lieutenant had told them to bill all meals to his account, but the restaurant screwed up and failed to do so.

A few weeks later, someone corrected the accounting and sent a note over to TBS looking for the lieutenant to settle the discrepancy. The leadership asked the lieutenant if he had stayed at the hotel and eaten at the Officers

Club, and he said "yes." They asked if the restaurant had charged him and he replied "no." Then they asked him if he had *known* they made an error and didn't charge him. "Yes." The young lieutenant was immediately removed from his training company and soon discharged from the Marine Corps for violating the Special Trust and Confidence granted to and expected from Marine Corps leaders.

"Gents, I know as recent civilians some of you might think this is harsh," said the colonel. "But I'm telling you, you will not do things like this in our Marine Corps. We will not tolerate it!"

He then went into additional examples of violations, and one lesson focused on strict enforcement of the policy against "fraternization." The term describes and the policy prohibits "improper personal and business relationships among Marines of different ranks or positions." This can cover a lot of different unethical or overly familiar relationships with subordinates—basically anything that can potentially damage or weaken the chain of command and imperil "good order and discipline." But it is most often thought of (and violated) in terms of romantic relationships between Marines of different ranks. [32]

I listened to this lesson with a little skepticism. I'd been an enlisted Marine for several years prior to earning my commission, and during that time had been aware of a few romantic relationships between enlisted Marines and officers, with little fuss made about any of them. In his next breath, the colonel acknowledged this history.

"Now, you former enlisted Marines: I know you've seen this happen," admitted the colonel. "You may have seen some of your officers dating lance corporals and all of that. It's always been illegal, but in recent years, the Marine Corps has really stepped up to stop this."

The lesson was noted, though I held on to my doubts. But sometime during the third week of TBS, the colonel unexpectedly strode into the classroom and interrupted the class that was in session.

"I spoke about fraternization a couple of weeks ago and I told you what would happen to any officer found to be guilty of this transgression," he said. "If you look at 3rd platoon's section of the classroom, you'll see an empty seat. Lt. [Smith] is not in that seat, he is no longer in your training company, and within a month, he will not be in the Marine Corps. He was found to be in an improper relationship with a female corporal. He admitted the relationship and that he knew that it was improper. This young man spent years following his dream of becoming a Marine officer and he threw it all away by willfully doing something he knew was wrong."

This woke me up. Maybe the Corps *was* serious about all of this character and integrity stuff!

Neither the Marine Corps nor its leaders can claim to be perfect. People are still people, and some Marines have violated their oath in large or small ways, and some have gotten away with doing it. But the institution sets and strives to enforce very high standards of conduct—backed up by harsh consequences for failing to meet them—to set the tone for *everything* a Marine leader does in his or her career.

The Corps is smart enough to realize that despite the tough screening process for officer candidates, these men and women come from civilian settings that are vastly different from the institution's ideal. Most of them are right out of college and accustomed to an environment where academic cheating, cutting corners, binge drinking, or being dishonest with authority figures is routine. It also knows that if these young leaders replicate those behaviors in the Marine Corps, it could ruin the institution. Thus, the Corps uses extensive training, education and cultural immersion to ruthlessly weed out bad seeds while expeditiously getting everyone else on the same page.

And, for the most part, the strategy works.

A Revolutionary Marine Leader

Leadership training has always been a part of Marine Corps history, but the Marine who is perhaps most responsible for developing the Corps' most enduring leadership philosophies and concepts is Lieutenant General John A. Lejeune. In a career that spanned nearly four decades, he distinguished himself as a leader in the Spanish-American War, numerous small campaigns, and World War I, where he became the first Marine to lead an Army division in combat and was awarded the French Legion of Honor and the Croix de guerre, as well as both the US Army and Navy Distinguished Service Medals. [33]

General Lejeune was appointed as the thirteenth Commandant of the Marine Corps soon after his exceptional service in World War I, and he quickly set to work shaping the future of the Corps. Among his lasting accomplishments, he reoriented the Marines toward a mission of modern amphibious assault—a visionary change that became an essential component of victory over the Japanese in World War II; and he formalized leadership, conduct, and professional development standards that are still used by the Marine Corps today.

Midshipman First Class William J. Moran and Major John Hatala described Lejeune's contributions in the book *Leadership Embodied: The Secrets to Success of the Most Effective Navy*:

> The eleven Marine Corps principles currently taught to all Marines were heavily influenced by John A. Lejeune. One of those principles is "set the example," a favorite theme of Lejeune's teachings. Through numerous speeches, letters, and ultimately the Marine Corps Manual of 1921, Lejeune expressed his theory of leadership that was intended to serve as the guideline for every officer. Lejeune emphasized that the behavior of the Corps' officers set the standard for the entire Marine Corps:
>
> "You should never forget the power of example. The young men serving as enlisted men take their cues from you. If you conduct yourselves at all times as officers and gentlemen conduct themselves, the moral tone of the whole Corps will be raised, its reputation, which is most precious to all of us, will be enhanced, and the esteem and affection in which the Corps is held by the American people will be increased."
>
> Lejeune's insight with regard to a Marine officer's personal accountability encompassed a total person, to include intellect, morals, conduct, appearance, and demeanor. While many of his remarks focused on military performance, Lejeune was keenly aware that officers should act responsibly in every environment. [34]

In addition to stressing the importance of setting the example and the essential qualities required of an officer, Lejeune *lived* them. He also redefined the relationship between officers and enlisted men, eschewing any perception of master and servant in favor of a paternal relationship based on care, service, comradery, and mutual respect.

Lejeune's philosophy has done much to shape the Marine Corps into the highly regarded institution that it is today, and it is worthy of study and emulation by the leaders of any organization.

The *Marine Corps Manual*—1921 Edition

What you are about to read is some of the *science* of Marine Corps leadership and the expectations that come with being a leader of Marines. The material that follows is taken verbatim from the 1921 edition of the *Marine Corps Manual*, but it remains largely the same in today's version.

As you read it, you'll easily grasp the major elements of the Marine Corps' philosophy and approach to leadership and the men and women granted the privilege and responsibility of leading Marines. The selected portion of the 1921 edition follows:

Military Leadership

1. Purpose and Scope

    a. The objective of Marine Corps Leadership is to develop the leadership qualities of Marines to enable them to assume progressively greater responsibilities to the Marine Corps and society.

    b. Marine Corps Leadership qualities include:

      (1) Inspiration—Personal example of high moral standards reflecting virtue, honor, patriotism, and subordination in personal behavior and in performance.

      (2) Technical proficiency—Knowledge of the military sciences and skill in their application.

      (3) Moral responsibility—Personal adherence to high standards of conduct and the guidance of subordinates toward wholesomeness of mind and body.

2. Responsibility

    a. The Commandant of the Marine Corps is directly responsible to the Secretary of the Navy for establishing and maintaining leadership standards and conducting leadership training within the Marine Corps.

b. Commanders will ensure that local policies, directives and procedures reflect the special trust and confidence reposed in members of the officer corps. Full credit will be given to their statements and certificates. They will be allowed maximum discretion in the exercise of authority vested in them, and they and their dependents will be accorded all prerogatives and perquisites which are traditional and otherwise appropriate. Except in cases where more stringent positive identification procedures are required for the proper security of classified material and installations, or those that are imposed by higher authority for protecting privileges reserved for eligible military personnel, the officers' uniforms will amply attest to their status, and their oral statements will serve to identify them and their dependents.

c. An individual's responsibility for leadership is not dependent upon authority. Marines are expected to exert proper influence upon their comrades by setting examples of obedience, courage, zeal, sobriety, neatness, and attention to duty.

d. The special trust and confidence, which is expressly reposed in officers by their commission, is the distinguishing privilege of the officer corps. It is the policy of the Marine Corps that this privilege be tangible and real; it is the corresponding obligation of the officer corps that it be wholly deserved.

(1) As an accompanying condition, commanders will impress upon all subordinate officers the fact that the presumption of integrity, good manners, sound judgement, and discretion, which is the basis for the special trust and confidence reposed in each officer, is jeopardized by the slightest transgression on the part of any member of the officer corps. Any offense,

however minor, will be dealt with promptly, and with sufficient severity to impress on the officer at fault, and on the officer corps. Dedication to the basic elements of special trust and confidence is a Marine officer's obligation to the officer corps as a whole, and transcends the bonds of personal friendship.

(2) As a further and continuing action, commanders are requested to bring to the attention of higher authority, referencing this paragraph, any situation, policy, directive, or procedure which contravenes the spirit of this paragraph, and which is not susceptible to local correction.

(3) Although this policy is expressly concerned with commissioned officers, its provisions and spirit will, where applicable, be extended to noncommissioned officers, especially staff noncommissioned officers. [35]

Even though what you've just read was written nearly 100 years ago, I don't think it will be difficult for you to reflect upon the words and think of how any organization, including companies of all sizes and in all industries, could benefit from having similar fundamental guidance for its leaders. Imagine what your company could achieve if leaders at every level were aligned on the concepts and philosophies described by General Lejeune … and lived them!

Applying this Leadership Philosophy

Any organization can benefit from the Marine Corps' ideal of integrity and responsibility. Just as a Marine leader's word is his or her bond, so should be the word of business leaders. Likewise, any leader should be expected to lead by example and treat subordinates with care and respect.

If effectively adopted within a company, these values can develop and shape good leaders with respect *for* the organization and its people, and *from* the people whom they lead. The values also have practical, bottom-line benefits in enhancing productivity and transparency while mitigating ethical lapses that can damage or even destroy an organization.

Special Trust and Confidence Applied to Corporate America

One of the lasting contributions of the leadership program I helped develop at Kforce is the company's adoption of similar standards, including fully embracing the specific concept of Special Trust and Confidence. The company made an implacable decision that its leaders at all levels would be expected to demonstrate impeccable integrity and ethics and painstakingly worked to get all of them "on the same page." Much like my TBS class on this topic was taught by the Commanding Officer (a full-bird colonel), the CEO of Kforce personally delivered the class on special trust and confidence during several leadership training events I conducted during the first year I was with the company.

The bottom-line philosophy he stated was essentially: "We're not going to increase your pay for being honest. Total honesty and integrity is the very minimum we expect of you, the price of admission for being part of the Kforce team. I want you to know that our great firm has a Zero-Defects policy on lapses in integrity and breaches of Special Trust and Confidence."

Crucially, this philosophy of Special Trust and Confidence was visibly backed up with consequences and benefits. Leaders (or any member of the company) who were caught violating it were terminated and the entire leadership team was notified in a memo that went like this: "Bob Schmuckatelli from our San Diego office is no longer with the firm. He committed a violation of Special Trust and Confidence."

The rewards were great trust, responsibility, and autonomy. Because Kforce put so much faith and trust in its leaders, senior leaders and executives tended to defer to a less-senior leader's decisions whenever possible. If a field leader thought that certain sales associates who were achieving their sales goals did not fit the culture and should be let go, senior leaders would usually back the decision. If a field leader requested expensive replacement equipment such as laptop computers or desk phones, it would be quickly shipped in good faith. If an expense report was submitted for a networking or team-building event, the company assumed the resources were used for legitimate purposes.

Essentially, the value gained by upholding these high standards was effective leaders who were empowered to make sound decisions. Accordingly, there was zero tolerance for any violation of this trust. And much like in the Marine

Corps, this concept and its associated high standards of conduct worked well within Kforce.

Cautionary Tales

Perhaps the best way to understand the value of Special Trust and Confidence is by looking at organizations that have clearly failed to set these expectations in their leaders.

The previously mentioned Wells Fargo example is a great one. Leaders who are steeped in a culture that has zero tolerance for dishonesty will be much less likely to pressure their workers into creating fake accounts to hit sales goals. The widespread scale of the fraud would have been nearly impossible if these rigid standards were set and enforced by top executives, and continuously emphasized to leaders at all levels.

Unfortunately, Wells Fargo is merely a recent example of this kind of behavior, and it seems like many other companies often have to relearn similarly harsh lessons on a recurring basis. The newest generation of business leaders may not be fully aware of the wave of fraud that gripped the corporate world in the late '90s and early '00s. Many of these incidents climaxed in 2002, which CNN labeled the "Year of the Scandal" while quoting a former chief accountant for the SEC (Security and Exchange Commission) who described the "year [as] almost unmatched in history" … likening the "scandals to the corruption that emerged from the 1929 stock market crash." [36]

That year, Adelphia, the fifth largest cable company in the country, imploded into bankruptcy and its senior executives were jailed for what the SEC described as "one of most extensive financial frauds ever to take place at a public company"; telecommunications giant Global Crossing filed for bankruptcy (the fourth largest ever, at the time) after it was caught artificially inflating its earnings; WorldCom, another telecom giant, also filed for bankruptcy (then the biggest in history) due to "an accounting scandal that created billions in illusory earnings"; and perhaps the most infamous case of fraud involved the massive energy trading and telecom company Enron, which "disintegrated almost overnight" when it filed for bankruptcy on Dec. 2, 2001 and became the subject of a criminal investigation launched by the Justice Department on Jan. 9, 2002. [37] [38] [39] [40]

Fortune magazine had named Enron "America's Most Innovative Company" every year between 1996 and 2001 based on its annual survey of executives, directors, and security analysts, and "[by] century's end Enron had become one of the most successful companies in the world, having posted a 57% increase in sales between 1996 and 2000." Behind this façade, however, the company had actually started losing money and building up debt by 1997—and its leaders began using fraudulent accounting tricks to hide the losses. [41]

Among other shady tactics, Enron "orchestrated a scheme to use off-balance-sheet special purpose vehicles (SPVs), also known as special purposes entities (SPEs) to hide its mountains of debt and toxic assets from investors and creditors. The primary aim of these SPVs was to hide accounting realities, rather than operating results." [42]

Several Enron executives were charged with and convicted of crimes, including CFO Andrew Fastow, founder and former CEO Kenneth Lay, and former CEO Jeffrey Skilling. The fraud was not limited to the top executives nor even the company itself; it was aided and abetted by the widely-respected Arthur Anderson accounting firm, which helped Enron cook the books and even shredded documents once the investigation was underway. Anderson was convicted of obstructing a federal investigation and eventually disintegrated into a holding company. Former partners bought the rights to the name in 2014 with an aim to resurrect the century-old firm and its once-sterling reputation. [43] [44]

This raft of scandals directly resulted in the Sarbanes-Oxley Act of 2002 (SOX), a federal law that comprehensively reformed corporate financial reporting and accounting practices. SOX makes specific demands of corporate officers and executives, such as a duty to certify financial statements and develop and maintain internal fraud controls, and puts teeth behind them with whistleblower protections and severe criminal penalties. This law has been beneficial for both companies and the American public—but it really just makes the transparency responsibilities that publicly traded companies have always had more specific and concrete. None of the organizations that influenced its creation had any justification for the fraud they committed. They were all, simply stated, led by liars and thieves.

Despite measures like Sarbanes-Oxley, ethical violations will always rear their ugly head in the business world, as we saw with some of the practices that drove the housing market collapse in 2006 and the crippling recession and government bailout that followed. There are also recent examples like Wells Fargo; the "massive fraud" by biotech company Theranos, which lied about its technology and income to raise $700 billion from unsuspecting investors; Volkswagen's emissions scandal, in which the company used software to cheat on US emissions tests; and the allegations of sexual harassment and intimidation that have rocked numerous organizations and powerful individuals in 2018. [45] [46]

Many of these infamous examples involve leaders at big companies doing things that radically impacted society. But ethical violations are not limited to corporate giants or people who make the news. Many more examples take innumerable forms and go unpublicized—and they can do just as much damage to organizations of all sizes.

Given the potential impact, training leaders to have high ethical standards isn't simply a noble ideal, or something that burnishes a company's image or makes people feel good about themselves. It's a strategy with a tangible return on investment—one that is just as practical and effective as instituting fraud controls or third-party audits. As the Marine Corps realized decades ago, leaders held to very high standards of personal and professional conduct are almost always the essential difference between an organization's long-term success and its inevitable failure.

I know that most readers will agree with the sentiments contained in this chapter, though they may think it all to be a bit idealistic. "This sounds good, but I'm not sure it will work in most companies." I think this skepticism is fair and to be expected, especially from those whose experiences have mostly been in companies in which concepts such as integrity and character were minimized, if discussed and emphasized at all.

But I assure you: The concept of Special Trust and Confidence works every bit as well in any company that chooses to embrace and enforce it as it does in the Marine Corps!

Chapter 13

TEACHER-SCHOLAR 360°

In addition to promoting ethical and moral standards for leaders, General John A. Lejeune defined enduring concepts that guide respectful relationships between Marine officers and enlisted personnel.

These changes were also expressed in the 1921 edition of the *Marine Corps Manual* through both "general instructions" and very specific, practical additions to the document. The latter included detailed proscriptions such as "No enlisted man will be employed by officers to perform any duty which in civil life is performed by a man or woman employed as a servant," and "Enlisted men will not be employed as chauffeurs of privately owned automobiles." [47]

Those items might seem like commonsense measures today, but the relationship between officers and enlisted soldiers was defined as a caste system in most militaries of that era, especially among European forces. The American military had some of this rigid hierarchy, but it still stood out in this regard—likely because of the strong independent streak in American culture, plus the high number of draftees in the American Expeditionary Force (AEF) during World War I.

In 1919, the Intelligence Section of the General Headquarters of the American Expeditionary Forces compiled a fascinating report titled "Candid Comment on the American Soldier of 1917-1918 and Kindred Topics by the Germans." The report evaluated the opinion of American troops by German "soldiers, priests, women, village notables, politicians and statesmen" that were collected through interviews and intercepted letters and telephone calls. Among the findings:

A postal agent in Dernau said that "[American] troops lack the snap and precision of the German soldiers but…the cordial relations between the officers and men more than make up for the lack of iron discipline."

Another German commented that "The attitude of the American officer towards enlisted men is very different than in our army in which officers have always treated their men as cattle."

And a German infantryman had the opinion that "the system of the American army and the comradeship of the men is far better in the making of good soldiers than the strict discipline and machine-like actions of the German system." [48] [49]

I want to emphasize what you just read. America was at war with Germany, yet we see that German soldiers and citizens who had observed the interactions between American officers and enlisted troops were impressed with the camaraderie and mutual respect among men of all ranks. Some Germans admired the Americans for these qualities, lamenting that their own military was much more of a caste system and that lower-ranking soldiers were often treated in less-than-admirable ways.

As a business leader, it would be a very high compliment if you ever discovered an "intelligence report" created by a competitor that described the *command climate* of your organization in a similarly positive manner! That said, I urge you to do some reflection and ask yourself, "If such a report was written about the current *command climate* within my team, would I be proud of what the report would convey? Or would I be alarmed or even embarrassed by its findings?"

Remember, the best leaders set the *tone from the top* and they continuously observe and supervise their teams to ensure that the desired leadership concepts and philosophies are actually being implemented—and that the desired organizational culture actually exists.

Formalizing the Teacher-Scholar Concept

General Lejeune and the Marine Corps sought to sublimate, nurture, and codify these types of collegial relationships in the 1921 Edition of the *Marine Corps Manual*, while stamping out any vestiges of the "master and servant" model that could manifest between officers and enlisted men. This goal was expressed in the first item of the section titled "Relations Between Officers and Men:"

> Comradeship and brotherhood. — The World War wrought a great change in the relations between officers and enlisted men in the military services. A spirit of comradeship and brotherhood in arms came into being in the training camps and on the battlefields. This spirit is too fine a thing to be allowed to die. It must be fostered and kept alive and made the moving force in all Marine Corps organizations.

The manual's next item formalized a "teacher and scholar" relationship between senior, experienced Marines and those of lesser experience and rank. It continues to serve as one of the Corps' most important leadership concepts:

> Teacher and scholar. — The relation between officers and enlisted men should in no sense be that of superior and inferior nor that of master and servant, but rather that of teacher and scholar. In fact, it should partake of the nature of the relation between father and son, to the extent that officers, especially commanding officers, are responsible for the physical, mental, and moral welfare, as well as the discipline and military training of the young men under their command who are serving the nation in the Marine Corps. [50]

I was first introduced to this concept during a class on Marine Corps history while attending boot camp at Parris Island in the summer of 1974. The words had an immediate impact on me and my understanding of what leading Marines truly means. Their significance only grew while serving as a non-commissioned officer during my enlisted years and became even more important during my eventual service as a commissioned officer.

My experience as an enlisted Marine was somewhat unique in that my promotion through the junior ranks occurred very rapidly, which resulted in me being assigned to leadership roles normally held by older, more experienced Marines. I fully understood the spirit and intent of the Teacher-Scholar concept, but was also very aware of the fact that many of my "scholars" were much older and had served longer in the Corps than their "teacher!" These situations created leadership challenges that resulted in me learning countless lessons. Naturally, some of these were more difficult or humbling than others.

A "Baby Marine" is Assigned to Lead Some "Old Salts"

I was only 18 years old when I was promoted to lance corporal in an infantry unit at Camp Pendleton in San Diego County, California. I was quickly made a fire team leader responsible for three other Marines and, within a few months, a squad leader who is responsible for 12 Marines. The leadership challenge was steep and unique. First of all, most of my Marines were only "junior" in rank—several of them had as much as ten years of age on me and had served combat tours in Vietnam, with a few of them rating Purple Heart medals for being wounded in action. They were a very salty and surly bunch, and most of them had little respect for authority.

It was 1975, and these Vietnam veterans had typically done a 13-month tour in southeast Asia during the late 1960's and gotten out of the Corps as soon as they came home from their combat tour. Most of them had less than two years of service when they left active duty and, for the most part, they'd only known a wartime Marine Corps. After several years in the civilian world, they decided to reenlist for a three- or four-year commitment and, pretty much to a man, they soon came to regret this decision.

These Marines had never served in the peacetime Marine Corps and most of them very quickly realized that they *hated* it. They hated the rules, the spit and polish standards, and, to use military slang, all of the "chickenshit" aspects of being a "peacetime Marine" vs. a "combat Marine." In addition, the Corps was going through a crisis just after Vietnam, much of it the result of the pressures and lowered standards associated with the draft; the institution was struggling with racism, drugs, and discipline and organizational issues. [51] [52]

Once these combat veterans decided they wanted to leave the Corps—immediately, if possible—many of them simply stopped caring. Some of them had been lance corporals like me, or even corporals or sergeants, but were busted down to private or private first class after brawling in bars in towns located outside of the base, failing to report for duty for several days or weeks at a time, refusing to adhere to various rules and regulations, and often for disrespecting or disobeying an officer or staff non-commissioned officer (SNCO).

They showed their dissatisfaction and defiance in any way possible, and most refused to maintain regulation haircuts or wear their uniforms in an appropriate manner. Many of them rated three rows of personal awards and service ribbons for their honorable combat service in Vietnam, which is a powerful currency in a combat organization like the Marine Corps. But they had become discipline problems who simply didn't care about following the rules. Sounds like a perfect leadership challenge for a fresh-faced 18-year-old who knows exactly nothing about real combat or leading men who are much older and more experienced than he is!

Nevertheless, I tried my best—and my best seemed to work. Crucially, I approached these "old salts" with respect and sincerity. Since many of these guys had valuable combat experience, I made it a point to learn from them, asking them about real-world situations that applied to the infantry tactics that we practiced in training. My combat-veteran Marines soon began sharing tips and tactics that I wound up carrying with me throughout the rest of my career.

I made it a point to continuously learn about leadership from these men. I would have sincere talks with them about the positive and negative aspects of leadership that they witnessed in combat. At first, I picked their brains about these issues but, soon enough, they started volunteering information, telling me "Hey, you might want to think about this."

Essentially, they saw me as a decent young Marine and pegged me as a *"lifer"*—someone who wanted to make a career in the Marine Corps. Once I earned their respect, I believe they decided to take it upon themselves to teach me things that would help me when I was eventually deployed to combat, plus make sure that I turned into a good NCO, SNCO, or officer—rather than like some of the bad ones they'd encountered in the past.

I also did my best to take care of them. Perhaps the most important thing I did in this regard was to get their pay squared away. Believe it or not, the Marine Corps paid enlisted men in cash back in the 1970s. Twice a month, an officer armed with a sidearm and accompanied by two "bodyguards" would pay Marines from a large canvas satchel that was stuffed with cash. Typically, the officer sat behind a "desk" that consisted of a standard issue olive drab

Marine Corps blanket placed over two stacked footlockers and positioned on the quarterdeck of the barracks.

Each Marine, with a fresh haircut and wearing a squared-away, inspection-ready uniform, would report to the officer, state his name, rank, and service number, present his ID card, and show that he was wearing his dog tags. Once the officer determined that the Marine's information was correct and that his uniform and personal appearance were within standards, he would dole out the appropriate amount of cash and repeat this process until every Marine in the unit was paid.

There were of course no computers at this level of the Marine Corps back in those days, and the antiquated accounting system was often an impenetrable nightmare. If a Marine's pay became screwed up, he might not get paid correctly for months. Naturally, this would only serve to further inflame the ill will of my combat veteran *"salt dogs"* who'd already decided that they were not meant for the peacetime Marine Corps!

One of the first things I did as their squad leader was to jump through many bureaucratic hoops to fix the pay of the Marines who were having problems in this area, and they never forgot that gesture of genuine concern and leadership. In hindsight, I think it was this single act of leadership that won them over; it was the thing that made them think, *This guy really does care about us!*

Finally, I made it my mission to teach *them* what they needed to know to be successful in garrison. While these Marines' combat experiences were unquestioned, most of them didn't know how to plan well. For example, if a unit inspection was coming up in three weeks, they had no idea how to prepare for it. I taught them the elements of an inspection, how to reverse-plan for one, guided them through a couple of "pre-inspections," and all of the other basic elements that would enable them to pass the formal inspection. I also appealed to their pride in a bid to adjust their attitudes and stop the disciplinarily problems.

I said, "Look, you guys have so much combat experience, more than most of the officers and many of the other senior Marines. Believe it or not, they actually have a lot of respect for you and what you've done as combat Marines. But you are frequently putting them in situations where they have no choice but to take disciplinary action against you. So, yes, you can get out of the

Marine Corps once your enlistment is up; we all know that is what you want. But I encourage you to maintain your honor on the way out."

Somehow, the combination of my sincerity, a willingness to learn, and the things that I taught them compelled these surly Marines to willingly take orders from me. I invested in them, and they invested in my success as a leader in return. The chain of command was amazed that I was able to convince them to get regulation haircuts and to wear their uniforms as they should be worn, with pride and looking sharp. In the end, I attribute this success to the fact that these were basically good men whom I approached in the right way. And, as is always the case with a leader, if you show people that you care about them—that you truly care—they'll usually respond in kind.

Responsibility and Care

It's an understatement to say that I learned a lot about leadership during my years as an enlisted Marine. The lessons from hands-on experience and the patient mentoring from more senior Marines during these years had a huge influence on how I ultimately lead people—both in peacetime and combat situations, during my subsequent service as a commissioned officer, through-out my 15 years as a senior executive at Kforce, and now, as I serve as an executive leadership coach who trains and mentors business leaders.

My understanding and appreciation for the wisdom of General Lejeune's guidance grew over time, especially when I married and had children of my own. As my wife and I cared for and developed our young children, I became even more aware of the awesome responsibility that had first been bestowed upon me as a leader of Marines.

I recall that one day, as an officer leading a training evolution in the woods of Camp Lejeune, I looked at the young faces of the Marines in my unit and thought, *Every one of these Marines is somebody's son, and their parents are placing a lot of trust in me to take care of them.*

I had always felt a special affection for the Marines I was entrusted with, but this was the first time that I actually thought of them as someone else's children. This was a powerful moment for me; one which further elevated my understanding of the responsibility of being a leader. I resolved to do every-thing in my power—every single day—to lead my Marines well, and to train and care for them as if they were my own flesh and blood.

During the last stage of my Marine Corps career, when I served on the staff of The Basic School at Quantico, Virginia, I was fortunate to be involved in various leadership development classes and discussion groups with newly commissioned officers. I used to tell these young lieutenants that if they could only remember one thing about the time I spent with them, I hoped it would be this:

> "Always remember that your Marines are the sons and daughters of loving parents just like yours, and that they have entrusted you with the life of their child. The very least you owe the parents of your Marines is the very most you can possibly do to ensure they are led well and fully prepared to face the realities of serving in combat."

I believe that the best leaders in non-military environments also embrace (even if unconsciously) a leadership style that is based on the Teacher-Scholar concept, and that they also feel a great sense of responsibility toward the men and women they are privileged to lead. If you are fortunate enough to serve in a leadership role at any level, always remember that you too are leading people who depend on you—and that their families are also counting on you to lead well!

Teacher-Scholar 360°

The Marine Corps teacher-scholar concept is written with the intent that an officer, SNCO, or NCO is the teacher and lesser-ranking Marines are the scholars. But this respectful relationship also implies that a senior Marine can and should learn from the men and women he or she leads.

When I teach and coach business leaders, I make this reciprocity explicit when explaining the concept of "Teacher-Scholar 360°." By adding the *360°* suffix, I am emphasizing that, as a leader, you should be willing to learn from anybody, no matter their position—including those above, below, or to the side of you on an organizational chart.

In the Marines, this might be a company commander learning about the operation of a new machine gun from a lance corporal, or an inexperienced lieutenant deferring to the judgement of a seasoned sergeant. In the business world, it might mean a senior executive learning something valuable from a warehouse manager, and the warehouse manager of course being open to ideas and suggestions from anyone in the company, including those at the lowest level of his own team. Knowledge and wisdom are incredibly valuable commodities that are not concentrated in title, role, or status. Be willing to seek them out wherever you can find them.

Application to Business

The Teacher-Scholar 360° concept was essential when I was appointed to lead Kforce's IT group. I knew a lot about leadership but next to nothing about information technology. Many of the individuals I was tasked with leading were exceptionally knowledgeable regarding various aspects of technology, but knew very little about planning, organization, and leadership, which un-doubtedly accounted for the fact that the IT group was generally considered the worst performing support entity within the entire company. For the pre-vious several years, critical technology implementations and associated proj-ects were routinely poorly planned and executed, with most being delivered late and over budget. And often, the new systems and tools simply didn't work as promised.

Once I was appointed Chief Information Officer, I immediately devoted my-self to gaining situational awareness and determining—with the help of my IT leaders—what actions needed to be taken to "stop the bleeding" within the department. I needed to understand both the basic technological issues and the practical impediments that were tanking efficiency. To uncover all of this, I showed my teammates that I was willing to learn from everyone—from the department heads who were my direct reports all the way down to some of the highly specialized technical experts.

I arranged weekly classes during which various subject-matter experts would come in and teach me about different aspects of the company's technology infrastructure. This gained credibility from a naturally skeptical staff, many of whom undoubtedly wondered why a guy with no technical expertise was charged with leading the technology group. They saw that I was interested in learning and, crucially, that I retained the knowledge from week to week.

In return, I taught them how to plan and manage projects more efficiently and accurately. The prevailing culture (as is common in many IT departments) was that a technology project always took longer and was more expensive than the initial projections that were provided to executives. In other words, they routinely overpromised and underdelivered!

The consequence was a department that was always rolling out projects late and, often, inadequately or ineffectively. This rightly frustrated other portions of the company that relied on timely delivery of technology. I stopped this intentional overestimating ("padding") of project timelines, instructing my leaders to generate accurate projections along with showing them how to plan more effectively, from the strategic down to the tactical level. I was very demanding of them, but the effort paid off.

My best leaders adopted the improved planning procedures and quickly became self-starters who could operate independently. Within 18 months, the IT group went from the worst performing support entity in the company to one of the best, and within two years, this group was unquestionably the best performing support team in the company. The IT group had been transformed from one of Kforce's biggest liabilities to an enterprise level force multiplier. Open, multi-way communication along the entire chain of command—along with establishing a strong culture of leadership and accountability—made this possible.

One of my direct reports and department heads was a man named Don Sloan. He was a tech wizard who taught me a great deal about the nuances of operating an IT group. I believe he also learned a lot about leadership from me in return. During an interview for this book, Don said:

"Mike was the first leader that we had that came in with a philosophy around instilling culture and driving execution in a disciplined manner. I know that sounds fundamental but that's what he brought to the table that no one else had."

"We had the knowledge, we had the skill; we had the experience within the organization," he continued. "What we lacked was the leadership to actually put a culture in place that ensured a level of discipline and execution that would bring us success."

"I knew project management long before I started working for Mike. But what I learned was more along the lines of how to ensure consistent execution of those plans in a manner that permeated the organization ... and not just within the context of a single project."

Six years later, Don replaced me as the Chief Information Officer for Kforce. Several years after that, he moved on to become the CIO at Randstad USA, a staffing and consulting company with 5,500 US employees and over $4 billion in annual US revenue. Of the many gifts bestowed on any leader, perhaps the sweetest is the satisfaction of seeing a leader you helped to develop excel and surpass your accomplishments. [53]

My tenure leading the IT group at Kforce is a good example of the Teacher-Scholar 360°concept in action, but it's not a perfect one. Since I didn't know anything about technology, *I had no choice* but to listen to and learn from my teammates!

A much greater challenge for any leader is the ability to assume a new position, and, although he or she may have prior relevant experience, still be willing to listen to and learn from—without bias nor preconceived notions—to the members of the team they will be leading.

The Marine Corps has an informal leadership maxim to the effect of, "If you really want to know what's important to carry into combat, look at the guys who have already been doing it for a while." If Marines are ditching chemical protective gear and other equipment and taking extra ammunition and water on patrol, there is likely a very good, practical reason for it.

The same lesson applies to the business world. If you're tasked with leading others, treat them and their opinions with respect, and always view each individual as a potential source of knowledge. Always be a teacher *and* a scholar, no matter your position.

Those who ignore this philosophy and let their title, role, and ego get in the way lose big—in terms of employee morale and performance and, ultimately, their success as a leader.

Chapter 14

SPEAKING TRUTH TO POWER

The very best Marine leaders deliberately create a culture in which Marines of all grades and experience levels are willing to *speak truth to power*—even when doing so may not be popular or it poses some degree of risk to the person delivering the message.

Those who've never served in or worked with the Marine Corps may have a difficult time believing this. It's hard to associate an organization known for its discipline and no-nonsense approach to accomplishing the mission with being one that intentionally seeks to develop this quality in its people. But Marine leaders know that a culture of candor—in which Marines at every level are encouraged to speak out to leaders *who are willing to listen*—is fundamental to the success of the institution.

Marine leaders are taught that creating a culture where the Marines, especially those of lesser rank or experience, are willing to speak truth to power is one of the most important tasks of a leadership role. General John F. Kelly, US Marine Corps (Retired), made these comments on the topic of speaking truth to power:

> "The one thing I was always told is you absolutely have to tell truth to power. Whether you're a second lieutenant working with a captain and a lieutenant colonel, or a four-star general working with the Office Secretary of Defense and the White House, the decision-makers have got to have ground truth." [54]

Of course, an individual speaking truth to power can be viewed by some leaders as a challenge to their authority, and this applies to Marine leaders as much as it does to their corporate counterparts. The Marine Corps is not perfect and there are leaders who discourage any form of dissent or debate. Suffice it to say that these individuals are often associated with mediocre or even underperforming units, and they earn professional reputations that cause talented and capable Marines to actively avoid serving with them.

Please remember that the initial sentence in this chapter began with, "The very best Marine leaders deliberately create a culture in which Marines of all grades and experience levels are willing to *speak truth to power.*" These leaders know the power that such a culture can bring to a unit, and they also know that creating this type of environment requires their genuine and sincere commitment. By "walking the talk" and encouraging and rewarding those who show a willingness to speak truth to power, this type of culture yields benefits for years and even decades.

"Leaders who follow their moral compass often feel lonely, but they never feel lost."

—Mike Ettore

Chapter 15

TRIBAL KNOWLEDGE

The word *tribe* describes a group of people who share common ancestry, heritage, culture, traditions, and rituals, and often live in their own enclosed society. Many Marines consider the Marine Corps to be a unique tribe to which they have earned the right to be a part of, and I share this view. In my opinion, the Corps is very much a modern-day tribe. And like all tribes, past and present, much of the information and knowledge that shape and guide the organization is based upon *"tribal knowledge."*

In the Marine Corps, this "tribal knowledge" refers to the philosophies, rules and guidelines, tactics, techniques, procedures, and other types of information known and preserved by a relatively small group of individuals. These stewards are the leaders of the institution—the Marine officers, SNCOs, and NCOs. Tribal knowledge is often undocumented; and it is typically distributed throughout the organization by leaders at all levels and other experienced Marines; verbally, through leadership by example, or by "hands-on" demonstrations. In my opinion, much of the most important information associated with the Marine Corps' vision, mission, culture, Core Values, history, traditions, customs, and best practices exist only in the form of unwritten tribal knowledge.

To fully grasp the concepts that you will be taught regarding the Trust-Based Leadership™ model, it's important for you to understand the tribal aspect of the Marine Corps, especially as it relates to the topic of leadership and leadership development. Today's Marine leaders, though operating in dramatically different and vastly more complex environments than their predecessors, still lead Marines in much the same way that the leaders of the "Old Corps" did 100 years ago—using time-tested concepts and techniques that have been passed on from one generation of the tribe to the next.

"If you're serving in a leadership role, you should remember that 'school is in session' every hour of every day and that you are both teacher and student!"

—Mike Ettore

Marines' Hymn

From the Halls of Montezuma,
To the shores of Tripoli;
We fight our country's battles
In the air, on land, and sea;
First to fight for right and freedom
And to keep our honor clean;
We are proud to claim the title
Of United States Marine.

Our flag's unfurled to every breeze
From dawn to setting sun;
We have fought in every clime and place
Where we could take a gun;
In the snow of far-off Northern lands
And in sunny tropic scenes,
You will find us always on the job
The United States Marines.

Here's health to you and to our Corps
Which we are proud to serve;
In many a strife we've fought for life
And never lost our nerve.
If the Army and the Navy
Ever look on Heaven's scenes,
They will find the streets are guarded
By United States Marines.

The Eagle, Globe, and Anchor

An emblem consisting of an Eagle, Globe, and Anchor is used to represent the Marine Corps. Whether it appears on a uniform, a printed page, or a flag, the Marine emblem is an icon of military prowess and a testament to the rich legacy and proud traditions created by previous generations of Marines.

The Eagle is the symbol of the United States, and it is the one part of the emblem that readily associates the Marine Corps with the country.

The Globe signifies the worldwide commitment of the Marine Corps and that Marines serve in any clime or place.

The fouled Anchor represents the amphibious nature of the Marines' duties and emphasizes the close ties between the Marine Corps and the U.S. Navy.

"The emblem of the Corps is the common thread that binds all Marines together, officer and enlisted, past and present," said retired Sergeant Major of the Marine Corps David W. Sommers. "The eagle, globe, and anchor tells the world who we are, what we stand for, and what we are capable of, in a single glance."[1]

I consider the emblem one of my most prized possessions. I will continue to strive to live up to all that it represents for as long as I live.

Chapter 16

DEFENDERS OF THE CULTURE

The Marine Corps is well-known for its unique culture and traditions that are passed from one generation of Marines to the next. The rituals and customs of the Marine Corps (official and unofficial) continue to sustain the rich legacy of the institution and a lifelong camaraderie that set the Corps apart from the other branches of the armed forces.

Along with its history of success on the battlefield, the Marine Corps' culture is continuously reinforced by various instruments or symbols—some tangible and others intangible—that foster a spirit of brotherhood and sense of purpose that are difficult to fully explain to those who haven't actually lived them.

The hard-earned title of US Marine; the revered Marine emblem consisting of the eagle, globe and anchor; "The Marines' Hymn"; the motto of the Marine Corps, *Semper Fidelis* ("Always Faithful"); the elegant and instantly recognizable dress uniforms, with the ceremonial swords and "blood stripes" earned and worn on the uniform trousers of officers and non-commissioned officers; the sacred yearly celebration of the Marine Corps birthday; nicknames such as *Devil Dogs, Leathernecks, Soldiers of the Sea*, and others; the blood-stained combat legacy earned by generations of Marines on countless battlefields across the globe; and, most notably, the faith that America has in its Corps of Marines. All of these things serve to reinforce and sustain the culture of the organization.

As you might expect, the Corps entrusts the preservation of its distinct culture to its leaders. No distinction is made between commissioned officers and enlisted Marines—if you're a leader of Marines, you are expected to serve as a *Defender of the Culture*.

Throughout this book, you will see repeated emphasis on the importance of leaders who lead by example and exhibit moral courage and a bias for action. As you read about how Marine leaders are trained and developed, it is important that you fully understand that without these individuals serving as passionate and active *Defenders of the Culture,* the Marine Corps that the American people love and respect will simply cease to exist.

This concept has direct application in the business world. And you should remember, as you read this book, that the success of your company or team will inevitably depend on the presence of well-trained leaders who possess impeccable character and ethics, as well as those who are capable of creating and, when necessary, defending a culture of excellence.

"Culture eats strategy for breakfast."

—Peter Drucker

"Leadership is the table the meal is served on."

—Mike Ettore

Chapter 17

Leaders Eat Last

If asked to summarize the Marine Corps' leadership philosophy in a single phrase, I might offer these words: *"Leaders eat last."*

This statement has been successfully used to guide the mindset and behavior of generations of Marine leaders, and the concept has even made its way into the business world in the form of a *New York Times* bestseller by organizational consultant Simon Sinek.

In its literal form, this statement describes the longstanding practice of Marine leaders placing themselves at the end of the chow line as they await their turn to receive a meal, while more-junior Marines take a place toward the front of the line. This, of course, implies that in the event that some or all of the food and drink runs out, the junior Marines will have been fed and the unit's leaders will go hungry.

This may seem a bit quaint or dramatic to some. But I assure you that this simple tradition is one of the most effective leadership tools in the Marine Corps' vast arsenal of leadership tactics and techniques. I can distinctly remember the first time that I became aware of this practice as a 17-year old recruit going through boot camp at Parris Island during the summer of 1974. While waiting to enter the chow hall one morning, one of my platoon's drill instructors gave an impromptu class on Marine leadership; specifically, that in the Marine Corps, leaders eat last. He told us that no drill instructor or series officer would ever go through the chow line until every single recruit in the series had done so.

He said that this practice was done not only in a garrison environment, but also in combat environments. He recounted that when he served as a junior-enlisted Marine in Vietnam, all of the unit's leaders—starting with his fire team and squad leader and progressing upward to the most senior officer—would eat last, bathe last, receive new field uniforms last, and, essentially, always ensure that the more junior Marines were taken care of before the leaders availed themselves of *any* type of benefit or comfort.

I began to pay attention during subsequent meals to see if what the drill instructor said was true. And I was quickly impressed by the fact that the drill instructors on duty *never* went through the chow line until the very last recruit had been fed.

In a broad sense, "leaders eat last" succinctly conveys and supports all of the concepts, philosophies, core values, and cultural aspects associated with the Marine Corps. Much like the North Star's importance to those navigating at night without the benefit of a compass or GPS, this powerful statement is a common thread that is woven through every single aspect of Marine Corps leadership.

The message is clear. Whether we're discussing the organization's relentless emphasis on character, integrity, servant leadership, self-leadership, special trust and confidence, the teacher-scholar relationship, or anything else associated with being a leader of Marines—you take care of your people first and your personal needs second.

Leaders Eat Last!

FUNDAMENTALS AND TECHNIQUES

Chapter 18

THE 5 LAWS OF LEADERSHIP

The previous portion of this book explained various aspects of the culture and philosophies that guide Marine leaders as well as the Marines who've yet to serve in leadership roles. It's important that you're exposed to this material because to fully understand Marine Corps leadership, one has to understand the fundamental culture, ethos, and approach to sustaining an institution known for achieving excellence.

In subsequent sections and chapters, you will learn about the specific elements of the *Science and Art of Leadership* as taught to and executed by Marine leaders. But first, I want to ensure that you learn and reflect upon what I refer to as the *Five Laws of Leadership*:

(1) Leaders are responsible for everything that does or does not happen within their organizations.

(2) Leaders can delegate authority, but they cannot delegate responsibility.

(3) The members of an organization will replicate the character, values and behavior demonstrated by their leaders.

(4) Leaders must be consistent in leadership style, personality, mood, behavior, interpersonal skills, and decision-making.

(5)   Leaders should never give an order they are unwilling or unable to enforce.

While there are countless leadership axioms, sayings, quotes, etc. (many of which are mentioned in this book) that can add great value to your development as a leader, I believe that the Marine Corps' leadership philosophy and all of its training and development programs are rooted in these time-tested Five Laws of Leadership.

My experience has been that while these fundamental truths are routinely emphasized by senior leaders as they mentor others, they are rarely presented as being *so* important—*so* critical as a foundation—that they should be considered the Five *Laws* of Leadership upon which all other tactics and techniques are built.

I believe that the vast majority of seasoned Marine leaders would agree with my assessment and rationale for declaring these truisms "laws." Equally important, my study of many other leadership development programs, systems, and books reveals that almost every one of them contains their own versions of them. No matter what the teacher's background or a program's specific purpose may be, both *leadership experts* and *expert leaders* seem to gravitate toward these maxims as fundamental building blocks of effective leadership.

Each of the *Five Laws of Leadership* will be discussed in later chapters. When you see exactly how they are applied and support other elements, I think you'll agree that they really are the linchpins of leadership success in any environment!

Chapter 19

THE 3 MAIN RESPONSIBILITIES OF A LEADER

At this point, I have explained various aspects of the Marine Corps and how they shape duty, teamwork, and leadership. I've also mentioned some of the most important philosophies, traits, and principles that all Marine leaders must learn and practice.

At the top of this detailed framework, I believe that there are <u>Three Main Responsibilities</u> that every leader must prioritize and strive to fulfill each day:

- Accomplish the mission

- Take care of your people

- Develop the next generation of leaders

1. Accomplish the Mission

For a Marine leader, this is not just a responsibility—it is *the* <u>fundamental duty.</u> Mission accomplishment is your responsibility and yours alone. Whether your unit succeeds or fails rests on your shoulders.

This obligation includes responsibility to your seniors and higher headquarters. You must accept and discharge the authority that accompanies your position, you must vigorously execute all orders, and you must show loyalty to your seniors. If you question an order, make known your objections so that they may be considered prior to compliance. But once the leader's decision is made regarding a plan or course of action, you are bound to carry it out regardless of your personal view.

The military places incredible weight on following orders for obvious reasons: expedited commands are essential in warfare. Disobeying a lawful order is a crime under Articles 90, 91, 92 and 94 of the Uniform Code of Military Justice (UCMJ). The only exception to this maxim is when an order violates a service member's oath to uphold and protect the Constitution, or it is otherwise unlawful. For example, a military leader has a duty to disobey an order that would be considered a war crime. [55]

This is a very narrow spectrum of exceptions, however. When a superior issues a lawful order in the military, you may (in most good commands) professionally question it to your superior. But once the order is officially issued, just get it done.

Application to Business

Business leaders must develop and exhibit the same type of "glass-half-full" attitude. If a given project is deemed "mission critical," you need to shrug off various forms of friction or irrelevant issues and focus on achieving the stated goals and objectives. As an executive coach, I routinely see leaders (and entire organizations) that allow themselves to become distracted by either disliking the mission or various problems, fads, or other "bright, shiny objects." This almost always results in a significant and harmful diversion of focus and resources from the actual purpose of the organization. In other words, these leaders begin to neglect the "main business of their business," and this is never a good thing!

Think of a shoe company, for example, that gets bogged down in a supply chain issue or becomes so tied up in putting in a new customer management system that it deprioritizes its core focus: producing the best shoes in the world. Or an IT department that gets so splintered by non-essential projects that it takes its eye off of the ball—which is making sure critical sales and support platforms are meeting the basic needs of the organization. Distractions should be ignored. And any friction needs to be assessed and matter-of-factly dealt with.

As a Marine or a leader in the business world, at the end of the day, whatever product or service you are expected to deliver must be delivered in a timely manner and according to established standards of quality. Everything else is a lower priority or even entirely unnecessary.

This is one of the situations in which leadership is the difference between success or failure. Poor leaders find excuses as to why things can't be done, or get distracted by things that don't *need* to get done.

Effective leaders zero in on what's important, accomplish the mission, and *find ways to win*.

2. Take Care of Your People

Marine leaders have an essential obligation to those whom they are privileged to lead. A leader is responsible for the physical and emotional well-being of the individuals in his or her unit. Marines, like all human beings, are infinitely complex individuals and their performance is influenced by a vast array of emotions, desires, and personal and professional ambitions.

Marine leaders are taught that they must take into consideration each person's unique abilities and weaknesses and figure out the best way to position each individual—depending on each situation—to accomplish the mission. And along the way, they must enable team members to develop personally and professionally. These leaders are taught that the quality of their leadership will be reflected by the emotional state—the morale and level of motivation—of those they lead, and that these factors play a huge role in whether the unit accomplishes the mission.

Another critical element of being a Marine leader is a willingness to defend your people when it is appropriate to do so. Effective leaders do this with absolute sincerity because *it's the right thing to do*. But there are also some very practical benefits, as doing so creates reciprocal loyalty and responsibility among teammates and increases their productivity. Caring for people is the right thing to do, it is a fundamental trait of the best leaders, *and* its rewards are exponential.

Application to Business

Many aspects of taking care of your people are very basic actions that are fairly easy to accomplish, and have clear practical benefits for accomplishing the mission.

One example that has direct application to the business world involves the simple step I took to make sure that my Marines made their dental appointments. Trips to the dentist are bizarrely important in the military—almost sacred. The Corps places such emphasis on making sure its Marines' teeth are taken care of that leaders can be relieved of command (fired) if a certain percentage of a unit misses dental appointments. Talk with any Marine leader and he or she will agree that one of the fastest ways to "get on the skyline" (become noticed in a very bad way) is to run afoul of the base dental clinic!

When I was commanding an infantry rifle company that had to become MEU SOC-certified in only four months (vice the typical 18-24 month training period), I had to figure out a way to get my Marines dental care while sticking to a very rigorous and compressed training schedule. I couldn't afford having my Marines miss critical field training evolutions for medical, dental, and other types of appointments.

The solution was pretty straightforward. I had my company first sergeant strike a bargain with the Navy master chief in charge of the dental clinic that if he could ensure that all of my company's dental appointments would be scheduled for Fridays, we would guarantee a 100% attendance rate. The master chief took us up on our offer and it was a win-win scenario for everyone involved; my Marines were in the field training from Monday through Thursday, and when appropriate, they were on-time for their appointments at the dental clinic every Friday.

In fact, if any of my Marines had to do anything, such as run critical errands for their families, they were instructed to try and schedule them for Fridays. This simple arrangement left field exercises on Mondays through Thursday unscathed, while allowing us to fulfill the strict medical and dental quotas we were facing. This also gave my Marines some breathing room to take care of their personal lives before deploying again on an accelerated timeline.

This technique worked extremely well, and I implemented it with the same level of success while at Kforce. Friday afternoons were deemed to be *flex time,* during which our teammates were encouraged to schedule various personal appointments and errands, if at all possible. We also switched several (and eventually, all) major technology deployments and systems updates from January 1st roll-outs to March 1st roll-outs to make sure individuals didn't wind up furiously working nights and weekends to complete any projects over the holiday season.

These very basic actions worked to accomplish the mission while giving our people the time they needed. And they were very popular, effective policies that *essentially cost me nothing to implement.* I've shared these simple techniques with many of my executive coaching clients and the attendees of my leadership training events, and many have adopted them within their companies. Clearly, this stuff is not "rocket science." But it does work and helps a leader take care of his or her people—and that's always a good thing!

Another good example of taking care of your people is how Kforce treated the employees who worked in our Manila office, which became part of my organization after our firm had acquired another staffing company. Most companies operating in the Philippines shut off the air conditioning in office buildings at 5pm to save money on energy bills. If you've ever been to the Philippines, you know that the weather is often sweltering regardless of whether the sun is out. And if you are working the night shift in a high-rise office building in downtown Manila, you are in for a very hot and humid experience, to say the least.

Kforce would never treat our employees in the Tampa headquarters or our domestic field offices like that. Thus, we ended the practice of shutting off the air conditioning at 5pm so the night shift in our Manila office would be able to work in comfort. We also installed water fountains and refrigerators that were stocked with free bottled water for all employees.

Pretty basic stuff?

The right thing to do for our teammates?

Increased morale and productivity?

Yes, yes, and yes!

But these elementary decisions and actions not only set our people up for success, they actually wound up becoming a huge competitive advantage. More qualified applicants in the Philippines wanted to work for Kforce—and they worked harder, simply because they wanted to work in the basic environment we had created.

Before long, the word got out about how we treated our teammates relative to most of our competitors in Manila, and the general sentiment among job-seekers was, "Go work for Kforce. They're paying higher salaries, and they have A/C and ice water for you!"

In the business world, you must also shield your people from unrealistic or unnecessary tasks. Always ensure that your team has the appropriate resources and tools necessary to accomplish the mission. And if you want quality, engaged employees, make sure they are paid at competitive levels for their profession, industry, and level of experience.

Loyalty is a two-way street and your team has to trust that you have their best interests at heart. Caring for them could involve easy, commonsense steps like turning on the A/C, or it could be difficult and professionally risky. Regardless, individuals must know that their leader will speak up and fight for them when necessary.

Bottom Line: As always, the first responsibility of a leader is to accomplish the mission. But the main lesson here is that by taking care of their people, leaders are greatly enhancing the chances of doing just that!

3. Develop the Next Generation of Leaders

If you speak with any Marine leader about what their main responsibilities are, they will all quickly mention *accomplishing the mission* and *taking care of their Marines*. But fewer of them will automatically mention their sacred responsibility to develop other leaders. You might be wondering why this doesn't make the cut—and I will do my best to explain it, based on my experience as a Marine leader.

While the Marine Corps is world-renowned for its culture of leadership development and it invests heavily in the development of its leaders, I have found that this critical task—the development of the next generation of leaders—is so "baked into the DNA" of the Corps that it is rarely mentioned in official strategies, plans, operational concepts, leadership curriculums, and training materials. In my experience, it's instead passed on verbally as *"Tribal Knowledge"* from one generation of Marine leader to the next.

Marine leaders reading this will almost assuredly think to themselves, "Mike's right on this. Developing future leaders is something we talk about constantly and consider in just about everything we do but we rarely see it in writing.

Everyone simply assumes that everyone else knows this is what we do—train the leaders who will follow us to preserve, protect, and sustain the Marine Corps."

Put It in Writing!

I'm a believer in the power of *simplicity* and *clarity* when communicating concepts, philosophies, and plans. In light of this, I have designated (as part of the Trust-Based Leadership model) the development of the next generation of leaders as one of a leader's *Three Main Responsibilities.* This responsibility is vital to the successful adoption and implementation of Trust-Based Leadership. Thus, it's been "officially" added to the other universally known and well-documented responsibilities of a leader.

There's a lesson here for leaders: if something is important to the success of your company, department or team, and you want it to become "baked into the DNA" of your organization, put it in writing and continuously emphasize it in all that you say and do!

The Leadership Factory

When I was a young enlisted Marine, I was immediately impressed by how much time senior Marines were willing to invest in developing me, both personally and professionally. Aside from the obvious personal benefits of this guidance, it was also a great example of what would be expected of me when I was privileged to lead Marines.

It may sound somewhat unrealistic to civilians, but even a 20-year-old lance corporal is expected to mentor 17 and 18-year-old privates and PFCs. The lance corporal's mentor is often a more senior lance corporal or corporal that may only be a few years older than him. In the Marine Corps, the development of leaders is not left solely in the hands of staff NCOs and officers. Every Marine, regardless of grade, tenure, or age, is expected to do everything within his or her power to nurture new leaders.

Personally, I always invested a great deal of time in developing my Marines. I saw this as a sacred duty and a debt to be repaid to the Corps that had invested so much effort in me. It was always very gratifying to see my Marines succeed. And many of them, enlisted and officer, served with distinction for many years and achieved way more success than I ever did. I am far prouder of their achievements than I am of mine, and I take great satisfaction in knowing that in some small way, I played a role in helping them develop as leaders.

Application to Business

I continued this practice of developing leaders when I entered the business world. There was a major difference, however. I came to realize that formal, dedicated leadership training and development, though almost universally appreciated by those who received it, was very rare in corporate America. In fact, I'd say that the absence of a culture of leadership development and its associated coaching is the rule rather than the exception in the vast majority of businesses.

This is low-hanging fruit that can easily be put into place in any organization. Over time, it snowballs into a huge competitive advantage—the presence of capable leaders who are consistently developing more capable leaders creates differentiation and success.

Being a Mentor

Mentoring isn't always easy. It's a fundamental responsibility, however, and it's almost always worth it. I don't claim to be the best mentor, but I do believe that I am good at creating environments that are good for mentoring. As leaders go about the business of leading—if they are doing it well, at least—they are naturally influencing and developing their people into leaders. It is also the responsibility of any good leader to consciously teach and mentor others.

When I was at Kforce, I had the pleasure of seeing Don Sloan grow as a leader and replace me as CIO. Eventually, I watched him achieve greater success than I did. And he wasn't the only example.

One of Don's employees was a gifted IT expert serving as a technician. "Fred" had expressed interest in becoming a leader. Don explained this to me, and we decided to give Fred a shot at taking charge of a small unit. Unfortunately, despite our best efforts to mentor and develop him, he did not do well in a leadership role. Fred's meetings were poor, he missed objectives, and he just didn't seem to have the natural or acquired people skills to lead effectively. We coached him, made adjustments, and gave him some time to develop—to no avail. We had to reassign him back into a technical role.

Roughly a year later, Fred asked for another chance to serve in a leadership role, and we agreed. The result was the same. I was convinced that this guy simply did not possess the aptitude to be an effective a leader.

"If you ever come to me again suggesting that we put Fred into a leadership role, I'm going to punch you in the face," I joked with Don at the time. "And if you ever suggest it to me and I agree to do it, I want you to punch me in the face!"

One day about two years later, Don came into my office and said, "Mike, I think we may be punching each other in the face. Fred insists that he's more than a techie. He wants to be a leader, says he's learned from his mistakes, and based on many hours of recent discussions with him, I believe him. I want to give him another chance."

By then I'd come to trust Don's instincts, so I reluctantly agreed. We spoke with Fred, mentored him, and rigorously questioned him about what he would do differently this time. Then we gave him another shot.

Remarkably, he succeeded. In fact, Fred did so well that after a couple of years, he decided that he no longer wanted to be confined to IT leadership and applied to head a sales team in one of the firm's business units. We gave him our blessing and he was assigned new duties as a sales leader. Fred excelled in this role and within a year, he was promoted into an executive position in the business unit. He was eventually "stolen" from Kforce and hired to become the chief information officer at a national healthcare company. Our former "problem child" is now at another large, well-known company and in charge of its nationwide sales operation. He is responsible for over 30 offices around the country and hundreds of millions of dollars in revenue.

Here is a guy that we mentored and gave several chances to—the first two of which he failed. But he kept trying and refused to be defined. Initially, leadership came hard to him; he wasn't a good delegator, he wasn't sufficiently organized, and he didn't take constructive criticism well. Those initial failures taught him valuable lessons, however. And through his sheer determination to learn how to lead, he turned the corner and achieved incredible success.

This situation served as a valuable lesson for me, and I hope it does for you, too. You must take the time to mentor and develop others. It's a fundamental responsibility of a leader, and the dividends can be huge—for both your organization and you personally. I couldn't be prouder of anyone than I am of Fred. Witnessing his success—and the success of others—is one of the most rewarding aspects of being a leader.

And, for the record: Don and I did not make good on our promises to punch each other!

"Leadership is an art in which the artist can continue to improve throughout his or her entire life."

—Mike Ettore

Chapter 20

THE 5 PILLARS OF LEADERSHIP

Leadership, as defined by the Marine Corps, is:

"The art of influencing and directing others in such a way as to obtain their willing obedience, confidence, respect, and cooperation to accomplish the mission." [56]

In addition to this formal definition, Marines are taught that leadership is the artful application of the intangible elements of the culture of the Corps, along with the specific, time-tested leadership philosophies and concepts practiced throughout the institution. These explicit elements include the guidance of the *Marine Corps Manual*, the Core Values, the Leadership Traits and Principles, and the oath all Marines take when enlisting or accepting a commission.

The 5 Pillars of Marine Corps Leadership

The Corps trains every Marine leader to have a thorough understanding of 14 specific Leadership Traits and 11 Leadership Principles that I'll cover in the next two chapters. There are broader elements that define the role of a leader, however, and I've summarized them by using a term that I have created: *"The Five Pillars of Marine Corps Leadership."* They are:

- Authority

- Responsibility

- Accountability

- Chain of Command

- Delegation of Authority

The first three pillars are commonly cited as basic elements in almost every leadership philosophy and training curriculum, military or civilian. The latter two show up in *some* other schools of thought, but they have particular resonance in the Marine Corps—fundamentally shaping how a Marine leader gets the job done. Likewise, these pillars are exceptionally important to the Trust-Based Leadership™ model that I promote throughout my leadership training and coaching programs and engagements.

1. Authority

Formal authority is the legitimate power of a leader to direct subordinates to take action within the scope of the leader's position. It is vested in an individual but is a transferable currency; authority, to varying degrees, can be delegated and used in the name of the leader.

All leaders, regardless of title or position, must exercise their authority to accomplish the mission. Equally important, however, is the essential requirement that whenever a leader of any rank is given responsibility for a mission, he must be granted the appropriate degree of authority to carry it out.

In addition to formal authority, it's important to recognize the existence of informal authority. This is possessed by individuals who may lack official title or charter but have natural, powerful influence borne of experience, aptitude, or expertise. For example, in the Marine Corps, the formal authority over a platoon resides in the commission of the second lieutenant platoon commander—but the platoon sergeant with a decade or more of experience naturally has immense informal authority and influence within the platoon, as well as formal authority over the enlisted ranks.

In the business world, a similar relationship might exist when a new executive takes over a department and discovers that everyone defers to and respects "Bob," one of his subordinates who has worked there for 15 years. Essentially, everybody is aware of the fact that "Bob knows his stuff and if he says do it—do it!"

Smart leaders with formal authority know how to avoid conflict with and effectively leverage subordinates who have earned informal authority among their teammates. This is usually done by delegating to and vesting them with some degree of formal authority. Or at least learning from what they have to offer and acting accordingly.

2. Responsibility

Responsibility is the obligation to perform an assigned job to a successful conclusion. It defines that which one must answer for, either to seniors or juniors, and includes assigned personnel, morale and leadership, tasks, money, equipment, and anything else required to accomplish the mission.

Responsibility is fundamentally intertwined with a leader's authority; it is the other half of the bargain. The *First Law of Leadership* reigns supreme regarding the concept of responsibility: "Leaders are responsible for everything that does or does not happen within their organizations."

Additionally, individual leadership responsibilities are not dependent on one's rank. All Marines are expected to exert proper influence within their units by setting examples of obedience, courage, zeal, sobriety, neatness, and attention to duty. While the exact cultural characteristics may change, every company in the business world should similarly communicate clear responsibilities and expectations at all levels.

3. Accountability

Accountability is the cornerstone of Marine Corps leadership. It is the reckoning wherein a leader answers for his actions and those of his unit and accepts the consequences, good or bad. As a Marine leader, accountability is the most important element of formally critiquing your performance. The poor performance of a unit will require honest review and recommended changes and may result in either administrative or disciplinary action toward the leader who has performed unsatisfactorily.

If any other factor—coercion, politics, favoritism, or something else—is allowed to intervene in holding Marines, regardless of rank, accountable, the structure on which the Marine Corps was created is weakened.

On August 31, 1988, Lance Corporal Jason J. Rother died during a training exercise in the Mojave Desert. His unit, Kilo Company, 3rd Battalion, 2nd Marines, had undergone desert warfare training at the Marine Corps Air-Ground Combat Center in Twentynine Palms, CA. Rother had been posted as a road guard—alone—after recently suffering from several medical issues, including dehydration and heat exhaustion. The solitary guard post was considered a "light-duty" assignment while he recuperated. Unfortunately, his unit failed to pick him up at the end of the exercise, and the chain of command didn't notice his absence until a weapons inventory was conducted 40 hours later. [57]

After a massive, three-day manhunt involving both Marine Corps and civilian personnel, Rother's remains were found about two miles away from the base. He had hiked roughly 17 miles with minimal water in temperatures that may have exceeded 120 degrees, but died within 24 hours—in sight of a highway.

The accountability for this incident was broad and harsh. Those who were directly responsible for Rother's welfare—the officer in charge, his platoon sergeant, and his squad leader—were court-martialed on various charges, including disobeying orders and dereliction of duty. And all of the key officers in the battalion—Rother's platoon commander, the company commander, the battalion executive officer, and the battalion commander—were relieved of command and/or formally reprimanded, which effectively ended their careers. The investigation had found that a series of avoidable and inexcusable errors and incompetent actions by specific, lower-ranking personnel were responsible for the failure to keep track of Rother, but accountability reached all the way to the top of the unit.

Application to Business

The Marine Corps is not, by any means, perfect about holding its leaders accountable. But from my experience, it tends to do it with more consistency and severity than the business world.

The recent retirement of Jeff Immelt, the former CEO of GE who replaced the legendary Jack Welch, is a very high-profile example. During his 16-year run, Immelt authorized "lavish spending on stock buybacks, especially over the last two years at the behest of the company's biggest and richest shareholders" while "underfunding ... its pension plans." In an article titled "The $31 Billion Hole in GE's Balance Sheet That Keeps Growing," Bloomberg reported that "GE's pension shortfall is the biggest among S&P 500 companies and 50 percent greater than any other corporation in the US" [58] [59]

In addition, insiders claimed that Immelt refused to hear bad news and created a culture of denial that included setting "unrealistic financial goals, poorly timed acquisitions and even mismanagement of the company's cash." But the most damning and *objective* assessment of his performance is GE's failed responsibility to shareholders: "[A]cross the 16-year tenure of recently departed Chief Executive Officer Jeffrey Immelt its stock was the worst performer in the Dow Jones industrial average." In contrast, the company's value had risen 4,000% under the twenty-year stewardship of his predecessor. [60] [61]

Despite what amounts to a critical weakening of one of the world's greatest companies, Immelt's successor praised him as "one of the greatest business leaders of our time" upon his resignation, and he will "take home nearly $211 million, on top of the salary and bonuses he has accumulated in his more than 35 years there." This includes $81.7 million in pension benefits—drawing from the same pool of resources that was underfunded during his run, which created the liability that now tanks GE's stock price. [62] [63] [64]

This isn't accountability.

General Electric may present an easy, well-known example but failures of accountability plague the business world at all levels. Sales personnel, vendors, and some contract workers tend to be held accountable, as do individuals with bonuses tied to specific, measurable performance objectives. Beyond that, many benchmarks for salaried employees are nebulous and fail to effectively measure performance, and key stakeholders often aren't held accountable for the results of projects or initiatives.

For example, if a new CRM system is installed in a business and it comes online six months late and 40% over budget—and a leader says, "I'm responsible"—does he commonly suffer some negative effects for this failure? Lose a bonus or otherwise take a pay hit? Frequently, the answer is none of the above.

In the end, much like Marine Corps leadership is designed to win battles, business leadership has an explicit purpose: To benefit the organization and further its goals, whether they're shareholder value, profit, growth, infrastructure development, or efficiency. Real accountability is essential to making this happen.

4. Chain of Command

Marine leaders are often in charge of extremely large units, which are often dispersed across huge areas of operation. This is why a leader must utilize the subordinate leaders who serve under his authority, and the reason this structure is rigidly defined.

For example, an order from an infantry company commander goes from him to his lieutenant platoon commanders, then down to the platoon sergeants and squad leaders, and then to the fire-team leaders and their individual Marines. This is the chain of command. Each subordinate leader at any level in the chain has only one immediate commander; this unity of command must exist if a unit is to operate effectively. Not surprisingly, the Marine Corps *lives and breathes* chain of command.

The civilian equivalent, of course, is the organizational chart. Pretty much every business has one, though not every company uses it effectively. Much like the military, the most successful businesses also tend to thrive with a clear chain of command—*however it is appropriately designed for their organization.* It could be tall, wide, flat, circular, matrixed, or whatever, but everyone should know who is in charge of what—where I go for this, who do I talk to if this problem happens, and who reports to whom. It is essential for assigning responsibility and accountability, as well as achieving operational clarity. Without a clear chain of command, chaos often takes over.

Poorly designed organizations often have teams and individual roles with fuzzy, overlapping responsibilities and functions and a lack of clarity regarding "who is responsible for____?" This typically results in individuals taking isolated and uncoordinated actions to meet their perceived obligations without much thought on how what they're doing will affect the rest of the organization.

A common example in the business world occurs when ad hoc teams are put together to complete a specific project. The individuals may span different departments and roles, and none of them may be senior to one another in title—but *someone* has to be given ultimate responsibility for strategy, oversight, *and* operational control. One individual must lead the group and set its priorities. While unstructured teams can be successful, the odds are stacked against them without a clearly defined chain of command.

The lesson here is that all organizations, teams, projects, campaigns, etc., must have a designated leader with the authority to organize and direct various individuals toward the successful accomplishment of the assigned goals and objectives.

5. Delegation of Authority

As mentioned above, the authority vested in a leader is a transferrable currency that can and should be given to subordinates. When a leader delegates some of his duties down the chain of command, he holds each subordinate responsible for the performance of these duties.

He must delegate sufficient authority to these individuals to enable them to carry out their assignments. Each level in the chain of command is given authority equal to its responsibilities, and each level performs its duties under the direction and supervision of the next higher level.

While a leader may delegate authority to her subordinates, she cannot relieve herself of any of her overall responsibility. She must ensure that she does not delegate authority to the point of losing control—and she must ensure that her subordinates understand the scope and limits of *their* authority.

A fundamental "law" of Marine Corps leadership is that while a leader is expected to delegate an appropriate level of authority, the leader can never delegate overall *responsibility* for the accomplishment of assigned missions or tasks. As previously stated, the Marine leader is ultimately responsible for all that his or her unit does or fails to do.

A Leadership Secret Weapon

When I teach the Trust-Based Leadership™ model, I get my students' attention when I mention that there are three "secret weapons" of successful leadership.

One of them—officially, "Secret Weapon #2"—is based around the way Marine units are organized. It's actually pretty simple: ***Delegate and Leverage***.

Bear with me as I provide the following example of how the Marine Corps does it. I promise that you'll ultimately realize that Delegate and Leverage can be extremely effective if utilized in the various teams and departments in your company.

A Marine Corps rifle company is typically led by a captain and contains a headquarters section, one weapons platoon that brings heavier weapons like mortars, machine guns, and anti-armor missiles to bear, and three rifle platoons that are the main assault elements of the company. In addition to the captain, the company typically has five other officers, all of them lieutenants—serving as the company executive officer and four platoon commanders. The headquarters element typically has two senior SNCO's: a company first sergeant and the company gunnery sergeant.

Roughly 42 to 45 Marines and one Navy Corpsman (medic) fall under each of the four platoon commanders, and each platoon is organized into three squads (or sections for the weapons platoon) led by a sergeant or corporal. Each of the assault squads is in turn broken down into three fire teams which are typically led by a corporal or even a more senior lance corporal. That's a total of about 181 Marines and five Navy Corpsmen who may fall under the command of a captain, who typically achieves this rank approximately 5-6 years after being commissioned as an officer of Marines. It's a very powerful and complex organization with a lot of moving parts, and the company commander has to possess a high level of leadership ability to unleash the full potential and combat power of the unit.

In my experience, some company commanders tended to mainly rely on their officers—trusting in the five lieutenants to follow mission-type orders and get the job done—while others bet on their officers *and* their SNCOs. Some commanders worked around their junior officers—or at least the platoon commanders, who tend to be inexperienced lieutenants—and bet heavily on certain experienced SNCO and NCOs to serve as the driving force within the unit.

All of these models are understandable but ultimately fail to leverage the true power of a rifle company, which actually has about *46 individuals who are specifically trained to be leaders*: 5 officers; about 9 staff NCOs; and 32 sergeants and corporals within the various platoons.

If a leader can get these individuals—especially the 32 NCOs; the sergeants and corporals—on the same page and taking initiative toward a shared goal—a mission-type order—the rifle company becomes exponentially more powerful and effective. This is the essence of the Marine Corps' intent when delegating authority, and it's a profound lesson with equally important applications in the business world.

I can honestly say that one of the main reasons for any success that I achieved as a leader in the Marine Corps was the fact that I set high expectations for the NCOs in my units; I expected them to lead and ensured that they were trained and empowered to do so. This applies to my business career, too. I taught my senior leaders to develop and leverage all of the leaders in the organization and we set the same high-expectations for our business "NCOs."

There is usually so much resident talent in any mid- to large-sized organization that smart executives develop, promote, and empower good leaders at every level of the chain of command. These leaders set the mission and its parameters, and simply get out of the way. As in a Marine Corps unit, when a company, department, or team harnesses the collective energy, knowledge, and experience of *all* of its leaders, success is almost inevitable.

Effective, widespread delegation is indeed one of the "secret weapons" of leadership. Smart leaders recognize this and ensure that this practice becomes part of the "DNA" of their organization's culture.

"Untrained leaders who are told to 'sink or swim' typically pull their teams underwater with them as they drown."

—Mike Ettore

LET NO MAN'S GHOST SAY MY TRAINING LET HIM DOWN.

(SGT. ETTORE – U.S.M.C.)

In 1975, as a young enlisted Marine, I saw this quote painted on the wall of an old barracks that was used by Marines during World War II. I thought its meaning was so powerful that I adopted it as one of the bedrock principles of my leadership philosophy.

I made this wooden plaque and placed it in every office that I had throughout my Marine Corps career. It served as a visual reminder of the great responsibility I had as a leader of Marines.

14 Leadership Traits

- Justice
- Judgment
- Dependability
- Initiative
- Decisiveness
- Tact
- Integrity

- Enthusiasm
- Bearing
- Unselfishness
- Courage
- Knowledge
- Loyalty
- Endurance

Fidelis Leadership Group
Developing World Class Leaders

Source: U.S. Marine Corps

Chapter 21

LEADERSHIP TRAITS

Special Trust and Confidence and other Marine Corps leadership concepts can only be effective if they are entrusted to leaders with certain characteristics. The Marine Corps outlines 14 specific leadership traits that every leader must possess in some measure. These traits are a fundamental part of the "science" of Marine Corps leadership—and many of them resemble the characteristics and philosophies of other well-known leadership schools.

Every Marine Corps leader is explicitly taught these traits and is expected to take the mandate to learn and implement them seriously; then naturally exhibit them as he or she lives the institution's Core Values, strives to lead Marines well, and lives up to the special trust and confidence he or she has been afforded.

Once taught, the Leadership Traits are developed and eventually mastered by Marine leaders through daily application and experience. They can be effectively applied in all situations and settings, and the key to their success is the sincerity and diligence with which a leader displays them. After a time, they become second nature. In fact, for many great leaders—natural or trained—these traits are simply part of an individual's basic personality and *"leadership DNA."*

MCTP (Marine Corps Tactical Publication) *6-10B: Marine Corps Values: A User's Guide for Discussion Leaders*, provides definitions for each trait as follows. As you read them (and remember they were written for Marines!), reflect upon their applicability to leadership in your profession or operating environment. I think you'll find them to be quite useful and actionable no matter what industry or leadership role you are serving in. I can assure you, based upon my experience as a high-level executive, that <u>these traits are applicable to all leaders in the business world</u>—from the C-suite down to front-line supervisors.

1. **Justice**

   a. <u>Definition</u>. Giving reward and punishment according to the merits of the case in question. The ability to administer a system of rewards and punishments impartially and consistently.

   b. <u>Significance</u>. The quality of displaying fairness and impartiality is critical in order to gain the trust and respect of subordinates and maintain discipline and unit cohesion, particularly in the exercise of responsibility as a leader.

   c. <u>Example</u>. Fair apportionment of tasks by a squad leader during all field days. Having overlooked a critical piece of evidence which resulted in the unjust reduction of an NCO [non-commissioned officer] in a highly publicized incident, the CO [commanding officer] sets the punishment aside and restores him to his previous grade even though he knows it will displease his seniors or may reflect negatively on his fitness report. (Also, an example of courage.) [65]

A sense of justice ensures that a leader is focused on fairness and merit when evaluating individuals and their actions. Subordinates should feel confident that they are being judged on their integrity, work ethic, skills, and, ultimately, the results of their work rather than any form of favoritism. Justice creates a level playing ground that inspires and enables individuals to rise and fall on their own merits, while giving them confidence in their leaders.

2. **Judgement**

   a. <u>Definition</u>. The ability to weigh facts and possible courses of action in order to make sound decisions.

   b. <u>Significance</u>. Sound judgement allows a leader to make appropriate decisions in the guidance and training of his/her Marines and the employment of his/her unit. A Marine who exercises good judgement weighs pros and cons accordingly to arrive at an appropriate decision/take proper action.

c. Example. A Marine properly apportions his/her liberty time in order to relax as well as to study. [66]

Sound judgement is the ability to not only make good decisions, but decisions that prioritize the organization, the welfare of its employees, and the mission. It almost goes without saying, but a leader can't be seen as credible without consistently displaying sound judgement.

3. Decisiveness

a. Definition. Ability to make decisions promptly and to announce them in a clear, forceful manner.

b. Significance. The quality of character which guides a person to accumulate all available facts in a circumstance, weigh the facts, choose and announce an alternative which seems best. It is often better that a decision be made promptly than a potentially better one be made at the expense of more time.

c. Example. A leader who sees a potentially dangerous situation developing, immediately takes action to prevent injury from occurring. For example, if he/she sees a unit making a forced march along a winding road without road guards posted, he/she should immediately inform the unit leader of the oversight, and if senior to that unit leader, direct that proper precautions be taken. [67]

Marine leaders have a bias for action, given the consequences of inaction in a quickly changing combat situation. A reasonable decision with a calculated element of risk that is executed quickly is vastly superior to a "great" decision that is made late.

While lives may not be at stake, the same principle applies in business. Indecision leads to inaction, which can ultimately result in missed opportunities or worse, a tangible loss for an organization. Taking action will move the mission forward and often create other opportunities, even if it doesn't wind up meeting the objective. Leaders should ensure that they don't allow the desire for perfection to be the enemy of adequate and effective!

4. Initiative

    a. <u>Definition</u>. Taking action in the absence of orders.

    b. <u>Significance</u>. Since an NCO often works without close supervision, emphasis is placed on being a self-starter. Initiative is a founding principle of Marine Corps Warfighting philosophy.

    c. <u>Example</u>. In the unexplained absence of the platoon sergeant, an NCO takes charge of the platoon and carries out the training schedule. [68]

Initiative also relies on having a bias for action, especially when no clear direction has been given. Marines tend to issue "mission-type orders," which define the objective and a commander's intent. Within the framework of that intent, each subordinate leader must take the initiative to accomplish the mission, even without specific instruction on how to make it happen.

In the Marine Corps or the business world, decentralized leadership that relies on qualified individuals taking initiative is an extremely powerful concept. Leaders at all levels can contribute something, and the whole becomes much greater than the sum of its parts.

5. Dependability

    a. <u>Definition</u>. The certainty of proper performance of duty.

    b. <u>Significance</u>. The quality which permits a senior to assign a task to a junior with the understanding that it will be accomplished with minimum supervision. This understanding includes the assumption that the initiative will be taken on small matters not covered by instructions.

    c. <u>Example</u>. The squad leader ensures that his/her squad falls out in the proper uniform without having been told to by the platoon sergeant. The staff officer, who hates detailed, tedious paperwork, yet makes sure the report meets his/her and his/her supervisor's standards before having it leave his desk. [69]

Dependability simply means that you can be relied upon to perform your duties properly. You can be trusted to complete a job. It is the willing and voluntary support of the policies and orders from your chain of command. Dependability also means consistently putting forth your best effort in an attempt to achieve the highest standards of performance.

To truly understand the value of dependability, think of the inefficiencies created by an employee who routinely fails to hit deadlines or complete assigned tasks successfully. Only a few weak links can result in complete failure in an organization that relies on successful delegation.

6. **Tact**

    a. Definition. The ability to deal with others without creating hostility.

    b. Significance. The quality of consistently treating peers, seniors, and subordinates with respect and courtesy is a sign of maturity. Tact allows commands, guidance, and opinions to be expressed in a constructive and beneficial manner. This deference must be extended under all conditions regardless of true feelings.

    c. Example. A Marine discreetly points out a mistake in drill to [an] NCO by waiting until after the unit has been dismissed and privately asking which of the two methods are correct. He/she anticipates that the NCO will realize the correct method when shown, and later provide correct instruction to the unit. [70]

Many civilians assume that a lot of shouting happens in the Marine Corps. But beyond the yelling that is done by drill instructors at our recruit depots, it's actually pretty rare. I can count on one hand the number of times I ever raised my voice at a fellow Marine outside of a combat situation during my 24 years of service. A Marine leader might get away with yelling at or "talking down" to a subordinate once or twice. But eventually, someone—who may not even be higher in rank—will call them out on their lack of professionalism and tact.

As a leader, you will run into a variety of personalities in the workforce, and it's important to be able to communicate appropriately with every member of a team. When people make mistakes, it is mutually beneficial to tactfully correct them and have them learn for the future, rather than undercut and humiliate them. Doing the latter is a leadership failure that often has long-term ramifications.

7. **Integrity**

> a. <u>Definition</u>. Uprightness of character and soundness of moral principles. The quality of truthfulness and honesty.
>
> b. <u>Significance</u>. A Marine's word is his/her bond. Nothing less than complete honesty in all of your dealings with subordinates, peers, and superiors is acceptable.
>
> c. <u>Example</u>. A Marine who uses the correct technique on the obstacle course, even when he/she cannot be seen by the evaluator. During an inspection, if something goes wrong or is not corrected as had been previously directed, he/she can be counted upon to always respond truthfully and honestly. [71]

We follow people we trust. If you want to lead others successfully, they must have faith in you. Lying, cheating, or stealing are unacceptable, as is tolerating anyone who exhibits any of these behaviors. In addition, a classic leadership axiom applies here: *as goes the leadership, so goes the organization*. A leader who lacks integrity will almost inevitably head a company, department, or team which lacks it as well.

8. **Endurance**

> a. <u>Definition</u>. The mental and physical stamina measured by the ability to withstand pain, fatigue, stress, and hardship.
>
> b. <u>Significance</u>. The quality of withstanding pain during a conditioning hike in order to improve stamina is crucial in the development of leadership. Leaders are responsible for leading their units in physical endeavors and for motivating them as well.
>
> c. <u>Example</u>. A Marine keeping up on a 10-mile forced march even though he/she has blisters on both feet and had only an hour of sleep the previous night. An XO [executive officer] who works all night to ensure that promotion/pay problems are corrected as quickly as humanly possible because he/she

realizes that only through this effort can one of his/her Marines receive badly needed back-pay the following morning. [72]

Endurance is required not only to perform when a situation calls for it, but to also set an example for others. Civilians may not need the endurance to lead a 10-mile forced march, but they certainly may need the will to endure stress and intense effort on a project.

There are many techniques that anyone can learn and practice in order to increase levels of endurance—either physical or mental. Just about any organization out there will experience tough times during which employees will take their cues from leadership. Leaders need to muster their strength and confidence to power through and execute solutions.

9. Bearing

a. Definition. Creating a favorable impression in carriage, appearance, and personal conduct at all times.

b. Significance. The ability to look, act, and speak like a leader whether or not these manifestations indicate one's true feelings. Some signs of these traits are clear and plain speech, an erect gait, and impeccable personal appearance.

c. Example. Wearing clean, pressed uniforms, and shining boots and brass. Avoiding profane and vulgar language. Keeping a trim, fit appearance. Keeping your head, keeping your word and keeping your temper. [73]

Marines place a lot of emphasis on appearance and fitness as components of bearing, and tend to evaluate each other on whether an individual is "squared away." Some of these elements of poise are certainly going to be less important in a Silicon Valley start-up—though presenting a professional appearance does benefit a leader in most settings. The primary factor in bearing, however, is how a leader behaves.

Subordinates can sense uncertainty, fear, and other weaknesses, and these feelings—or their opposites—can spread like a virus. When a leader is faced with a tough situation, he or she should suppress undue personal doubts and project confidence. Your manner should reflect alertness, competence, confidence, and control.

10. Unselfishness

a. <u>Definition</u>. Avoidance of providing for one's own comfort and personal advancement at the expense of others.

b. <u>Significance</u>. The quality of looking out for the needs of your subordinates before your own is the essence of leadership. This quality is not to be confused with putting these matters ahead of the accomplishment of the mission.

c. <u>Example</u>. A Marine leader ensures all members of his unit have eaten before he does, or if water is scarce, he will share what he has and ensure that others do the same. Another example occurs frequently when a Marine receives a package of food from home: the delicacies are shared with everyone in the squad. Yet another form of unselfishness involves the time of the leader. If a Marine needs extra instruction or guidance, the leader is expected to make his/her free time available whenever a need arises. [74]

Unselfishness is key to developing the teacher-scholar aspect of leadership envisioned by Lieutenant General John A. Lejeune, and the best leaders care for their Marines as if they were extended family.

In the business world, every business decision a leader makes should be in the best interest of the company's objectives and its people. No leader should ever personally profit at the expense of others or the mission. Probably the most common situation where business leaders exhibit selfishness is by taking credit for successes while blaming others for failures. The inverse should be the standard.

11. Courage

a. <u>Definition</u>. Courage is a mental quality that recognizes fear of danger or criticism, but enables a Marine to proceed in the face of it with calmness and firmness.

b. <u>Significance</u>. Knowing and standing for what is right, even in the face of popular disfavor, is often the leader's lot. The business of fighting and winning wars is a dangerous one; the importance of courage on the battlefield is obvious.

    c. <u>Example</u>. Accepting criticism for making subordinates field
    day for an extra hour to get the job done correctly. [75]

Physical courage means that you can continue to function effectively when
there is physical danger present, which is obviously an essential trait for a
Marine leader operating in combat.

Moral courage is just as important in the Marines, and paramount in the
civilian world. It means having the inner strength to do what is right and
to accept blame when you are at fault. Often, it may mean standing up to
superiors to defend subordinates, making smart or just decisions that are
professionally hazardous, or any situation where doing the right thing carries
significant risk.

12. Knowledge

    a. <u>Definition</u>. Understanding of a science or an art. The range
    of one's information, including professional knowledge and an
    understanding of your Marines.

    b. <u>Significance</u>. The gaining and retention of current develop-
    ments in military and naval science and world affairs is import-
    ant for your growth and development.

    c. <u>Example</u>. The Marine who not only knows how to maintain
    and operate his assigned weapon, but also knows how to use
    the other weapons and equipment in the unit. [76]

It should always be a leader's goal to learn as much as possible about the
operations and people he or she is responsible for. Typically, your teammates
do not expect you to be an expert at all aspects of the operations they are
executing, but they do need to see that you are interested in learning more
about what they do and how you might be able to better enable them to perform their duties well. The Lifelong Learner and Teacher-Scholar 360° concepts detailed in this book are the cornerstones of obtaining this knowledge.
Use personal time to research material related to your field and *never* stop
learning—from *anyone* or *anything* that has something valuable to teach you.

13. Loyalty

    a. <u>Definition</u>. The quality of faithfulness to country, the Corps,
    and unit, and to one's seniors, subordinates, and peers.

b. <u>Significance</u>. The motto of our Corps is Semper Fidelis, Always Faithful. You owe unswerving loyalty up and down the chain of command: to seniors, subordinates, and peers.

c. <u>Example</u>. A Marine displaying enthusiasm in carrying out an order of a senior, though he may privately disagree with it. The order may be to conduct a particularly dangerous patrol. The job has to be done, and even if the patrol leader disagrees, he must impart confidence and enthusiasm for the mission to his men. [77]

Leaders should be loyal to the organization, its mission, and its people. But because all of the leadership traits must work in conjunction with one another, it's important to understand that *loyalty cannot be blind*. This trait doesn't include letting someone senior to you act in an unethical way out of a misguided sense of loyalty. You must also have enough moral *courage*, sound *judgement*, and *integrity* to do what is right.

14. Enthusiasm

a. <u>Definition</u>. The display of sincere interest and exuberance in the performance of duty.

b. <u>Significance</u>. Displaying interest in a task, and an optimism that it can be successfully completed, greatly enhances the likelihood that the task will be successfully completed.

c. <u>Example</u>. A Marine who offers to help carry a load that is giving someone great difficulty while on a hike despite being physically tired himself, encourages his fellow Marines to persevere. [78]

Be enthusiastic, optimistic, and willing to accept any challenge that comes your way. Subordinates, colleagues, and superiors will feed off of this energy.

Leadership is a complex skill defined by an individual's possession of characteristics that are worthy of respect, emulation, and even admiration. While some individuals are hardwired to have many of these qualities, they don't simply materialize in the vast majority of people—it takes a conscious effort to internalize and practice them.

These leadership traits I hold dear. They helped me become a better leader throughout my years of serving in leadership roles in various environments. They're timeless and interchangeable in any career field or personal role, and I encourage all leaders—in all capacities—to deliberately and continuously invest in their mastery.

"The best leaders are more focused on getting it right, than being right."

—Mike Ettore

11 Leadership Principles

- Know yourself and seek self-improvement
- Be technically and tactically proficient
- Know your Marines and look out for their welfare
- Keep your Marines informed
- Set the example
- Ensure the task is understood, supervised, and accomplished
- Train your Marines as a team
- Make sound and timely decisions
- Develop a sense of responsibility among your subordinates
- Employ your command in accordance with its capabilities
- Seek responsibility and take responsibility for your actions

Fidelis Leadership Group
Developing World Class Leaders

Source: U.S. Marine Corps

Chapter 22

LEADERSHIP PRINCIPLES

In addition to the *14 Leadership Traits*, all Marine leaders are taught *11 Leadership Principles* that help guide their attitudes and behavior. When carefully studied and implemented, these principles serve to raise the caliber of leadership displayed by individuals. The Leadership Principles directly support the Leadership Traits, and vice versa. And much like the traits, applying them consistently causes them to become second nature to experienced leaders.

The following are the 11 Leadership Principles that Marine leaders are taught early in their training. The quoted descriptions are also found in *MCTP 6-10B: Marine Corps Values: A User's Guide for Discussion Leaders*:

1. **Know yourself and seek self-improvement.**

   - This principle of leadership should be developed by the use of leadership traits. Evaluate yourself by using the leadership traits and determine your strengths and weaknesses. Work to improve your weaknesses and utilize your strengths. With a knowledge of yourself, and your experience and knowledge of group behavior, you can determine the best way to deal with any given situation. [79]

The Marine Corps instructs its leaders to learn about and improve themselves through "reading and observing," as well as asking for input from seniors and colleagues. Once weaknesses are identified, a leader should set a goal to improve these qualities and develop a plan to make it happen. Marines should also study the "causes for the success or the failure of other leaders." This is a superb bit of advice for business leaders, too. You can learn how to avoid making many mistakes by studying the actions and decisions made by other leaders in your industry, company, department, etc.

Bottom Line: Being a lifelong learner and continuously seeking knowledge and self-improvement should be your "default setting."

2. Be technically and tactically proficient.

- Before you can lead, you must be able to do the job. The first principle is to know your job. As a Marine, you must demonstrate your ability to accomplish the mission, and to do this you must be capable of answering questions and demonstrating competence in your MOS [military occupation specialty]. Respect is the reward of the Marine who shows competence. Tactical and technical competence can be learned from books and from on the job training. [80]

Good business leaders know their job thoroughly and possess a wide range of knowledge in related topics. In addition to being necessary for basic competence and success, this principle is closely related to the leadership traits of knowledge and judgement—if you don't display either the traits or the principle, your subordinates will not respect you.

Almost everyone has dealt with a leader who issues directives without really knowing what they're doing. If you haven't, you're fortunate. If you have, you're even luckier, because you can use how you felt about that leader as motivation to not repeat their mistakes. Know your stuff. If you don't, learn it.

3. Know your Marines and look out for their welfare.

- This is one of the most important of the principles. You should know your Marines and how they react to different situations. This knowledge can save lives. A Marine who is nervous and lacks self-confidence should never be put in a situation where an important, instant decision must be made. Knowledge of your Marines'

144

personalities will enable you, as the leader, to decide
how to best handle each Marine and determine when
close supervision is needed. [81]

Knowing who will perform is crucial for delegating tasks in a combat situation where lives are at stake but it's also essential in any organization. Who is good at a variety of tasks? Who has excellent communication skills that are well-suited for a certain role? Who will fold under the pressure of a tight deadline, and who will rise to the occasion?

A business leader must make a conscientious effort to get to know his or her people and understand how they deal with different scenarios. This enables optimal use of their skills and identifies any weaknesses that can be remedied with mentorship or training.

While it's possible to go overboard in a professional setting, try to learn a little bit about your team's personal lives, goals, and any challenges they may be facing; this enables you to help them accomplish the objectives and overcome the problems. A key tenet of knowing your people is caring for them, which is closely related to the Teacher-Scholar 360° concept and the leadership traits of unselfishness and integrity.

4. **Keep your Marines informed.**

    •   Marines by nature are inquisitive. To promote efficiency and morale, a leader should inform the Marines in his unit of all happenings and give reasons why things are to be done. This, of course, is done when time and security permit. Informing your Marines of the situation makes them feel that they are a part of the team and not just a cog in a wheel. Informed Marines perform better and, if knowledgeable of the situation, can carry on without your personal supervision. The key to giving out information is to be sure that the Marines have enough information to do their job intelligently and to inspire their initiative, enthusiasm, loyalty, and convictions. [82]

Junior enlisted Marines are often asked to do unpleasant or incredibly boring things, from standing post in 100+-degree temperatures or digging fighting holes on a new defensive position, only to be told to move a few meters an hour or so later, and begin digging *new* fighting holes. I've been the junior enlisted Marine in scenarios like this, and it's not fun. In fact, situations like this can be incredibly frustrating, if not infuriating, for those at the lowest levels of an organization who are repeatedly given conflicting or ever-changing orders, guidance, goals, and objectives.

In situations like this, leaders can minimize confusion, misalignment, and ill-will by providing some rationale and context to their teammates. Nobody likes to feel as if they are being "kept in the dark," and effective leaders know it is their responsibility to minimize this from happening in their units. This anecdote from a well-respected sergeant who led a squad of junior Marines in combat in Iraq illustrates the concept:

> The newly married twenty-six-year-old's easygoing nature permeated his management style. Only rarely did Dockter yell, barking at his guys when he had no time to baby the naturally unruly nineteen-and twenty-year-old PFCs and lance corporals. Usually he would ignore his men's endless complaints about whatever facet of the "colossal suck" of being in Iraq had drawn their ire. After all, according to him, "Marines ain't happy unless they're bitching."
>
> Sometimes, however, Dockter took the time to outline the rationale behind orders when the youngsters bucked, because junior Marines often gripe due to being kept in the dark. The most common response offered by a lance corporal when asked why he was doing something was a blank stare followed by, "Because the Gunny [gunnery sergeant] told me to do it." Dockter found that by occasionally explaining important things to them, he could get the men to quiet down and perform even the most difficult or boring tasks with workmanlike efficiency. [83]

Marines are no more "inquisitive ... by nature" than anyone else. Everyone likes to know that what they are assigned to do has a purpose, especially if the job is unpleasant. And leaders in the business world usually have a lot more latitude in explaining the rationale for a task. Don't feel constrained to justify every assignment or decision, but getting buy-in on the importance of a task, project, or new initiative can often work wonders in results.

5. Set the example.

- As a Marine progresses through the ranks by promotion, all too often he/she takes on the attitude of "do as I say, not as I do." Nothing turns Marines off faster! As a Marine leader your duty is to set the standards for your Marines by personal example. Your appearance, attitude, physical fitness, and personal example are all watched by the Marines in your unit. If your personal standards are high, then you can rightfully demand the same of your Marines. If your personal standards are not high you are setting a double standard for your Marines, and you will rapidly lose their respect and confidence. Remember your Marines reflect your image! Leadership is taught by example. [84]

The best leaders will not ask something of their team that they aren't willing to do themselves. A leader must also strive to show professional competence, an exemplary work ethic, a positive attitude, an impeccable appearance, and strength of character at all times. Setting an example is tied to all of the Leadership Traits. The more of them you display consistently, the more your people will emulate them.

6. Ensure that the task is understood, supervised, and accomplished.

- This principle is necessary in the exercise of command. Before you can expect your Marines to perform, they must know first what is expected of them. You must communicate your instructions in a clear, concise manner. Talk at a level that your Marines are sure to understand, but not at a level so low that would insult their intelligence. Before your Marines start a task, allow them a chance to ask questions or seek advice. Supervision is essential. Without supervision you cannot know if the assigned task is being properly accomplished. Over-supervision is viewed by subordinates as harassment and effectively stops their initiative. Allow subordinates to use their own techniques, and then periodically check their progress. [85]

Instructions or orders cannot be ambiguous. Your people must know exactly what is expected of them. They must understand the mission's desired end-state as well as the various steps to get there. Micromanagement is the mortal enemy of delegation, but you must establish benchmarks or check-ins that allow supervision of a task.

This communication is a two-way street. A subordinate should be encouraged to ask any questions that enable successful execution.

7. **Train your Marines as a team.**

- Every waking hour Marines should be trained and schooled, challenged and tested, corrected and encouraged with perfection and teamwork as a goal. When not at war, Marines are judged in peacetime roles: perfection in drill, dress, bearing and demeanor; shooting; self-improvement; and most importantly, performance. No excuse can be made for the failure of leaders to train their Marines to the highest state of physical condition and to instruct them to be the very best in the profession of arms. Train with a purpose and emphasize the essential element of teamwork.

- The sharing of hardships, dangers, and hard work strengthens a unit and reduces problems, it develops teamwork, improves morale and esprit and molds a feeling of unbounded loyalty and this is the basis for what makes men fight in combat; it is the foundation for bravery, for advancing under fire. Troops don't complain of tough training; they seek it and brag about it.

- Teamwork is the key to successful operations. Teamwork is essential from the smallest unit to the entire Marine Corps. As a Marine officer, you must insist on teamwork from your Marines. Train, play, and operate as a team. Be sure that each Marine knows his/her position and responsibilities within the team framework.

- When team spirit is in evidence, the most difficult tasks become much easier to accomplish. Teamwork is a two-way street. Individual Marines give their best, and in return the team provides the Marine with security, recognition, and a sense of accomplishment. [86]

As evidenced by the length of this section, teamwork is a *vital* concept for the Marine Corps or any military organization. Warfare is possibly the ultimate team endeavor. Much smaller, integrated forces that communicate and work in concert can defeat forces that are vastly superior in numbers. Beyond the tactical advantages, forming a team of individuals who respect each other and work well together creates comfort, shared purpose, and productivity.

There are many ways to nurture effective teams, but perhaps the most important is for a leader to treat individuals *as* a team. This means being cautious about providing too much effusive, public praise or blame for a specific person—a team succeeds or fails together. And shared accomplishment and difficulty bond them tighter.

8. Make sound and timely decisions.

- The leader must be able to rapidly estimate a situation and make a sound decision based on that estimation. Hesitation or a reluctance to make a decision leads subordinates to lose confidence in your abilities as a leader. Loss of confidence in turn creates confusion and hesitation within the unit.

- Once you make a decision and discover it is the wrong one, don't hesitate to revise your decision. Marines respect the leader who corrects mistakes immediately instead of trying to bluff through a poor decision. [87]

The impact of this principle on a leader's credibility and the success or failure of a mission is self-evident. It is closely tied to the traits of decisiveness and judgement, and the principle of being technically and tactically proficient.

9. Develop a sense of responsibility among your subordinates.

- Another way to show your Marines that you are interested in their welfare is to give them the opportunity for professional development. Assigning tasks and delegating the authority to accomplish tasks promotes mutual confidence and respect between the leader and subordinates. It also encourages the subordinates to exercise initiative and to give wholehearted cooperation in the accomplishment of unit tasks. When you properly delegate authority, you demonstrate faith in your Marines and increase their desire for greater responsibilities. If you fail to delegate authority, you indicate a lack of leadership, and your subordinates may take it to be a lack of trust in their abilities. [88]

A good leader will always ensure that his or her people have the opportunity for growth. In addition to inspiring loyalty and confidence, it has practical benefits in all environments: Individuals become more competent, more jobs are completed successfully, and the overall strength of the organization grows along with their abilities.

10. Employ your command within its capabilities.

- Successful completion of a task depends upon how well you know your unit's capabilities. If the task assigned is one that your unit has not been trained to do, failure is very likely to result. Failures lower your unit's morale and self-esteem. You wouldn't send a cook section to "PM" [conduct preventative maintenance on] a vehicle nor would you send three Marines to do the job of ten. Seek out challenging tasks for your unit but be sure that your unit is prepared for and has the ability to successfully complete the mission. [89]

This principle may have even greater relevance in the business world, as the Marines Corps—though highly adaptable—has a well-defined hierarchy and responsibilities. It also has an incredibly-strong vision and core focus: Winning battles. *Everything* supports this mission.

In contrast, many businesses or their individual departments fail to define a mission or core focus, or they struggle to keep it whole as they are dragged in different directions by (what often seems like) operational necessity—or ostensible opportunities that really create failures and inefficiencies.

My experiences as Kforce's new CIO provided some great examples of this drift. Among other reasons, the department had been failing because it attempted to do too many different things as requests for IT infrastructure poured in with little rhyme or reason.

Perhaps the first major decision I implemented was a change freeze, halting all new projects until the department got the basics right. We focused on improving processes, instilling core values of integrity and discipline, and completing essential deliverables successfully. From there, we implemented a Program Management Office that organized the suite of new and existing initiatives so that they were prioritized according to the company's overall mission and *well-suited to the department's capabilities.*

These changes were successful, but they weren't magical or incredibly complex. It was simply a matter of using an effective tool—a competent team of IT employees—for tasks that it was designed to do well. Follow the principles of knowing your people and developing the proficiency required to understand the mission; then use this knowledge to focus your team on what matters, and they will accomplish assigned tasks successfully.

If you are assigned to do something that you truly believe your team cannot (or should not) complete—either through lack of training, time, focus, or tools—respectfully make the case to your leader, and back up the argument with facts. Doing this looks out for the welfare of your team and employs the traits of integrity and moral courage.

11. **Seek responsibilities and take responsibility.**

- For professional development, you must actively seek out challenging assignments. You must use initiative and sound judgement when trying to accomplish jobs that are not required by your grade. Seeking responsibilities also means that you take responsibility for your actions. You are responsible for all your unit does or fails to do. Regardless of the actions of your subordinates, the responsibility for decisions and their application falls on you. You must issue all orders in your name. Stick by your convictions and do what you think is right, but accept justified and constructive criticism. Never remove or demote a subordinate for a failure that is the result of your own mistake. [90]

Seeking responsibilities is key to becoming a good leader—though it's a balancing act in light of the previous principle. You should *almost always* attempt to take on things that challenge you personally, and *often* look for tasks that challenge (and improve) your team. But in a bid to excel, many a young, hard-charging Marine leader has made the mistake of going after missions that don't make sense—or worse, get people killed unnecessarily.

Whether you're leading in combat or business, be sure that "your eyes aren't bigger than your stomach." Ensure that the mission is viable and that your people have the tools and skills they need to succeed. Once these elements are in place, by all means, *go for it!*

The key here is using judgement—weighing the challenge within the context of your team's abilities and core focus, as well as the fact that you will accept responsibility. Your willingness to do so shouldn't be a factor in whether you decide to take on something difficult—a good leader will *always* be responsible and accountable.

As previously mentioned, the Leadership Traits and Principles are fundamentally connected. In a nutshell, if you constantly work on developing and implementing one, by default you will be leveraging several of the others. Study, diligence, focused and deliberate practical experience, and a self-reflective "feedback loop" measured against these time-tested traits and principles can help shape you into an exceptional leader.

"I was a Captain in the Marine Corps and it's not lost on me how that helped me develop as a leader and the impact it's had on business and my career."

—Charles Phillips, CEO of Infor, former Co-President of Oracle and philanthropist

Chapter 23

DELEGATION

An essential element of the *Science of Leadership* taught to all Marine leaders is the concept of *delegation*—the assignment of various tasks, along with an appropriate level of authority, to subordinate leaders and individuals within their units. It is emphasized early in a Marine leader's development that one of the most effective ways to maximize speed while successfully attacking assigned missions is to tap into the wide range of knowledge and experience that resides within their unit. New Marine leaders are taught that during the stressful situations in which they may one day find themselves, being able to effectively delegate is one of the most important skills they can possess.

This training is based on the concept that effective delegation is a potent force multiplier, enabling the unit as a whole to achieve more and do it faster than if the execution of tasks is tightly controlled by senior leaders. These young leaders are also taught that *multi-tasking* is usually a bad idea. It's largely been proven to cause excessive risk and often yields poor results; many tasks or missions are done poorly because the leader was overloaded with too many priorities. And predictably, he or she did none of them as well as they could have been done, or actually did them at all.

Simply put, it is emphasized—relentlessly and forcefully—to new Marine leaders that one of the fastest ways of becoming an effective leader is to actively practice and master the science of delegation, to the point that they can artfully employ this critical skill and achieve far better results.

The Flag Pole Test

There is a classic lesson used in Marine Corps leadership classes at The Basic School that conveys the importance of delegation. The instructor presents the class of newly commissioned second lieutenants with a scenario:

> "You are told by your company commander on Monday morning, 'Lieutenant, you see the flagpole next to the parade deck? We need to take it down and put the new one up. We need it done by 1700 (5pm) on Saturday; we're going to have a battalion change of command ceremony at that time. This is your mission. Get it done.'"

The instructor provides a list of the dozen or so Marines under each new lieutenant's command and their ranks—including a gunnery sergeant, who is the lieutenant's direct report—and also provides "a detailed list of materials and equipment," and gives the class 30 minutes to individually plan and write down their orders. Some of the new lieutenants create incredibly detailed schemes and step-by-step orders; invariably, most of the class tries to ace the test by writing orders that are complex. It was a trick question, of course. [91]

At the end of the lesson, the instructor collects the orders and tells the students the correct answer:

> "Lieutenants, this is what you should do in this situation. Approach the gunnery sergeant and tell him, 'Gunny, the Captain just told me that we need to have the new flagpole installed by 1700 on Saturday for the battalion change of command ceremony. Let's meet again later this afternoon so you can brief me on your plan and discuss any resources and support you will need. Once the plan is approved, you can assemble the Marines and begin the work. I'll meet with you early each morning and late each afternoon to discuss the project's progress and to provide any support you may need from me. I'll also visit the work area a few times each day to see how things are going and to talk with the Marines.'"

The lieutenant approves the plan and he must now supervise it well. He'll be held accountable if the new flagpole fails to go up on time—but he's appropriately *delegated authority* to make it happen.

This simple lesson helps instill in new Marine leaders how fundamental delegation is to the way the Corps operates. It's a maxim in the Marine Corps that the officers may be in charge by formal title and authority, but the SNCO's and NCO's—who can think and act independently when given "mission-type" orders—are the backbone of the institution.

Maneuver Warfare

This independence is a force multiplier that enables a level of adaptation and agility which runs circles around opposing military organizations with top-heavy structures—those where senior officers tend to hoard authority and are reluctant to delegate it. On a dynamic battlefield (and in the business world), trust in qualified subordinates is crucial!

Marine leaders are taught that becoming effective delegators is vital to the Marine Corps' warfighting doctrine, which is known as *Maneuver Warfare*. This operational philosophy calls for speed of action and effective decision-making by leaders at all levels—often in the absence of orders and guidance from senior leaders—in the disciplined pursuit of achieving the *Commander's Intent*.

You'll learn about Maneuver Warfare and some of its key elements in the next section of the book, and you'll see how much this operational concept has influenced the Trust-Based Leadership™ model that I teach.

Application to Business

The importance of delegation isn't limited to the Marine Corps. Most business professionals recognize that delegation can generate efficiencies and serve as a force multiplier. What is different in a trust-based organization is the degree to which you can delegate those tasks as a leader, as well as the complexity of those delegated tasks. By focusing your efforts on developing all of your subordinate leaders—and ideally, there is an organization-wide focus on doing this—there will naturally be more people capable of successfully executing things delegated to them. And these tasks can become more complex over time, as junior leaders continue to gain experience and confidence.

Overcome the Barriers to Delegation

Nevertheless, many leaders struggle with delegation and there are innumerable business coaches, advice columns, and think pieces about how to overcome this challenge; specifically, outlining what to delegate and when. Writing in the *Harvard Business Review*, career and business strategist Jenny Blake describes this threshold as "peak ping":

> When I reach Peak Ping—a sense that I don't have room for yet another request without sacrificing my sanity or my strategic projects—I take a moment to focus on what matters most, and remind myself that I don't have to fly solo in my day-to-day work.

She then goes on to list 6 types of tasks that are delegable: Tiny, Tedious, Time-Consuming, Teachable, Terrible At, and Time Sensitive. [92]

Management consultant Jim Schleckser, CEO of the Inc. CEO Project, establishes a "70% Rule" for delegation among CEOs: "Put simply, if the person the CEO would like to perform the task is able to do it at least 70 percent as well as he can, he should delegate it." Others have put the threshold at 80 percent for *any* leader using this threshold. [93] [94]

And a variety of business and organizational gurus have established a host of systems and litmus tests, spanning anywhere from four to seven to 10 rules that attempt to define when and how to delegate. These systems are fine, and they are especially relevant in smaller units like start-ups or company departments, where executives or other leaders naturally wear a lot of hats and must learn to let go of some of their responsibilities as the organization grows. But these rules become less vital when the organization implements the Trust-Based Leadership™ model, for two reasons:

(1) **In the Trust-Based Leadership™ model, roles, responsibilities, and standards are clearly defined.** A CEO of a reasonably sized company will likely never be handling customer service requests, and a line manager at a manufacturing plant probably won't be reconciling invoices.

(2) **Trust-Based Leaders already make a concerted effort to develop other Trust-Based Leaders.** When this culture of leadership development is combined with clear standards, standard operating procedures, a common culture, and other elements, the number of individuals who meet that 70 or 80 percent rule increases dramatically.

A smart strategy to define delegation is to spend some time upfront organizing (or reorganizing) your company, department, team, or whatever unit you lead. With the help of your leaders and other key teammates, define who does what including setting very clear objectives for yourself as a leader. This doesn't mean you won't ever deviate from these rules—after all, adaptability is key—but it will minimize time spent wrestling with what to delegate. For example, a CEO of a small-to-midsized company should be focusing on how to grow the business as well as establishing its long-term goals. If she gets bogged down in the minutiae of daily operations, she's not really doing her job. It's time to delegate!

One of the first things I do with new executive coaching clients is ask them to show me their weekly schedule. If it's completely packed with no room for maneuver (and it usually is), something isn't right. I then challenge them to find a way to reduce their commitment to various meetings and appointments by 10 hours a week, and usually this time is reclaimed by pruning their existing meeting schedule. The leader should propose a number of meetings or other tasks that can be eliminated, and then ask subordinates: "Which of these can go and which of them need to stay, and what other ideas do you have that can save all of us time and free up our schedules?" Engaging your direct reports in this process is key!

Another technique for figuring out what to delegate is by auditing your tasks to find those where you are a single point of failure. The test is simple: Which of the essential things you do would go undone if you were taken out of the picture, and which of them would give *your* boss a fit if he or she didn't have you do them. These tasks should be prioritized for both delegation and the training to make that delegation possible.

The real challenge of delegation is when a complex task requires both the experience to do it well *and* a complex set of skills. Leaders meet this challenge by actively developing subordinate leaders and other key teammates. One vital aspect of doing this involves developmental assignments. Let's say you're a department head who is the only one who knows how to manage a certain type of project. You've got to change that in order to focus on the core functions of your job. You should work on the next project with one of your subordinate leaders, teaching them the relevant skills along the way. On the next project, you'll assign them to be the project leader with your supervision, but without your direct daily presence or management.

If that goes well, that subordinate leader's next project will come with a new assistant and the directive to develop *that* person into a competent project manager. Their job is to bring the project home successfully; but by about the midway point, the assistant should really be serving as the de facto project manager. This process should be repeated as long as it's feasible within the size of the unit, until you have multiple competent leaders for complex tasks. It develops leaders and important redundancies as well as makes the struggle over what to delegate a lot easier.

If it's a simple task that's outside of your defined responsibilities, delegate it. If it's a complex job outside of scope, develop the leaders required to delegate it and have them, in turn, develop others. The latter takes discipline, but it is a core requirement of Trust-Based Leaders within a trust-based organization.

Issue Mission-Type Orders—And Put Up Those Flagpoles!

Like teamwork, delegation is one of those organizational principles that everyone says is great, but fewer individuals and organizations do it effectively. The Marine Corps typically doesn't have this problem. Through clear standards and responsibilities, a strong culture, dedicated training, and the development of leaders at all levels, there is often less confusion about who should or can do something than there is in much of the business world. The private sector can embrace these principles too, and many great companies and other organizations already do it.

Being a Trust-Based Leader means hiring, developing, and relying on trustworthy people. You must delegate to your leaders and key teammates often. Solicit their suggestions on how to do something properly and support them with anything they need. Revise plans and instructions when necessary to adapt to new circumstances or a better plan. Then supervise—*while otherwise getting out of their way!*

Chapter 24

SUPERVISION

The military loves its acronyms (official or otherwise) and the Marine Corps is no exception. A civilian might overhear an exchange between two Marines and—between the acronyms, jargon, and slang—understand only about half of the conversation!

One official acronym that has been taught to generations of Marine leaders is BAMCIS (pronounced "bam-sis"). It's the acronym for a planning process known as the *Six Troop Leading Steps*. These steps are a succinct guide to planning and issuing orders at the tactical level, which often means those that come from the battalion commander all the way down to the individual fire teams of four or less Marines. These six steps are a logical and well-organized sequence of actions which enable a leader to make the best use of time, resources, and personnel while preparing for and executing a task.

The Six Troop Leading Steps are listed below:

Begin Planning: During this phase, the leader determines how much time he can devote to each required action before the operation begins. Usually, the unit leader will create a "reverse-planning" schedule for his unit. The leader issues a preliminary order that allows members of his unit to make preparations until the final orders are given.

Arrange for Reconnaissance: The leader contacts all necessary personnel needed for conducting reconnaissance of the area in which the unit will be operating.

Make Reconnaissance: Once all arrangements have been made, the unit leader meets with necessary parties and, to the extent possible, they go out and view the terrain, assess the enemy forces, and coordinate with adjacent units.

Complete the Plan: The unit leader uses the information gained from the reconnaissance to revise and complete a plan of action. At this point, he can make changes to the initial warning order by incorporating new information. Marine leaders use a five-paragraph-order format for small unit tactics. It uses another acronym called SMEAC, which stands for: **S**ituation, **M**ission, **E**xecution, **A**dministration and Logistics, **C**ommand and Signals. This detailed format means no vital information is left out when relaying the plan to troops.

Issue the Order: The unit leader gathers his unit and issues the order. The confidence and conviction with which this order is presented often influences how well a unit will perform.

Supervise: Mission success depends heavily on how effectively a leader supervises Marines and ensures that they are ready and able to complete the assigned task. [95]

Supervision is Another "Secret Weapon of Leadership"

The objective of this chapter isn't to teach you how to plan or issue orders and directives. Rather, it's to provide context to the technique of *supervision* and how much emphasis the Marine Corps places on it to leaders at all levels.

The Six Troop Leading Steps and their widely known acronym BAMCIS have been somewhat eclipsed in recent years by newer operational planning concepts and methods. However, the Marine Corps wisely chooses to teach all leaders to continuously supervise (and ensure that others appropriately supervise) the operation and administration of their units. Marine leaders know that while warfare is always evolving, adequately supervising all aspects of their organization is still one of the most essential ingredients of individual and unit success.

Like many others, the acronym has earned a lasting place in Marine Corps culture and lexicon and BAMCIS is still heavily referenced to put an emphasis on supervision. It's still common to hear an SNCO advising his NCOs to *"remember to execute the S in BAMCIS"* as they leave a meeting and return to their squads and teams.

Likewise, a company commander may tell his lieutenants, "The SNCOs will be running the live-fire exercise next week. Each of you will be assigned duties as the Range Safety Officer (RSO) on specific days. However, even when you're not the RSO, you're still expected to execute the S in BAMCIS and be vigilant for anything that might deviate from safety procedures and creates a dangerous situation on the range."

In some instances, junior Marines may see the battalion commander and sergeant major walking through the barracks after normal working hours talking with Marines. Some of the newer Marines might ask an NCO, "Why are they in our barracks? Are we in trouble?" The NCO will tell them, "No, we're good. The colonel and sergeant major visit us just about everywhere we go; they're just doing the S in BAMCIS like all good leaders do."

Applying effective supervision is one of the most important duties of a leader, and it's a cornerstone of the mission-type orders and decentralized command and control that are key to the Trust-Based Leadership™ model.

The Marine Corps defines supervision as a leader ensuring "compliance with the details of his plan until the mission is accomplished. This includes the timeline the commander set forth (operating environments often require that timelines are non-negotiable), the mission rehearsals defined (as combat realistic as possible), the inspections ... of personnel prior to execution, and the complete execution of the mission. Delegation to subordinate unit leaders is utilized, however check, do not assume, that your plan is being executed by subordinates to your standards." [96]

The above passage amplifies the need for all leaders to supervise in an appropriate and effective manner and to never, ever simply assume that everything is being planned, executed, sustained, and otherwise supervised effectively.

The Marine Corps depends on delegation to well-trained, responsible, and highly motivated Marines who carry out orders while taking initiative to fulfill the commander's intent. But, as you have learned from previous chapters, whatever happens or fails to happen remains the leader's responsibility—and he or she will always be held accountable for the results. The bridge between this cause and effect is the expectation that a leader will effectively supervise any plans, orders, operations, and tasks to make sure they are executed properly.

Application to Business

As a leader, it is imperative that you always stay on top of where things stand and how your plan is progressing. This rule also applies in any business organization that has a relatively flat structure which depends on employees who show initiative. And frankly, most of the best companies have exactly that structure.

What Constitutes Effective Supervision?

Effective supervision can be a tricky thing to design and implement. A version of *The Goldilocks Rule* applies—too little supervision and your team probably won't achieve the desired results; too much supervision means subordinates won't have the opportunity to develop or take initiative, and they may view their leaders as micromanagers.

Any leader, whether she is a Marine sergeant or a senior vice president in a Fortune 500 company, should know her people well enough to understand who might need more supervision and who can be trusted to follow instructions independently. It is also essential that she ensures that her people have everything they need—in terms of time, training, supplies, and equipment—for the task they've been assigned. The simplest framework for effective supervision involves these four elements:

- Create a process and schedule for tracking progress.

- Maintain open communication with all parties involved.

- Have contingency plans ready in case they're needed.

- Supervise at every level of leadership—but adjust the supervision accordingly based on the experience, knowledge, and competence of the people you are leading.

1. Create a Schedule Based on Clear Goals and Standards

Any unit or team should first have clearly defined goals, with clearly defined standards for accomplishing them.

In the machine gun section of a Marine weapons platoon, for example, a lance corporal machine gunner must be intimately familiar with the components of his weapon and its rate of fire, have the ability to react to stoppages and clear them effectively, conduct regular maintenance, and know how to disassemble and then reassemble the machine gun in six minutes or less. [97]

A Marine battalion commander's responsibilities and standards are vastly different, of course—but no less clear. And the business world obviously has its own measuring sticks, whether that's to provide technical support to a client within four hours of a support request being filed, hit a quarterly sales target of $5,000,000 in gross revenue, or achieve at least a 2% response on a direct marketing email campaign. These objectives form the basis of supervision, as well as providing the milestones used when designing a schedule to oversee the operation or task.

Once you have established clear-cut mission, goals and objectives, along with any standards or clarifying guidance germane to the situation, you should create a schedule to oversee execution. In the business world, the management aspect of leadership often takes the form of reviewing Key Performance Indicators (KPIs) and other specific, periodic reports.

In terms of more generalized leadership, supervision usually boils down to a schedule of effectively organized and focused meetings with subordinates, personal observation of the work environment, and interaction with those working on the "front lines." Read that last sentence again; it effectively illustrates how leaders can execute the S in BAMCIS in any environment or situation.

As a leader, set a meeting schedule that enables you to get an accurate grasp on progress from members of your team plus ensures that they have everything they need as the mission unfolds. Design the schedule *with* your subordinate leaders: Do we need to meet twice a day on this? Once a week? Create a realistic, informed timeline for reviewing the work. This initial schedule will inevitably change, however, in light of unanticipated events associated with your industry, company, project, product roll-out, etc.

Remember, meetings should adapt to the environment and operational tempo that your people are working in. Most important, these meetings should be enablers of progress; your subordinates should ultimately look forward to your meetings because they are where plans are refined, actions coordinated, friction is mitigated, problems are resolved, and new opportunities are chosen to be exploited.

2. Maintain Open Communication with All Involved Parties

You must consistently communicate with your teammates to understand what they need to accomplish their mission and any obstacles they are facing that affect their ability to do so. Open communication is essential for identifying the right benchmarks, key performance indicators, revenue targets, etc., as well as how often you need to evaluate them. At some point, once the wheels are in motion and you see the mission is being executed properly, you should ask your people: "Are we meeting too much? For example, would backing off to a weekly meeting be more efficient than meeting twice per week?"

"Sir, you're right on the money, I was just about to come to you and recommend that," a Marine first sergeant or executive officer might respond to his commander. "We're at the point where I think meeting once a week is fine. We know your guidance and expectations, you know our capabilities, you're asking the right questions, and to be honest with you, things are going well; I recommend that we meet once a week from this point forward."

Proper communication entails a lot more than setting a schedule, of course. It should enable you to fully understand any challenges that crop up, identify situations and issues that need to be quickly corrected, and assess whether the team has all of the resources and support they need—many of which only a leader can provide.

Some basic rules of thumb: A leader must have a clear conscience that he or she is supervising appropriately and effectively. And it's imperative to communicate openly and frequently with the team, asking them questions like:

- Are you getting what you need?

- Am I asking the right questions?

- Am I asking these questions too often; am I not asking them enough?

- What can I do right now that will enable you to do your job more effectively and efficiently?

Competent and trusted subordinates will give you invaluable feedback on any and all of these items.

3. Have Contingency Plans Ready in Case They're Needed

Effective supervision relies on open and responsive communication to identify problems that imperil the mission. The mandate then becomes how to fix any issues that crop up—quickly.

The best leaders know that effective supervision includes being proactive and having contingency plans to address various issues that are likely to arise. If a Marine leader is overseeing a 20-mile conditioning hike and the supply of water runs out, what contingencies are in place to quickly remedy the situation? If he's done his job well, he and his staff will know where water points are located and how they'll get the unit resupplied.

Likewise, if a business leader or member of a project team is injured, has a family emergency, or decides to exit the company, who will take their place? When a crucial vendor closes up shop in the middle of a project, where will you quickly get an equivalent product or service?

It's wise (and very practical) to assume that no original plan will survive contact with the reality of an ever-changing business environment, and a leader must be poised to provide essential direction and support. Effective leaders in agile, decentralized organizations are always superb facilitators and they know that contingency plans provide them with the flexibility to find ways to win when challenges and obstacles surface.

4. Supervise at Every Level of Leadership—But Adjust Accordingly

Inadequate supervision is what gets everyone from Marine generals and Fortune 500 executives to human resources and marketing department heads in trouble. Every leader must supervise at every level. There are obviously vastly different ways to get it done, however.

Generally speaking, the lower you go in an org chart toward the front line—in the Marine Corps or the business world—the more supervision tends to involve leaders closely observing the actions of their teammates and ensuring that established policies and procedures are being followed.

> "This is how we load our products on our custom-built delivery trucks."

> "We have set procedures for entering customer data in our contact management system."

"Customer service requests must be dealt with through these communication channels, on this timeline and in this sequence."

Front-line leaders conduct a lot more of this hands-on, direct supervision.

The front-line leader's boss does less of it in continuous proximity to the front-line employees. She'll tend to lead by walking around and observing operations and by asking the appropriate questions during meetings. While walking around, she might stop and talk to a subordinate leader or teammate: "Hi, how are you doing? How's the new equipment working? Is there anything you need that I might be able to get for you?"

At the *front-line* and often *customer-facing* point of the leadership spectrum, the team leaders and managers are often physically located with their people. This enables them to provide on-the-spot supervision and guidance to their teams. Often, they may even be the only onsite leader.

This situation is only possible when the company's version of SNCOs or officers—directors, vice presidents, and other senior executives—know that the NCOs/front-line leaders are trained, competent individuals who can take initiative and execute the *commander's intent*.

In other words, they know that their leaders demonstrate the essential qualities of the Trust-Based Leader and are capable of producing the desired results with a minimum of guidance and supervision.

Move one or two levels up the chain of command, however, and a senior leader often isn't on the same floor, in the same building, or even the same geographical location as the teams and functions they are responsible for. The leader's *span of control* widens immensely, as do his or her responsibilities. Supervision must adapt accordingly.

Consider a Marine lieutenant colonel leading a battalion in combat, for example. While his company commanders (captains) and platoon commanders (lieutenants) are focused on the current battle, the battalion commander may be called up to a hastily called meeting at the regimental command post to participate in the planning of a mission that has just been assigned from the division commander—and must be executed later that day.

While junior officers, SNCOs, and NCOs are leading their units and, of course, executing the *"the S in BAMCIS"* on the immediate battle, the battalion commander (and several members of his staff) must fulfill his higher-level responsibilities of planning the new mission to be conducted later that day. But while doing this, he must *also maintain effective control and supervision on current operations*, many of which are happening a significant distance from his location. Similarly, business executives and other senior leaders must ensure the adequate supervision of a company's daily operations while formulating long-term plans and dealing with other strategic issues.

Failing to Adapt Supervision with Greater Responsibility is a Common Problem

Properly supervising as you move into higher levels of leadership involves striking a balance. It relies on less direct observation (which is often physically impossible) and a lot more on effective organization of objectives, people, and resources, as well as management techniques such as policies, procedures, and a well-designed meeting and reporting schedule.

Again, this form of decentralized and delegative leadership is only possible when the leaders and key members of the team are well-trained and adequately engaged and motivated. If a senior leader supervises his people in an appropriate manner, all will usually go well. If he does it every hour of every day—or if a twice-a-week check is appropriate but he's doing every day—that's micromanagement, which is a fatal blow to any organization attempting to employ the Trust-Based Leadership™ model.

Micromanagement not only prevents senior leaders from spending time on what they're paid to do—think, plan, and act strategically—it also develops subordinate leaders who will not make a decision or do anything unless they are directed to do it. It kills initiative, resulting in a rigid and overly bureaucratic organization that reacts only upon the direction of the most senior leaders (much like a dictatorship). And in many instances, entire companies, divisions, departments, or project teams are paralyzed with indecision and inaction when the senior leaders are unavailable.

A Failure of Supervision. And a Terrible Example of Accountability

The 2018 shooting at Marjorie Stoneman Douglas High School in Parkland, Florida shocked and saddened the nation while putting intense scrutiny on local leadership.

At 2:19 pm on Valentine's Day, a former student entered the school and used an AR-15 rifle to shoot staff members and students during a roughly six-minute attack. The shooter then dropped the weapon and fled the premises, only to be captured in a nearby neighborhood a little over an hour later. Seventeen people were murdered, including 14 students, and 17 others were wounded. The tragedy filled the nation with outrage and grief, sparking political activism and calls for improved school security. [98]

In the aftermath of the attack, video and testimony showed that an armed Broward County sheriff's deputy—the school's dedicated resource officer—as well as at least two other deputies hesitated to move toward the gunfire and engage the shooter or help victims. Other law enforcement officers, many of them with the Coral Springs Police Department, reported that they moved past two Broward County deputies to enter the school. The posture of the deputies was contrary to standard police active shooter training, and these reported failures naturally focused criticism on the Broward Sheriff's Office and its leader, Sheriff Scott Israel. [99]

What was Sheriff Israel's response to this criticism—specifically, questions about the reaction of Marjory Stoneman's onsite school resource deputy?

> "Leaders are responsible for the agency. Leaders are not responsible for a person," Israel told a local NBC News affiliate. "I gave him a gun. I gave him a badge. I gave him the training. If he didn't have the heart to go in, that's not my responsibility." [100]

> "I can only take responsibility for what I knew about," Israel said during a separate interview with CNN. "I exercised my due diligence. I've given amazing leadership to this agency." [101]

Suffice it to say that I almost fell out of my chair as I watched this interview and heard Sheriff Israel make these comments!

Let's unpack what he said.

Leaders are *Always* Responsible *and* Accountable

The tangible link between responsibility and accountability is the guidance, support, and supervision a leader must provide to ensure that individuals are properly trained, equipped, and assessed as being willing and able to do their jobs. Whether a deputy has "the heart to go in" may not be under a sheriff's direct control in a tactical situation, but it's certainly within his scope of responsibility—which includes vetting, training, and supervising a police officer who is explicitly charged with and expected to serve and protect students in even the most dangerous situations.

Complete and total on-scene supervision is often impossible and good leaders can be genuinely let down by an individual—but they remain responsible and accountable. The consequences may or may not be fair. Nevertheless, this is simply the burden of being a leader.

Finally, proclaiming one's own "amazing leadership" is like a professional comedian having to explain a joke. "It's funny, trust me on this." Amazing leaders don't have to tell people they are amazing leaders. They simply lead well, and others perceive it.

The deputy who failed to immediately respond to the gunfire arguably showed more immediate accountability than his boss. "It's haunting," he told *The Washington Post* in a June 2018 interview. "I've cut that day up a thousand ways with a million different what-if scenarios, but the bottom line is I was there to protect, and I lost 17." He was eventually arrested for these failures the following year and now faces "11 charges of neglect of a child, culpable negligence and perjury." [102] [103]

In my opinion, Sheriff Israel's statements and demeanor are the antithesis of sound leadership, including its supervision component. He *owned* Broward County from a law enforcement standpoint. If Israel were serving as a Marine leader and a similar incident had taken place—especially if he publicly denied accountability—I feel confident in saying that he would have been promptly relieved of his leadership role.

Apparently, many of his subordinates agree with my assessment. On April 26th, 2018, The Broward Sheriff's Office Deputies Association held an unprecedented no-confidence referendum on Israel's leadership. 534 out of the 628 union members who participated voted no confidence. [104]

"The sheriff is a complete liar, capital letters on that!" commented union president Jeff Bell, who called on Rick Scott, Florida's governor at the time, to remove Israel. "He fails to listen to the membership. And he wants to blame everybody else for his problems."

After the no-confidence vote, the union put up two billboards calling for Scott to fire Israel. The governor's office responded that it was waiting for the completion of a Florida Department of Law Enforcement investigation before taking any action. Israel was in the middle of his second term as Broward County Sheriff and wouldn't have faced re-election until 2020. But newly elected Florida Governor Ron DeSantis finally suspended him from office on Jan. 11, 2019. Nevertheless, Israel is appealing the suspension and plans to run for sheriff again. [105] [106] [107] [108]

All of this said, I cannot say that Sheriff Israel is a bad person or is completely lacking in character. What I can say, based upon what I've observed and read about his handling of the tragic school shooting, is that he clearly lacked an appropriate understanding of some of the most basic concepts of leadership, most notably authority, responsibility, delegation, supervision, and humility. As I was writing about this tragedy and Israel's attitude and actions, I found myself wondering if he had ever received any form of formal leadership training and development throughout his career in law enforcement.

If you are ever forced to weather a setback as a leader, do not double down on failure with stupidity and arrogance. Shirking responsibility and trying to pass off accountability are anathemas to good leadership and are especially toxic when done in an organization that uses the Trust-Based Leadership™ model. In the above example, doing so directly led to more criticism, significant morale problems, and a revolt from those who were being led.

Take responsibility for failures and setbacks. Hold yourself accountable for results. And if accountability isn't severe enough to cost you your position, press ahead with grace, humility, and a resolve to investigate and fix any errors, to ensure that they never happen again.

Being held accountable for the actions of everyone in your organization may not always seem fair, but that's the ultimate price of leadership. And proper supervision is an essential link between having great power and responsibility and being accountable for them.

"Regarding leadership development, of these things, I am certain:

- The major factor in an organization's success is the quality of its leaders.

- Leaders are not born, they are trained and developed.

- Effective leaders master the Science and Art of Leadership, in that order.

- Leadership development can be greatly accelerated via focused training and coaching.

- Anyone with the proper desire and initiative can become a World Class Leader."

—Mike Ettore

The Four Indicators of Leadership

1. Morale

2. Esprit de Corps

3. Discipline

4. Proficiency

Fidelis Leadership Group
Developing World Class Leaders

Source: U.S. Marine Corps

Chapter 25

THE 4 INDICATORS OF LEADERSHIP

As you know, a Marine leader's three main responsibilities are accomplishing the mission, taking care of his or her teammates, and developing the next generation of leaders. Marines are taught that their ability to execute these responsibilities determines the quality of their leadership as well as that of subordinate leaders within a unit.

Throughout this book, a heavy emphasis is placed upon the time-tested leadership axiom, *"As goes the leader, so goes the team."* Another way of saying this is that the success of any unit depends upon the leadership exercised by leaders at *all levels* of the organization.

One way that Marine leaders are taught to assess the state of leadership within units is to evaluate what are known as *The Four Indicators of Leadership.* As defined in various Marine Corps leadership training programs and courses, they are:

- Morale

- Esprit de Corps

- Discipline

- Proficiency

Morale: Morale is the individual's state of mind. It depends on and defines the Marine's attitude toward everything.

Esprit de Corps: The loyalty to, pride in, and enthusiasm for the unit shown by its members. Whereas morale refers to a Marine's attitude, esprit de corps is the unit's spirit.

Discipline: Discipline is the individual or group attitude that ensures prompt obedience to orders and appropriate action in the absence of orders.

Proficiency: Proficiency is the technical, tactical, and physical ability of the Marine and the unit to perform the assigned mission. [109]

I don't think I have to go into much detail to ensure that readers understand how critical these four elements are to the success of any Marine Corps unit, especially during high-stakes combat operations. Likewise, I am sure that you can understand why they are continuously observed and assessed by leaders, and the sense of urgency that happens whenever a deficiency exists and is in need of remedial action.

Like so many leadership concepts, there are also many additional factors involved in the Four Indicators of Leadership that are not mentioned in the definitions shown above.

Seasoned Marine leaders know this, and they develop an intuitive sense of the factors through training and experience. I like to refer to this as "Old eyes that are backed up by 20/20 hindsight, wisdom, and lessons learned." This intuition enables them to simply observe a unit as it prepares for or executes its duties, and very quickly formulate an assessment of the current state of its morale, esprit de corps, discipline, and proficiency.

These leaders long ago learned the value of continuously exercising the *S in BAMCIS* and they often do this by utilizing the technique of *Leadership By Walking Around*—simply being amongst their units and individual Marines on a routine basis.

Application to Business

As in the Marine Corps, people working in the various departments and teams within companies will only be as effective as their leaders. When properly adapted to specific business environments, the Four Indicators of Leadership can be quite useful for business leaders who seek awareness of the current state of their teams and the leadership that is being provided to them.

Morale: In any company or business unit, morale consists of various tangible and intangible factors. As you might expect, how members of these teams feel about themselves and one another is perhaps the most important aspect the current state of morale. Members of a team that has high morale typically exhibit enthusiasm, confidence, a willingness to cooperate with others, and a general sense of well-being as they perform their duties. Because it is so important to the long-term success of a company, the current state of morale must be continuously assessed by leaders.

Esprit de Corps: The Marine Corps is famous for its esprit de corps. Marines typically and proudly demonstrate a lifelong loyalty and spirit of *"Gung Ho"* for their beloved Corps that is rarely matched by members of other branches of the armed forces. Some of the very best companies have also managed to tap into the dynamic of esprit de corps; a positive and fraternal unit spirit demonstrated by teammates at all levels. Leaders in these companies understand the very real benefits associated with teammates who believe in their company's vision, mission, and core values, and feel a strong sense of pride in belonging to something bigger than themselves.

Discipline: Discipline is no less a factor in the long-term success of a company than it is for the Marine Corps. While the members of a company may exhibit superb morale and esprit de corps, the full potential of the organization will never be realized unless they also possess discipline while executing their individual and collective duties. The Trust-Based Leadership™ model emphasizes the importance of individual discipline and a willingness to follow established plans, policies, and procedures. And, when appropriate, team members must demonstrate initiative and a bias for action in the absence of guidance, as long as they're aligned with achieving the Commander's Intent.

Proficiency: In the business world, proficiency is the ability of individuals at all levels of a company to effectively execute and sustain the technical and tactical requirements of their specific roles and responsibilities. Clearly, it is the responsibility of leaders to ensure that members of their teams are proficient and are provided with the training, tools, and resources to remain so. A company may have superb morale, excellent esprit de corps, and individual and organizational discipline, but without adequate proficiency, its success is doubtful.

Like their Marine counterparts, business leaders should constantly assess the Four Indicators of Leadership within their organizations. The very best leaders know this, and they're typically known for their habit of *Leadership By Walking Around.* The appearance of these leaders eating lunch with teammates in the cafeteria, walking around various departments and work spaces, and talking to workers are the rule, rather than the exception.

As they stay close to the teams they lead—in an appropriate manner that doesn't disrupt business operations—these leaders can easily observe and assess the current state of morale, esprit de corps, discipline, and proficiency.

"Leadership is a force multiplier
that can catapult a company
to the heights of its industry!"

—Mike Ettore

Chapter 26

PROFESSIONAL REPUTATION

The simple definition of the word *reputation* is the common opinion that people have about someone or something, or the way in which people think of someone or something. Your *professional reputation* is how those at your place of work and others in your profession and industry think of you.

Leaders should always be cognizant of how important their professional reputation is to their long-term success in leadership roles. This awareness is not merely based on self-interest but the realization that a solid professional reputation is a byproduct of consistently exhibiting sound character, competence, leadership traits and principles, moral courage, and other qualities associated with the very best leaders.

Marines are taught early on that <u>their professional reputation is one of their most precious assets</u>, and that they began building theirs from the very moment they stepped off of the bus at Boot Camp or Officer Candidates School. One's professional reputation is exceptionally important, and this is especially true for those serving in leadership roles.

You Have Two Professional Reputations

There are two forms of reputation. First is the *"official"* one that people see on paper. For Marines, this is usually encoded in years of Marine Corps fitness reports that are stored in their personal records; and for business leaders, its what's contained in their human resources file, professional biography, and resume. The second reputation is the *"real"* one that is created over time through your actions and interactions with others.

Many individuals can get pretty far based on the former, but the latter is almost always closer to the truth. And if the two reputations don't match, inevitably the real one will almost always override the official reputation among a person's colleagues.

You'll Never Outrun Your True Professional Reputation

There's an old saying that emphasizes the point I'm trying to make; "Good or bad, your reputation will always enter the room before you do!"

A great example can be seen in the recent *#MeToo* movement and the rash of sexual harassment and assault accusations made toward powerful people in various industries. While some of these charges may wind up being unsubstantiated or isolated examples, in many cases, numerous accusers came out of the woodwork with additional allegations once the first one surfaced. And if three, five, or dozens of people are accusing the same person of similar behavior, the allegations quickly gain immense credibility.

This maxim goes far beyond sexual harassment and similar accusations. Favoritism, bullying, creating a toxic work environment, cheating on reports, or misallocation of funds are all things that others will likely observe—and all varieties of shady behavior may come back to haunt a leader who exhibits them.

A professional reputation can also have very *practical effects* on both professional success and the ability to lead.

Your professional reputation—good or bad—will follow you throughout your career and impact how well you do your job. It affects how others interact with you, including your ability to influence people and the degree to which your leaders will entrust you with opportunities to lead.

Many excellent leaders have personally slipped at certain points and damaged their reputations. This could be a lapse in their personal lives, becoming known as a micromanager who fails to develop other leaders, or simply a colossal failure that may or may not have been within that leader's control. Regardless, the good and bad aspects of an individual leader accrue to form a reputation, and the negative examples tend to resonate more with others.

Some Leaders Don't Take This Advice Seriously—And Eventually, They Pay for It

I've said previously that the Marine Corps, like almost all organizations, has its ten-percenters— those on the bad end of what I refer to as the *"Leadership Bell Curve."* These people simply cannot or will not meet the high expectations associated with being a Leader of Marines.

Surprisingly and frustratingly, in some cases, Marines with less than stellar professional reputations still seem to get promoted and assigned to prestigious roles and career-enhancing assignments. I dare say that every Marine knows at least one senior leader who meets this description.

Marines like this often appear to be "one step ahead" of their professional reputations and never held accountable for their actions. They present a good appearance on paper and to higher leadership, but most individuals within their chain of command know the real deal.

The Marine Corps is a relatively small institution and, in most instances, justice prevails. Substandard Marine leaders eventually find themselves alone inside a room with their professional reputation. One or more of their senior leaders will then enter the room, slam the door shut, and proceed with some form of disciplinary hearing. Those who have failed to live up to the *Special Trust and Confidence* associated with being a Marine leader will finally be held accountable for current and past transgressions.

I know of one Marine leader (a senior officer), for example, who always seemed to get away with everything. Fraternization, taking unethical or unsafe shortcuts, not following established rules or guidelines, concealing or misstating the truth—he seemed to do it all. And while this officer somehow maintained an excellent reputation with his superiors and got promoted, many Marines who had worked with him throughout his career knew the truth regarding his poor character and habitual disregard for the expectations and responsibilities of a Marine officer.

Eventually, as he continued to engage in what had been a career-long habit of inappropriate activity with young, enlisted female Marines, someone reported him to senior leaders. The subsequent investigation then looked back at other aspects of his behavior and the charges grew on a daily basis. And once the dam broke, individuals who had worked with him in the past came forward to testify about his poor character and behavior.

After seemingly getting away with unethical and unacceptable behavior for over two decades, all of his past lapses of character and indiscretions suddenly dropped on him like a ton of bricks. He eventually was found guilty of various offenses at a court-martial and was dismissed from the Marine Corps in disgrace.

Application to Business

The above is a pretty extreme example, but the lesson remains the same for business leaders: How you live and behave as a leader accrues over time and will catch up with you. It's simply a lot easier to sleep well at night when you consistently do the right thing, and this has benefits for your professional reputation and long-term leadership success.

Let's be honest, all of us know at least one person like this Marine officer in the business world; if not from a personal perspective, certainly from watching the never-ending litany of news stories about high-level leaders who were caught behaving badly.

I've known more than a few business leaders who displayed many positive leadership qualities, but their professional reputations suffered because of their history of making bad decisions, poor temperament, and a tendency to take unethical shortcuts that put themselves and others in jeopardy.

For example, as in the Marine Corps, there are clearly some leaders in the business world who get things done and have a record of success—but routinely fail to develop subordinate leaders. Their organizations perform brilliantly while they are present and personally directing routine operations. But the results are often fleeting.

When leaders like this leave their organizations and someone new steps in to lead, the new leader often discovers that the initiative and a bias for action are lacking among the members of the leadership team and, in many instances, throughout the entire organization. Faced with a new leader with a more delegative leadership style, the organization often begins to fail in various ways as the leaders struggle to satisfy a new boss who actually expects them to lead, make decisions, and take appropriate actions without being provided with continuous guidance and detailed direction.

This is because the previous leader was leading almost entirely through his personal talent, experience, and *force of will* rather than empowering junior leaders by training and developing them. Once this type of leader leaves the organization, things often fall apart quickly because other leaders have not been developed and cannot function effectively without constant, detailed guidance. I've seen this situation play out a number of times and it's always sad to see the less-senior members of the leadership team realize that they haven't at all been developed as leaders by their previous boss.

The negative implications for this type of leader's professional reputation may take longer to accrue, but eventually this person will be known as *"one who can get the job done, but doesn't develop other leaders capable of doing the same."*

My personal experience is that, like the Marine Corps, which prioritizes the development of current and future leaders, the very best companies in the business world take a similarly dim view of any leader who fails to train and develop a strong bench of junior leaders—even if their teams are otherwise successful.

Elements of Your Professional Reputation

By now, you may be wondering what one's professional reputation consists of and how it can be effectively developed and maintained. These are excellent questions and the good news is that the answers are quite simple and, for most, easy to do! Some of the elements of a solid professional reputation include:

- Success. Perhaps more than any other factor, a consistent track record of strong results is crucial to forming a good professional reputation.

- Displaying impeccable character and behavior, and providing consistently good leadership. Does this person effectively live the concepts, philosophies, science, and art of leadership outlined in the previous chapters? Is this individual hypocritical about any of them?

- Investing in and caring for subordinates. Does a leader develop other leaders and allow them to grow? Does he or she do everything within reason to support team members in trying circumstances, whether they are professional or personal challenges?

181

TRUST-BASED LEADERSHIP™

- Lead by example—always! Most important of all, do you lead by example in all that you do and say?

Repairing a Damaged Professional Reputation

Everyone makes mistakes, so it's not about achieving perfection. But even if a big mistake or repeated ones are enough to tarnish a reputation, it's often possible to recover.

Doing this is a lot tougher in the Marine Corps than in civilian life. If a Marine leader receives a DUI, gets caught submitting a dishonest report, or an individual under his or her command dies during a training exercise, it's almost always a "career-ender." While there have been instances when this type of zero-defects discipline has not always consistently applied, the Corps tends to have a "no mercy" policy on major lapses in a leader's judgement, including ethical and moral ones. A Marine officer could otherwise be considered the next Chesty Puller (look him up, he's a big deal!), but it doesn't matter: If he commits a single integrity violation, he's done.

Thankfully, the business world is often more forgiving—and I think this is a good thing. Human nature being what it is, people will make mistakes. Some of them will be honest and some of them quite dumb, but everyone, at some point, makes mistakes. As a business leader, you may be blessed with the opportunity to recover from errors and reinvent yourself as a better leader. You may also be able to use your own authority to provide similar opportunities for your teammates when they deserve them.

An Example of Repairing a Reputation

I once worked with an executive who successfully repaired his less than stellar professional reputation. He was very intelligent and was usually the smartest guy in the room, but he *knew it* and was often arrogant and condescending—which of course tended to put people off. He was also not a team player and, in general, made no effort to serve as a colleague to those around him.

This manifested in him always putting his department's goals first, while dragging his feet when the company set priorities that called for resources and effort to be steered toward other departments and projects. In other words, when his department was the main effort, he was happy and energized. But when other departments were given priority, he withdrew and did the minimum required to get by.

Several of his peers addressed this problem with him but got no relief, so the complaints were eventually kicked up to the next level and he was counseled by his C-level executive. Despite the counseling, he still failed to adapt, and finally did something that caught the attention—in a major and negative way—of senior executives. I was told that he was slated to be fired in a couple of weeks.

This executive was saved at the last minute by the fact that his boss suddenly fell ill. There was no way the company could fire him now that his boss was going to be recovering from his illness for several months. Senior executives assured me and several others that he would still be terminated when his boss returned to work but, for now, he would be allowed to remain and fill some of the void.

Here's the positive ending: I'll never be sure whether someone had a powerful conversation with this guy or if he sensed that his head was on the chopping block, but to his credit, he changed for the better. He started cooperating with other leaders and departments—working to integrate his team and resources with new initiatives, even when his team wasn't the main effort. He went from being aloof to becoming an enthusiastic teammate. It was a complete turnaround in attitude and behavior.

As a result, he prospered, going from "about to be fired" to eventually being promoted a couple of times within the organization. These days, he's a high-level executive in a very large organization and his professional reputation among his peers and within his profession is quite good.

Nevertheless, think about all of the self-inflicted damage this individual caused earlier in his career. He tanked his reputation and if it weren't for a twist of fate (not being fired due to his boss getting sick), there is a very good chance he wouldn't have the level of success he enjoys today. The bottom line: You *can* recover from a bad reputation, but it's a lot smarter to avoid creating one in the first place.

Leadership by example is perhaps the most fundamental way to establish and keep a good reputation. The way you treat people is similarly crucial. Don't just practice some of the elements of good leadership or preach them to others; try to *live* all of them.

Application to Business

Beyond healthy ambition and self-interest, such as the effect it can have on promotions and career advancement, your professional reputation can have a profound impact on your long-term success as a business leader.

For example, senior executives are often hired based on their previous successes <u>as well as their demonstrated ability to attract and nurture talented people</u>. Skilled professionals at all levels will often flock to work for this type of leader, including many people who have previously worked for him or her. When people hear about a leader who is competent, treats their teammates well, and invests heavily in their professional development, <u>they naturally gravitate toward them and seek out opportunities to join their teams.</u>

In contrast, inadequate leaders often cause avoidable voluntary turnover within their teams, as people simply "vote with their feet" to escape poor leadership and stagnant or even toxic work environments. This type of leader almost always has a professional reputation that aligns with his or her substandard leadership style and, in many instances, <u>people will go to great lengths to avoid being associated with them, much less having to work for or with them!</u>

This is why the best companies often put immense effort and financial resources into hiring the best leaders. They know that they're not simply hiring one person; they are essentially acquiring this individual's exceptional professional reputation—and the goodwill, experience, professional contacts, and competence that go along with it.

One of the best examples, other than a high-profile business leader, is that of a marquee coach in the National Football League (NFL). The owners of NFL teams aren't investing in the head coach because he's a nice guy and merely has the appropriate level of experience. They are betting on his *professional reputation* and the *mystique* associated with it. They will spend millions of dollars to hire this coach in hopes of attracting talented players and subordinate coaches to the organization, as well as maximizing the development of those already in it.

They are willing to invest heavily in a proven leader because they know that's the price an NFL team has to pay for the chance of success on the football field. If the bet pays off, it will yield financial results exponentially greater than the cost associated with hiring an exceptional leader.

Great Opportunities for Proven Leaders

Thus far, I haven't mentioned the elevated monetary compensation that's typically associated with leadership roles in the business world, and for good reason: <u>one should never aspire to serve as a leader simply because doing so can result in enhanced salary and benefits.</u>

In almost every instance that I've observed someone who is in a leadership role primarily because of compensation, the individual typically achieves mediocre results at best. Often, he or she doesn't last long in the role or soon embodies the *Peter Principle*: they reach a level at which they are no longer able to perform adequately (or maintain the façade of doing it) <u>because their heart isn't in serving people as leaders are expected to.</u>

That said, those who develop stellar, legitimate professional reputations as leaders capable of consistently achieving superior results and attracting, developing, and retaining other exceptional teammates will inevitably be offered opportunities to serve in leadership roles of significant scope and responsibility. And most of these jobs *are* associated with high compensation. Get the essentials of leadership right and the money usually follows.

I can say that from personal experience, it's very good to be viewed by others as being one of the *marquee leaders* or *franchise players* within the ranks of one's profession. One of the many benefits of being known as an "A-Player" in your industry's "Leadership League" is that the companies that seek you out *know what you are worth* relative to the potential impact you can have on their organization and its bottom-line results. <u>They are very willing to pay top dollar for proven leadership talent</u>.

It typically takes several years or more of success in roles of increasing responsibility to legitimately be included in this upper tier of professional leaders. But once you get there and demonstrate the ability to remain there via continued performance, the financial benefits of being a top-level leader can be life-changing for you and your family.

How does one gain entrance to the upper echelon of leaders within their company, profession, and industry?

By building and maintaining a solid professional reputation as a leader!

Section I:

SUMMARY

How the Marine Corps Develops Leaders: Now You Know the Essentials

The section that you've just read has introduced you to the concepts and training methods involved in creating Marine leaders. But believe it or not, there is a lot more to it. For example, there are various elements of "tribal knowledge" that go unwritten as well as routine, real-world situations that have a lot to do with Marine Corps leadership. But what we've covered is the foundation that sets leaders on the path—from day one—to striving for these ideals.

Some of it may seem abstract or unbending to some readers, such as the Zero-Tolerance policies or the mandate to live the Core Values and other ideals every day and for the rest of a Marine's life. Other concepts might seem quaint or idealistic; often to those who have a skeptical view of the military, large institutions, or human nature. I understand this doubt ... even if I'll knowingly smile and politely but firmly disagree.

The reality is this: A strong culture and high standards, put in place from the outset, have been proven—for generations—to create good leaders who do exceptionally hard things. This often means fighting and, if necessary, dying for one's country, Corps, and fellow Marines, despite intense risk and overwhelming odds.

Think about that for a minute. You may have a job where getting people to work as a team on a new project is difficult, or even compelling folks to *do* their job is tough. You and your leaders might have trouble motivating others to put out appropriate effort—much less exceptional effort. Yet, the Marine Corps consistently develops leaders who motivate others to give their all, often in intensely difficult situations.

This may be special, but it's not rocket science.

Yes, some of it is the mystique of the institution and the powerful call to service most Marines feel, as well as the high stakes of the job. But much of it—most of it—is the time-tested formula that the organization has evolved to create Marines and leaders of Marines.

And if there is one lesson that I urge you to take from this section, it is this: **Marine Corps leadership concepts are replicable in the business world.**

I've successfully used all of them while serving as a business leader, and I've taught many others to do the same. Now, many of these concepts may need to be adapted to suit your specific environment and culture, and this is where wisdom and judgement enter the picture. But if you study these concepts and strive to live them on a daily basis, with time and diligence, you have the opportunity to not only become a better leader, but perhaps even a great one—a World-Class Leader.

Now that you've learned how the Marine Corps sets these leadership wheels in motion, let's look at where the rubber meets the road. The next section gets into more detail and practical examples of how these concepts translate to the business world, as well as outlining my leadership development program that's based on them: the Trust-Based Leadership™ model.

"Executives continue to say,
'Our people are our greatest asset.'

Yet, the vast majority of companies do not have a leadership development strategy, nor do they conduct any form of leadership training or mentoring.

They don't invest in leadership in any way, which means they are not investing in their greatest asset."

—Mike Ettore

Section II:

TRUST-BASED LEADERSHIP™

Introduction:

*T*RUST-*B*ASED *L*EADERSHIP ™

Since I retired from the Marine Corps in 1998, I've effectively adapted and employed many of the concepts of Marine Corps leadership in the business world, and I've helped other business leaders do the same. My experiences have resulted in what I call the *Trust-Based Leadership™* model. It is the foundation of all of the leadership training, coaching, speaking, and writing that I do under the auspices of my company, Fidelis Leadership Group. This section of the book outlines the major *enabling philosophies* of the Trust-Based Leadership model.

I've thrown a lot of material at you so far, and now I'd like you to step back and consider it for a few minutes. View the components in sequence and at a 30,000-foot level. As you do, think of each element as a building block. Once all of the blocks are in place, the completed structure positions an organization to perform in a very specific way. In the case of the Marine Corps, this structure is used to win battles, quickly and decisively. In business, it is applied to rapidly conquer challenges and meet established goals and objectives, whatever they may be.

Let's go through these elements step by step:

- Marine recruits and officer candidates learn about and are continuously immersed in the Core Values of the Marine Corps: Honor, Courage, and Commitment. These values serve as the bedrock of everything that follows.

(1) Other values are added that form *The Marine Mindset*, which is essentially the "corporate culture" of the Corps.

(2) Being a Marine is a privilege, not a right. Marines are taught to always work as a team and seek to achieve excellence as they strive to honor the example of legendary Marines who have come before them. The Marine Corps believes that it is the best and teaches new recruits that this is true. This belief becomes a self-fulfilling prophecy.

(3) "Every Marine a Rifleman:" A fundamental identity and singular purpose are embedded in every Marine. The organization's focus—winning battles—starts with the individual and everything he or she does within a team or function is designed to support that focus.

After outlining these basic building blocks that mold every Marine, we moved on to the *science* of Marine Corps leadership:

(4) Special Trust and Confidence are placed in leaders. They have significant responsibility and accountability, and are vested with great authority in return. Marine leaders are expected to fulfill this bargain by displaying total integrity and commitment, and through seeking constant self-improvement.

(5) Leaders must care for subordinates, teach them, and learn from them. This "Teacher-Scholar 360°" concept strengthens the organization by developing leaders at *every* level— and caring for people ensures that they will in turn care for their leaders by striving for success.

(6) We discussed the Five Laws of Leadership, the 14 Leadership Traits, the 11 Leadership Principles, and The Five Pillars of Marine Corps Leadership.

(7) I explained the three fundamental responsibilities of Marine leaders in order of priority, and how they serve as a compass to guide their decisions and actions:

   o   Accomplish the mission

- o   Take care of your people

- o   Develop the next generation of leaders

(8)   I discussed the *S in BAMCIS*, explaining how supervision is the essential link between a leader's responsibility and his or her accountability—and how doing it right is necessary for delegation that allows subordinates to take initiative. Within this framework, all members of a team work to fulfill the leader's *intent* while accomplishing the mission.

Read through these items again, if you'd like. As you do, consider how they interact and build upon each other, *and what they ultimately create*.

The Marine ethos—its culture, values, and traditions—winds up transforming young, often self-centered recruits into highly motivated members of an incredibly strong team. Marine Corps leadership training forges leaders who care for their people and develop them, while displaying integrity and viewing their mandate to lead as a sacred responsibility that requires impeccable character and constant self-improvement.

Once all of these pieces are in place, it unleashes something that is incredibly powerful: A relatively nimble organization that works together to strike hard and fast.

All Marines are expected to take initiative and lead, to some degree. They have the ability to work as a team—with or in the absence of orders—to accomplish the mission, regardless of the challenges that get in their way. In other words, when the inevitable friction and fog of war appear in dangerous, chaotic environments, Marine leaders know they are expected to find a way to win—to achieve the commander's intent and effectively exploit opportunities that may surface while doing so.

This is the framework from which everything else flows. From there, the Trust-Based Leadership model and the Marine Corps experience it is based on get more specific on tactics, techniques, the methods for handling any challenges, and other elements of executing successful leadership. Let's dive in.

"In the Marine Corps, leadership by example matters most when operating in darkness and danger.

The business world is no different.

Leaders must lead by example… Always!"

—Mike Ettore

Trust-Based Leadership™

The Trust-Based Leadership™ model is a concept for winning . . . it is a business-oriented leadership doctrine based on rapid, flexible, and opportunistic decisions and actions.

The essence of Trust-Based Leadership is that all members of an organization are enabled and encouraged to take action that can generate and exploit some kind of advantage over competitors or the business environment as a means of accomplishing stated goals and objectives as effectively as possible.

Especially important are decision-making and actions in time—we generate a faster decision-making and operating tempo than our competitors or market conditions to gain a temporal advantage. It is through decisiveness and actions in all dimensions that enables a company of any size to achieve decisive superiority at the necessary time and place.

Fidelis Leadership Group
Developing World Class Leaders

fidelisleadership.com

Chapter 27

TRUST

If you had to boil down how the Marine Corps functions in one word, that might be "trust." If you were only allowed to do it in four words, they'd probably be "trust," "delegate," "execute," and "win." And while trust has always been a component of Marine Corps leadership and operations, it's taken on even more importance in the last 35 years or so.

In the mid-1980s, the Marine Corps adopted a warfighting doctrine named *Maneuver Warfare*. This doctrine depends first and foremost on a culture of absolute trust among Marines of all ranks and roles. That trust is created through the adoption and effective application of the various concepts, fundamentals, etc., that were covered in Section I. When embraced and lived by all Marines—especially those in leadership roles—every element of the Science of Marine Corps Leadership plays a role in the development of a *Culture of Trust* that is essential to the success of the Maneuver Warfare doctrine.

Maneuver Warfare is described in *MCDP (Marine Corps Doctrinal Publication) 1: Warfighting*:

> The Marine Corps concept for winning ... is a warfighting doctrine based on rapid, flexible, and opportunistic maneuver. ...
> The essence of maneuver is taking action to generate and exploit some kind of advantage over the enemy as a means of accomplishing our objectives as effectively as possible. ...

> Especially important is maneuver in time—we generate a faster operating tempo than the enemy to gain a temporal advantage. It is through maneuver in all dimensions that an inferior force can achieve decisive superiority at the necessary time and place.[110]

Maneuver Warfare relies on teamwork, mission-type orders, and the delegation and supervision that enable them to be carried out. Again, all of the elements of Marine Corps culture and leadership training build this framework. If your people are unqualified and poorly motivated, and your leaders aren't very good, *it simply won't work*.

Compare this philosophy with an organization that has a very centralized, rigid, top-down structure. I'll use the Iraqi military under Saddam Hussein as an example, though we've all dealt with analogous "dictators" and the rigid-minded organizations they create in the business world.

In the Iraqi Army, non-commissioned officers and lower-level officers had very little independent authority. All of the power and the ability to make decisions were gathered toward the top of the organization. Subordinate leaders wouldn't make a move without explicit instruction, and this hesitance was reinforced by severe punishment for taking initiative. This created a slow moving, extremely reactive organization. One that, despite having 900,000 men under arms in 1990 (making it the fourth-largest army in the world), was rolled up very quickly in a fight against opposing forces who took initiative and applied Maneuver Warfare. [111]

Trust-Based Leadership™: Applying Marine Corps Leadership Concepts in Business

Since I retired from the Marine Corps in 1998, I've adapted Maneuver Warfare and other Marine leadership concepts for use in the business world. These are the main elements of the Trust-Based Leadership™ model.

There may not be an "enemy" in the business world—but there are competitors, and we all wage a daily struggle to solve problems and seize opportunities in rapidly changing, sometimes chaotic environments. Trust-based leaders and the organizations they lead are able to adapt, conquer challenges, and seize initiative at a pace that leaves other organizations—those working within a rigid, centralized model of leadership and decision-making—in the dust.

Directly adapted (and "civilianized") from the Marine Corps' definition of Maneuver Warfare, the Trust-Based Leadership model that has proven so effective for so many organizations and companies is defined as follows:

> *The Trust-Based Leadership™ model is a concept for winning … it is a business-oriented leadership doctrine based on rapid, flexible, and opportunistic decisions and actions. … The essence of Trust-Based Leadership is that all members of an organization are enabled and encouraged to take action that can generate and exploit some kind of advantage over competitors or the business environment as a means of accomplishing stated goals and objectives as effectively as possible.*

> *Especially important are decision-making and actions in time—we generate a faster decision-making and operating tempo than our competitors or market conditions to gain a temporal advantage. It is through decisiveness and actions in all dimensions that enables a company of any size to achieve decisive superiority at the necessary time and place.*

Reflect upon this for a moment and ask yourself, "Who wouldn't want to be part of a company that can execute and operate like this?!"

And the best part is that once the Trust-Based Leadership model is learned, implemented, and nurtured, it becomes natural and sustains itself. The companies and leaders that implement Trust-Based Leadership grow stronger and stronger over time and accrue lasting advantages and success.

When applied to any organization, the key to understanding this philosophy is the power of enterprise-level leadership by example, mutual respect and trust, speed, focus, and adaptability. A company that embraces the Trust-Based Leadership model is one that develops a culture that propels itself forward, adapts to challenges, and seizes opportunities. It continuously focuses on the development of competent leaders who can think and act independently.

Again, consider how this concept may apply to your professional environment; specifically, how a trusted subordinate could be afforded the latitude to demonstrate initiative in accomplishing a goal while still fulfilling your overall intent (and that of leaders more senior than you). Would you rather have an organization with reactive employees who can't make a move without direction? Or would you prefer a trust-based organization that has a cultural bias for action and leaders who seize and exploit appropriate opportunities?

As is often the case, Warren Buffet provides an interesting, if extreme, example. The formula of Buffet's Berkshire Hathaway is pretty simple and hugely effective: It buys successful companies and generally doesn't mess with them too much. The multinational conglomerate holding company sets goals, establishes a common culture, and gives trusted executives great latitude to accomplish their mission. It provides minimal (but effective) guidance and supervision while ensuring teammates receive adequate levels of support.

Stanford professor David Larcker and researcher Brian Tayan described Berkshire's management style in a case study for the university's Graduate School of Business:

> [U]nique was the operating structure that the company employed to manage these operations. It was a model based on extreme decentralization of operating authority, with responsibility for business performance placed entirely in the hands of local managers.
>
> While many publicly-traded corporations implemented strict controls and oversight mechanisms to ensure management performance and regulatory compliance, Berkshire Hathaway moved in the opposite direction. The company had only two main requirements for operating managers: submit financial statement information on a monthly basis and send free cash flow generated by operations to headquarters. Management was not required to meet with executives from corporate headquarters or participate in investor relations meetings; nor was it required to develop strategic plans, long-term operating targets, or financial projections.
>
> Instead, local managers were left to operate their businesses largely without supervision or corporate control. Vice Chairman Charles T. Munger described the Berkshire Hathaway system as "delegation just short of abdication."[112]

Larcker and Tayan also "surveyed approximately 80 Berkshire subsidiary CEOs to determine how Buffett's acquisition and management style translates on the ground." One respondent from a successful company under Berkshire Hathaway said "The only change is that I now discuss any major capital acquisitions with Warren. We run the business the way we always have."

Respondents reported that "their companies' performances are better under Berkshire (and even better than if they were stand-alone companies)," citing the ability to focus on long-term strategy plus the resources and brand value provided by the parent company. Respondents also mentioned the strength of a "common culture ... shared across Berkshire's subsidiaries," one that is "focused on honesty, integrity, long-term orientation, and customer service." [113]

This strong, universal culture is a civilian mirror of many of the leadership and organizational principles that guide the Marine Corps, as well as the ones I and many other leaders have implemented while serving as senior executives. A culture of honesty and integrity combined with clear standards and a focused mission are essential for successfully implementing the Trust-Based Leadership™ model.

The Berkshire Hathaway example of "delegation just short of abdication" is pretty extreme, but my personal experience and study have shown that most of the very best companies in the business world all rely on *some form and degree* of decentralized command and control (C2). And trust-based organizations are only becoming more vital as businesses work in a globalized environment spanning many different locations, governments, sectors, and economies. Their success in diverse settings depends on decentralized C2 and the presence of competent, trusted leaders who take initiative and use sound judgement to achieve objectives.

Let's say your company is faced with a last-minute, time-sensitive deal that carries some personal and organizational risk. You want to have trusted leaders who will say:

> "My boss is on vacation. My regional vice president is at a conference and I cannot reach her via phone, email, or text message. My division president is on a business trip in Europe. But despite my inability to communicate with my senior leaders, I know the stated intent is to engage in deals that raise the division's gross profit. I've got a deal right in front of me. And

while I usually need approval for some of the modifications and accommodations the client is asking for in this contract, I'm going to approve it. Because I believe the boss and *his* leaders would allow me to if I were able to communicate with them. It's a good deal and it increases our gross profit."

Reflect upon this example for a moment. I can't think of a good reason why any leader would not want his subordinate leaders and other key teammates to be empowered in this way and be willing to take decisive action in the absence of guidance. This is the type of decisiveness, judgement, and bias for action found in an organization that embraces a Trust-Based Leadership model!

The subsequent chapters included in this section of the book address what I refer to as the *Enabling Concepts of Trust-Based Leadership.* As you read each chapter, I encourage you to remember that <u>the fundamental element in each of them is trust</u>; the complete and unshakable trust that is promoted, developed, and maintained among all members of a trust-based organization.

"Leadership is an art in which the artist can continue to improve throughout his or her entire life."

—Mike Ettore

Chapter 28

MISSION TACTICS

Maneuver Warfare relies on an operating philosophy known as *"Mission Tactics"* and an associated technique of issuing guidance to subordinates that is referred to as *"Mission Orders."* Mission orders are used by Marine leaders to assign missions, goals, objectives, and tasks to individuals.

This technique depends on and enables trust. And it's essential to the effective delegation of all types of missions to members of a Marine unit. It also promotes the concept of accomplishing the mission at all costs, even if junior leaders have to deviate from established plans and orders to adapt to rapidly changing circumstances on the battlefield.

Bear with me as you read about the Maneuver Warfare-related concepts, techniques, and examples in this and other chapters in this book. They may seem esoteric or only applicable to the military—but please keep in mind that I've successfully adapted and employed all of them in the business world. And I've taught many other business leaders to do the same.

Mission Tactics

MCDP (Marine Corps Doctrinal Publication) 1: Warfighting defines mission tactics as follows:

> Mission tactics serve as a contract between senior and subordinate. The senior agrees to provide subordinates with the

support necessary to help them accomplish their missions but without necessarily prescribing their actions. The senior is obligated to provide the guidance that allows subordinates to exercise proper judgement and initiative.

The subordinate is obligated to act in conformity with the intent of the senior. The subordinate agrees to act responsibly and loyally and not to exceed the proper limits of authority. Mission tactics require subordinates to act with "top sight"—a grasp of how their actions fit into the larger situation. In other words, subordinates must always think above their own levels in order to contribute to the accomplishment of the higher mission.[114]

Marine Corps Major Peter E. Higgins also summarized mission tactics well in a 1990 thesis for the Command and Staff College (CSC): "Historical Applications of Maneuver Warfare in the 20th Century." As you read the following, consider how this concept can be applied in the business world (emphasis added):

Mission tactics are also called "trust tactics". Leaders are expected to make decisions without constant supervision and without asking for permission as long as their decisions are within the framework of **the commander's intent**. Mission tactics replace control with guidance and allow the subordinate leader to do without question or doubt whatever the situation requires—**even the disobedience of orders was not inconsistent with this philosophy**. ...

The situation may dictate changing the mission to comply with the commander's intent. Of course, we want initiative on the battlefield, and when subordinates know the commander's intent, it will synchronize their efforts to support the will of their commander. **In the absence of orders, a subordinate will still know what to do if he knows his commander's intent.** He now has the latitude to take advantage of fleeting opportunities.[115]

Commander's Intent

The key term in the example cited is *"Commander's Intent."* The Marine Corps defines it as follows (emphasis added):

> We achieve this harmonious initiative in large part through the use of the commander's intent, **a device designed to help subordinates understand the larger context of their actions**. The purpose of providing intent is to allow subordinates to exercise judgement and initiative—to depart from the original plan when the unforeseen occurs—in a way that is consistent with higher commanders' aims.
>
> There are two parts to any mission: the task to be accomplished and the reason or intent behind it. The intent is thus a part of every mission. The task describes the action to be taken while the intent describes the purpose of the action.
>
> The task denotes what is to be done, and sometimes when and where; the intent explains why. <u>Of the two, the intent is predominant.</u>
>
> While a situation may change, making the task obsolete, the intent is more lasting and continues to guide our actions. Understanding the intent of our commander allows us to exercise initiative in harmony with the commander's desire.[116]

There are three major benefits to setting clear commander's intent.

First, it fundamentally gets everyone on the same page, aligning the organization toward a goal.

Second, knowing the "larger context of their actions" gives subordinates the ability to adapt effectively while carrying out orders.

Finally, by communicating commander's intent, Marine leaders ensure that their subordinates are better informed of what the "big picture" looks like, and this results in them becoming more engaged and vested in the successful accomplishment of the mission. It also serves to inspire them, as they fully understand the key role they and their teammates are playing in any operation.

Examples of Commander's Intent in Combat

In this first example, a Marine infantry captain is ordered to capture a bridge and to subsequently occupy specific defensive positions on its eastern side. He's told that the commander's intent is to prevent the enemy from moving forces across the river at that specific location, while preserving the bridge so Marine and allied units can use it to cross the river during future operations.

Once he and his unit seize the bridge, the captain discovers that the terrain isn't as expected. The specific defensive position he was directed to occupy on the eastern side of the river is not conducive to preventing the enemy from crossing the bridge. He determines that his unit will need to move to the western side of the river and occupy better defensive positions to protect the bridge while simultaneously preventing enemy forces from crossing it.

In this example, the captain had been issued orders that became unrealistic once he was able to actually see the terrain on the eastern side of the bridge. And he appropriately adapted his tactics within the framework of the order to accomplish the commander's intent; both the immediate intent (prevent enemy crossing) and the longer-term intent (maintain a way for Marine and allied units to subsequently use the bridge).

Here's another example of commander's intent being used in a combat situation: When Marine infantry units are engaged in combat operations, junior Marines have historically been ordered to dig *a lot* of fighting holes and other defensive positions, which is difficult, back-breaking work done with small shovels. Often, after these Marines have been working for a good amount of time and have expended a lot of energy digging, they receive word that the unit is moving to a new location where they will have to begin working on *new* fighting holes. As you might imagine, the morale of these Marines often suffers; they begin to feel like pawns on a chessboard that they cannot see.

At the same time these Marines are preparing their new defensive positions, some of them are also routinely ordered to man forward-observation posts for hours, often at the expense of precious sleep and recovery time. Simply put, they're placed under stress and they're in the dark. Marines may have already been fighting enemy forces for days or weeks without adequate sleep, rest, food, or water, and they don't know exactly what their unit is trying to accomplish—nor what their particular role is in the tactical plan.

Consider the difference in these Marines' energy, motivation, and engagement if their sergeant had communicated the fact that an enemy force has been spotted moving in the unit's direction, and *the commander's intent is to guard the unit's left flank.*

These Marines are going to dig much deeper fighting holes and remain a lot more attentive while on watch at the observation posts, simply because they know the enemy situation and the commander's intent. It conveys the context of the difficult tasks they are being ordered to execute, and the gravity of failing to execute them well.

An Example of Commander's Intent in Business

In this example, two sales managers are told they must complete tedious and time-consuming end-of-week sales reports. One is told "Just do it, the Chief Sales Officer wants to review these reports no later than 2 p.m. every Friday."

The other sales manager is told the intent of the guidance from the corporate office: "We recently had several discrepancies between what some of our clients understood and expected as deliverables and what we thought we were contracted for and paid to deliver. In the end, we wound up modifying these contracts to specify a lower level of service, and some of your sales reps' monthly commissions will be affected. We need a way to identify and reconcile any problems quickly so we can ensure your teammates are paid correctly."

The second sales manager understands the intent and the importance of the end-of-week reporting. He's probably going to work with more enthusiasm and better tolerate doing that boring task, whereas the less-informed sales manager may not. In addition, there is a chance that well-informed teammates at any level—not just the leaders—may suggest *a better way* to *fulfill* the intent to solve this reporting issue.

An individual sales rep may say to her boss, "Hey, I think we can create and fill out an automated form with the exact terms of the contract upon the close of any sale; integrate this form into our client management system and accounting platforms to reconcile invoices with contracts. Or instead of doing this custom, weekly report, why don't we add these simple fields to current reporting that's already filled out as sales are made?"

Simply knowing the intent often spurs innovation or effective suggestions from within a team, because its members understand *why* they are being asked to do something.

Commander's Intent and Mission-Type Orders are Adaptable to any Organization

The higher up you go in any trust-based organization, the more important delegation becomes, and the more that delegation relies on clearly communicated commander's intent and mission-type orders.

A janitor is not going to require a mission-type order to clean the hallways, meetings rooms, and bathrooms on the third floor of an office building every night. In contrast, a salesperson selling technical solutions and support services will need this type of adaptive guidance to do his job effectively.

In that example, the intent of a sales team order could be "we are going to increase top-line growth (gross revenue) for the next two quarters."

Whatever the aim—increase gross revenue or net profit, roll out a new IT system by the end of Q3, or design and implement an effective marketing campaign—a leader must define the mission and the standards, *and* set the intent. Within that framework, subordinates can strive to meet their goals while *always* keeping their decisions in line with the intent.

That salesperson in an effectively led trust-based organization will be someone capable of thinking: "My boss is on vacation, but I know the intent is to increase our gross revenue. I've got a deal here that requires some adaptations of how we do things; but those changes are minor, and this increases our gross revenue. Let's do it."

Now, this example may seem a bit simplistic, but I assure you: There are countless companies in which the salesperson does not have the latitude to make that deal if he is unable to receive approval from the boss. Lacking the freedom to make decisions that support the intent of his leaders, this salesperson will likely watch in dismay as the contract remains unsigned and is lost to a nimble and empowered competitor.

Take an honest look at your own situation, be it as an individual contributor, a team leader or a senior executive. Are people in your organization trained and enabled to make decisions that will benefit the company? Or are they operating in a *"do only what you are told to do"* environment?

If you don't like your answers, take action and make things right!

Micromanagement is Fatal to Mission Tactics

A *non*-mission-type order doesn't just communicate the mission and the intent; it prescribes exactly what an individual must do. The only settings where this may be appropriate are those at the lowest levels of organizations; when an individual is needed for a task (for the moment) but does not have the knowledge, experience, or skills to take initiative; or for vital tasks which require consistent and specific processes and procedures.

Now, in some instances, various operations and tasks simply *must* be executed in a rather rigid or prescribed manner, often with a high level of supervision from senior leaders. There's nothing wrong with this, as long as the situation truly warrants such detailed guidance, direction, and continuous scrutiny from leaders. An extreme example of the latter would be the decision to initiate the launch sequence for a nuclear missile. You sure as hell don't want to see much front-line initiative in this situation!

In the aforementioned sales example, however, a <u>mission-type order</u> to a salesperson might look like this:

"Our goal is to increase top-line growth (gross revenue) for the next two quarters. We would like to do this by focusing on businesses in these four industries: hospitals, surgical centers, physical therapy practices, and orthopedic surgical partnerships."

A <u>***non*****-mission-type order**</u> would be something along the lines of this:

"We want to increase top-line growth. Here is a list of 13 companies; call on them within the next 5 days and in this order. Only accept deals that generate at least 26% gross margin. There can be no deviation from our established billing rates and customer support procedures."

The leader issuing this order, who may not even be based in the same zip code, is dictating to a salesperson—who best understands her geographic market and the companies in it—exactly how she must go about accomplishing the mission. That salesperson may be thinking, "Of the 13 companies on your list, four of them just had massive layoffs and are focused on cost reductions. We're probably not going to be able to sell them anything for quite some time!"

As a Trust-Based Leader, <u>don't try to dictate every aspect of how your teammates will accomplish the mission.</u> Formulate mission-type orders *with prior input* from those who are going to be receiving them, as well as *subsequent input* that may require you to modify the order moving forward. Let the front-line leaders and teammates you trust interpret your intent and use their initiative to make things happen.

Of course, there's that word again: *trust.* Mission tactics, mission orders, and commander's intent are *very* powerful techniques, but they are useless (or worse) if the individuals who are executing them cannot be trusted to exercise sound judgement and appropriate initiative.

As with many things in this book, the sum is greater than its individual parts. Each element of the Trust-Based Leadership™ model works in concert with others to make great things possible. Specifically, the use of mission tactics and mission-type orders requires a culture of integrity and excellence, an active effort to develop and delegate to subordinate leaders, and leaders who use judgement to put the right people in the right positions.

"Great leaders apply the science of leadership in an artful manner, consistently achieve superior results, and develop other leaders who can do the same."

—Mike Ettore

Chapter 29

DECENTRALIZED COMMAND & CONTROL

Maneuver Warfare and the derivative Trust-Based Leadership™ model rely on a philosophy of decentralized command and control (C2). In addition to the benefit of empowering leaders to devise adaptable solutions, decentralized C2 creates much *faster* ones. The Marine Corps cites this quick pace as the most important element of Maneuver Warfare in the "Philosophy of Command" section of *Warfighting*:

> It is essential that our philosophy of command support the way we fight. First and foremost, in order to generate the tempo of operations we desire and to best cope with the uncertainty, disorder, and fluidity of combat, command and control must be decentralized.

> That is, subordinate commanders must make decisions on their own initiative, based on their understanding of their senior's intent, rather than passing information up the chain of command and waiting for the decision to be passed down.

> Further, a competent subordinate commander who is at the point of decision will naturally better appreciate the true situation than a senior commander some distance removed. Individual initiative and responsibility are of paramount importance. The principal means by which we implement decen-

tralized command and control is through the use of mission tactics ...[117]

In both the Marine Corps and the business world, decentralized C2 and mission tactics—that implicit contract between leaders and subordinates to fulfill the commander's intent—promote an adaptive *culture of execution* in which individuals at all levels seize on opportunities and find a way to get the job done quickly and effectively.

The Marine Corps instills this culture because when tactical radios and other communication networks get jammed or are otherwise rendered inoperable, the senior commanders or key leaders are killed or incapacitated, or whatever other challenges and obstacles arise, the remaining leaders—the junior officers, SNCOs, and NCOs—can quickly assume more senior leadership roles and continue the mission.

On the battlefield, it is also necessary to seize and keep momentum. The Marine Corps trains its leaders to know when to press the initiative against an enemy in the absence of orders, as long as doing so fulfills the commander's intent. The previously mentioned scenario of a Marine captain exercising sound judgement and initiative while seizing and defending a bridge is an example of this.

The business battlefield has similar needs, though the stakes are obviously not as high as those in an actual combat zone. Leaders get sick or have family issues that cause them to be absent; they take vacations and some of them suddenly resign or are asked to exit the company.

If this happens in a *centralized* C2 organization, what happens when that "hands-on" leader is suddenly gone or unavailable? Subordinates are unused to having the latitude and authority to exercise their judgement and initiative, and business operations may become inefficient or even paralyzed. While the operational tempo and decision-making cycle in most companies tend to happen at a much slower pace than they do in a combat scenario, *decentralized* C2 enables members of a company that embraces the Trust-Based Leadership model to strike while the iron is hot and exploit fleeting opportunities.

The Marine Corps explicitly states the key to making decentralized C2 work:

> **Our philosophy requires competent leadership at all levels.** A centralized system theoretically needs only one competent person, the senior commander, who is the sole authority. A decentralized system requires leaders at all levels to demonstrate sound and timely judgement. Initiative becomes an essential condition of competence among commanders.[118]

Decentralized C2 and the need for competent leaders with a bias for action are becoming even more important in the modern business environment, which continues to become more global, culturally diverse, and technologically and operationally complex.

The decentralized C2 approach championed by the Trust-Based Leadership model provides leaders throughout the chain of command the ability to use their judgement. They can deviate from established plans, policies, and procedures to adapt to local political, economic, and market conditions, culture, weather, or any other unique aspects of the environment that affect business operations.

Things may be quite different in the western region of a company versus the eastern region, for example. And differences and associated complexities become exponentially greater when companies with global operations have to navigate different national governments, laws, languages, and cultures.

In a well-designed decentralized C2 organization, a company's overall mission, goals, and objectives (commander's intent) are typically the same throughout the organization, but the regional vice presidents, local managers, and other leaders have the authority to decide to do some things differently—as long as they're all striving to achieve the stated intent.

Fortunately, technology—including the broad range of communication systems and other business platforms—has greatly enabled the concept of decentralized C2 and the effective supervision needed to make it work. In today's business world, worldwide communication is instantaneous, and many teams can almost seamlessly work together at great distances from each other. This supports an unprecedented degree of decentralized C2 and its associated flexibility, responsiveness, initiative, and decisiveness at all levels.

Examples of Successful Decentralized C2

First, it's important to recognize that very few successful organizations are *completely* decentralized. Highly-directive and appropriately rigid orders and guidance still flow through the chain of command in the Marine Corps when necessary. And even companies under Warren Buffet's highly decentralized Berkshire Hathaway model of "delegation just short of abdication" are beholden to a common culture and must still submit financial and operational reports and perform other tasks that leave little, if any, room for deviation or modification.

The traditional franchise business model provides an example of a mix of decentralized and centralized C2. National or international brands such as Matco Tools, Pearle Vision, McDonald's, or Chick-fil-A set specific, very detailed standards. In the case of a restaurant franchise, for example, the corporate leadership determines the menu, recipes, portion sizes, and more. But individual franchisees often have the flexibility to modify some of their business practices to account for local conditions, as long as they remain within the broad intent and the standards set by corporate headquarters.

The Johnson & Johnson Company is a famous example of highly decentralized command and control. J&J has over "200 operating companies that produce consumer goods such as baby shampoo and medical products." This diverse structure is unified by the company's "Credo," which "states that the company's primary responsibility is to the people who use their products, secondary responsibility is to their employees, tertiary responsibility is to the communities they operate in, and final responsibility is to their shareholders. And as a result, J&J historically has deployed an operating strategy to invest in people and innovation, both through their own employees and external parties through acquisitions." [119]

In 2008, then Chairman and CEO William Weldon had this to say about Johnson & Johnson's structure in an interview with the Wharton School of Business:

> I think J&J is probably the reference company for being decentralized. There are challenges to it, and that is you may not have as much control as you may have in a centralized company. But the good part of it is that you have wonderful leaders, you have great people that you have a lot of confidence and faith in and they run the businesses.

If you look at Japan, for example, we have the local management running the companies. They understand the consumer, they understand the people they are dealing with, and they understand the government and the needs in the marketplace. Whereas it's very hard to run it from the US and to think that we would know enough to be able to do this. And so, I think it really affords us a lot of opportunities by being decentralized; what you do lose is control. But, with our credo and the value system that we work under, we feel very confident about our leadership and our management—and you have to have trust and confidence in them.[120]

Reflect upon Mr. Weldon's comments and contemplate how beneficial it would be if your company, department, or team could operate in a trust-based environment with a decentralized C2 similar to Johnson & Johnson.

Another great example: Back in 1999, Illinois Tool Works was dubbed "The most decentralized company in the world" by *Forbes.* At that time, ITW had "$6 billion in sales, [but was] broken into 400 units with an average revenue of just $15 million." Fast forward to 2016, and the company had grown to over 50,000 employees and $16.6 billion in sales. Here's how its decentralization worked:

There aren't any companywide, preset benchmark profit goals, such as those GE and AlliedSignal impose. Instead top management imposes standards based on a particular unit's competition. Each general manager must usually submit to grillings about six times a year by one of Farrell's seven executive vice presidents: "Why don't you have that account? Why does our competitor have it? What will you do to get it?"

When a unit starts to outperform—or underperform—the competition, Farrell splits it into more pieces, usually along tightly focused product lines. This corporate mitosis, Farrell argues, acts to capitalize better on what's working—or to isolate what's wrong. "When you separate the pieces, you can grow faster than if you keep them together, and that growth far outstrips the duplicate costs," he says. [121]

Various models of decentralization C2 can be applied to the entire structure of a company or the way individual departments are organized and interact within a company, all the way down to how small teams of employees work on specific projects. To be successful, the exact nature and level of decentralization often varies according to the unit's size and goals. Here is a good rule of thumb: Companies can effectively utilize the concept of decentralized C2 to the extent they can create and maintain a strong culture of execution, set high standards, and develop effective leaders—who in turn develop other effective leaders capable of sustaining the culture while achieving stated goals and objectives.

The benefits of decentralized C2 are varied but a huge one is *organizational resilience*. Nicolas Bloom, a Professor of Economics at Stanford University, conducted research that proves the worth of decentralized command and control:

> "Decentralization helps firms perform better, particularly in bad times," says Bloom, coauthor of "Never Waste a Good Crisis? Growth and Decentralization in the Great Recession," a working paper.

> Bloom's paper, coauthored with Philippe Aghion of Harvard University, Raffaella Sadun of Harvard Business School, and John Van Reenen of the Centre for Economic Performance at London School of Economics, examined company performance just before and during the Great Recession and found that firms that decentralized their decision making had lower falls in their sales and faster increases in their productivity than those with a centralized structure.

> Uncertainty rises and conditions change quickly during a recession, increasing the need for companies to respond to such dynamic times, the researchers say. That's more likely to occur when managers are empowered to make decisions instead of waiting for orders to filter down from the executive suite. "It's really costly to have big response times, so that would suggest pushing decisions down," Bloom says.

> These findings, Bloom says, sharply contrast with the long-standing notion that centralized firms perform more strongly during recessions because they allow C-suite executives to

make the tough and unpleasant decisions about plant closures, layoffs, and other types of aggressive cost-cutting, assumed to be the primary survival strategy in a downturn. Although the researchers examined midsized manufacturing companies, the findings apply to various industries, says Bloom.[122]

An Example of *Centralized* Command and Control Failure

A few years ago, one of my executive coaching clients told me about a situation in which he left a high-level executive position to take a job at another company—and the new leader who was appointed to replace him did massive damage to the department, effectively setting it back several years in productivity and efficiency.

When my client left this company, senior executives, who had years before embraced the concept of decentralized C2, decided not to replace him. Instead, they chose to break up the very large organization he had led and assign various departments and functions to other executives. My client supported this plan, with one exception: one of the leaders they had chosen to inherit some of his departments had a very "hands-on" and dictatorial style. My client warned senior leaders that this person's oppressive and micromanaging leadership style would likely clash with some of the leaders and teams he was about to assume control of. [123]

This new executive took the reins of several previously successful departments and teams and immediately began making unnecessary and sweeping changes. He demanded that a large number of highly capable remote employees who'd been working offsite for many years convert to working in-office at all times; he centralized all decision-making, declaring that no one could authorize a project, make a decision, or take the slightest form of initiative without consulting him first; and he integrated his newly inherited teams into his *existing* group. This was a problem because his longtime employees were used to his oppressive style, had been part of an average-performing department (at best), and suffered from poor morale.

As you might imagine, these changes caused a precipitous drop in morale among the teams this executive took over, resulting in rapid and massive turnover of high-quality employees who had been excellent performers for years. Many of them resigned within several weeks of exposure to the dictatorial leadership style of their new executive.

Sadly, this executive was in an automobile accident a few months later and he sustained very serious injuries that put him in the hospital for several months. Because he had deliberately trained his subordinate leaders to only act on his orders and directions (with dire ramifications for those who dared do otherwise), they simply *didn't know what to do* now that he was absent.

The recent loss of so many quality, long-tenured employees, the vast intellectual capital that left with them, and the department's culture of all decisions being made by this executive effectively paralyzed everything once he was gone. Operations ground to a halt and the entire company began to suffer from the fact that various support units were no longer capable of providing adequate support.

Eventually, another executive was assigned to take temporary control of the organization while the injured executive was recovering. He quickly discovered that the department was used to a domineering and dictatorial manner—that leaders and key players had been trained to never make a decision unless they obtained permission and detailed guidance.

Sorting out this mess took far more time and effort than the senior executives had ever imagined it would, and the company lost significant revenue and suffered serious operational decline for months. Worse, more quality, longtime employees quit in disgust, taking with them vast operational expertise that was impossible to replicate in the near-term.

Eventually, the injured executive returned to work and he immediately attempted to reinstate his oppressive style of leadership. This didn't go over well with his teammates, as they had become accustomed to more freedom and latitude under their temporary leader. Numerous complaints flooded the human resources department. Many of these were about his oppressive leadership style, whereas some cited verbal abuse and other instances of poor leadership. Within several weeks of his return, senior executives finally took action and fired the executive.

The worst part of this story is that by the time this individual was "found out" to be an ineffective leader, he had caused several dozen extremely valuable teammates to leave the company. Many of his ill-conceived reorganization efforts had also created great turmoil within teams that had performed very well for many years. In other words, this executive's ego, controlling personality, and micromanaging leadership resulted in him "fixing what wasn't broken." In several instances and almost immediately, the poorly reorganized teams showed a steep decline in effectiveness.

I have witnessed many situations like this in both the business world and the Marine Corps. A leader who hoards authority and decision-making almost always sets the organization up for failure. Subordinate leaders and key players are not empowered, nor do they learn to take initiative. And if the centralized, "hands-on" leader is out of commission, the entire unit typically devolves into paralysis and chaos.

A Marine battalion commander has no business micromanaging daily rifle counts in the company armories (I've seen some do this), and a senior executive should not be reviewing and approving every individual employee's vacation schedule and daily work tasks (I've also seen this, which is a gross misuse of an executive's time).

Within your own sphere of leadership—whether that is as a senior executive or the leader of a three-person team—invest in your people's development and strive to decentralize command and control, to the extent that it makes sense. Do not strictly centralize authority and decision-making in yourself, and resist the centralization of it in others. Doing the latter may produce short-term results from some individuals who cling to this authority; but it often ends poorly when someone is taken out of commission, or a big decision must be made quickly.

"The true test of your leadership
begins when you're gone."

—Mike Ettore

Chapter 30

PRIORITY OF EFFORT

In Maneuver Warfare, great emphasis is placed on leaders stating clear and concise mission statements, and they use various planning and communication techniques to ensure their units are focused on what's important.

Marine leaders often have to deal with conflicting priorities. Whether they are operating in high-stress training exercises or combat operations, there's often an overload of competing demands with not enough time to address all of them. Thus, leaders are taught to remain focused on the assigned mission and commander's intent, and to assess and prioritize the tasks that are most relevant to mission accomplishment.

When faced with rapidly changing situations and established plans that are no longer relevant, Marine leaders must remain calm and consciously avoid becoming overwhelmed. They know the onus is on them to assess the situation, adjust priorities, and issue new orders and guidance to their teammates.

As always, great attention is paid to the proper application of the "S" in "BAM-CIS" by leaders throughout the chain of command. This supervision ensures that the prioritized goals and objectives critical to mission accomplishment are being adequately executed.

A particularly effective way to prioritize and execute under pressure is to stay at least a step or two ahead of real-time problems. To "pull themselves off the firing line," leaders at the top of the organization step back and focus on maintaining the strategic picture. This perspective helps correctly set priorities for the team.

Just as in combat, priorities in business can rapidly shift or become irrelevant. When this happens, leaders must communicate that shift to the rest of the team—both up and down the chain of command.

Application to Business

The Trust-Based Leadership™ model utilizes these same general concepts. Trust-Based Leaders must be capable of assessing the mission, the commander's intent, and individual goals and objectives to create a prioritized sequence of actions that must be executed to achieve success.

There are many superb methods and techniques that leaders can use to do this, and I encourage readers to explore this topic in depth by reading books, articles, and other resources that are specifically dedicated to helping you gain clarity and prioritize. For the purposes of this chapter, we are discussing the high-level concept of Priority of Effort. Thus, only the major elements are covered.

Trust-Based Leaders will generally take the following two-phased approach as they assess a mission and the commander's intent; prioritize goals, objectives, and tasks; and create a plan of attack that allows for flexibility and initiative during its execution.

Phase I: Assessment, Prioritization and Planning

1. Review the Mission and the Commander's Intent: The leader must ensure that he and his subordinates have a thorough understanding of the mission, its objectives, and the commander's intent. Leaders are responsible for asking questions of their leaders until these elements are clear.

2. Create a List of Goals, Objectives, and Associated Tasks: This is a draft of these items; one that will be refined as the mission progresses and new challenges and priorities are identified.

3. Assess and Identify What's Critical vs. Important: Critical tasks are non-negotiable unless something substantially changes. Important tasks follow in prioritization but also must be completed.

4. Create a Prioritized Task List: Order tasks by their status (critical, important, or desired) as well as when they can be completed (some critical tasks may require other steps before they can be accomplished).

5. Create and Issue the Plan: Design it clearly and only make it as complex as it needs to be. Ensure that all of the plan's executors understand their role, the mission, and the commander's intent.

Phase II: Execution

6. Execute All Tasks: Get it done by issuing mission-type orders.

7. Be Vigilant, Flexible, Adaptable, and Decisive: Vigilance includes leaders properly supervising teammates (The S in BAMCIS) to ensure executors diligently fulfill their role. Flexibility, adaptability, and decisiveness are relevant because leaders must be capable of overcoming unforeseen obstacles and alter course when necessary.

8. Deviate from Plans When Necessary: No plan survives its execution 100 percent intact. New challenges and scenarios will arise that call for a change. When this happens, a leader must be able to recognize that an adaptation is needed and decisively issue orders.

9. Remain Focused on the Mission and Commander's Intent: Of course, it all comes down to the mission and the intent of your senior leaders. Never let go of this focus at any stage of the process.

10. Determine Follow-on Actions, If Necessary: What could have been done better? What still needs to be done? And what can be done to take advantage of new opportunities that are either beyond the scope of the original mission and commander's intent, or augment them. Powerful organizations are relentless about relevant follow-on actions.

In addition to the leadership philosophies and principles covered in previous chapters, all of the *enabling concepts* contained in the remaining chapters of this section directly and indirectly affect a leader's ability to prioritize and execute plans.

Chapter 31

SIMPLICITY

Combat is complicated and confusing, to put it mildly. But so is business and, for that matter, life. Running any organization or tackling a new initiative involves numerous moving parts, processes, and people. This truism—that everything is complex—drives the need to effectively manage the human element by keeping things simple.

Marine Corps leaders are trained that when it comes to leading their Marines in all types of environments, the concept that "simple is better" is one that they ignore at their peril. They are ingrained with the philosophy that they must, to the extent possible, ensure that plans, operations, tactics, techniques, orders, and communications should be kept as straightforward as possible.

This simplicity enables quick understanding and execution, both of which enhance the likelihood of success during rapidly changing and chaotic environments.

Simplicity in Everything, Including Plans, Orders, Communications ... and *Purpose*

The need for simplicity applies to nearly every element of leadership, but let's first think of its value in formulating plans. The plan (and the orders that flow from it) must be uncomplicated enough to be easily understood and executed by numerous people. It also has to be sufficiently straightforward to weather the inevitable changes that challenge its viability, such as casualties among key leaders, failing radios, or the intangible confusion that is the "Fog of War."

The plan, say, for a Marine unit to "secure that bridge" must be simple and clear enough so that the people carrying it out easily understand the objective and the commander's intent, while not being hamstrung by self-imposed complications when things don't go as expected. To put it another way, simplicity reduces *internal* friction which enables Marines to better handle *external* friction—a concept we'll detail more in a subsequent chapter.

Napoleon Bonaparte is considered one of the greatest military leaders in history, and his success largely stemmed from certain exceptional leadership qualities. Notably, he had the ability to intensely motivate his soldiers and adapt much quicker than his enemies using a 19th-Century version of maneuver warfare. But a famous story known as "Napoleon's corporal" implies that he valued simplicity as well:

> The story goes that during the battle planning stages Napoleon would have one of his ... corporals shine his boots, with the understanding that he knew the corporal would be listening in on his conversation with the rest of his commanders. Following the brief he gave to the other leaders in his army, Napoleon would look to the corporal and ask him if the plans made sense. If he answered "yes" then they would go forward with the plans. But if he did not understand them then Napoleon and his staff would make changes or draft new plans. [124]

This story may or may not be apocryphal but it's wise, regardless. Good leadership requires plans and orders to be clear and specific, hence the military's emphasis on the principle and its use of various tools to accomplish it. One of these tools that's taught to leaders is the five-paragraph operations order, often known by the acronym **SMEAC**. Marine Corps Officer Candidates School (OCS) describes it as follows (emphasis added):

> **S**ituation. The Situation paragraph provides details on both friendly and enemy personnel operating in your area of operations. We combine our understanding of the terrain with an understanding of the enemy force we are facing, and what friendly support we may have around us to help our decision-making process for finding our solution.

Mission. A short statement containing all five "W's". **When** is **who**, doing **what**, to **whom**, and most important of all, the **why**. This is the problem that we have to determine the solution for. Using all of the information we have at this point, we determine a course of action to accomplish the mission.

Execution. This is where we communicate the plan (solution) for our problem (the mission) we are tasked to accomplish. Starting from our present location, we brief how we get to the point where the "what" has been accomplished that leads to the "why" of the operation. We provide enough detail to direct how to accomplish the mission without being too detailed where we lose initiative from subordinates. We imply discretion to subordinates in determining how they accomplish their tasks.

Administration & Logistics. Providing some of the smaller details of the operation, this paragraph focuses on medical issues, Enemy Prisoner of War handling, food, water, and ammunition needed to accomplish the mission. We remember the details involved in this portion through the use of four "B's": **Beans, Bullets, Band-aids, and Bad Guys.**

Command & Signal. Here we wrap up the order by discussing how we will communicate key events throughout the operation. We also discuss where key personnel are going to be located, and what the order will be for succession of command in the event the unit leader becomes a casualty.

Marine leaders are taught this and other planning templates because "Standard order formats expedite understanding, communication, prevent omissions and facilitate ready reference." Further, "A short, simple order that conveys your will is superior to a lengthy, complicated order."[125]

As another example, communications also require clarity and simplicity. The Marine Corps (and the US military as a whole) uses standardized brevity codes in communications that leverage a common language. Take these examples of multiservice brevity code words used in air-to-air, air-to-surface, surface-to-air, and surface-to-surface engagements:

- Abort: Cease and desist an action or mission.

- Champagne: Specifies an attack of three distinct groups with two in front and one behind.

- Cleared Hot: Ordnance release is authorized.

- Go secure: Use encrypted voice communications.

- Gorilla: A large enemy force of indeterminate numbers and formation has been spotted.

- LZ: Landing Zone

- Brevity: This is a directive call indicating the radio frequency is becoming saturated, degraded or jammed and briefer transmissions must follow.[126]

Brevity codes can communicate *a lot* of information in an extremely simple, efficient manner. When used effectively, they greatly reduce the length of messages and minimize the possibility of confusion among units operating on the same battlefield.

Simplicity is not limited to these two examples. It's an essential part of almost all aspects of Marine Corps leadership as well as the Trust-Based Leadership™ model that derives from it.

This directness is enabled by having a common operating language, simple plans and orders, straightforward processes, and clear standard operating procedures (SOPs)—all of which will be covered in more detail in the following chapters. These elements, of course, have similar value in the civilian world. And never forget that the quest for simplicity applies to *nearly everything*—including your basic purpose and mission.

Application to Business

When I first joined Kforce, I knew nothing about the staffing industry. As I began studying the nuances of the business, I started getting lost in vast detail. The various policies, practices, systems, and tools that our recruiters and account managers used to conduct business on a daily basis seemed hopelessly complicated.

Sensing my confusion, Larry Stanczak, my boss at the time, sat me down and said something similar to what one of my previous Marine Corps leaders would have said: "Mike, don't get consumed in the minutia. At its core, our business is very simple: we interact with companies that need individuals with certain skills to help them with their business. We find these individuals and connect them with the companies. If a company feels that the individual is a good fit, the company agrees to hire them. No matter what else we do, everything is supposed to support this simple process of finding the right candidates for companies that are in need of their skill sets."

I never forgot this lesson throughout the rest of my career with Kforce. I always viewed operations, projects, systems, or whatever element from the perspective of how they would enable and simplify our people's ability to find qualified candidates and place them with companies that needed them.

When I transitioned from the Marine Corps into a role as a business leader in 1999, I took the concept of simplicity with me—especially the techniques associated with planning and communications. I applied them to practically everything I was involved with from a leadership and operational perspective. Though I was new to business, I had a gut-feeling that these techniques could be used effectively in this new setting. And I quickly realized that this instinct was correct.

In my executive role, I found that despite not having the *combat* rationale for clarity, brevity, and precision, these guidelines had just as much benefit in the modern business world. And they still applied to all types of communications and plans.

My teammates at every level responded well to the methods I'd learned and used in the Marine Corps. Even better, others at Kforce adopted these techniques. Within a couple of years, the entire company was using many of them, and they enhanced our internal and external planning and communication competence. Most of my civilian counterparts had received no formal training on planning and organizing tasks, projects, or business operations. Thus, when I taught them some of these tools, they saw that they worked and seized upon them.

There are many management concepts and techniques that can help a business leader keep things simple and, again, the chapters following this one will get into some of them. For now, I just want you to understand the concept of simplicity and its value in almost everything you do. Simplicity should be the goal in all types of operations and tasks, from planning and executing a big new IT project to the organizational design of a department to the individual emails you send every day.

- Keeping things simple ensures common understanding and consistent execution by teammates at all levels—even when chaos and uncertainty, such as the loss of key leaders or resources, come into the picture.

- Focus on developing the simplest way of achieving the mission and the commander's intent. For example, don't create a 7-step process when a 4-step process is just as effective—and much easier for everyone to understand and execute with consistency.

- Utilize specific, smart management techniques that simplify things. Examples include clear and succinct communications that rely on a common operating language; the effective use of meetings that have clear agendas, well-structured discussions, and realistic time-frames (such as "60 minutes, max"); and devising templates for complicated projects—such as onboarding the IT components of a newly acquired company—that break down the steps and make priorities and actions easy to understand and execute. There are numerous rules and techniques that can help leaders and their teams simplify all that they do.

It is a leader's duty to introduce and reinforce the concept of simplicity throughout his or her sphere of influence. This habit cuts through the clutter and enables consistency, despite any storm swirling around you and your people. Life and business are complicated enough. Your leadership—including all plans, orders, processes, and communications—shouldn't compound this confusion.

Chapter 32

STANDARD OPERATING PROCEDURES

Despite its reliance on decentralized command and control and developing initiative in individuals, the Marine Corps remains a hierarchical organization with many *very centralized* aspects. The decentralized vs. centralized elements are largely determined by what makes the most sense. While the Marine Corps wants leaders who are free to take initiative on the battlefield, it also needs individual Marines to adhere to established standards for routine tasks that demand consistency and reliability.

To accomplish the latter, the Marine Corps has a seemingly endless number of standard operating procedures (SOPs), for everything from securing a landing zone, to cleaning and maintaining a machine gun, to handling various administrative issues.

The best way to think of well-designed SOPs: they set standards for basic performance that enable delegation and supervision. And when the process, procedures, steps, etc., of administrative and operational tasks are standardized into well-designed SOPs, the resulting efficiency sets individuals free to focus on the things that require creative thinking and innovation.

SOPs can be short, or they can be lengthy. For example, *Marine Corps Artillery Fire Support Training Standing Operating Procedures (SOP)* is a long document that outlines the exact roles, responsibilities, equipment, qualifications, training, and organizational structure of "all fire support teams within [an] artillery regiment." [127]

The artillery training materials get into even more specific SOPs, such as the tactics, techniques, and procedures (TTPs) and essential fire support tasks (EFSTs) for artillery Marines. Take this example of an ESFT for a "deliberate attack;" the standard operating procedure for each one demands outlining a Task, a Purpose, a Method, and the Effects:

- Task: Disrupt the enemy on objective from effectively engaging attacking forces with direct fires.

- Purpose: Allow infantry to close and engage the enemy with direct fires.

- Method: Echelon close air support (CAS), artillery and mortar suppressive fires across the objective. Priority of fires to TF 2-64, target AD0018, Bn 6 rounds (rds) with marking round and 2 sorties A-10 CAS. airspace coordination area (ACA) Blue in effect.

- Effects: CAS destroys 1 platoon; artillery and mortars provide continuous (sustained rate of fire) fires within 200 meters (m) of other 2 platoons until cease or shift fire is ordered. [128]

A great deal of information, common terminology, and other SOPs are packed into that example, enabling the quick execution of a complex task that involves very high stakes. To the trained eye, the brief statements contain complex guidance that is easily understood and promotes rapid, coordinated actions of various units participating in a combat operation.

When designed and implemented wisely in any environment, SOPs provide explicit direction, ensure consistency, and increase efficiency. They free up leaders and individual team members to focus their critical thinking skills on problems that are not covered by the procedures. SOPs also contribute to the "common operating language" shared by members of a team. This means that an organization can immediately replace one member with an alternate individual who already knows the role and its actions.

SOPs are Also Vital in the Business World

The best companies, departments, and teams have well-designed SOPs that

228

enable consistent execution of essential tasks.

The distribution arms of successful manufacturers have figured out standard procedures for quickly and economically shipping their products. Human resources departments use SOPs to create a consistent hiring and onboarding experience for new employees. Most successful sales organizations have devised outlines and templates that help their sales reps sell to, upsell, and retain customers.

For example, a salesperson may have a pre-call checklist that involves:

- Researching the prospect

- Setting and sending a meeting agenda

- Gathering supporting materials

- Summarizing key features and benefits of the product or service

- Setting goals

- Summarizing action items after the call

In a decentralized trust-based organization, an individual salesperson will be encouraged to adapt within this framework as various situations require it. But having a checklist like this is a great way to ensure consistent communication, quickly train new sales associates, and ensure that time-tested, successful steps are followed.[129]

When I worked to integrate newly-acquired companies into Kforce, we used a range of SOPs for everything from making initial contact with the leaders of the new company to the content of initial meetings. We also had a checklist of the specific policies, processes, and systems that needed to be addressed to achieve the dates and objectives established by senior executives.

How to Formulate Effective SOPs

SOPs are usually born from experience, and behind many of them lie a problem or even a disaster. Commercial aviation uses countless SOPs, from the preflight checklists for ground crews, pilots, and flight attendants to criteria for grounding aircraft in certain weather conditions—all of which improve safety and efficiency.

In many situations, leaders find that they are having good results in certain areas and they want to reproduce these results at scale. In these cases, they will study the operations that are producing the positive results and reverse-engineer every action from start-to-finish. Once codified into logical sequences and steps, these newly created SOPs are broadcast and continuously emphasized and supervised by the appropriate leaders. In other situations, the need for an effective SOP will stem from mistakes and poor results. They are born from the thought, *Alright, whatever we do, let's make sure we never do **that** again.*

The Three Big Questions

Whether an SOP evolves from a good or a bad experience, it should ideally always come from experience. All good SOPs and, for that matter, all operational activity within an organization should start with the leader asking the *Three Big Questions*:

- What should we start doing?

- What should we stop doing?

- What should we be doing differently?

Note: This highly effective leadership technique—asking the Three Big Questions—will be covered in more detail several times throughout this book.

If you are a leader who is looking to develop a standard operating procedure, creating it closely mirrors how you should execute plans, orders, and other directives. Set the intent and solicit input from key stakeholders; in this case, *the individuals who actually do the task* that an SOP will govern.

An assembly-line manager and his teammates in a manufacturing plant will intuitively know some of the operational inefficiencies that could be eliminated, as well as when suggested procedures will not work. Design your SOPs with input from the front-line executors, with the intent of having them supervised by leaders at that level and perhaps one or two levels above it. If you've developed a trust-based organization with strong values and quality leaders, this input becomes exponentially more precise and actionable.

Walk the Fine Line Between Standardizing and Micromanaging

SOPs can get a bad rap. This usually happens when they are cumbersome or overly precise. When a poorly crafted SOP is put in the hands of a petty or oppressive bureaucrat with little initiative and fewer critical thinking skills, it can tank efficiency and kill morale, as well as common sense.

Relegate SOPs to the things that individuals should not have to think much about, or make them broad enough to be interpreted within the scope of the commander's intent. For example, a specific SOP for a company's preferred method of issuing press releases or other external communications may be as precise as "place the company logo in the upper-right corner of the document, use 12-point Arial font, and employ a standard cover sheet format." It's simple, specific, and easy to implement, and serves to make all written communications look consistent and professional.

In contrast, a good SOP for onboarding a new client may involve weekly follow-up communications that indicate the status of the account for six weeks; initial deliverables provided within two weeks; and scheduling a review meeting with the client at the end of the first month. Again, each SOP should serve to provide a consistent framework to actually speed up operations and make them simpler while ensuring quality results—not slow them down or hamstring initiative.

SOPs Are an Iterative Process

As a leader, it is your responsibility to create and maintain effective SOPs within your sphere of influence. This is once again accomplished by getting feedback from subordinates and front-line executors, who—if you've established a Teacher-Scholar 360° environment—will have the confidence to tell you when something doesn't work.

Leaders may hear teammates make statements like these:

> "I can't get my job done on time because the people ahead of me in the workflow are taking too long."

> "I have to create, read, and sign off on too many reports."

> "Every day, people repeatedly ask me the same questions when they are trying to complete routine tasks."

Comments like these indicate various operational inefficiencies and problems. They may be an indicator of poorly designed SOPs or surface the fact that there are no SOPs at all! Always remember this: If you want to find out which SOPs are not working well, *ask the people who are using them.*

One of your subordinate leaders may tell you, "Look, everybody knows that the SOP for this task says we will do Steps A, B, and C during a certain situation. The truth is that nobody ever does Step B, and this is why…"

This type of input from the front-line executors provides the opportunity to refine the procedure by getting rid of Step B and making other recommended modifications. If you take the time to solicit feedback from your teammates on SOPs and other operational guidelines they are required to use, they will likely say, "Hallelujah!"

The lesson here is that a leader must constantly assess if existing SOPs are effective or not—whether they are actually enabling efficiency and consistency, or they are simply slowing things down, are overly restrictive, or causing other problems.

SOPs Should Set You Free

Again, it is always prudent to create SOPs with input from front-line people. Use them to develop a "common language" of terms and definitions, tactics, techniques, and predetermined actions that increase efficiency and consistency. Tailor them to be broad or specific in relation to the task and the level of initiative and critical thinking it involves.

If they are designed correctly, they will support decentralized leadership in a trust-based organization. SOPs simplify routine tasks and facilitate communication. They also allow individuals to quickly take on new roles and free up your team to spend their time and energy on bigger challenges and new opportunities!

Chapter 33

COMMON OPERATING LANGUAGE

In modern military organizations, the use of standardized terminology and interpretations plays a critical role in various types of activities. This practice enables unit leaders to organize, plan, train, and execute operations using a *common operating language* that is clearly articulated, universally understood, and enforced at all levels. This language helps *simplify* things, as covered in the previous chapter of the book.

Since 1948, military terms have been codified in the Department of Defense Dictionary, and these terms are constantly evaluated for operational relevance and effectiveness; terms are added, deleted, and modified as appropriate. The Marine Corps in particular places great emphasis on the use of a common operating language. The organization leverages definitions and interpretations from this dictionary and other official sources, plus maintains a supplemental Marine Corps-centric dictionary.

These resources enable Marine leaders to effectively plan and execute Maneuver Warfare as well as routine operational and administrative tasks.

Benefits of a Common Language

One of the most significant challenges Marine leaders face during combat operations is the need to quickly assess a situation, make decisions, and direct their unit to adapt to the ever-present *"Fog of War"* on the battlefield. Experience has shown that one of the greatest sources of *internal friction* during situations like this is when various units and individuals use different operational terms and interpretations.

Within a single unit, there may have been several different "dictionaries." As you might expect, this leads to confusion and delayed actions at best—and chaos, failed missions, and unnecessary casualties, at worst. Tragically, in some instances, Marines who were shrouded in the *Fog of War* and confused by the lack of a common operating language unintentionally killed or wounded fellow Marines or noncombatants.

Marine leaders conducted post-operation meetings and after-action reviews in these scenarios, and the lessons led to the use of a common dictionary. The resulting operating language has greatly enhanced the capabilities of Marine combat units.

Application to Business

History has shown the need for a common operating language in companies in any industry and of any size. Most successful companies have created a language that consists of industry- and company-specific terms, definitions, interpretations, and metrics which enable transparency, accountability, and rapid planning and execution. Additionally, the use of a common language helps identify and refine the best practices and standard operating procedures (SOPs) that play a critical role in the Trust-Based Leadership™ model.

This standard communication also influences the establishment and sustainment of a performance-driven culture. When all members of the various divisions, departments and business units speak the same language, great efficiencies are gained in the planning, execution, and supervision of almost any effort.

As an executive leadership coach, many of the clients that I've worked with—both individuals and teams—had not taken the time to establish a common operating language. And some of those who possessed one failed to routinely update and refine it, or enforce its use within their organizations. The results are predictable: precious time is lost as people struggle to interpret what others are saying or requesting.

These challenges and many more can be solved by establishing a common operating language. Identify the routine concepts that are relevant to your operations. Set the terms and definitions. And enforce their use to drive clear communication and smart standard operating procedures.

Chapter 34

FRICTION

Legendary Prussian general and military strategist Carl von Clausewitz used the term "friction" to describe the innumerable, random factors—everything from inclement weather to personality conflicts—that distinguish "real war from war on paper." He described it as "the force that makes the apparently easy so difficult."

MCDP (Marine Corps Doctrinal Publication) 1: Warfighting addresses friction, as it did when it was originally published as *Fleet Marine Force Manual (FMFM) 1* in 1989. *Warfighting* was "drafted by Captain John Schmitt under the direction of the USMC Commandant, General Alfred M. Gray," and both cited ancient Chinese military strategist Sun Tzu as their main inspiration—but there is clearly a lot of Clausewitz in there:[130]

> Friction is the force that resists all action and saps energy. It makes the simple difficult and the difficult seemingly impossible. ...
>
> Friction may be mental, as in indecision over a course of action. It may be physical, as in effective enemy fire or a terrain obstacle that must be overcome. Friction may be external, imposed by enemy action, the terrain, weather, or mere chance. Friction may be self-induced, caused by such factors as lack of a clearly defined goal, lack of coordination, unclear or compli-

cated plans, complex task organizations or command relationships, or complicated technologies. Whatever form it takes, because war is a human enterprise, friction will always have a psychological as well as a physical impact.

While we should attempt to minimize self-induced friction, the greater requirement is to fight effectively despite the existence of friction. One essential means to overcome friction is the will; we prevail over friction through persistent strength of mind and spirit.[131]

The presence of friction is inevitable in combat and a Marine leader must be able to account for and deal with it. But any leader, including those in the business world, will encounter friction. A sudden loss of resources. A lack of time to get something critical done. A failure by a critical supplier or some other random event that threatens a project. Business leaders must remain composed and propel the organization forward, despite any challenges.

As in warfare, every industry, profession, company, or team encounters two main types of friction:

External Friction

These are things you have little control over that arise from outside of the organization. In combat, it could be the presence of a much bigger enemy force than anticipated or inclement weather that prevents close air support from helping ground forces. Examples in business might be a broad economic crash, the unexpected loss of a critical supplier of raw materials, or even a natural disaster or a fire at a facility which disrupts operations. Leaders may not be able to control whether or not external friction happens, but they can certainly control how they react to it with proper planning and the establishment of effective standard operating procedures (SOPs).

Internal Friction

Sometimes referred to as "self-imposed friction," internal friction includes unplanned challenges and situations that happen within the organization, such as a key team member getting sick or leaving for another job, or a critical IT system going down. In some cases, a leader can influence and minimize the occurrence of internal friction. In other instances, he or she cannot.

During military operations or an intense period in a business, internal friction may be self-imposed, such as when a leader is unable (or unwilling) to decide which course of action to take or otherwise reacts too slowly to rapidly changing circumstances. Internal friction can be the result of defective leadership, personality clashes among team members, poor coordination or communication, inadequate planning or training, lack of mental or physical preparation, or many other things that are generally controllable, to some extent.

In other words, the way to reduce these internal sources of friction is to lead your organization well and create an environment in which the possibility of friction is minimized—and when it happens, quickly addressed and rectified. There is no substitute for engaged leadership in situations like these. In most instances, any type of internal friction can be quickly eliminated or minimized by isolating the sources of "friction points" and properly addressing them.

How you respond to and overcome challenges is key to leading well in an adaptive organization. And this maxim applies to both types of friction.

Dealing with Friction in the Trust-Based Leadership™ Model

The Trust-Based Leadership™ model assumes that there will be friction during all types of business operations—and many of its concepts and techniques are specifically designed to help leaders deal with it.

If you can effectively implement all or most pieces of the Trust-Based Leadership model within your team, you'll directly and indirectly reduce the existence of friction, especially the type that stems from the organization itself. The following techniques help a leader specifically mitigate internal, *self-imposed* friction while making his or her team better equipped to deal with *all* types of friction:

- **Mission-type orders with clear commander's intent minimize friction.** Trusted subordinates who are empowered to take initiative have the latitude to deal with unexpected events. They can either propose solutions when problems with the initial plan or existing SOPs surface or, when appropriate, simply adapt to the situation and take immediate action to remedy it.

  In many instances, some of this friction may not ever even come to a more-senior leader's attention, because her empowered subordinate leaders have been trained to have a bias for action and to exercise initiative in the pursuit of achieving the commander's intent. And remember, simplicity, brevity, and clarity in orders, communications, and plans make mission-type orders possible.

- **Standard Operating Procedures (SOPs) and detailed planning can minimize friction.** Marine leaders can't exactly predict what the enemy's going to do in a given situation, but they can account for internal factors with relative certainty. For example, a leader knows what kind of ammunition his Marines need to carry and in what quantities as well as what the resupply methods are, even during an active combat action.

  There are SOPs for executing this resupply and countless other activities, such as calling in air strikes or artillery support, evacuating casualties, linking-up with an adjacent unit, and even communicating if radios are suddenly rendered ineffective due to technical problems or enemy electronic countermeasures.

  All of these scenarios create significant amounts of friction. Having effective SOPs can help minimize it to manageable levels.

- **Having a clear core focus minimizes friction.** In the Marine Corps, this core focus is winning battles. When this couples with mission-type orders, both elements serve as a compass to guide decisions at all levels during challenging times.

- **Core values and a strong culture minimize friction.** A culture of integrity, execution, and excellence ensures that a team will rise to meet challenges, rather than procrastinate, evade responsibility, or fold under pressure.

- **Train like you fight.** Proper training that replicates some of the impact of friction is incredibly valuable in combat, and it also has importance in the business world. While it's impossible to exactly replicate real-world combat conditions, great training serves to prepare Marines for the stress and uncertainty that arise from friction.

Business leaders have an advantage here because their teams are operating daily in the *real-world* conditions of their industry, company, department, or team. The opportunity to observe and evaluate the performance of your teammates as they conduct business operations is something that should be exploited. This evaluation serves as the basis for continuous improvement in all aspects of employees' roles and responsibilities.

All of the above elements particularly minimize ***self-imposed*** friction. Some companies wonder why their team members suddenly leave for other jobs, and perhaps why they have such a high overall rate of turnover. Others don't understand why they continually miss deadlines or often roll out failed products or services. Avoidable friction is often the culprit.

An effective trust-based organization is not only better at dealing with external or unexpected internal friction—it naturally minimizes the *self-imposed* variety that stresses people out and causes inefficiencies or failure. Employees who are fairly compensated, trained and developed professionally, and given clear standards and the necessary autonomy to do their jobs don't tend to leave suddenly.

Mitigating Internal Friction Frees Up Resources to Tackle External Friction

Think of a simple Marine Corps analogy: A Marine unit is located in a forward operating base in Afghanistan and told to be ready to execute offensive operations within an hour of being notified of a mission. The unit commander and his staff will ensure that all administrative, logistical, and operations details have been worked out, with appropriate back-ups and contingency plans in place. The unit has trusted, well-trained leaders at every level and the unit's pre-deployment training, existing SOPs, mission-type orders, and other trust-based elements make it as ready as possible to successfully execute difficult missions on short notice.

In this example, the combined impact of effective leadership and the best-practices of a trust-based organization have greatly minimized potential sources of internal friction or even eliminated them from the equation. Because the unit leader has taken steps to ensure that his team is in a high-state of readiness, the unit will have more "gas in the tank" to use when executing complex, dangerous missions on short notice. And they'll better handle the various forms of *external* friction that *always* appear during combat operations.

As you already know, this unit commander and his Marines are simply applying and executing the concepts and techniques of traditional Marine Corps leadership and Maneuver Warfare. And the Trust-Based Leadership model that I teach to business leaders looks very much like this when its applied to companies of all sizes, within any industry.

External Friction Tends to Come in Waves—Reverse the Momentum

Sources of internal friction sometimes overlap with a period of intense external friction, such as the loss of a major client, an economic collapse, or the sudden emergence of a "disruptor" like Uber, Airbnb, or SpaceX in an industry or business niche. If you haven't built an organization that minimizes internal friction and can effectively handle external sources of it, your company could be swamped by waves of intense friction.

I spoke to a very experienced member of a Marine Corps special operations unit about the effects of friction during combat operations and asked him to provide some of his thoughts on the topic. He had this to say:

> Your examples of internal and external friction are spot-on; both types of friction can be found in almost everything my unit does, whether it is during training or while on real-world ops. Our experience has enabled us, through honest and detailed self-assessment of our team members and our actions, to pinpoint most of the areas in which internal friction can exist.

> To be honest, we found that most of our internal friction issues were associated with personality clashes and inadequate communication between the unit leaders and the guys at the tip of the spear, so to speak. We've done a lot of work to ensure that our leaders and team members are on the same frequency regarding the objectives and plan of attack throughout all phases of an operation. We have done a lot to eliminate the inevitable personality clashes that can arise when you have so many strong-willed, high-achieving, "Type-A" personalities operating with each other.

> If you look at various professional sports teams, many of them seem to be dominated by or overly focused on the personality

or talent of one or perhaps just a few of the players. And many of these teams end up having problems due to this. In our unit, we do our best to eliminate the "prima donna" or "superstar" mentality that might exist; it simply isn't tolerated.

When it comes to external friction, we've just come to accept that it will exist despite our best intelligence and planning efforts, and that like any other combat unit, our success will always depend on our operators being able to think on their feet and make the right decisions when things happen that make our game plan unworkable.

To sum it up, we do everything possible from an individual and unit perspective to minimize instances of internal friction, and we train relentlessly to enhance our ability to successfully cope with every imaginable type of external friction.[132]

Don't minimize the psychological impact of friction. To continue the above sports analogy, you often see a team that has lost momentum get rolled over by their opponents. The losing players are put on their heels and play reactively and ineffectively. A leader must understand that when enough friction occurs, it can send you or your team into a spiral of doubt, frustration, and confusion.

How you react as a leader to external friction—ideally, with decisiveness and poise—will help set the tone for your team and prevent this losing spiral. You may not be able to control external friction, but if you accept and meet it head on, you are more likely to prevent it from devolving into something that's even more negative. Also, be sure to support members of your team who have a harder time dealing with friction. Firm leadership and a helping hand can go a long way toward completely shifting someone's outlook. They are incredibly powerful tools.

Good leaders expect to experience friction and develop the focus, poise, and mindset to deal with it. They set up the trust-based elements necessary to minimize internal friction and contingency plan for sources of external friction that are reasonable possibilities. Otherwise, they quickly, confidently, and decisively adapt to the unexpected.

Focus your energy and effort on the things you can control (internal friction), and don't waste much time worrying about the things that you can't (most sources of external friction). When those bad things happen—and they will—don't get consumed by stress or inaction. If you're a real leader, you know it's simply part of the job!

"There are two types of friction. The best leaders know how to adapt to the first and minimize the second."

—Mike Ettore

Chapter 35

DETACHMENT

In addition to "friction" (and many other brilliant military observations), Prussian general and military strategist Carl von Clausewitz wrote about a concept that led to the commonly used phrase *"the fog of war"* which describes confusion in battle:

> "War is the realm of uncertainty; three quarters of the factors on which action in war is based are wrapped in a fog of greater or lesser uncertainty. A sensitive and discriminating judgement is called for; a skilled intelligence to scent out the truth." [133]

Combat is perhaps the ultimate stressful activity. When you combine that intense stress with confusion, randomness, and complexity, clear judgement is often a casualty. This is why combat leaders must learn to mentally detach and literally or figuratively *"step outside of the firefight"* to gather their thoughts and gain perspective on the situation they are dealing with.

Detaching to Achieve Clarity

Picture a Marine company commander or platoon commander leading a combat operation in an urban environment. He may be situated on the rooftop of a building 30 meters or more to the rear of his lead elements that are actively engaged in a firefight. This somewhat detached position enables him to see things that the Marines who are fully engaged in intense combat can't see, plus it removes some of the intense stress of direct combat from his decision-making process.

"From my elevated vantage point, I can see three enemy armored vehicles coming down an adjacent street. My Marines on the ground can't see them. I'm directing them to change their location so they can protect their exposed flank and I am calling in close air support on the enemy vehicles."

Call it detachment, reflection, gaining perspective, or something else, but leaders of all types must often remove themselves, even if only slightly, from the chaos, pressure, and tunnel vision of a situation to make the right decision. The sayings *"can't see the forest for the trees"* and *"you can't view the picture if you're inside the frame"* are good descriptions of this concept.

Gaining Perspective and Clarity Apply in Any Complicated Situation

In the above example, having less immediate fear of getting killed has obvious value for the combat leader. But the benefits of *stepping outside of the firefight* can apply to any leader who must make a difficult decision or assess a complicated situation.

Removing yourself from the stress of a *business* "firefight," if it's feasible and realistic, can result in better analysis and decision-making. Of course, some stress can be a good thing, physiologically-speaking:

> A moderate increase in heart rate can improve performance because it increases the amount of blood in the brain, and the neurotransmitter activity that enhances cognitive processing, according to Lee Waller, director of research at the UK's Hult International Business School.
>
> "We think clearly, make good decisions and learn well," she says. But too much stress causes the opposite response as more blood flows to the limbs—known as "fight or flight" and that reduces cognitive function. [134]

Intense stress—and too much of it, for too long—has a variety of negative short- and long-term effects on an individual. Scientists have conducted numerous studies that outline the impact of stress on decision-making. Much of this research involves rats, not humans—but it has still led to interesting insights. (Plus, there's probably a great rat-race metaphor for these studies.)

One neuroscientist from the University of Washington drew this conclusion from his study:

> "The stressed animals took longer to learn and weren't adjusting their behavior in the maze," said Jones. "From this research we can see the effects of stress on rats and how one episode of stress impairs their decision making for several days.
>
> We know humans have to make numerous higher-level decisions, some of which are complex and require deliberations. Rats are guided by survival, and seeking out the larger of two rewards for the same effort should be fundamentally easy. The fact that stress can have such an effect on a simple but critical task is amazing." [135]

And long-term stress has been tied (in humans, this time) to both impaired decision-making as well as lasting brain changes, including dementia. [136]

As a leader, briefly removing stress during intense situations can help you make much better decisions. And making a practice of identifying and mitigating *ongoing* forms of stress—including through coping techniques that help you frame it differently—will benefit both your health and durability as a leader.

Time and Space = Opportunity for Reflection and Gaining Perspective

As a business leader, sometimes it's best to force yourself to take a break, go grab a cup of coffee, or take a short walk outside. These are simple ways to make it a practice to step outside of "business firefights," when you have the opportunity to do so.

Leave your office or the conference room, politely step away from people talking to you, and get into an environment in which you can think clearly. Deliberately consider scenarios or potential solutions to a problem that may not otherwise occur to you when you are sitting in a meeting. If the situation allows for it, don't be afraid to tell the members of your staff, "Let me sleep on this tonight. I'll have some thoughts and recommendations to share with you tomorrow morning."

When I was making non-combat decisions in the Marine Corps, I would sometimes tell my subordinate leaders, "Okay, I got it. Is there any more information that anyone wants to give me before I go have a cup of coffee and think this over?" Often, I'd go out for a run and mull over the situation while I exercised. Some of the very best decisions I've ever made were the result of reflection while conducting physical exercise, and I know many leaders who've had similar success doing this to step outside of "firefights." As a business leader, I'd often leave my office and take a drive or head to a local Starbucks to get some alone time with my thoughts.

In either scenario, several things would happen: I'd usually think about some important questions that I had forgotten to ask my colleagues during a recent meeting on the challenge we were facing. By stepping away and putting myself in an environment in which "I could hear myself think," I could view the specific scenario or problem from a different angle. And often, potential solutions would suddenly present themselves, clear as day.

I'm not telling you anything novel; we've all done this. What is relevant to your development as a leader is the fact that <u>you have to train yourself to do this when it's appropriate</u>. Don't routinely get so sucked into situations that you forget to "step outside of the firefight" to gather your thoughts and gain perspective. Learn to consciously decide to "take yourself out of the picture frame" when necessary.

Enlist Others to Gain Perspective

Stepping outside of the firefight doesn't always involve thinking about a scenario on your own, especially when you are so close to a problem that truly independent or unbiased thinking is difficult to do. This is one of the biggest benefits of cultivating a team of great mentors, trusted colleagues, and friends. If there is someone whom you respect and is more detached from an issue than you are, he or she may be able to provide you with some surprising insights. Tap into these resources routinely—you'll be better off if you do!

Also, work to develop the practice of detachment in your subordinate leaders. Everyone can benefit from this technique when formulating plans or making complex decisions, including leaders at every level of any organization. Encourage them to mentally detach when the situation allows for it. Many of my junior leaders in the Marine Corps quickly learned the value of stepping outside of the firefight, either naturally or through my emphasis on them doing it.

And at times, my leaders felt the best thing to do was to detach *me* from a situation so they could reflect and gain perspective on an issue. The words "time for a cup of coffee" were often the code for "please leave us alone for a while, sir" in these situations.

"Sir, this might be a good time for you to go get a cup of coffee. When you get back, we'll have some recommended courses of actions ready for your review."

My absence enabled my leaders to discuss issues and potential solutions without their commander hovering over their shoulder. As a senior executive, I would also often ask my leaders:

"Is this a good time for me to go get a cup of coffee?"

"Yes, it is, Mike. In fact, have two cups and come back in a couple of hours. We'll have some options ready to discuss with you."

Mentorship Includes Kicking Back Plans to See if They Can Be Improved

Not only would I teach my subordinate leaders that they should look at an issue from another angle, I often *insisted* on it. While this practice can be abused, applying it judiciously can vastly improve decisions and plans.

When approached with an issue on Monday morning, I'd ask them, "When do we have to make this decision?"

"Friday."

"Okay. How about this? Each of you step away and think about this situation by yourselves for the rest of the day and evening. Then, get together tomorrow, brainstorm it as a team, and come back to me Wednesday morning with some options based upon your collective wisdom and expertise."

Nearly every time my leaders brought me options based upon their combined efforts, they were better than any I would have produced on my own— even though in many instances, my experience was far greater than theirs. Likewise, the options they arrived at by collaborating with each other were almost always better than they would have produced individually. The lesson here is that—if time permits—it is almost always better to <u>leverage the experience and ingenuity of your teammates to solve problems!</u>

Stepping Outside of the Firefight Requires Judgement and Balance

A leader who steps out for a break before *every* decision is indecisive and ineffective. One who *never* does it may be impulsive and equally ineffective. Pick and choose when you need some time to detach from your surroundings. Do it when you know you have the time *and* that inner voice tells you that a quick decision may be an inferior one.

Marine combat leaders often literally "step outside of a firefight" to make decisions, but many times, they don't have the luxury. The ability to function under fire is essential in a combat leader. Fortunately, the business world affords many more opportunities for reflection. We're not typically being shot at, though it may feel like it at times!

The vast majority of business decisions afford the time to think and reflect, especially more-complex scenarios that have naturally longer timelines. Sometimes, just a night's rest will give you an entirely different perspective and, in some instances, issues may actually resolve themselves or new opportunities could arise before taking a course of action.

In my experience, business leadership is almost always the direct opposite of combat leadership in this regard. There is a time and a place for instantaneous decision-making in business, but in most scenarios, there's usually more time to consider various options and courses of action. A lot more time. Don't rush to make a decision today that must be made three days from now, unless you're absolutely confident you've got all of the information, it's not going to change, and moving now is going to help your team have more time to plan out the execution.

I'm a very Type-A personality, and as such, I tend to be very decisive. I'm the type of person who is always looking for problems that I can help other leaders solve. I want to lead and help my teammates achieve their goals and objectives! Those are generally good qualities in a leader, but they can also be flaws. In the business world, I eventually learned to tell myself:

> "Mike, this isn't combat. You don't need to decide everything right now. In fact, you don't need to decide everything at all. You have a lot of smart people on your team—give them some room to run!"

I wish I'd learned this earlier!

Chapter 36

THE FORCE MULTIPLIER

The Trust-Based Leadership™ model helps create adaptive, powerful organizations that can succeed in dynamic and often chaotic environments. These organizations are resilient and durable—they can take a hit and keep functioning despite unforeseen challenges and even the loss of key leaders.

Once again, think of all of the elements that make up a trust-based organization:

- A strong culture, a core focus, and core values which shape all teammates into a tight, unified team that executes with excellence.

- The training and development of leaders at all levels, with a focus on integrity, mission accomplishment, accountability, responsibility, delegation, and effective supervision.

- A decentralized command and control (C2) model that includes:

  o Mission-type orders that enable individuals to execute them with initiative.

  o Simple, clear plans, orders, and communications.

  o Standard operating procedures that increase efficiency and free up individuals up to innovate in other areas.

- o Personal and organizational strategies that minimize internal friction and prepare for external friction.

- o Leaders who know the value of *stepping outside of the fire-fight* to reflect and gain perspective.

I've told you that the Trust-Based Leadership™ model is being leveraged by many successful organizations. But by now, you may wonder, "Ok, you've said it's great. But what makes it *better* than some other models? What's the *secret sauce* of Trust-Based Leadership?"

The main reason for the success of the Trust-Based Leadership model is a senior leader's ability to *delegate to and leverage* the experience, ingenuity, and initiative of a highly trained and capable multi-level leadership team.

The Force Multiplier

The Marine Corps places a lot of faith in its junior officers and non-commissioned officers (both *staff* non-commissioned officers (SNCOs) and regular NCOs), and in many ways, they are the engine that powers the institution. Newly commissioned lieutenants are taught, "Listen to your SNCOs and NCOs. Learn to delegate effectively and leverage their experience and wisdom." In turn, the SNCOs and NCOs are told, "Teach and develop your young officers. Show them that you're worthy of their respect and confidence in you."

As a Marine leader, I invested in and relied on *all* of my leaders, not just my officers and SNCOs, as some other commanders tended to do. Of course, I greatly leveraged the more-senior leaders, but I also bet heavily on the many sergeants and corporals within the unit. Throughout my entire Marine Corps career, I ensured that my *entire* leadership team—all officers, SNCOs, and NCOs—were completely aligned on the most important concepts and operational priorities. A leadership team that is in sync to this degree is a very powerful force that is capable of delivering amazing results!

This synchronization can also be successfully utilized in the business world. I've done it—repeatedly and at every level of leadership—within a large, publicly traded company. Even better, I have taught many other leaders to do it. They soon realized that the most effective way to ensure organizational success is by continuously developing *other* leaders and forging them into a cohesive and focused leadership *team*.

I've said it before about applying Marine Corps leadership concepts to the business world, and I'll say it again: <u>this stuff really works!</u>

Leadership Team > Senior Leaders

In my experience, leadership training and the expectation of leadership competence at all levels are far less common in the business world than they are in the Marine Corps. The concept of executives ensuring that their "junior officers, SNCOs, and NCOs" are being developed as a unified, fully aligned leadership team is foreign to the vast majority of organizations.

Instead, a lot of emphasis is placed solely on executives. Essentially, the company "bets on the senior leaders" to get things done. Trusting these executives isn't always a bad thing, as long as those senior leaders have other strong leaders within their teams who are capable of executing and supervising plans and operations.

But sadly, in too many organizations, the reliance on senior leadership results in a failure to invest in the development of more-junior leaders. These individuals are often expected to succeed with minimal, if any, leadership training, coaching, and mentoring.

The solution to this problem: Getting senior leaders to understand that one of their main responsibilities is to *develop* current and future leaders.

Junior Officers, SNCOs, and NCOs = Directors, Managers, Supervisors, and Team Leaders

The titles of leaders may vary from one company to another, but as you read this chapter, I am sure you'll be able to figure out who the junior officers, SNCOs, and NCOs are in your organization. Make it a priority to develop them to the point that you can rely on them to consistently produce outstanding results with minimal guidance and supervision. The critical point is that <u>you must focus on continuously training and developing leaders at every level</u>. This conscious and consistent effort is needed to forge them into a fully aligned and highly capable leadership team.

To do this, you must become comfortable delegating your authority in various ways to your leaders, while effectively supervising them as they execute orders. Unless you're Einstein, Superman, or some combination of the two, at some point, you aren't going to be able to do it all yourself. You may do things as well as you can, but you'll never match the combined mental and operational horsepower resident in your leadership team.

The Flagpole Lesson Applies in the Business World

We've previously mentioned the flagpole example; an instructional exercise in which new Marine lieutenants are taught the importance of delegation and leverage. Let's go over it again:

> A Marine instructor presents a class of newly commissioned second lieutenants with a scenario:
>
> "You are told by your company commander on Monday morning, 'Lieutenant, you see the flagpole next to the parade deck? We need to take it down and put the new one up. We need it done by 1700 on Saturday; we're going to have a battalion change of command ceremony at that time. This is your mission. Get it done.'"
>
> The instructor provides a list of the dozen or so Marines under each new lieutenant's command and their ranks—including a gunnery sergeant, who is the lieutenant's direct report—and also provides "a detailed list of materials and equipment," and gives the class 30 minutes to individually plan and write down their orders. Some of the new lieutenants create incredibly detailed schemes and step-by-step orders; invariably, most of the class tries to ace the test by writing orders that are complex. It was a trick question, of course. [137]
>
> At the end of the lesson, the instructor collects the orders and tells the students the correct answer:
>
> "Lieutenants, this is what you should do in this situation. Approach the gunnery sergeant and tell him, 'Gunny, the Captain just told me that we need to have the new flagpole installed by 1700 on Saturday for the battalion change of command ceremony. Let's meet again later this afternoon so you can brief me on your plan and discuss any resources and support you will need. Once the plan is approved, you can assemble the Marines and begin the work. I'll meet with you early each morning and late each afternoon to discuss the project's prog-

ress and to provide any support you may need from me. I'll also visit the work area a few times each day to see how things are going and to talk with the Marines.'"

As the senior leader in charge, the young (and inexperienced) lieutenant approves the plan, he knows that he must supervise it well by applying the *S in BAMCIS*, and that he alone is responsible if the new flagpole fails to go up on time—but he's delegated to the Gunny the appropriate level of authority required to accomplish the mission, and then stepped back to allow the Gunny and his Marines the freedom to operate without being micro-managed.

This simple lesson can also help business leaders understand that delegation should be a "default setting." And to do this, they must prioritize the growth of their team's *other* leaders.

A trust-based organization that's *firing on all cylinders* develops and fully leverages leaders at all levels, from senior executives down to front-line managers and supervisors. If a leader can get these individuals unified and focused on achieving the mission and intent, the organization becomes exponentially more powerful.

My time in the "leadership trenches" (that has imparted a few tough lessons along the way!) showed me that my teams were *always* more successful when I bet on all leaders—and when I made it clear to senior leaders *that one of their main responsibilities was the development of other leaders.*

When leaders are nurtured and all of their efforts are synchronized, these individuals become a team—one that's an exponential, virtually unstoppable force-multiplier.

Section II

SUMMARY

Let's go over what we've just learned.

I've explained why **Trust** is essential to how the Marine Corps functions, as well as the Trust-Based Leadership™ model that's based on Marine leadership concepts and my experience as a military and civilian leader.

You've learned how **Mission Tactics**, **Mission-Type Orders**, and **Commander's Intent** rely on and develop this trust by leveraging competent leaders and teammates at all levels. These elements enable **Decentralized Command and Control (C2)** in the military and in business. And decentralized organizations tend to run rings around rigidly centralized ones—seizing opportunities faster, making better decisions, and adapting more quickly to new challenges.

I've explained how Trust-Based leaders must be able to adapt **Priority of Effort** in the face of rapidly changing conditions and keep all things—plans, communications, orders, processes, and more—**Simple**, to the extent possible. Well-designed **Standard Operating Procedures (SOPs)** and a **Common Operating Language** enable this simplicity, as well as the efficiency and consistent execution that free up teams to spend their energy on tasks that require innovation and critical thinking.

You've learned what **Friction** (internal or self-imposed, as well as external) is, why it is often inevitable, and how to deal with it. I've explained how minimizing the former gives you resources to tackle the latter; plus how **Detach-**

ment that achieves clarity ("stepping outside of the firefight") enables better decisions.

And finally, I've revealed one of the "secret weapons" of leadership: Why leveraging leaders at all levels is **The Force Multiplier** that unleashes the true power of any unit, department, or organization.

These are the main components of the Trust-Based Leadership model. You've got the basic blueprint. But just like the Marine Corps needs certain types of leaders to execute maneuver warfare doctrine, so are leaders with specific traits required to make Trust-Based Leadership work.

That's where this next section comes in. I will explain the key characteristics, skills, and attitudes of Trust-Based leaders while encouraging you to develop these elements in yourself.

As you read this section, keep the following in mind: While these traits are essential for operating in a Trust-Based Leadership™ model, know that they will also serve you well as a leader in *any* organization or situation. If you diligently focus on developing and applying them, you will undoubtedly go far in leadership, business, and life.

Let's dive in.

"I've found that the very best leaders in Corporate America almost all practice some of the Trust-Based Leadership™ concepts and principles that I experienced in the Marine Corps and teach to clients. That said, the *majority* of business leaders I encounter do not approach leadership from the perspective of trust.

Ultimately, my discussions with the '*non-trusters*' lead to the fact that they have been 'burned' or 'stabbed in the back' in the past, and this has soured them on the idea of empowering and trusting their peers and teammates. Some of these leaders muster the courage required to 'trust again' but some cannot bring themselves to do it, fearing poor results or even betrayal at the hands of their colleagues.

I applaud those in the former group and feel genuine sadness for the latter—knowing that without the ability to trust others, it's unlikely that they will ever attain their maximum potential or that of the teams they lead."

—Mike Ettore

Section III:

THE TRUST-BASED LEADER

Introduction:

THE TRUST-BASED LEADER

In the first section of this book, we reviewed what I view as the *science* of Marine Corps leadership training, including but not limited to:

- Core Values

- Servant Leadership

- Special Trust and Confidence

- Teacher-Scholar 360°

- The 5 Laws of Leadership

- The 14 Leadership Traits

- The 11 Leadership Principles

- The 5 Pillars of Marine Corps Leadership

- The 3 Fundamental Responsibilities of a Leader

- Leaders Eat Last

These fundamentals are timeless and enduring. Marine leaders serving 100 years ago would recognize most of them. The actual terms and definitions used in today's Marine Corps may be somewhat different, but the core concepts and guiding principles remain the same as those used by generations of leaders.

The second section of this book introduced you to the more recent Marine Corps warfighting doctrine of *Maneuver Warfare* and its derivative, the Trust-Based Leadership™ model that I have developed, implemented, and taught for more than two decades in the business world. This section also covered some specific techniques and procedures that enable this leadership model.

In this third section, we're going to expand upon some of the concepts from these two sections, as well as introduce new ones—with a specific focus on **how and why a leader should possess *certain traits*** in an organization that embraces the Trust-Based Leadership model.

The Need for Trust-Based Leaders

The Marine Corps' traditional leadership philosophy evolved along with the institution's focus on Maneuver Warfare during the 1980s.

While the Corps had naturally embraced some elements of Maneuver Warfare in the decades after World War II, the concept was codified as doctrine with the publication of *FMF-1 Warfighting* in 1989. In addition to defining the strategic, tactical, and organizational elements required for this doctrine, the change called for *a very specific type of Marine leader*.

"Like war itself, our approach to warfighting must evolve. If we cease to refine, expand, and improve our profession, we risk becoming outdated, stagnant, and defeated," wrote General Alfred Gray, 29th Commandant of the Marine Corps, in the preface to a later edition of *Warfighting*.[138]

In some ways, the Marine Corps has always been a pretty flexible military organization compared to others of its time, but it used to have a more rigid hierarchy; there was less emphasis placed on initiative from junior Marines. But the reorientation toward Maneuver Warfare surfaced the need for a new type of Marine leader at all levels. From *Warfighting*:

> Various aspects of war fall principally in the realm of science, which is the methodical application of the empirical laws of nature. ...
>
> An even greater part of the conduct of war falls under the

259

realm of art, which is the employment of creative or intuitive skills. ... The art of war requires the intuitive ability to grasp the essence of a unique military situation and the creative ability to devise a practical solution. It involves conceiving strategies and tactics and developing plans of action to suit a given situation. [139]

The facets of Maneuver Warfare and the Trust-Based Leadership model that we've discussed—such as a decentralized command and control and mission-type orders—simply won't work without competent leaders who possess good judgement, creative thinking skills, initiative, and a bias for action.

This section of the book covers the characteristics and qualities that you must have as a leader—as well as the ones you must develop in other leaders—to thrive in the Trust-Based Leadership model.

Many Marines Have Successfully Transitioned to the Business World

Some employers specifically seek to hire Marines with leadership experience because they know they have had dedicated leadership training and exposure to great responsibility throughout their military careers. The experience, knowledge, and individual traits these civilian employers hope to leverage include:

- All Marine leaders have received continuous formal and informal leadership training and mentoring. This is very rare in the business world. A 25-year-old Marine leader—officer or enlisted—has typically already operated in dynamic operational environments. They've been routinely thrust into leadership roles and have been expected to perform well at a much earlier age than most of their civilian counterparts.

- Marines are often individuals with good character and a strong work ethic, and they come from an organization that prizes mission accomplishment above all else.

- Marines have the ability to plan, lead, delegate, and supervise. In particular, Marine leaders typically have significant experience in operational planning and execution. Through training and experience, they have developed the ability to take the strategic vision, mission, and intent and boil them down into actionable tactical plans.

- Business needs people who can execute and accomplish the mission. There are a lot of "idea people" in the business world; much rarer are the individuals who can translate ideas into action.

- Marine leaders have the ability to thrive in chaotic and unpredictable environments. Combat experience is the ultimate test of this trait, but even peacetime Marines have significant experience conducting complex operations and training exercises. They've also been heavily involved with leading and supervising routine unit and individual training programs, as well as administrative and logistical operations that have a lot of moving parts.

I want to once more emphasize that the Marine Corps does not have a monopoly on good leadership and that all Marine leaders are not, by any means, perfect. I've worked with and observed many civilian leaders who are as competent as the very best leaders the Marine Corps has to offer. But the key difference is that Marine leaders have been steeped in dedicated leadership training and then quickly pushed to use and develop these skills. They've been raised in a culture of leadership. And they are continuously surrounded by high-quality leaders, mentors, and coaches throughout their time in uniform.

That said, I do believe leadership can be learned by motivated individuals of any age and in any setting. All of the traits and qualities covered in this section are highly desired for any leader. While some people may be born with certain natural abilities and aptitudes—maybe the universe blessed them with a bit more in their *leadership rucksack* than another person—all of the qualities and characteristics associated with becoming an effective Trust-Based Leader are learnable skills.

Some of these attributes and skills can be learned from this book, but you must take this knowledge and fuse it with experience to develop wisdom and sound judgement. This involves putting yourself in positions to lead and learning from your mistakes and successes. While I am a huge proponent of all forms of study and self-development, I honestly feel that it is almost impossible for a person to become an effective leader, much less and exceptional one, unless he or she actually serves in leadership roles, however minor.

And while some of the ideas in this book were developed and/or applied in a military setting, they are all *very* applicable in the business world. Most of the leadership, organizational, and operational issues I dealt with in the Marine Corps exist in some form in the business world. And, there's no doubt that the need for effective leadership is identical in both environments.

Who Would Not Want a Leader in Any Environment with These Traits?

- Impeccable character

- A strong sense of accountability

- Courage

- A bias for action

- The ability to thrive in chaos and uncertainty

- Resilience

- A team player

- Someone who develops other leaders and shares hardship with their team

- A lifelong learner

You may not have or perfectly develop all of these characteristics. Leadership, like life, is an endlessly iterative process. But the more of them that you study, accumulate, practice, and make part of your natural leadership philosophy—and your way of being—the more successful you will be. I guarantee it.

Chapter 37

CHARACTER

I've written a lot about character in previous chapters; how the Marine Corps demands it of leaders and why creating core values and a leadership culture that require good character are essential to the success—and sometimes the survival—of an organization. The concept of individual character is so important, however, that I feel it deserves additional emphasis that specifically explains why a leader in the Trust-Based Leadership™ model must possess it.

Aristotle defined "A Man of Character" as someone "who does the right thing, at the right time, and in the right way." He further defined four types of character, one of which you really want to strive for: The Virtuous Character:

> "The Virtuous Character ... feels no conflict between emotional inclinations and moral duty. Why? Because the virtuous character has trained his emotional system to be aligned with his moral inclinations. In short, at a deep emotional level, the virtuous character wants to do the good." [140]

Not all, or even perhaps many people (a cynic would say) achieve this ideal. Most of us, at least partially, fall into Aristotle's definition of "The Continent Character," someone "who has selfish, amoral, or immoral desires, but exhibits control over them in the service of acting morally." [141]

But there is an important lesson in trying to be a person with virtuous character. The more you can align doing the right thing with the positive emotions you experience from it, *the easier and more natural it is to do the right thing.*

In order to develop this strength of character, Aristotle suggested that it is necessary for individuals to develop habits of thought and action (ethos), which result in an ability to manage emotions and make decisions wisely. By habitually responding to situations and scenarios using the four cardinal virtues as guidance—prudence, courage, temperance, justice—our character will consequently be virtuous.

Let's Put This in Terms of Leadership

Leaders who do the right thing reap the extremely practical benefits associated with leading well. People respect them. These leaders develop superb professional reputations. And the loyalty and trust they inspire in colleagues at all levels make their job much easier and far more effective. These are powerful incentives for having and displaying good character.

As you know, one of the primary responsibilities of Marine leaders is to set the example for other Marines to follow. In order for an individual of any rank to be worthy of being respected enough to be emulated and followed by others, he or she must first and foremost be a "Person of Character." The habits and work ethic of each Marine leader demonstrate how dependable, trustworthy, and driven he or she is. It is through actions that these characteristics are revealed. And again, it is through virtuous actions that you develop virtue.

For the Marine Corps, it is critical to ensure that mission accomplishment is at the forefront of each individual's thought process. It is vital that every Marine knows, unequivocally, that no matter how overwhelming the odds, how perilous the job, or how seemingly hopeless the situation, he or she must always be willing to do whatever is necessary to accomplish the mission.

These Marines, because of the ethos by which they live, are also trusted by their leaders to make sound, ethical decisions—even in the absence of orders or guidance. It is this absolute, unspoken trust in each other that defines the ideal character of Marines.

The rigorous training of Marine officer candidates and enlisted recruits is the first step in developing this character, with great emphasis placed on the Core Values: Honor, Courage, and Commitment. Marine leaders are taught that they must be committed to constantly seek self-improvement to achieve excellence in all aspects of their role as leaders. They are also dedicated to the team and will do everything possible to make their unit successful. This means caring for your teammates as much, if not more, than you care about yourself.

In the Marine Corps, everyone is of value, regardless of race, nation of origin, religion, or gender. Leaders are expected to uphold this critical element of the Marine Corps' culture; and also work to improve the level of character, intellectual development, combat readiness, and quality of life for the Marines they are privileged to lead.

Character is a Very Practical Necessity in any Organization

What organization *doesn't* want leaders with good character? An example of one may be hard to find, but it's all too easy to encounter companies that *don't do anything* to develop character in their leaders. The Trust-Based Leadership™ model places extra emphasis on impeccable character and its associated traits—because it assumes that leaders at every level will be left unsupervised for extended periods of time, often in difficult and fluid environments.

In this leadership model, trust means that teammates are not subjected to micromanagement and they are afforded freedom of action; the freedom to make decisions on their own in pursuit of achieving the commander's intent. The Trust-Based Leadership model requires leaders who are decisive about this and have a bias for action.

The Strategic Corporal

Former Marine Corps Commandant General Charles Krulak described how this trust extends all the way down to the lowest levels of leadership with the concept of "The Strategic Corporal."

In a paper titled "The Strategic Corporal: Leadership in the Three Block War," he described how the complexity of post-Cold War conflict puts Marines in situations where decisions by individuals—including the most junior leaders—can have a drastic impact on the success of a mission. To adapt, he argued that the Marine Corps must decentralize even further than it already had, and redouble its investment in developing junior leaders with character:

The clear lesson of our past is that success in combat, and in the barracks for that matter, rests with our most junior leaders. Over the years, however, a perception has grown that the authority of our NCO's [non-commissioned officers], has been eroded. Some believe that we have slowly stripped from them the latitude, the discretion, and the authority necessary to do their job. That perception must be stamped out.

The remaining vestiges of the "zero defects mentality" must be exchanged for an environment in which all Marines are afforded the "freedom to fail" and with it, the opportunity to succeed. Micro-management must become a thing of the past and supervision—that double-edged sword—must be complemented by proactive mentoring. Most importantly, we must aggressively empower our NCO's, hold them strictly accountable for their actions, and allow the leadership potential within each of them to flourish. ...

Every opportunity must be seized to contribute to the growth of character and leadership within every Marine. [142]

General Krulak published that piece in January 1999, before the wars in Iraq and Afghanistan and the rise of social media and today's instantaneous, digital-media landscape—all of which have made his observations even more prescient.

Now, in warfare or in business, special trust and confidence in leaders and their judgement must *really* go all the way down to the lowest level—because an individual Marine or a civilian employee at any level can do or say something that could almost immediately become an "international incident." Individual mistakes can have negative or even disastrous consequences for an entire organization.

Let's look at some recent examples:

- A soldier with the Wisconsin National Guard, a member of a mortuary services unit that handles the remains of fallen servicemen and women, was relieved of duty when she posted Instagram pictures of "comedic poses around an empty, flag-draped coffin." This is a violation of perhaps the most sacred duty station in the military. [143]

- A leaked video of Marine snipers urinating on dead Taliban insurgents went viral on YouTube and became an international news story. [144]

- So did (on a much larger scale) the abuse of inmates by soldiers at Abu Ghraib prison in Iraq, which was revealed by a whistleblower and followed up with reports published by The Associated Press and CBS News in 2003 and 2004. [145] [146]

Each one of these examples of misbehavior varies in severity but the latter two, and Abu Ghraib especially, were used by the enemies of the United States in information, propaganda, and recruiting campaigns against the US war effort.

"Abu Ghraib represented a devastating setback for America's effort in Iraq," wrote US Army General Stanley McChrystal, who led an effective special operations campaign in Iraq and was later the Commander of the International Security Assistance Force (ISAF) in Afghanistan. "Simultaneously undermining US domestic confidence in the way in which America was operating, and creating or reinforcing negative perceptions worldwide of American values, it fueled violence that would soon worsen dramatically." [147]

Think about it: The poor decisions of some of the most junior service members and the failure of their leaders can influence the entire conduct and perception of a war. And these examples don't even touch on the incredible responsibility that every individual serving in war has when they have to decide whether or not to pull a trigger in a chaotic environment filled with non-combatants.

The Consequences in the Business World Can Also Be Serious

In business, the impact of mistakes includes but certainly goes beyond social media and public relations fallout. Think of all of the national scandals that have shaken major corporations in recent years. Here are just a few examples:

- A passenger "is suing United Airlines for allegedly failing to protect her from an off-duty FedEx pilot she says touched her sexually three times during a flight from Hong Kong to San Francisco."

- The suit alleges that a United flight attendant "'suggested' that [the

267

accuser] return to her seat and talk to [to the assailant]" when the woman asked to be moved. The reputations of both FedEx and United have taken a hit, simply based on bad decisions by two individual employees.

- The Equifax data breach that compromised the records of 146 million Americans in 2017—the largest in history—was attributed by the company's former CEO to "an 'individual' in Equifax's technology department who had failed to heed security warnings and did not ensure the implementation of software fixes that would have prevented the breach." One decision by one person potentially affected 146 million Americans. [148]

- To make matters worse, Jun Ying, former CIO of Equifax's US information-solutions business, was subsequently charged by the Department of Justice with insider trading after he reportedly "used confidential information entrusted to him by the company to determine it had been hacked" and "exercised all of his stock options." A software developer employed by Equifax was also charged "for allegedly selling stock while knowing of the breach before it was made public." [149] [150]

- One of the best examples is mentioned earlier in this book: how Wells Fargo employees, who were steeped in a culture of gaining accounts at the expense of doing the right thing, created fake accounts and charged "as many as 570,000 customers for auto insurance they did not need." One former employee claims that he called the company's ethics line and was fired. [151] [152]

- The fines and other remediation that Wells Fargo has been forced to pay are huge, but the loss of reputation and damage to the brand are far more significant. And all of these issues stem from or were abetted by leaders and a culture that did not prioritize good character above other things.

If You Must Focus on One Thing, It Should Be Character Development!

As the saying goes: "Actions speak louder than words." How you act and react as a leader; how you handle situations; the way you present yourself to the world—whether you are on time, care about your health and fitness relative to the demands of your role, always work to the best of your ability, constantly strive to increase your knowledge, and help and take care of others—are just some of the basic actions that define your character on a daily basis.

Being conscious of them and ensuring that you can be considered a "man or woman of character" by those around you is a decision that will have a major impact on your success in life. And it also has a major impact on the companies you work for and the people you work with—especially in a trust-based model.

If you haven't done so already, I would encourage you to look back and think about occasions when you displayed the qualities of good character discussed in this book. Think about how these made you feel; think of the pride that you still feel when you reflect on them. Think also of how each instance was received by others.

On the flip-side, think about the times when you may have fallen short. If those occasions do come to mind, don't get too down on yourself. Simply commit them to memory and make the decision here and now that you won't fall short again—and that integrity and honor will be the guides for your actions moving forward.

The definition of who you choose to be is projected by your character. It is a deliberate choice that takes effort, discipline, strength of will, and plenty of thoughtful reflection. Your character will affect how you are viewed, how you are treated, how you are remembered, and most importantly, how you judge yourself. If you wish to be an effective leader in any field or arena, you must first invest in becoming a Man or Woman of Character.

Chapter 38

ACCOUNTABILITY

We've previously discussed the importance of accountability and its place as one of the 5 Pillars of Marine Corps Leadership:

> Accountability is the cornerstone of Marine Corps leadership. It is the reckoning wherein a leader answers for his actions and those of his unit and accepts the consequences, good or bad. As a Marine leader, accountability is the most important element of formally critiquing your performance. The poor performance of a unit will result in either administrative or disciplinary action.

> If any factor—coercion, politics, favoritism, or something else—is allowed to intervene in holding Marines, regardless of rank, accountable, the structure on which the Marine Corps was created is weakened.

A trust-based organization must have leaders who hold themselves and those they lead accountable for their responsibilities. Accountability is an exceptionally important trait in the Trust-Based Leadership™ model and without it, leaders who possess all other desired traits such as character, integrity, a bias for action, etc., will eventually fall short. In this model, a leader's long-term success relies on an individual's willingness to take complete ownership of everything, good and bad, that happens within the organization that he or she is privileged to lead.

Marines are taught two different variants of the term accountability; one deals with the physical responsibility for various types of assets (facilities, equipment, money, etc.) and the other, as emphasized in the formal definition, is specific to one's actions and behaviors. And again, in addition to being responsible for their own actions, Marine leaders are held accountable for the actions of all Marines within their chain of command; they are responsible for everything. The Trust-Based Leadership™ model applies the same two variants of accountability to business leaders.

Authority vs. Responsibility and Accountability

A fundamental *Law of Leadership* that is taught to all Marines is that as a leader "you can delegate authority, but you cannot delegate responsibility."

In other words, Marines learn that they have the authority to make decisions and issue directives appropriate to their role; and while they are encouraged to delegate authority to Marines in their chain of command so that they can accomplish assigned tasks, leaders are always responsible *and accountable* for the success or failure of their unit. This uncompromising standard of accountability is heavily enforced at all levels of leadership within the Marine Corps.

Accountability drives productivity and quality. Leaders must first hold themselves accountable for getting their own work done well and on time. Otherwise, they risk becoming so comfortable with procrastination that they will fail to meet stated deadlines. A day becomes a week; a week, a month. Worse, non-accountable leaders often become complacent to the point that their deliverables are mediocre or even sub-standard.

And poor leadership accountability at the top levels will inevitably lead to inefficient and inferior work by subordinates. Delays caused by leaders will have a viral effect throughout their organization, resulting in widespread delays "downstream," and often, the failure of the entire unit to achieve goals and objectives. When leaders fail to hold themselves accountable, the adverse results trickle down and grow exponentially.

Marine Leaders Do Not Have a Monopoly on Accountability

The leaders within many highly successful organizations and companies place an equally forceful emphasis on holding themselves and their teammates accountable. Like their Marine Corps contemporaries, the best business leaders have learned that an organization with a strong culture of accountability is one that can meet almost any challenge that may arise.

Trust-Based Leaders seek and embrace accountability, as do trust-based organizations in which a *culture of accountability* exists. In companies that do not enforce accountability, leaders tend to shy away from it—these individuals are often figureheads and not what most of us consider *real* leaders.

Instead of being decisive and willing to be held accountable for their actions and those of their teams, they prefer to seek detailed guidance on practically every issue or situation that arises. Sadly, these individuals are not only allowed to do this in many organizations, they are actually encouraged to do it by senior leaders who prefer to micromanage rather than invest in their team members' development.

The Trust-Based Leadership model assumes that a leader is not only comfortable with authority, responsibility, and the uncompromising accountability that goes along with both, but that he or she <u>actively seeks these things out and thrives on them.</u>

Some individuals (wisely) turn down a leadership role because they think, *That's a tough job with too much opportunity to fail. I want no part of it!*

Let's face it, the demands associated with being an effective leader are not for everyone. I actually admire those who know themselves well enough to realize that, despite the lure of elevated compensation and title, they are simply not the right person for a leadership role. These individuals are not to be ridiculed or otherwise looked down upon, because they can still play essential roles within an organization and are often some of the most valuable and productive members of a team.

What Does Accountability Look Like?

Accountability varies at different levels within an organization, of course, and directly mirrors a leader's sphere of responsibility. A Marine battalion commander is responsible and accountable for the basic welfare of all of the Marines under his command, as well as the overall accomplishment of any mission he is assigned.

The measures of this accountability can be either broad, or highly specific: Did the battalion successfully secure a critical airfield and do it on time? In a peacetime setting, are all of the Marines in the battalion current on individual and team training requirements? Accountability in the Marine Corps can be fairly swift and somewhat harsh at higher levels, and may involve a leader being relieved of command for what many would consider a relatively minor issue or event—even if it isn't something within the leader's immediate observation and control.

Marine leaders at lower levels of the chain of command operate with a narrower accountability that includes making sure their Marines are appropriately cared for, adequately trained, that their weapons are maintained, and that their specifically assigned goals within the overall mission and commander's intent are achieved.

Accountability is both a "stick" and a "carrot." It motivates individuals to avoid failure while giving them the opportunity to shine when they succeed. Let's go back to our previous example where a Marine captain is assigned to take his unit and set up a blocking position at a key bridge. The commander's intent is "do not let enemy forces cross that bridge."

Remember, he arrives at the bridge and the terrain is completely different than reconnaissance photos (if they exist) or other assumptions about the area. There are no great positions from which to defend the bridge. He may or may not have communication with his superiors, and even if he does, he must now use his judgement to adapt while fulfilling the commander's intent. This may involve moving farther forward than the area he was assigned to, in order to set up on high ground overlooking the avenues of approach to the bridge.

The opportunities to take initiative like this are exponentially greater in a trust-based organization, and so is the accountability. In a combat situation, there is also a natural and powerful accountability—often, the *ultimate* accountability: don't make a decision that gets everyone killed.

But Marines are trained to make decisions and accomplish the mission despite this fear. And even in a training exercise, the captain knows: *I have the opportunity to take initiative. I also have the opportunity for praise and respect if I make the right decision and it accomplishes the mission. And if I fail, I will suffer repercussions.*

Think of accountability in other situations. If the individual Marines in a platoon do something stupid or unethical, such as abuse prisoners or gratuitously shoot a civilian because of poor fire discipline, their leaders, officer and enlisted, will be held accountable. Character and judgement are ideals that any organization wants to develop in its people to mitigate the possibility of these actions. When human nature is a factor, accountability is the main enforcement mechanism for doing the right thing.

Application to Business

The culture and dynamics associated with the sales force of a company provide a good example of accountability, though all aspects of a business should have it. Sales organizations typically have tangible sales goals and revenue objectives, and there are almost always specific measures of accountability that are enforced through various reports, metrics, and frequent meetings with appropriate leaders.

Within that framework, however, there is still significant room for subjectivity. Let's say a salesperson is negotiating with a prospective client who makes a counteroffer that is outside of the normal scope of a deal that the sale's rep is authorized to agree to, and then says, "I'm ready to sign this deal but it's got to be today."

Oh, and it's also the last day of the quarter, and the last day to realize commission in the salesperson's next bonus check. She has to decide what to do, balancing personal goals with what's right for the company and her leader's intent. If she makes the right decision and the deal is profitable, she'll be rewarded in the form of extra pay and praise for making a good deal.

If not, and the boss says, "I wish you wouldn't have agreed to those terms," her pay may or may not suffer in the short-term—but her standing in the eyes of her leader may be lastingly diminished, as her boss realizes that he needs to provide more restrictive policies and guidelines for future deals, now that she has demonstrated questionable or even very poor judgement.

The lesson here is that if you are that person's leader, you must judiciously hold her accountable—balancing giving the salesperson the freedom to show initiative (knowing that she may make some mistakes) while also not creating an environment without accountability.

Because you will *also* be held accountable for her actions!

All Organizations, Teams, and Functions Benefit from Accountability

The key is setting clear standards. A broad and fundamental standard should be "do not lie, cheat, or engage in unethical activity or tolerate those who do it." A narrower standard might be "sell as many new accounts that generate as much gross revenue as possible, but ensure all actions are lawful, ethical, and remain within our established policies and procedures."

If Wells Fargo had prioritized these broad and narrow standards and actually held people accountable for them, they wouldn't have wound up in a scandal for selling and creating fake or unnecessary accounts. Leaders at various levels of the company would have nipped illegal and unethical behavior in the bud by holding employees and their colleagues accountable, rather than the media and the government having to step in to do it.

As a leader, expect and embrace accountability—and *increasing* levels of it as you move up the chain of command within your organization. Enforce it among your subordinates. Accountability is essential for the success of the Trust-Based Leadership model. When it's implemented correctly, a culture of accountability pays vast dividends as it disincentivizes bad decisions and behavior and rewards initiative and good judgement.

"Impeccable character and ethical behavior are contagious, especially when demonstrated by senior leaders!"

—Mike Ettore

Chapter 39

COURAGE

Courage is one of the Marine Corps' Core Values for an obvious reason. Leaders are trained under the assumption that they will probably, at some point, have to lead their Marines into battle. A form of courage is needed to convince and motivate young men and women to follow you into combat and risk their lives to accomplish a mission—and physical courage is of course required to face these dangers oneself.

All individuals experience fear when facing dangerous situations. It is through constant training that Marines learn how to recognize the reactions that the human body has to it, and to neutralize these effects before they can impact the ability to function effectively.

Marines leaders must especially have and display physical courage. Though senior leaders are not always at the very tip of the spear, they are taught that an effective leader *never* asks his Marines to do something he wouldn't be willing to do himself. And just as with many other qualities shown by a leader, <u>courage is contagious</u>.

The Marine Corps Requires Leaders with Physical Courage—But *Moral* Courage is Similarly Important

As a young Marine officer, I was told that I would have many more opportunities to use moral courage during my career than physical courage—because I would probably be serving in peacetime environments far more often than in combat situations. This was sound advice and it turned out to be completely accurate.

Moral courage can take many forms. It is, of course, also required in combat situations. For example, moral courage must be combined with physical courage to avoid pulling the trigger if doing so could harm innocent people—despite being in fear for one's life.

But in its most basic sense, it is the courage to follow the other two core values (honor and commitment) along with displaying sound leadership—<u>even when doing so carries personal risk</u>. This risk may involve coming into conflict with others, jeopardizing one's career, or fulfilling a duty to care for subordinates despite any consequences.

Application to Business

There are few civilian professions that require leaders to demonstrate physical courage, but almost all of them call for leaders who possess moral courage. In the business world, you *will* be faced with repeated opportunities to exhibit or withhold moral courage, especially if you are a leader, and even more so if you lead within a decentralized organization.

In the Trust-Based Leadership™ model, you are routinely left to operate with great autonomy and wide latitude to take appropriate actions. Often, whether or not you exhibit moral courage will be apparent only to yourself—at least in the short run.

Here are some hypothetical examples of moral courage, big and small:

- You're a team leader in the shipping department of a company. While walking around the shipping floor, you notice that some members of your team are packaging items incorrectly; probably because it takes less time than following established procedures. It may seem like a simple thing to correct them—and yes, it's part of your job description as their leader—but you want to be liked and you have to work with these individuals every day.

  Thus, even just saying, "Folks, let's stop for a moment. We're not supposed to pack the product like this. Let's get back to following the established procedures" requires some moral courage by the leader. And your senior leaders who are likely off site are counting on you to do the right thing in situations like this.

- You're a salesperson who becomes aware that one of your colleagues is falsifying sales reports to receive commission. Do you report him? Speak to him about it first? Do nothing? If you work in a trust-based organization and a position that you value, moral courage always means taking some form of judicious action.

- You're the leader of a team of financial analysts and a senior leader asks you to alter a report; to simply *"massage the numbers"* so that the quarterly sales projections presented to senior executives look more positive than they are. Refusing to do so may, of course, have personal and professional repercussions. You could lose the "friend-ship" of your boss and may even be fired due to your unwillingness to compromise your integrity. But given the fact that senior leaders are depending on accurate projections—and your name will be on those projections after they fail to materialize—figuring out a smart way to display moral courage is the best course of action.

There are consequences to lacking moral courage or even feeling (incorrectly) that you failed to show it. For example, in the military, symptoms of post-traumatic stress (PTS) as a result of combat are often caused by what is called a "moral injury," or what the Marine Corps terms "inner conflict." One study showed that about a third of troops suffering from PTS reported a moral injury as being their "main problem." [153]

Many returning servicemembers may have done nothing wrong; they were simply put in impossible situations that may have forced them to be unintentionally responsible for the death of a noncombatant; or they simply witnessed the suffering or death of others and could do nothing about it. But the mere *perception* of a moral failing is enough to haunt them. [154]

In the business world, the damage from failing to have moral courage is also a significant form of stress. Think back to the Wells Fargo example we've repeatedly mentioned. Almost all of those managers and many other employees knew that what they were doing was wrong. And I'm sure many of them went home at night with their stomach in knots, thinking, *We're going to get caught. This is on us. Am I the only one who thinks this is wrong? Should I speak up, and what will happen to me if I do?*

Usually, in situations like this, someone finally *does* speak up. Most publicly traded companies, for example, have an ethics hotline on which employees are supposed to report malfeasance without fear of repercussions. And when someone finally uses it or otherwise sounds the alarm, a subsequent investigation sometimes reveals systemic ethical and moral problems in the leadership and practices of individuals, departments, and even entire companies.

Courage Also Drives Innovation and Success

Think of the innovative leaders and businesses. Sure, some were simply lucky. But many, many others took a risk—often a big one—that paid off exponentially. Bill George, a Senior Fellow at Harvard Business School and a former CEO, outlined several examples of courageous leaders who took a stand and significantly impacted large companies, including a contrast in courage between two of the world's largest automakers:

> **Alan Mulally.** When Mulally arrived at Ford, he found a depleted organization losing $18 billion that year and unwilling to address its fundamental issues. To retool Ford's entire product line and automate its factories, Mulally borrowed $23.5 billion, convincing the Ford family to pledge its stock and the famous Ford Blue Oval as collateral. His bold move paid off. Unlike its Detroit competitors, Ford avoided bankruptcy, regained market share, and returned to profitability.

> **Mary Barra.** In contrast to Mulally, General Motors CEO Rick Wagoner and his predecessors refused to transform GM's product line, even as the company's North American market share slid from 50% in the 1970s to 18%. When the automobile market collapsed in late 2008, Wagoner was forced to ask President George W. Bush to bail the company out. Even so, GM declared bankruptcy months later.

> Mary Barra, GM's CEO since 2014, demonstrates the difference courage can make. Immediately after her appointment, she testified before a hostile Senate investigating committee about deaths from failed ignition switches on Chevrolet Camaros. Rather than make excuses, Barra took responsibility for the problems and went further to attribute them to "GM's cultural problems." Three years later, she is well on her way

to transforming GM's moribund, finance-driven culture into a dynamic, accountable organization focused on building quality vehicles worldwide.

The rest of George's examples also involved actions at large companies, but of course that's not always the case and those aren't always the best examples. Think of the courage it took for Bill Gates to drop out of the safety of a Harvard education to start a company in a burgeoning industry, though he expressed that his decision was also driven by the fact that he was "'a little worried' that the revolution—putting personal computers in every home, office, and now pocket across the world—would happen without him." [155]

Michael Dell famously started his business of putting together upgrade kits for computers in his freshman-year dorm before winning bids as a Texas state contractor and going on to found a massive company and accumulate wealth of nearly $30 billion. Dell started his venture with $1,000. In 2018, he tweeted a copy of his original company's first financial statement, which he "used to convince [his] parents that it was OK for [him] to not go back to college." [156] [157]

Less well-known is someone like Limor Fried, who similarly started her "do-it-yourself electronics company for hobbyists" in her dorm room at MIT. Adafruit Industries is now a unique, innovative company that "makes hundreds of different kits, including ones for electronics experimentation built around an open-source prototyping platform to make gadgets such as smartphones, handheld video games, and a wearable for GPS-enabled clothing so 'you'll never get lost again.'" And it's worth millions. [158]

There are numerous entrepreneurs, high- and low-profile executives, and everyday businesspeople who start or shape the companies they work for in huge ways. And the ones who make the biggest impact tend to consistently display courage.

There Are Also Consequences for *Having* Courage. That's Why it's Called "Courage!"

There is a reason why that shipping floor manager may hesitate to correct employees; why a salesperson won't address a colleague submitting false reports; why an analyst may consider "massaging the numbers" on a report; why high-powered executives hesitate to make waves at huge companies;

and why potential entrepreneurs instead opt to abandon a great idea and finish that degree. Rational individuals will weigh doing the seemingly safe thing against jeopardizing themselves.

And while leaders in an ideal, trust-based organization will always want you to do the *right* thing, other situations, companies, and individuals will come down on you like a ton of bricks for showing courage. It's not just possible that you'll encounter a situation like this—if you lead for any length of time, it's almost *inevitable* that you will face this at some point in your career. What do you do?

Show Courage and Stay True to a Moral Compass

Take smart risks that will improve your team, your business, and your future. A saying popularized by the British Special Air Service (SAS) motto is applicable here: "Who Dares, Wins."

You might not be the founder of a once-in-a-lifetime startup like Elon Musk or Mark Zuckerberg, or a high-powered executive deciding the fate of a Fortune 500 company, but you will have opportunities to make courageous decisions. You can shape your organization, your team, and your mission to perform better, and doing that will require you to take on some degree of personal and professional risk. Never be so afraid to fail that you shy away from judiciously bold moves.

When it comes to moral courage, know what's right in any specific situation; what is morally, ethically, and procedurally correct. For example, if there is an ethics hotline, use it. If it is a human resources issue or it requires a conversation with your immediate supervisor, utilize the appropriate channel. If the appropriate person blows you off, move on to someone else that can help you address the problem. Be smart about it. Document whatever steps you take and be methodical about doing the right thing. But show courage and act.

Know that even if you do the right thing in the right way, it still may cost you. But take comfort in the fact that you will triumph—as a leader and a person—in the long run.

There are good and bad aspects to the modern digital media environment, and one of the good things is that malfeasance is a lot harder to get away with. So, from a practical standpoint, you may eventually be vindicated if showing moral courage costs you your job or advancement, or results in other hardships.

But even if you aren't vindicated quickly, know that displaying courage and, fundamentally, having character work to your advantage over time. This may sound like a naïve or idealistic thing to say, but it's actually very practical.

Good character is essential for good leaders, and character means drawing a line: "I will never need a job so badly that I will lie, cheat, or steal. I will never shy away from doing something that is right. I'd rather quit and go on unemployment until I find another job at a company that values people with character and integrity."

I've seen people live by these principles and make very hard choices. And often, they either come out on top or they simply resign, move on, and ultimately find success somewhere else. Even in the worst-case scenarios, at least these individuals can live with themselves.

Nevertheless, I'll give you the same piece of practical advice I gave my children (all of whom are adults working in various industries) and anyone else who will listen: Steadily save enough money to have a "Freedom Fund" that will ensure that you and your family can weather the potential short-term consequences of displaying moral courage. In other words, don't put yourself in a position in which the need to make your next mortgage payment causes you to contemplate or rationalize compromising your integrity.

Trust-Based Organizations Need Courageous Leaders

Trust-Based Leaders have wide discretion in a decentralized model, and exponentially more opportunities to show or lack courage, along with integrity, initiative, and judgement. Be a courageous leader. Take smart, calculated risks. Always do the right thing, even if doing so carries some degree of personal or professional risk. And remember that it is your duty to develop subordinate leaders who will also demonstrate courage when the time calls for it.

Coupled with the other elements of the Trust-Based Leadership model, courage plays a huge role in creating and maintaining incredibly powerful organizations that get things done—*right*. And competent, courageous leaders tend to go pretty far in the business world!

Chapter 40

BIAS FOR ACTION

Maneuver Warfare and the Trust-Based Leadership™ model require leaders who have a *bias for action*. Marine leaders must develop an instinct for when changing circumstances call for decisions to be made quickly to create and sustain positive direction and momentum.

This characteristic is developed in all Marines during their earliest days of training and well before some are assigned to leadership positions. Having a bias for action means instinctively being able to recognize that current plans and orders have been rendered ineffective by new information and rapidly changing situations.

In combat operations and in the business world, dynamic environments often dictate that decisiveness and speed are the difference between success and failure. There may be little time to conduct extensive analysis as part of a preferred decision-making process; leaders must exhibit a bias for action and make the best decisions possible.

A bias for action is an acquired leadership instinct that can be developed and refined over time. It helps a leader avoid becoming a victim of *"paralysis by analysis"*—a condition that can literally be fatal on a fast-moving battlefield; and one which can also lead to disaster in today's business environment.

Some leaders delay making decisions while waiting for that *one additional piece of information* which, in their view, seems to be all that stands between them and total clarity and situational awareness. This hesitation causes failure to exploit unanticipated opportunities that surface during these situations. And in some instances, these leaders lose momentum and are totally overcome by the events and friction that surround them.

Trust-Based Leaders Often Make Decisions Alone

Trust-Based Leaders must have a bias for action, especially in rapidly changing environments. They need to have the ability to recognize that something has changed, a new opportunity exists, or the plan has been rendered moot, unprofitable, or even dangerous to the company. In a trust-based organization, senior leaders encourage other leaders to use their experience, judgement, and initiative to react decisively and ensure that the organization's efforts remain aligned with achieving the commander's intent.

A Trust-Based Leader takes action. Do what you think your boss would want you to do. Mistakes may be made, but as long as you're trying to achieve the intent, a bias for action should dominate. Leaders who have to be nudged and prodded to make decisions aren't leaders at all.

During my experience spanning more than four decades in the Marine Corps and the private sector, I have worked for and with many leaders. Some were exceptional, many of them were average performers, and still others were inept. I have found that one of the biggest differentiators between the first category and the latter two is a leader's willingness to make decisions and take action when it is warranted—even if it's risky.

- High-performing leaders prefer to *have their decisions develop the situation*. Instead of allowing themselves (and their teams) to become paralyzed by dynamic situations with fast-paced operations and often contradictory information flow, these leaders demonstrate a bias for action via the rapid assessment of what is happening—*after* having conducted basic due diligence on the best available options and the potential impact of their execution.

- Their training and experience have taught them that a good decision today is almost always more effective than a perfect decision that is implemented next week.

- Average and ineffective leaders are content to *allow the situation to*

develop their decisions. These leaders always seem to have plenty of reasons for not making a decision, like waiting for more information … more options, more opinions. In my experience, organizations led by this type of leader rarely perform at high-levels. They are typically mediocre (or worse) in practically all that they do.

You may have had the experience of failing to act on an issue or seize an opportunity that comes your way due to basic fear, including the anticipation of the worst-case scenario happening. You might think, *What will happen if I'm wrong?*

If you do this frequently, the negative impact accrues. Routinely failing to meet challenges head-on or exploit fleeting opportunities signifies reactive, slow-moving leaders and organizations. This is especially true for individuals in leadership positions that require setting the direction for very large or numerous teams. It's essentially the difference between thriving and merely surviving.

Having a Bias for Action Does Not Mean Being Rash or Impulsive

… and it doesn't always mean definitively taking a final action or making a final decision.

Action, as we're defining it, doesn't equate to reckless action. *Routine inaction* is almost always wrong. However, a bias for action doesn't imply you've got to lash out with a decision just to show others that you are decisive!

Sometimes judgement, wisdom, and experience tell a leader that the best option is to wait an hour or another business day. A bias for action may also manifest in the fact that a leader is actively looking at the situation—doing so may represent decisive action, whereas not actively evaluating the matter is punting on the issue.

The action could be comprised of active planning, refining a solution, or gathering key stakeholders together to review options. Any definitive action requires basic due diligence. A bias for action never means plunging into a situation with no information; it simply means recognizing when you have *enough* information—and the *consequences of inaction are so potentially negative*—that a decision is required *now*.

At first glance, this may seem like confusing, contradictory advice, but it's really pretty clear. The key is to hone your leadership skills, analytical ability, and decision-making instincts to the point where you're able to make sound decisions quickly during rapidly changing situations.

Some Examples of Having a Bias for Action:

- A key IT system goes down unexpectedly, and the repercussions of this failure mean significant lost revenue within the next 24 hours. The IT leader who is responsible for the system has no real opportunity to consult with her superiors. After reviewing basic options to fix the problem with her team, she finds that one solution has a high probability—but not a certainty—of success, whereas another, safer option will take much longer to implement. This leader makes the decision to go with the quick option, balancing the chance of success with the tangible consequences of inaction.

- In a different scenario, a critical IT system has developed an issue that won't have a negative impact until next week or perhaps a few weeks later. In this case, a bias for action means that the leader will work with her team to scope the problem and proactively research potential solutions. Since she has the time to consult with her leaders, action means she will present them with several viable solutions and recommendations. She will seek their input on which solution to choose, rather than merely telling them about the problem and what actions she'd already taken to remedy it.

In either of the above scenarios, a bias for action also means assessing the issue and devising ways to prevent it in the future. A passive leader might just oversee a fix that meets the immediate challenge; in other words, she may simply *"treat the symptoms, but fail to address the disease"* associated with that particular IT system. A Trust-Based Leader with a bias for action will gather her team to do an after-action review: "What happened here? What did we do wrong? And what can we do, starting right now, to adapt our existing SOPs to prevent this from happening again?"

She will then supervise her team as they explore potential long-term solutions and proactively present them to senior leaders: "These are the best options and hardware solutions available to fix this systemic problem over the long term. In addition to the new hardware, I will need your support as my team creates and implements some new policies and procedures that will affect the desk-level users of this system."

The experienced and effective Trust-Based Leader does not have to be asked to do this; she just does it instinctively. Her default setting is having a _bias for action_ and all that it entails!

In my experience, leaders in the business world run into far more of the _extended-timeline_ scenarios than Marine leaders do. Marines—especially those in a combat situation—must be extremely decisive. They often must gather options very quickly and act to press momentum or avoid a calamity.

Fortunately, we usually have a lot more time to make decisions in the business world. Nevertheless, a leader must always act—whether that action involves making a key decision, rapidly moving to gather enough information to make it, or devising and presenting plans to improve the organization going forward.

Leaders Must Also Create a Culture That Has a Bias for Action

Just as this quality is valued in a Trust-Based Leader, it is similarly valued in every member of a trust-based organization. Leaders with a bias for action shouldn't be the only ones that have this personal trait; they need to develop an organization that defaults to it. It must be made part of the company's culture.

Some individuals take action by nature. Others have to be coaxed into doing this. Anyone who has led others has likely led passive individuals, and doing so can be frustrating.

Let's look at an example—anonymized and paraphrased, but real—of an IT team leader on a website development project. He instructs a website developer to add a series of new pages with expanded functionality to a website according to design and performance specifications. A day later, the developer reports that the job is complete. When the leader checks on the project, he finds that the intended design is not an exact match to the specifications, two functions are missing, and the website is now running slowly, with an unacceptably sluggish load time for each page. He tells the developer to fix these issues, but the subsequent conversation goes something like this:

Web Developer: "I fixed the site."

Team Leader: "That is better, but the site is still loading very slowly. This will kill the performance of any marketing campaigns tied to the new pages. Why is this happening?"

Web Developer: "I ran an analysis. These are the speed statistics."

Team Leader: "Yes, and what is your interpretation of them? How do they compare with acceptable parameters?"

Web Developer: "It's running a bit slow."

Team Leader: "What are the reasons?"

Web Developer: "Not sure. I think it may be due to outdated site plugins, or the images and other elements may not be fully optimized."

Team Leader: "OK. How do we fix this?"

Web Developer: "Well, we could …"

This sequence is passive, slow, and incredibly frustrating for a team leader working in a trust-based company—I actually found myself becoming a bit aggravated while writing the example conversation! Obviously, this website developer is not a Trust-Based Leader *or* even an effective follower and teammate.

This entire cycle of execution and communication should have been vastly shortened. The website developer should have properly accomplished all of the assigned tasks on the first pass before reporting that the project was complete. Failing that, he could have proactively assessed and identified the page load problem, providing potential reasons for it (or definitively determining them), and recommending a course of action … or just taking that action if it did not pose an unacceptable risk. The developer should have done all of this without the team leader having to *"pull"* this level of initiative and proactive problem-solving out of him.

You will run into and lead individuals who lack initiative or critical thinking skills. A good leader nips this passivity in the bud. Make it clear, in polite but no uncertain terms, that if a team member comes to you with a problem, he or she must also come to you with a potential solution, or at least enough information to devise one. If possible, this individual should have solicited feedback and advice from his colleagues before coming to you with one or more proposed courses of action.

Develop other leaders and team members with a bias for action. Individuals who can't acquire this trait, or those who show incredibly bad judgement when making decisions, will almost always need to be culled from the organization if it truly desires to have a team of "A-Players." This doesn't mean they are bad people; just that they are not the type of person suited for a company that embraces the Trust-Based Leadership™ model. Helping people move on and find environments in which they fit is what a Trust-Based Leader does, even when it is difficult or emotionally tough to resolve.

Trust-Based Leaders are Action-Takers Who Lead Action-Takers!

I've seen executives fired for being incapable or unwilling to take action without detailed direction from their boss, as well as junior employees let go for routinely failing to take the initiative to solve basic problems that are well within their ability to do so.

Whether it's through your natural personality (if you're fortunate) or training and development, embrace a bias for action tempered with sound judgement—and develop and expect the same from the trusted individuals whom you are privileged to lead. Develop this quality successfully and you and your team will run circles around those without it!

"Good leaders win battles. Great leaders know which battles are worth fighting!"

—Mike Ettore

Chapter 41

THRIVING IN CHAOS

"No plan survives contact with the enemy."

This common military saying is sometimes attributed to General Dwight D. Eisenhower and various other military leaders. But the original author of the sentiment was likely 19th Century German Field Marshall Helmuth von Moltke, who wrote: *"No plan of operations extends with any certainty beyond the first contact with the main hostile force."* [159]

Marine leaders are trained to achieve success across a wide range of military operations while operating in complex environments. Achieving the commander's intent—or, more simply put, winning—in settings clouded with uncertainty and fraught with danger requires leaders who are innovative and clear-headed.

The combat history of the Corps, including recent combat operations in Iraq and Afghanistan, has validated the requirement for agile-minded leaders at all levels who are capable of making sound decisions in highly-fluid environments while fighting against adaptive, relentless enemies. Marine leaders know that they are expected to not only survive, but thrive in the chaos and friction of today's battlefield. Their training is designed to help them develop the ability to sense and seize opportunities as they emerge in the moment.

The key is becoming a leader *who views the difficulties and rapid change found in situations as the norm*, rather than something that is unexpected and devastating to the ability to accomplish the mission. Marines are trained to be hypervigilant to emerging threats and subtle changes in their area of operations, even when—perhaps especially when—all is going well. They must assume conditions will inevitably turn against them, at perhaps the worst possible moment.

These concerns are channeled into action as leaders continuously prepare and develop contingency plans, place their units in the most advantageous situations possible, and seek to maintain the largest margins of safety possible—without stifling the initiative of their Marines and the positive momentum of the battle.

Expect Change, Deal With It, and Make It Your Ally

My battalion commander, when I was a second lieutenant, was a Marine Corps legend. Then a lieutenant colonel (LtCol) who went on to become a major general, Ray Smith had been awarded the Navy Cross, two Silver Stars, the Bronze Star for Valor, and three Purple Hearts as a platoon and company commander and advisor to the South Vietnamese Marines in some of the most difficult battles of the Vietnam conflict. He is considered by many to be one of the best combat commanders in Marine Corps history. And he is certainly someone who knows how to thrive in chaos and uncertainty.

LtCol Smith was a strong advocate of Maneuver Warfare as well as developing adaptive leaders, as I soon found out. He liked to inject friction and stress during training exercises to see how his leaders would respond. For example, just as one of his three rifle companies was preparing to board helicopters to kick off a major field exercise, he surreptitiously stopped the company commander from getting on the bird—he just pulled him out of the exercise without telling anyone he'd done so.

When the company landed at the landing zone (LZ), everyone asked, "Where the hell is the captain?" They tried to reach him and the battalion headquarters via their radios. There was no response, because LtCol Smith had instructed the radio operators at the command post not to answer the lieutenants in the field.

The company's junior leaders had been briefed properly by their company commander prior to the exercise, but now they had to adapt to not knowing where their captain was with no communication from higher headquarters.

They were on their own, armed only with the mission and the commander's intent. LtCol Smith wanted to see how the company's lieutenants and senior noncommissioned officers would react to this form of friction.

Would they sit there in the LZ, scratching their heads as they dealt with radio silence and no sign of their company commander? Or would the lieutenants shoulder the burden and take initiative to hike to a key road intersection that was three kilometers away, dig defensive positions, and achieve the mission to serve as a blocking force? Initially, some of the lieutenants *did* sit there and do nothing. Soon, others took initiative, as they'd been trained to do. They got the company moving and effectively executed the mission and commander's intent.

After this exercise, all of the leaders in the battalion realized that LtCol Smith would probably do this again. They knew what was expected of them should leaders become casualties, communications were not working, or the situation on the battlefield took another unexpected turn. Suffice it to say that the company and platoon commanders spent a lot of time training their subordinates on how to deal with such situations. And, in the process, they rapidly elevated the operational skill and survivability of the entire battalion.

You can't completely and accurately simulate the fear of death and injury that exists during combat operations, but LtCol Smith figured out ways to accurately simulate a lot of the friction, confusion, and stress. We all learned many lessons during our field exercises, especially those that called for leaders to be agile-minded and resilient, and to demonstrate a bias for action and initiative to ensure the commander's intent was achieved.

Operation Urgent Fury—Grenada

These lessons helped me immensely while leading my platoon during Operation Urgent Fury—the liberation of the tiny Caribbean island nation of Grenada in 1983. The battalion's operational plan dictated that Fox Company, 2nd Battalion, 8th Marines would conduct a helicopter-borne air assault into an LZ that was a large open field outside of a town named Grenville, located on the northeast section of the island. My rifle platoon would be the first to land in the LZ and we would be spread out on three different helicopters, with me riding in the one that would be the first to land.

I could not see anything outside of the helicopter during the pre-dawn, low-level flight toward the island. I knew that the trip would not take long, and I knew which portion of the landing zone my platoon was tasked with securing. Again, I was expecting to be set down in a very large, open field. You can imagine my reaction when the helicopter suddenly flared before landing and I realized that we were being inserted into a small, fenced-in soccer stadium!

I tried to speak with the crew chief and tell him we were in the wrong landing zone, but one of the pilots waved to me from the cockpit and signaled that I needed to get my Marines off of the bird. I did so. The adrenaline was flowing that morning and the helicopter's crew chief later said that he'd never before seen Marines get off a helicopter that fast!

As I ran out of the helicopter into the fenced-in soccer stadium, my first thought—seriously—was, *Come on, Colonel Smith! Don't do this to us now; this isn't the time to play games!* I remember feeling aggravated by the thought that he'd actually done this to our unit at such an important moment.

Several minutes later, my company commander arrived in the LZ and his first words to me were, "Mike, do you have any idea where we're at?"

"No sir, no idea."

We had not been provided with maps of Grenada (that's a story for another time!) and had to adapt by acquiring some from a nearby gas station. With the help of some friendly locals, we soon figured out that the soccer stadium was located just outside of Grenville and we started moving toward our objective. Landing in a completely unanticipated LZ—which is sort of a big deal in combat operations—had only slowed us up by about 15 minutes or so.

Later that day, we found out that landing inside the soccer stadium wasn't done on the orders of LtCol Smith. It turned out that a couple of our Cobra attack helicopters had flown over the intended LZ (the large field) a few minutes before we were scheduled to land and spotted several telephone poles and power lines that satellite and aerial reconnaissance photos hadn't picked up. A decision was made at the last second to change the LZ. It would have been nice if the helicopter crew chiefs would have passed this info to us while we were diverting to the soccer stadium, but that's part of the chaos and uncertainty of any combat operation. This is a prime example of the "Fog of War."

Fortunately, LtCol Smith had prepared us to deal with something like this by consistently putting us in unexpected situations during our pre-deployment training exercises. He had prepared us to *expect the unexpected* and still figure out a way to accomplish the mission.

Adaptive Leadership Training is Less Common in Business

Civilian leaders need this skill as well, considering the ever-increasing degrees of chaos and uncertainty in today's business environment. In the book *Great by Choice: Uncertainty, Chaos, and Luck—Why Some Thrive Despite Them All*, Jim Collins, a former executive and Stanford professor, and Morten Hansen, a faculty member at Harvard Business School, argue that change and chaos are constants and certain individuals do especially well in these circumstances. The two men argue that "uncertainty is permanent, chaotic times are normal, change is accelerating, and instability will likely characterize the rest of our lives." [160] [161]

Given shocking political and economic events and the rise of social media platforms as well as Amazon, Uber, Airbnb, SpaceX, and other "disruptors," this maxim has proven to be accurate.

Organizations of all types have a need for leaders who possess the ability to thrive in this abnormal new-normal.

The Most Basic Application of This Principle is the Ability to Solve Challenges

There is plenty of internal and external friction in the business world, and the very best leaders and the very best companies are usually the ones that show resilience; the ability to bounce back from challenges and not only perform adequately in difficult environments, but shine.

Let's say you're an IT leader who is rolling out a new customer management system. The development and integration cycle is meticulously planned out and should take 18 months. In a time horizon of that length, things *will* go wrong:

- A critical vendor will have problems delivering equipment or services.

- Key team members will get sick or exit the company.

- There will be various technical problems with the new system.

- New features or capabilities will be requested by the user base and senior leaders throughout the project, causing many changes to the project plan and execution timeline.

- A newly created law like Europe's GDPR or New York state's cybersecurity regulation will be put into play or expanded, placing additional demands on the platform and the software developers.

Hopefully, there are contingency plans for some of these events. When there aren't, a leader must *step outside of the firefight* and think:

Okay, things are going to hell. I need to focus: What's the mission? What's the intent? Rather than sit and moan about it, what can I do right now to get us back on track?

The advanced application of this ability is when leaders are not only able to deal with these unforeseen challenges and emergencies—but are able to identify and exploit any opportunities that may have surfaced during these times. These opportunities come in different forms:

- In a personal sense, a leader who handles these challenges gains experience. He or she also has the opportunity to shine—leaders who show that they can adapt, improvise and solve problems gain status and reputation.

- Abraham Lincoln and FDR aren't considered two of the greatest presidents in US history because they were snappy dressers, nor even mainly because of most of their policy accomplishments. They are routinely at the top of presidential-ranking lists because they adroitly dealt with the greatest calamities in US history. A leader who comes to expect challenges and deals with them energetically can take comfort in knowing that he or she is being tested and gaining invaluable experience, plus a great reputation if they succeed.

- Unanticipated friction can also be the catalyst for huge opportunities. A good leader may see an opening to improve the way things are done. Let's say you've just been promoted to serve as the head of a troubled department from which several key teammates had recently and suddenly resigned.

Beyond identifying which problems caused the turnover and fixing them, this presents an opportunity to restructure the department; elevating competent junior leaders and otherwise figuring out if there is a more efficient way to get things done. The solution might involve better leveraging technology. Often, many organizations would never have voluntarily arrived at these refinements and solutions, as they were entrenched in the old way of doing things. The unforeseen situations caused them to "think outside of the box" and find new ways to accomplish the mission.

- In a bigger sense, huge external events, like a downswing in the economy or the disruption of an entire industry by a new player or technology can present opportunities—if an organization has the right type of leaders who can think of new and innovative ways to leverage the change. Consider the example of many leaders in the Fintech (financial technology) industry, who seemed to make the claim that cryptocurrency and the blockchain technology that underlies it would make banks obsolete.

  In reality, the opposite has happened; many traditional banks are adapting by establishing key partnerships with Fintech players, integrating a range of automation software to streamline operations, and actually trying to leverage blockchain for many transactions. J.P. Morgan Chase, Citigroup, Barclays, and many other banks are working to use this new technology, and one estimate believes it "could cut banks' infrastructure costs by up to $20 billion each year by 2022." [162]

In a room full of leaders, only a few will have the natural ability to adapt to uncertainty and chaos—but just about everyone can be trained to do it. The development of this skill comes from:

- Training yourself to step back from a problem and devising ways to solve it. Maintain calm and focus as you do so.

- Develop a Teacher-Scholar 360° atmosphere. Press your subordinates for solutions. They will soon learn that they should never approach you with a problem without first formulating potential solutions and courses of action. If you create such an environment, you will unleash the full power of your team and great things will happen! For your part, stay intensely educated and informed about your role, your teammates, and your industry. This will enable you to more easily solve new problems and spot opportunities.

- Experience, experience, experience. When you step up to lead, you will inevitably be put in a position of having to adapt to new challenges. Volunteer for any and all opportunities to lead that are a match with your capability, and a few that may even seem beyond it. Seek out opportunities to lead!

Thriving in chaos and uncertainty doesn't mean that you have to have all the answers. It means you can adapt and lead effectively. Develop the skill and mindset in yourself, as well as in your team. And remember: Great leaders put themselves out there, roll with the punches, *and find ways to win*.

"The best leaders don't always have all of the answers, but they always ask the best questions."

—Mike Ettore

Chapter 42

RESILIENCE

Marine leaders have to be resilient, whether they're engaged in training or actual combat operations. Challenges, conditions, and situations will vary, but all are best handled by highly trained leaders possessing an inner strength that enables them to prevail over whatever is facing them at the moment.

Marine leaders routinely deal with situations where it might seem logical for them to abort a mission or retreat in the face of unexpected enemy threats or events. During these situations, they tap the reservoir of resilience and "iron will" that is developed through education, training, and continuous practical application of the science and art of leadership. This "gas tank" of resilience enables them to endure and achieve when many others would simply quit.

Now, Marines do encounter setbacks—things don't always go as planned, especially in combat. Plans go awry, helicopters break down or even crash, radios and communication networks fail at critical moments, and, in some instances, teammates are killed or wounded. But Marines' training and inner resolve are what enable them to quickly recover, assess the status of their plan, and adapt it appropriately to accomplish the mission. Marine leaders actually tend to flourish in such situations; they learn a lot from them and incorporate these lessons into their training, tactics, and SOPs.

The very nature of warfare is such that Marine leaders must be mentally tough and possess the ability to "get the job done," no matter what it takes.

Quickly bouncing back from setbacks and losses is expected of these leaders and a great amount of institutional, unit, and peer pressure exists to ensure they do it. As a result of their training, Marine leaders expect a lot of themselves in this regard, and they hold themselves and each other accountable to a standard in which <u>the only acceptable outcome is success</u>—accomplishing the mission.

This focus on results and mission accomplishment has resulted in a culture in which sympathy is not offered nor expected should a Marine leader fail to achieve his assigned mission. This may sound a bit cruel, but it reflects the harsh and unforgiving world in which these men and women often operate. This aspect of Marine Corps culture produces leaders who *simply will not quit*. There are numerous examples of them persevering when all logic tells them to give up and accept failure.

Application to Business

Like their Marine contemporaries, business leaders—especially those within a Trust-Based Leadership™ model—must possess a reservoir of inner strength and an "iron will" that enables them to be resilient in the face of serious and nearly continuous challenges. In business, as in warfare, there is a need for leaders who are capable of remaining calm, self-aware, optimistic, and focused on resolving the problem at hand. This valuable quality enables a business leader to effectively operate in environments and situations that are associated with high-levels of stress, and the friction and chaos that often reside within the "Fog of Business War." More than many other qualities that are desired in a leader, resilience is often the determining factor in achieving professional success.

Here's another take on what the quality of resilience can do for a business leader and his or her team. In an article published in *The Wall Street Journal*, Former Krispy Kreme CEO Daryl Brewster discussed the tough times the company was going through at one point due to a serious and controversial financial issue. "We would be turning over a rock, and some other new issue would come up," he said. "It was good to get those issues out into the open, but it was unproductive to just stew on them."

Sensing that his team was becoming demoralized, Brewster directed a well-respected leader to move into an office that was closer to some of his colleagues who were starting to show the effects of the high stress associated with this situation. This leader had a positive attitude and was known by all to be a "problem solver." His enthusiasm and "can-do" attitude showed a level of resilience in the face of adversity that had a positive and calming effect on his teammates. "He brought a wonderful sense of optimism—a good old 'let's get it done and figure this stuff out' attitude," Brewster said.[163]

The main lesson here is that a resilient leader is capable of quickly recovering from challenges, setbacks, and even abject failure. They maintain their bearing, poise, and positive attitude as they lead by example while helping their team deal with friction, uncertainty, and stress.

The Trust-Based Leadership model demands resilient leaders because of its focus on delegation, latitude, adaptability, and durability. Leaders need to have the confidence that other leaders and teammates won't fold under pressure, especially when detailed supervision isn't possible. Everyone is expected to adapt to difficult circumstances while accomplishing the mission and achieving the commander's intent. And leaders must always lead by example when the chips are down. A trust-based leader rolls with the punches and bounces back to move the mission forward—again and again—thereby inspiring others to stand strong as well.

"In business, as in warfare, there is a need for resilient leaders who are capable of remaining calm, self-aware, optimistic and focused on resolving the problem at hand."

—Mike Ettore

Chapter 43

TEAM PLAYER

We've gone over the importance of teamwork in some detail, and how it is particularly essential when a Marine unit is engaged in combat operations. Again: warfare might be the ultimate team activity; smaller forces that work together can and often do beat much larger forces that fail to work well as a team. Thus, the Marine Corps uses powerful and time-tested methods to shape recruits into Marines with a "team-first" mentality that puts mission accomplishment, other Marines, and the needs of the institution before the needs of any individual.

Marines embody *esprit de corps*, defined by the *Collins English Dictionary* as "a feeling of loyalty and pride that is shared by the members of a group who consider themselves to be different from other people in some special way." Esprit de corps is the faith and trust that Marines have in their fellow Marines, their leaders, and what the Marine Corps stands for. A Marine is willing to put his life on the line for the person to his left and to his right. He is willing to do this because he knows that they would do the same for him.[164]

Esprit de corps is an incredibly powerful force. It helps leaders develop groups of individuals into cohesive teams that can accomplish insanely difficult tasks.

A Trust-Based Leader Develops Strong Teams—But First Views Him or Herself as *a Member* of the Team

In a trust-based organization, everyone needs to deprioritize the concept of "self" in favor of being a team member, including those serving in leadership roles. Yes, a leader still needs to be able to inspire, motivate, direct, and set the example for others to follow; but you are first and foremost a part of the team.

One of the best ways to achieve this perspective is to view *leadership as service*, and *leaders as servants*. The *reason* for your existence as a leader is your team. Your *responsibility* is to take care of them, to ensure that they have the tools to accomplish the mission, and to mold promising individuals into effective leaders—thus making *them* more effective members of the team.

Do you notice the cycle?

The Marine Corps emphasizes the continuous development of good leaders; good leaders create, lead, and sustain good teams; better teams perform better; and the better they perform, the more the Marine Corps succeeds and further invests in good leadership.

Lessons about the importance of teamwork abound, and this quality is recognized as being vital in any organization that strives for success. Everyone, from the coach teaching your kid's soccer squad to the folks running a restaurant and the executives of a Fortune 500 company understands the basic value of teamwork and strives to obtain its benefits.

But one of the reasons that Marines prioritize it so highly—and put real muscle into developing it to an incredibly strong degree—is that teamwork takes on even greater importance in an organization that practices Maneuver Warfare and decentralized command and control. And it's of course similarly vital in a company that uses the Trust-Based Leadership™ model and all that is associated with it.

Teamwork, if employed well and instilled into a decentralized culture, will result in an organization that can respond and adapt much more rapidly than its competitors. The decision cycle is quicker. Trust enables the leader and all members of the team to swiftly identify and call for action on opportunities and threats, plus automatically expect viable ideas, plans, and lower-level actions.

A Special Type of Team Player is Required in the Trust-Based Leadership Model

As you know, the Maneuver Warfare concept calls for somewhat centralized planning and very decentralized execution. A well-trained Marine unit understands what's supposed to happen or not happen; its members have a mission and the commanders' intent and know that they will be successful if they achieve this intent. For example, let's say a platoon is ordered to "Keep the enemy on the eastern side of the river. Do not allow him to move into the western side."

The original plan may go to hell, but as long as the team's actions result in the enemy staying on the eastern side of the river, they succeed. When the plan *does* go to hell (and it often will), this calls for a change in plans and focus, initiative, and quick action.

Traditional business organizations may also value teamwork, but things are typically planned out over weeks, months, and years in a highly centralized model rather than hours, days, or weeks. Trust-based organizations move faster and not everyone can naturally be the free-thinking, nimble-minded team player that's required. Why?

For one thing, it takes a combination of initiative and *humility*. An individual may be the person or part of a department or team that is in the spotlight one day, but on the following day finds himself in a supporting, non-glamorous, less visible, and underfunded role when the company's priorities suddenly shift. He may have to cease what he has been doing and change direction to make the new goals happen. If you become a leader who can handle this type of change, you will be incredibly valuable to the organization.

Here are Some Examples of Teamwork in Action

Shortly after I took over the IT department at Kforce, we had just started to get the department running smoothly and had several major projects fully funded and underway. The organization was beginning to hit its stride and the team was finally firing on all cylinders to get things done—then everything changed. All of a sudden, my boss took me aside and said:

> "Mike, look, we're bringing you into the loop on this. We've decided to pursue the acquisition of another staffing company. If all goes well, the acquisition will be completed within 90 days, after which you will serve as the executive sponsor for most of the activities related to the integration of the acquired company. We know this will be a lot of work and place

heavy demands on your teams, especially the IT team. So, we're willing to delay all current and planned IT projects by at least two quarters while your teams complete the integration of this new company."

As a team player, I had to immediately work with my IT leaders to revise the department's priorities, stop or slow work that had required a great deal of effort to get moving, and otherwise quickly pivot to change the department's focus on the new mission of integrating the acquired company. I had to quickly divorce myself from any negative emotions or attachment to what my team had worked so hard to build—and just get everyone focused on getting the new task done well and on time.

I immediately went to my IT leaders and said, "We've got a new priority. Please get together and devise your recommended courses of action for putting current and planned projects on hold while we effectively integrate the company we are acquiring. We have to brief our high-level plan to the executive team in two days."

In contrast, a non-team player—and trust me, I've seen this happen many times—is only a team player when his team is getting its way. This type of executive (I won't call him a leader) may pout. He finally has a well-funded project set up and he and his team are enjoying executing the plan, and now someone is essentially coming in and flipping over the chess board.

Rather than just say, "Okay. The main effort has changed," this individual does not conceal his disappointment and grumbles about the shift to his seniors, peers, and subordinates. He slow rolls any changes related to the new priority while stubbornly and selfishly holding onto previous priorities that he felt were more important. He might even say to his team, "This is what we've been told to do, but really, nothing's going to change," mistakenly believing that it's possible to accomplish both the original mission and the new priority—a move which typically ends in disaster.

There are a lot of different personalities in any company and many of them can be selfish, often at higher leadership levels. The best organizations stamp out this instinct. A bad leader will say, "You took my ball from me, and I'm going home." In truth, he or she needs to be reminded: "It wasn't your ball in the first place."

Leaders at *All* Levels Must Be Team Players

Continuing the Kforce example: Perhaps an IT project manager is heavily invested in the original mission; she loves working on this project and was specifically hired to manage it. This opportunity is a tremendous résumé-builder that can help her achieve her lofty career aspirations. But a third of the way through the project, it's suddenly put on hold in favor of a new priority that this project manager is less enthusiastic about. The team player in a trust-based organization adapts in situations like this, even when they are disappointing or unpleasant—she charges after the new mission with enthusiasm. In contrast, the non-team player takes a selfish approach, as if the entire company exists to further her interests and career.

In another example, perhaps a critical technology system goes down and fixing it requires a department to put in work over a couple of weeks of 18-hour days, including working through the weekends. Most IT teams of significant size find themselves in this position and willingly do whatever it takes to get technical systems and tools back up and running.

In this example, let's say that numerous other employees will not be paid next month unless this system, which controls the company's payroll, is repaired. It has to get fixed quickly. A well-led IT team that has a team player mentality will accept that they have to go the extra mile to get this urgent task done, whereas a team that has not been taught the importance of team play will often resist, drag their feet, or simply complain about difficulties or inconveniences the entire way.

How to Be a Team Player

These are the qualities a Trust-Based Leader must cultivate and display to be a team player and inspire teamwork in others:

- Lead by example: If you require adaptability of your team, demonstrate this trait as you execute your duties and emphasize it at every opportunity. If you want employees to weather hardship, show them that you are willing and able to weather it yourself. Even if it's merely sharing their hardships, stress, and inconveniences—such as giving up your weekend to be present on the job site, even though you have nothing essential to contribute to the actual work being done—do it. And make the working conditions as comfortable for your team as possible. People notice and appreciate little things like this, far more than you might imagine.

- Subsume the self: View yourself as a servant, to both your organization and especially your people. Leadership is a responsibility, not a perk. Have good character, follow the core values, leadership traits, and principles, and dedicate yourself to the concept of service, not entitlement.

- Be adaptable: Things can change very quickly in a decentralized organization that rapidly tackles challenges and pounces on opportunities. Adapt to legitimate new priorities and prioritize mission accomplishment. Stay flexible. As you know, the Marine Corps motto is *Semper Fidelis*, which is Latin for "Always Faithful." But in situations that require quick adaptations to changing circumstances, many Marines like to say *"Semper Gumby,"* meaning that one must be Always Flexible!

- Communicate with teammates at all levels: Changing priorities, new missions, and unforeseen problems will be accepted by your team much more easily if you take the time to communicate why the priorities have shifted or the extra effort is needed. The lower down you go on an org chart, the less of the "big picture" strategy an individual will see. Sometimes, simply explaining what's going on and how it will affect certain individuals and teams works wonders for morale and motivation.

Coach Your Team and Develop Team Players

All of the above, especially leading by example and communicating well, will help most individuals develop into team players. For those who still don't play ball, however, dedicated coaching and counseling—and putting consequences behind failing to adapt—are required.

Set the standard. Live the standard. Enforce the standard.

Despite your best intentions and the application of sound leadership, you *will* run into individuals who are not and do not want to be team players. And some of them are, for various reasons, essentially incapable of it. Typically, the latter survive in an organization for a time that is in direct proportion to their talent and/or unique experience, knowledge, or skills.

Nevertheless, even the most valuable sales reps, technicians, or specialists who don't work well in a team environment will damage the organization over the long haul. If someone displays behavior that is detrimental to team unity, counsel them in an appropriate manner. This may simply involve taking them aside and saying, "Hey, look: it seems to me that you're not pitching in and playing ball. Now is not the time for debates or half-hearted effort. We've been given a mission. We need action from the entire team, including you."

Maintain a positive, respectful tone and stress the importance of the mission. That usually gets most people on track. If it doesn't, counsel that individual in more detail. And if that doesn't work, take whatever actions are appropriate for the situation. Usually, individuals who refuse to be team players have issues related to previous, negative situations in their careers and often, they simply are not used to working in a trust-based model. As a leader, you have to be patient enough to coach these individuals while remaining objective enough to know when it is necessary to discipline or even terminate someone.

Be a Trust-Based Leader—And a Team-Based One

Combat may be the ultimate team activity, simply because of the stakes involved—but any organization exponentially increases its flexibility and "firepower" when it builds a culture that places great value on teamwork. The senior leaders in these companies have seen what happens when individuals come together and energetically work toward a common goal—when they are willing to make sacrifices and dedicate all of their talent, experience, and energy to their colleagues.

The most successful companies rely on leaders who have the ability to develop and sustain this quality among teammates. And this skill often plays a critical role in a leader's eventual elevation to the most senior levels of leadership.

As always, remember that anywhere you go and anything you do, it is the sum of your actions and words that define what kind of leader you are. And the kind of leader you are will determine whether your team trusts you, will follow you, and will perform at optimum levels for you. The Trust-Based Leader is a *part* of the team, just like those whom he or she is leading.

Being a team player means leading by example; asking questions of and listening to your people; considering yourself a servant and sacrificing for them; communicating effectively with subordinates as well as higher-ups; and putting as much trust in your team members as they place in you.

"Only when the tide goes out do you discover who's been swimming naked."

—Warren Buffett

"Leaders of Substance > Leaders of Image."

—Mike Ettore

Chapter 44

DEVELOPING LEADERS

The ability to mentor and develop other leaders is something that separates average leaders from truly great ones, and it has crucial importance in the Trust-Based Leadership™ model. Specifically, the need for this skill has three main components:

- It develops vital redundancies. In a centralized organization, the loss of a leader can often cripple the organization—it is paralyzed without that individual's presence, authority, and decision-making ability. A trust-based organization seeks to create a culture in which leaders are developed throughout the organization, so they can assume the duties of other leaders quickly and effectively.

- It exponentially increases the speed and effectiveness of the organization. Trust-Based Leaders demonstrate a bias for action, take initiative, and use good judgement when making decisions. The more of this type of leader you have—and the more discretion (freedom of action) you give them within the framework of accomplishing the mission and fulfilling the commander's intent—the more novel, effective solutions they can devise.

- It creates lasting success. Companies that prioritize leadership development and recognize and reward leaders for developing other leaders create a deep pool of talent. These trained, capable individuals (who continue to create other leaders) can serve the organization well for years, decades, and even generations.

It is for these reasons—as well as the basic fulfillment of the contract of special trust and confidence placed in a leader—that the Marine Corps places a huge emphasis on leadership development at *all* levels.

Marine leaders are taught to prioritize developing subordinate leaders who have the capability to function one or two levels above their current responsibilities. When I was a young lieutenant, one of my battle-hardened battalion commanders gave me some sage advice; he matter-of-factly told me, "Mike, as a rifle platoon commander, there is a good chance you will get killed or seriously wounded during a combat operation. You *need* to have sergeants and corporals who can step up and take charge when, not if, this happens."

Examples of this grim need litter Marine Corps history. One of the most powerful is found in the assault on Sugar Loaf Hill during the Battle of Okinawa in 1945:

> Company G of the 22nd Regiment's 2nd Battalion, commanded by Captain Owen T. Stebbins, kicked off seven days of agony with an infantry-tank assault on the afternoon of May 12. Confident that a speedy operation lay before them, Company G encountered minimal gunfire in its first 900 yards. Suddenly, all hell broke loose as small arms fire, machine guns, mortars, and artillery ripped into their ranks and pinned down two of the three platoons before reaching Sugar Loaf's slopes. Captain Stebbins and Lieutenant Dale W. Bair led 40 men of the remaining platoon toward the hill, but before they advanced 100 yards, 28 Marines fell to Japanese gunfire.
>
> Stebbins collapsed when machine-gun bullets riddled his legs. Bair assumed command, but before he could shout his first order, Japanese bullets shredded his left arm. With the limb hanging useless, Bair gathered 25 Marines and, after grabbing a light machine gun with his good hand, resumed the attack. Upon reaching Sugar Loaf's crest with 10 men, the six-foot, two-inch tall, 225-pound officer boldly stood atop the hill and sprayed the enemy with machine-gun fire.

Bair's total disdain for danger stirred his men. One Marine stated, "It was impossible to be afraid when you saw him standing up there." ... Two more bullets slammed into Bair before he went down. ...

Company G repeatedly stormed Sugar Loaf throughout May 12, even seizing its summit on three occasions, but each time Japanese mortars and hand grenades drove them back. When nightfall arrived, the hill remained in Japanese hands, while Marines tended to their wounded. DeMar's platoon suffered 50 percent casualties, while only 75 of 215 men in Company G were able to man their posts that night. The most demoralizing aspect was that, despite the appalling losses, Marines faced further attempts in the days to come. Sugar Loaf had to be taken, which meant that more young Americans would perish.

Marines repeated the gruesome pattern over the next six days.[165]

The Marines eventually took Sugar Loaf Hill and never let it go, but "the 6th Division Marines suffered 2,662 men killed or wounded. They lost another 1,289 men evacuated because of either exhaustion or battle fatigue." And while Okinawa is a very extreme leadership example, involving particularly extreme combat, the need for training junior military leaders to step up has endured, including in the most recent wars:

Of the more than 6,600 troops killed in Iraq and Afghanistan, thousands have been in leadership positions: captains, lieutenants, staff sergeants and corporals. Which means that thousands of times over this decade of war, a junior and often less experienced leader has had to assume his dead boss's job, and those under him have had to adjust to new leadership during the most stressful time of their lives. Add to those the many thousands of leaders who have been grievously wounded and sent home, leaving more empty slots to fill ...

And those taking over for them often don't get even a few hours to process what has happened and mentally prepare themselves for the new role; they take over amid the cries of the wounded and the crack of rifle fire.[166]

Application to Business

Most business leaders will of course likely never know this form of leadership under fire, but ask yourself: How strong do an organizational culture and leaders have to be to continue functioning in the face of a loss of numerous key leaders and still be able to accomplish something that difficult?

How knowledgeable and confident do junior business leaders need to be to be able to take over when *their* leaders are taken out of the fight?

And how can some of these leadership lessons from the Marine Corps be applied to strengthen teams in the business world?

Vital Redundancies in Business

Obviously, business leaders are not leading their teams into enemy-controlled territory like a Marine leader in combat. But the modern business world and increasingly diverse and dynamic operations are increasing the need for the development of subordinate leaders who can step up and make decisions. The Marine Corps often calls for situations in which various units are spread out across vast distances "distributed operations," and this term also describes the operational footprint of many companies.

Very rarely nowadays are companies of significant size all housed in one building. Often, not all employees are even in one time zone, or even one country. Some companies' claim to fame is that the sun never sets on their operation; they've got teams of remote employees and vendors working on their programs and products around the clock and around the world. Different corporate and regional offices. Multiple service centers around the country. Warehouses spread across the globe. One senior leader might be in charge of all of a company's facilities east of the Mississippi, and they've got 23 of them in various states. That's obviously a very distributed operation.

This leader needs to be able to develop subordinate leaders, many of whom he will probably not have daily or even weekly contact with. He may only see them personally once a quarter or maybe twice a year at regional sales meetings. The implicit special trust and confidence in junior leaders is an increased requirement in distributed operations vs. the traditional business environment, the latter a scenario where you generally get to see your people every day or at least several times per month.

And over the past decade or so, the rapid rise of the remote workforce brings forth a new challenge for leaders. Can you lead remote teams and develop other leaders who are capable of leading them? This trend has thrown a whole new aspect of leadership competence into the mix. In today's environment, it's almost a given that you're going to have some people working remotely if you're leading a team of any size, whether they're employees who are organic to the company or external contractors or vendors.

If you've trained your leaders well, they know the mission and your intent, they've got the right type of initiative and bias for action, and they are guided by sound SOPs and other established business practices. One of your project leads working in India or in the Philippines for example, knows that a certain task needs to get done, and knows that he won't have the luxury of calling a senior leader multiple time zones away when confronted with a problem or an obstacle. This junior leader has to be empowered to make proper decisions in the absence of his boss and maybe even his boss's boss. When he can communicate with you again, he can say, "We were presented with these challenges. These were the options that we considered. I went with option B, and here's what's going on right now. Please let me know your thoughts."

Marines naturally take to this responsibility because of the combat element; they know that a leader being taken out of action is a definite possibility. It's a little harder to convince people in the business world that this is going to happen, but what leader does not want to have subordinate leaders capable of making good decisions with minimal guidance? While he takes a vacation? When he's sick? When he's in a business meeting with a client, and an opportunity presents itself to one of his sales representatives 300 miles away—from a prospective client they've been trying to crack into for months, if not years?

Essentially, leaders at every level should embrace the concept of replicating their mind, experience, business savvy, and decision-making ability in every single one of their subordinate leaders, to the extent possible.

How Do You Develop Other Leaders?

Leaders range in ability and effectiveness from terrible to World-Class. To move into the far-upper end of that spectrum, you must empower others by doing the following:

1. Create a culture of education

Just as you should be a lifelong learner, you should strongly encourage—in many cases, mandate—that subordinate leaders schedule time to develop their knowledge and skills. And you must *give* them that time.

When I was at Kforce, it wasn't unusual for the Amazon delivery guy to come by and drop off a couple of dozen books. If I'd read a book that I thought was particularly valuable, I'd buy and distribute it to my leaders and discuss it once they'd had a chance to read it. Some of my departments and teams actually created discussion groups that met frequently to go over a book, journal article, or whatever professional development material was relevant to their mission and operations.

Eventually, members from different teams asked to sit in on some of these sessions and other leaders asked if they could roll their people into the program. Some of these other leaders started holding sessions like these of their own. And sometimes, another leader would approach me and say, "Hey Mike, I'm doing this for my team. Would you like your guys to sit in on it?"

I'd typically respond, "Absolutely, because I don't know anything about that topic—and I can see where it could benefit them."

Not only did the specific material benefit the people in all of these departments, it showed everybody that "Hey, knowledge is out there. We want you to take advantage of it."

Don't be too prideful to let your position or your departmental boundaries hinder this type of culture. Learn and teach. Share the knowledge. Turn your entire team, to the extent possible, into an organization in which learning is continuous.

2. Send your leaders to training and development opportunities—and go with them!

A leader who wants to train and develop other leaders can't learn everything on his or her own. You need to stay relevant by attending leadership workshops and training seminars both geared toward your industry and subjects outside of it. These are the settings where you're going to find emerging concepts and technologies, new concepts and recent innovations, and perhaps even some very old, time-tested techniques that you've never heard of—

which can be brought back and applied to your organization.

The Marine Corps is very good at doing this and it has the unique latitude to do it long term. It's not uncommon for an infantry officer to do several years of his 20-year (or more) career in assignments that have little or nothing to do with the infantry, as the Corps wants to shape individuals into well-rounded leaders capable of handling many different tasks as they rise in rank. While not every Marine leader is going to attain the senior grades of first sergeant or colonel, and even fewer of them will become sergeants major or general officers, the Corps tends to invest in all leaders with the idea that they have the *possibility* of doing so. And the organization ensures that it has the budget, the manpower, and the time horizons required to make this investment.

There is less flexibility to do this in business, as many more individuals jump around between jobs ... though it does happen in some companies. At Kforce, I was able to send several of my leaders to graduate school so they could obtain an MBA. Unlike most companies, Kforce did not require them to sign a contract to pay back the cost of their education if they left the company before a certain point. This was a leap of faith. But we assumed that we would reap benefits as they used their newly acquired knowledge to become better leaders more capable of developing other leaders.

These and other types of training and development opportunities may be less common in many companies, but leverage them whenever possible. And if they don't exist, discuss the concept with your boss and see if starting such a program is possible.

3. Be a mentor and encourage mentorship

Leaders improve their skills by gaining wisdom and guidance from internal and external mentors. An internal example could be someone within the individual's chain of command or in a different part of the company. An external mentor is obviously outside of the company, and this could be a friend, a professional colleague or former boss who's moved on, or a professional leadership coach. Unfortunately, active and aggressive mentorship programs—much like dedicated leadership training—have been in decline for some time in the modern business world, in a period when the need is arguably even greater:

> Peter Cappelli, a Wharton management professor and direc-

tor of the school's Center for Human Resources, says mentoring has assumed a different guise in recent years in response to the disintegration of the traditional employer-employee contract as a result of downsizing and outsourcing.

"If you go back a generation ago, your immediate supervisor had the responsibility to develop you; the mentor was your boss," says Cappelli. "Bosses knew how to be mentors. They knew what employees needed to do and they knew how to give employees a chance to accomplish things. Mentors were assessed based on the number of subordinates who got promoted and how the subordinates moved along in their careers."

But the boss-subordinate model of mentoring shifted in the 1980s. "Companies had a surplus of white-collar managers, and reengineering waves in corporations were about getting rid of people," Cappelli notes. "Companies told mentors, 'We're trying to get rid of people, so we can't promote your mentee.'"

Although bosses continued to play an important role as mentors when they could, the supervisor-subordinate model waned, and companies sought other ways to help workers navigate their way in the workplace. According to Cappelli: "Companies said, 'What do we do for these folks? Bosses aren't helping them anymore.' The idea became to find mentors who weren't necessarily someone you worked closely with or for. Instead of your supervisor, your mentor became somebody you could bounce ideas off of and get career advice from. It became more low-impact."[167]

Nevertheless, many larger companies still have dedicated mentoring programs, and the value of mentorship is clear:

Various academic studies since the 1980s have demonstrated the many benefits of mentoring. "Clearly, employees who have mentors earn more money, are better socialized into the organization and are more productive," [Terri A.] Scandura [a management professor and dean of the graduate school at the University of Miami] says. "They experience less stress and get promoted more rapidly. Because of the positive benefits shown to mentors, companies are still very interested in this process."[168]

For example, researchers from several universities studied youth, academic, and workplace mentoring and their summary, published in the *Journal of Vocational Behavior*, found particular benefits in the latter two categories:

> Results demonstrate that mentoring is associated with a wide range of favorable behavioral, attitudinal, health-related, relational, motivational, and career outcomes, although the effect size is generally small. Some differences were also found across each type of mentoring. Generally, larger effect sizes were detected for academic and workplace mentoring compared to youth mentoring.[169]

Practical Experience Through Developmental Assignments: A Crucial Method for Developing Subordinate Leaders

Do you want to get a developing leader truly up to speed? Find or create any possible situation, event, meeting, or assignment that lets them face new challenges.

For example, take someone who's never been a project manager before, teach them how to do it, and assign them to lead a project. Once that person has successfully led a few projects, put him or her on another project with a specifically chosen subordinate and say, "Listen, your job is to make sure this project goes well … but it's also to make sure that by about halfway through, your assistant is capable of running the show by herself. Next year at this time, she should be able to lead a similar project like this without you."

You have to put people in positions where the stakes are *significant*, but *not a potential company- or career-ender.* These inexperienced leaders are probably going to make mistakes early on because leading an effort by oneself is not the same as doing it with continuous oversight. But you've got to give your subordinates these opportunities to lead and, if necessary, fail a little bit.

I believe that many aspects of leadership—*the science*—can be learned via training and study, but the only way anyone really gets better at *the art* is to apply these lessons and learn from practical experience. Two fatal leadership flaws in the business world tend to be a lack of investment in dedicated, continuous leadership training and development; and that most individuals are placed into leadership roles without *any* training or practical experience.

The classic sales organization example illustrates this. Many companies take great salespeople and make them into sales managers without providing them with any leadership training. They simply throw these individuals into the deep end, and it's a *sink or swim* mentality.

Unfortunately, a lot of them sink because leading a sales team is a very different skill set than selling. And even more unfortunately, these untrained leaders often grab onto other people as they sink and bring them underwater with them! Change this practice. Develop your current and future leaders through culture, training, and providing subordinates with the opportunities to lead.

Can you be a force multiplier? Can you produce other leadership force multipliers? That's the true power of this stuff. Once it gains momentum, it's like an avalanche, or perhaps a perpetual motion machine. If you can learn leadership skills, live them, use them in your organization, *and* teach others to do the same—and better yet, be able to teach them how to teach *others*—you'll have a leadership legacy that theoretically never ends.

Chapter 45

SHARING HARDSHIP

In the Marine Corps, being a leader means sharing the same difficulties—including the danger and privation—as those whom you lead. This is of course directly tied to the previously mentioned concepts of leading by example and "leaders eat last."

As with many things in the Corps, the most important application of sharing hardship is when leading during combat situations. Marines will master their fear and follow a leader who masters *his or her* fear, despite incredible danger. Think of the example from the previous chapter: the lieutenant who led the assault on Sugar Loaf Hill during the battle of Okinawa:

"One Marine stated, 'It was impossible to be afraid when you saw him standing up there.'"[170]

That man may have been overstating things—it's certainly normal and possible to be afraid. But often the example of both colleagues and especially leaders helps overcome this fear. Another great example is the leadership of Sergeant Major John Canley during the Battle of Hue City in January 1968. Canley's Navy Cross was finally upgraded to the Medal of Honor decades later when he received it—at 80 years-old—on Oct. 17, 2018. The accounts of those who were there suggest the award was long, long overdue.[171]

"I call it 'the three missing days in Marine Corps history' which were never documented anywhere. Due to the nature of the battle, we had no officer," explained John Ligato, who served as a private first class under Canley during the battle. "We were in firefights, when we'd be all hugging mother earth, he'd be standing up directing us … he stood up in firefights. … I know that might sound unrealistic to people listening, but you will hear that from every Alpha Company Marine."

"We all considered him totally, completely, and absolutely without fear," added retired Major General Ray L. Smith, who also served with Canley at Hue and later commanded my battalion during the Liberation of Grenada and subsequent operations in Lebanon when I was a lieutenant. "He had a piece of shrapnel, still in there, sticking out, in between his eyebrow and his eyeball. And I pulled it out. And he said, 'I want that on-the-spot report.'"

"He loved his enlisted Marines, and he never scolded us. He instructed us but you could feel the love, you really could," said Ligato. "And I know that's maybe a tough word in combat Marines, but you could feel the love. And I would screw up or something and it was never a chewing out, it was just 'This is the way we do it.' So, you wanted to do it right for him after that."

"He is individually and uniquely responsible for saving and/or protecting the lives of a lot of good young Marines," added Smith. "All of us, the lieutenant included, literally worshipped the ground he walks on. He's a special human being."

Think of how great of a leader Canley must have been—and exactly what he must have done—to inspire these words from those he led. Individuals are far more likely to follow a leader whom they know is not ordering them to do something that he would not do himself.

"The only thing I was doing was just responding," said Canley. "The Marines, the young Marines, it just shows them it's not do as I say, it's do as I do. And just being that close to them brings motivation to them. My Marines, because they believed in me, they would follow me to death. And I had no doubt about that."[172] [173] [174]

It is my belief that almost every company has one or more leaders at least somewhat like Sergeant Major Canley. These leaders are often a bit reserved and do not seek the spotlight, but they project a leadership presence that inspires and enables everyone who works with them. Do whatever it takes to find these leaders and place them in roles in which they can not only continue to serve as superb leaders, but can actively train and develop other leaders.

Leaders Eat Last

As mentioned previously in this book, the principle "leaders eat last" shows how the Marine Corps stresses sharing hardship outside of and far beyond combat. And the business world has now been widely introduced to this phrase and the philosophy behind it. Author and organizational consultant Simon Sinek wrote a book called *Leaders Eat Last: Why Some Teams Pull Together and Others Don't*. Its title sprang from "a conversation with a Marine Corps general" in which Sinek learned the leadership maxim "Officers eat last."[175]

The general's statement was true, if incomplete. In the Marine Corps, this custom is expanded to all leaders, not just officers. In any group of Marines, the senior ranking individual is last in the chow line and will always be the last to be taken care of in any situation involving basic comfort. The leader must first ensure that his or her people are taken care of, and then look to his or her own personal needs.

This is a great ideal that rightly stresses the concept of leadership as service. It also has very practical benefits. Leaders who take advantage of their position while those they lead are subject to hardship breed immense resentment, a hostility and disrespect that are sometimes surprisingly intense for seemingly small things. In contrast, those who are seen as sharing difficulties are respected and, in many cases, admired.

For example, if the officers' sleeping quarters are air conditioned, then the enlisted quarters had better be air conditioned as well. If there is only one air-conditioned space available, then the most junior enlisted Marines are assigned to it. Some Marine leaders in certain roles must often, out of strategic and tactical necessity, operate from the rear of frontline units—but they do not hesitate to lead from the front in any combat situation that demands it.

Unfortunately, a small percentage of leaders don't live up to this standard— every Marine knows at least one bad example who hasn't—but every leader is taught this principle and it is fundamentally baked into the culture of the Marine Corps.

These lessons directly apply to leading in the business world. Always put the personal needs of those you lead above yours. It's the right thing to do. It is what is expected of great leaders and it obtains the respect that is necessary to lead—as well as to ask individuals to do difficult things.

This seems like a simple thing to do, but you might be surprised (or not) at how many business leaders prioritize their personal comfort or basic needs above those of their subordinates. In addition to being selfish, it's a fundamentally stupid thing to do as a leader. You *must* share difficulties with your people and care for them if you want their respect and loyalty.

Former Secretary of Defense and retired general James Mattis is somewhat of a Marine Corps legend for his tough talk, a scholarly bent, the vital command positions he's held, and his leadership skill. One story about Mattis that illustrates the importance of willingly sharing hardship was related by his former commander and a previous Commandant of the Marine Corps, General Charles Krulak.

One Christmas day, General Krulak and his wife were visiting various units' headquarters and delivering homemade cookies to the Marines who were unlucky enough to draw duty on the holiday:

> Back in 1998, [Krulak] was making his final delivery to Marine Corps Combat Development Command headquarters at Quantico [on Christmas Day] when he asked the Marine on duty who the officer of the day was.
>
> "The young Marine said, 'Sir, it's Brigadier General Mattis.'"
>
> Krulak thought the Marine had misunderstood him, so he asked again, but he got the same answer.
>
> "I looked around the duty hut and in the back, there were two cots: One for the officer of the day and one for [the] young Marine. I said, 'OK, let me cut through all of this: Who was the officer who slept in that bed last night?'
>
> "And the Marine said, 'Sir, Brigadier General Mattis.'"
>
> At that moment, Mattis walked around the corner.
>
> "So I said to him, 'Jim, what are you standing the duty for?' "And he said, 'Sir, I looked at the duty roster for today and there was a young major who had it who is married and had a

family; and so I'm a bachelor, I thought why should the major miss out on the fun of having Christmas with his family, and so I took the duty for him.'"

Never before or since has Krulak run into a general officer standing duty on Christmas Day.

"I think it says volumes about Jim Mattis and his leadership style," Krulak said. "He did it very unobtrusively. He just took the duty."[176]

The story has been repeated numerous times as a testament to Mattis's leadership skill. It's a simple and relatively minor example of sacrifice by a leader. But think of its enduring power and how it applies to your daily practice of leadership. Namely, what will people say about you?

Leadership by Example—Always!

As an infantry company commander, I gave my officers and SNCOs a piece of advice prior to deploying to participate in the Persian Gulf War:

"Listen, I've had some experience in past combat operations where some leaders sometimes selfishly availed themselves to a level of comfort and privileges that the average Marine, enlisted or officer, did not have available to them. Do not do this, *under any circumstances*. The Marines will be watching us to see if we are living the same way we are asking them to live. Whatever we do, good or bad, they will see it and they will never forget it. They will forever tell others about how we led, treated, and cared for them while operating in combat and austere environments. Our professional reputations will reflect how we chose to lead during this time. As always, we will lead by example in every aspect."

Leaders Are Always Being Inspected

Prior to the start of combat operations in Kuwait, my entire unit was living in dug-in positions; essentially, deep holes in the ground. I was talking to one of my lieutenants and the company first sergeant one day while sitting on ammunition crates and drinking some MRE coffee we'd heated on a standard-issue squad stove. At some point, we saw a couple of my unit's vehicles roll by very slowly, perhaps at a distance of 25 yards or so, with all of the Marines in the vehicles looking toward us. These Marines were living in dug-in positions perhaps 300 yards to our front, which was appropriate for the tactical situation. I said to the lieutenant:

"Lieutenant Yoas, do you know what that is?"

"Sir, it's obviously a couple of our Humvees."

"Yes, but not exactly. *That* is some of our Marines heading back to their positions but coming close enough to ours to see how the captain and the first sergeant are living. They know that we're back here 300 yards behind them, and to them, that's considered the rear echelon. They want to know if we're living the same way they are."

Later, I asked my vehicle driver: "Hey, Lance Corporal Barcia, do you ever get any questions about how the old captain lives?"

"Oh, yes, sir. When we first deployed to the desert, I used to get questions like that. What's the captain eat? Where does the captain sleep? I tell them, 'He eats MRE's and sleeps in a hole in the ground, just like us.'"

Marines are always inspecting their leaders, and the same thing happens in the business world!

Shared Hardship in the Business World

It is just as important for business leaders to "eat last" and lead by example in every way. You obviously will not have to lead from the front in combat situations, but there will be tough times and your people will expect you to share the burden and make sacrifices with them. Here are some examples:

- If a company is not doing well and the executives have decided to say, "The company did poorly last year. We have to cut costs in order to remain profitable, so there will not be any pay raises this year," then the executives had better not be getting raises.

  Much like those young Marines checking out my living situation in the desert of Kuwait, in this situation, individuals at all levels of the company will wonder if the compensation of upper management is following suit, and that means all the way to the top. They will inevitably find out whether or not their leaders are leading by example and foregoing their raises like everyone else is.

When leaders continue to reap rewards while most of their team-mates are being asked to make sacrifices, the resentment it breeds is immense and hugely counterproductive to morale, engagement, and productivity.

- A leader in a large open-air manufacturing plant may have the benefit of working in an air-conditioned office, but he or she had better do everything possible to make sure the people working in high heat and humidity on the plant floor are as comfortable as possible. In situations like this, poor leaders would likely say, "It is what it is," without sparing any thought or effort for the wellbeing and comfort of their people. Good leaders reflexively know to check on their team's working conditions, and they will ensure that cooling fans, water-misters, and cold-water fountains are installed if the space can't be closed off for climate-control purposes.

- Asking your people to work late and on weekends will go over a lot better if you do it as well. When I was at Kforce, we typically needed IT technicians and members of various business and support teams to work through several weekends at various stages of major technology projects.

  As the CIO, my job description was to lead and set the direction for the IT group, but I obviously could contribute nothing in the way of technical expertise or advice related to actually getting the IT work done. Nevertheless, I considered the sharing of hardship part of my duty as the CIO and a leader who was asking people to sacrifice their weekends.

  Thus, I would go in on these weekends and bring the project team food and coffee. I'd walk around and ask team members how things were going and if they needed anything. I'd then go to my office and otherwise get out of their hair. I may have been catching up on some paperwork—at some point, I'm sure I was reading a newspaper or magazine—but I was there, sacrificing my weekend. And that was not lost on the members of the project team.

  Now, I don't state this in an attempt to get you to think, "Mike showed great leadership by sacrificing his weekend, too." No, this type of behavior is *simply what good leaders do*. And they do it willingly and cheerfully!

Leaders Must Be Hypervigilant About Avoiding Hypocrisy

Even the *slightest perception* of hypocrisy on the part of a leader can have a poisonous effect on his or her credibility among teammates. Conversely, even small or symbolic gestures and examples of leaders *leading by example* can have a very positive impact on the morale and sense of urgency within an organization.

When Kforce went through an almost-fatal downturn after the dotcom crash—the company's stock price had tumbled and there was concern that it would be delisted from the NASDAQ—the organization conducted a massive reorganization and a comprehensive cost-cutting effort. There were significant layoffs. Departmental budgets were slashed. Salaries were frozen, and in some instances, reduced. Annual performance bonuses were eliminated. Nothing was considered "off limits;" we looked at every expense as something that could be removed, reduced, or deferred. (We even stopped providing free coffee in our offices.) These were tough times and everyone on the team felt the pain!

There were weekly executive meetings of the senior executives that had always included a lunch that was brought in from a local vendor; no foie gras or filet mignon, but pretty much what you'd expect at a buffet at a decent restaurant. We didn't stop the meetings after the budget cuts went into effect, but we certainly stopped the catering in favor of bringing in less-costly soup and sandwiches for the lunches. And sure enough, some employees checked with our administrative assistants to see what we were eating during these weekly lunches. Thankfully, we were indeed leading by example and that our call for company-wide cost-cutting was being applied to the food we were eating in these day-long executive meetings.

During this time, I even started ordering ink refills for my pens rather than ordering new pens. It may have saved only about a dime per pen, but this small gesture communicated to my team how serious I was about cutting costs. A few of my teammates never forgot that practical, minor, and somewhat amusing action. During the following years, the phrase "ordering ink refills" became code for the need to remain vigilant about spending.

A *culture of shared hardship* was set during these tough times. It enabled leaders throughout the company to approach our tenuous situation from a common perspective:

"We are all feeling the pain and we are all cutting costs. And if the senior leaders can forfeit pay raises and bonuses (some actually had their salaries reduced), eat low-cost lunches, and screw in ink refills instead of buying new pens, how and where can I find ways to save *real money* in my team?"

For example, as the CIO, I encouraged my IT leaders to contemplate questions such as:

- Can we extend the service life of our computers rather than buying new ones?

- Can we squeeze another year out of our current servers?

- Can we terminate some levels of external tech support for now and fix some of our equipment in-house?

These leaders and many more with the company responded magnificently, and Kforce got through this difficult period. And it did so much more easily and with a lot less resentment when leaders found ways, big and small, to lead by example and share the hardships facing their teammates.

Sharing Hardship Shouldn't Just Be a Calculated Effort by a Leader—It Should Be an Instinct

I've outlined some of the practical benefits of sharing hardship; how it's necessary if you want to be respected and obtain compliance and loyalty from those you ask to do difficult things. But it's important to not only do it because it's *smart*, but also because it's *wise*.

Trust-based Leaders realize that leading well is really a function of choosing the type of person you want to be. The more of the Leadership Traits and Principles you adopt and practice in your daily life, the more naturally you will lead others.

If there are any elements of Trust-Based Leadership™ that encapsulate the concept of sharing hardship with subordinates, they are leading by example and suppressing ego to view leadership as service rather than a power trip or perk. Care for your people. The more you instinctively look out for others and take satisfaction from doing so—the more you want to share in their triumphs *and* their pain—the more successful you will be … in leadership, business, and life!

"A leader is always being inspected and evaluated by others—nothing you do is '*off the record*.'"

—Mike Ettore

Chapter 46

LIFELONG LEARNER

"A leader without either interest in or knowledge of the history and theory—the intellectual content of his profession—is a leader in appearance only."—*MCDP 1 Warfighting*[177]

The Marine Corps prioritizes the professional development of every Marine, especially those who serve or aspire to serve in leadership roles. This includes the instruction that broadening the mind is critical to a leader's preparation for the day he or she will lead Marines in combat. All Marine leaders are expected to devote significant time and effort toward the pursuit of knowledge, whether it is through formal education and training courses or self-directed study—with a heavy emphasis on the latter.

Every exceptional Marine leader that I've ever served with, observed, interacted with in some way, or studied (including legendary Marine leaders like Generals John Lejeune, Ray Davis, Robert Barrow, Al Gray, James Mattis and John Kelly) showed a high level of curiosity about the profession of arms. They all had an insatiable thirst for knowledge, and all were known to be voracious readers.

These leaders were the personification of the term *lifelong learner*. And perhaps most notably, they all had a reputation for instilling this passion for the pursuit of knowledge in the leaders they mentored and developed during their careers. This aspect of the teacher-scholar relationship has been in practice for nearly 100 years and it has had a very beneficial impact on the Marine Corps.

Developing a 5,000-Year-Old Mind

American military historian Jay Luvaas said, "There is no excuse among professional military officers for not having a 5,000-year-old mind." What he was trying to convey was that the entirety of mankind's experiences in war over the course of recorded history are available to anyone willing to study and learn from them.[178]

History tends to repeat itself, especially in geopolitics and war. The lessons found in the study of history can provide today's military leaders with perspective and insights on almost every dilemma or challenge they could potentially face on the battlefield—assuming, of course, that they factor modern warfighting concepts and technologies into their analysis and operational planning.

As a Trust-Based Leader, Becoming a Lifelong Learner Takes on More Importance

As you know, the Marine Corps doesn't just bet on its generals, colonels, or sergeants major; it relies on all of its leaders at every level of the institution. In fact, the science and art of Marine Corps leadership specifically acknowledges that lower-level leaders—captains, lieutenants, sergeants, and corporals—often lead the main effort. They are the individuals who are going to do the most of the actual leading during the fighting that wins battles, not the generals or senior staff personnel.

In the Marine Corps and the business world, the leaders who will excel are those who are agile-minded and have a bias for action. They can operate with guidance and structure or without them; they can discern when to adhere to plans, as well as when to adapt them after they've become obsolete or irrelevant due to unique circumstances; and they can supplement or replace guidance with initiative, *creating their own structure* when doing so is called for.

The ability to do this relies greatly on being a lifelong learner. Let's look at some very practical examples of how having a thirst for knowledge has benefited Marines—plus how staying even more true to this principle could have helped them to a greater degree.

The most recent US war in Iraq kicked off on March 19, 2003, and "major military combat operations" were declared over on May 1, 2003. Through overwhelming firepower and Maneuver Warfare, the US military had defeated Iraq's conventional military forces and toppled its government in only 43 days.

Of course, that wasn't the end of the story. The conflict morphed into an asymmetric insurgency that meant many more years of war for America. These years were particularly difficult, as the US military struggled to reorient itself to the concept of using counterinsurgency doctrine, which was finally, officially made the standard in 2006, just prior to US Army General David Petraeus leading a "surge" of US troops into Iraq. This strategy yielded comparative success—but only after several years of poor results and in some instances, even failure. The US officially withdrew most of its forces from Iraq on Jan. 1, 2010.[179] [180]

Here's the thing, though: The US military actually has a wealth of experience fighting insurgencies—in some cases, very effectively—from its own history. And beyond that, there are thousands of years of history and numerous exceptional books that illustrate key concepts of counterinsurgency, many of which were broadly implemented in 2006. There is also a wealth of material on Iraqi tribal society and culture that has immense value to leaders tasked with operating in that region. Many of the best US military leaders in the conflict proactively studied this material and were prepared to use this knowledge to carve out areas of success even before the Surge kicked into gear in 2007. These lifelong learners relied on continuing education to excel compared to other leaders.[181]

The above example—understanding the nature of insurgencies, counterinsurgency doctrine, and Iraqi culture—had benefits for all leaders, from generals to lance corporals. But there are also good lessons that specifically illustrate the impact of lower-level leaders. For example, a Marine company commander near Fallujah needed to figure out a way to organize a flood of intelligence he was receiving after making an alliance with a local tribe. He required a way to track and assess which individuals were friends (many of whom were former enemies) and who were foes, as well as make sense of all of the rapid events that were shaping his battlespace.

Fortunately, he had a corporal—an infantryman—who knew how to create searchable and actionable databases. The company commander put this junior Marine leader to work in an "intelligence cell" which developed a database that made sense of what was going on—and this information paid off in a big way for the security in the area and the accomplishment of the mission.[182]

In many ways, the latter is an even better example of how being a lifelong learner benefits a trust-based organization. It involves innovation at a comparatively low level—the knowledge of a corporal—that had an exponentially larger impact on the conduct of the war. That simple database helped improve security in one of the most historically insecure areas in Iraq. It's a great example of how lifelong learners can powerfully and surprisingly apply knowledge.

Business Also Needs Leaders with 5,000 Year-Old Minds

Being a lifelong learner has a direct application to the development of leaders in all types of organizations, especially those operating in the business world. I'd venture to say that in the majority of instances in which organizations and companies have failed during the past 50 years, the leaders of these entities made many of the very same mistakes that were previously made by others in similar situations.

For example, the majority of mergers and acquisitions in the business world fail, often to the detriment of the company that acquires another one. It is quite common for a very sound company to acquire a similarly sound company and very quickly produce what is inarguably a larger, but much-less-effective entity—one that struggles to achieve what once seemed simple. Sometimes, the poorly managed integration of acquired companies results in problems so significant that the acquiring organizations are forced to file for bankruptcy and restructure or, in some instances, they simply shut down operations and cease to exist.[183]

During my time at Kforce, I was assigned as the executive sponsor for the majority of the administrative and logistical tasks associated with integrating various companies our firm acquired. Knowing that our company had experienced significant difficulties while carrying out several integrations years earlier, my colleagues and I studied everything we could find on how other organizations had executed these operations successfully—and also why and how others had failed to do so.

In a relatively short period of time, we produced a concise list of *best practices* and "Do's and Don'ts" that helped guide our decisions as we integrated any new organization. Over time, Kforce actually developed a reputation among industry experts and Wall Street analysts as being the very best within our peer group of professional staffing firms at successfully integrating acquired companies.

Lifelong Learning and Business Innovation

There are numerous examples that show how business leaders and companies with a bias for lifelong learning have adapted in the face of challenges or seized opportunities. Let's look at a great one, which tech blogger Keith Rozario wrote about and dubbed "The greatest Crowdsourcing story ever told" [punctuation modified]:

> Rob McEwen took over a mining company called Goldcorp that owned a gold mine in Canada. After a couple of unsuccessful years, Rob was continually frustrated by the failure of the mine to yield meaningful profit. One day at a meeting with his geologists, he gets up and tells them, "We're going to find more gold on this property, and we won't leave this room tonight until we have a plan to find it." The meeting ends with Rob giving the geologists nearly $10 million dollars to find the gold.

> The meeting seemed a success; after just 2 weeks, the geologists came back reporting happily that there could be as much as 30 times the gold in the mine that Goldcorp was currently mining. Everyone was happy—but not for long. You see, there is a difference between pointing to the mine in general and saying, "there's a lot of gold there," and another thing to pinpoint exactly where Goldcorp should have mined. Years after the geologist had reported on the gold deposits, Goldcorp still hadn't seen much of it.

> Then, in 1999, something serendipitous occurred. [CEO] Rob McEwen ... found himself in an unusual conversation about Linux, and how [software engineer] Linus Torvalds basically gave the world free access to the code to his operating system and how thousands of coders and developers around the

world helped Linux become a world-class operating system. All by getting volunteers from around the world and working for free in a loosely structured organization—but an organization that yielded superior results.

Rob was bitten by the crowdsourcing bug [and] he rushed back to Canada, went straight to his head geologist, and proposed the idea of publishing all the geological data of the mine from as far back as 1984.

The geologists were appalled; geological data was considered confidential [and] they didn't want anyone looking at it that wasn't on the Goldcorp payroll. Rob McEwen thought differently; he was looking at a dire situation in which his own geologists didn't know where the gold was, he thought someone else in the world might be able to find it, and he soldiered on to release the proprietary data online.

In March 2000, Goldcorp started the "Goldcorp challenge." [F]or a total prize ... of $575,000, anyone from around the globe could compete to find the gold in this Canadian mine based on the wealth of data that Goldcorp was literally giving away for free. This was by no means a safe bet; the risk[s] were high, particularly for Rob. [H]ad the initiative not worked, Goldcorp would be back where it started, but this time with [a] huge amount of proprietary data 'lost' to the public domain.

The people that answered the challenge weren't just geologists like the team working at Goldcorp, but a mixture ... of people from different backgrounds and cultures. The entries were judge based on a selection panel, and the top 5 winners were award[ed] prize money. [T]he winning entry was a combination of 2 Australian groups, one of which had never been to a gold mine or even Canada up until then.

Out of the top 5 entries, 4 have been drilled and all 4 have literally—struck GOLD!

Goldcorp today has grown to a $9 billion-dollar company from just $100 million before the Goldcorp challenge ... [184]

What's the lesson here?

The non-lifelong learner would likely have never even known that the concept of crowdsourcing exists. This new way of solving the problem happened because the CEO of a mining company "found himself in [an] unusual conversation about Linux." That example is a great one, because of the stakes and innovation involved. But there are innumerable other instances of solving problems and seizing opportunities, large and small, by leaders whose thirst for knowledge gives them an advantage over their peers.

Think of a business owner who realizes she can pay a freelancer an hourly rate to run her company's social media accounts for a fraction of the cost of a full-time salary, simply because she learns about the existence of an outsourcing-focused website like Upwork.com. Or the hospital administrator who sees, early on, how the use of iPads loaded with custom applications could serve as data storage and diagnostic tools that significantly improve efficiency among emergency room doctors and nurses. Or the bank executive who realizes that embracing the blockchain concept—instead of simply fighting this new technology—may usher in a new era for the financial industry rather than killing it.

Consider how a Trust-Based Leader who prioritizes learning will handle the upcoming disruptions caused by 3-D printing, artificial intelligence, and other emerging technologies. Or how the best ones have already handled the rise of the Internet economy and the move to a service economy from a manufacturing one over the past decades.[185]

Stay Hungry for Knowledge, Make Time for Learning, and Apply What You've Learned

This quest for knowledge may manifest in reading books, taking classes, going to seminars and conferences, keeping up with current events, or soliciting opinions from colleagues, friends, subordinates, or *anyone else* who has valuable information. It often just means having the ability to listen to others with an open mind; the capacity to check your ego and realize that you do not have all of the answers.

During the entire time that I worked at Kforce, I made an effort to stay aware of innovative concepts and technologies (and new uses of existing ones) by reading five newspapers every morning while I was on the treadmill. At the same time, CNBC was playing on the gym's TV and I could see if anything of note was happening that could affect any aspect of our business operations.

UPS and FedEx trucks certainly knew the path to my door, delivering a good number of new books to read each week. I subscribed to and read all sorts of publications, from professional journals to all types of books and magazines about various industries and topics, simply because I wanted to see what was going on. I wanted to learn what was happening in other industries and organizations that might be useful in some way within one or more of the many departments and functions that I was leading.

I did all of this because my previous studies reinforced the fact that many of the disruptive concepts, technologies, etc., that have a profound impact on an industry *rarely come from within* that industry. Instead, these "disruptors" have usually been implemented, often for quite some time, by someone else, somewhere else, perhaps in a totally unrelated industry. Someone said to the new adopter, "We've been using this technology for more than a decade. Where have you guys been?"

A Trust-Based Leader must have a thirst for knowledge and professional curiosity. All else being equal, a lifelong learner will almost always be a superior thinker and decision-maker over a non-lifelong learner. Knowledge is one of the most powerful tools you can obtain as you journey through life and business, specifically because it helps you develop sound judgement. And remember that to be a successful leader, it isn't enough to know about *your* profession, role, or industry; you must also acquire and increase your knowledge on other topics, as well as maintain your study of the science and art of leadership.

The amount of information available to us today is astounding, especially when you consider that the sum of all human knowledge is now instantly available via a smart phone sitting in the palm of your hand. Take advantage of it!

Chapter 47

Adaptability: Leadership Styles

This book has presented a series of Marine Corps and Trust-Based Leadership™ concepts and now the essential qualities needed in a Trust-Based Leader. But within this framework, there is the latitude for choosing and applying a specific leadership style that works for you, your organization, and the individuals you lead. It's a dynamic choice that adapts to the situation.

In 1939, the German-American psychologist Kurt Lewin and his colleagues formulated one of the main leadership theories in psychological study. It broadly defined three distinct styles:

- Authoritarian (autocratic) leadership involves unilateral decision-making, task-assignment, and problem solving with little or no input from subordinate team members. An authoritarian leader sets clear operating procedures and deadlines, and then tightly manages output from beginning to end.

- Democratic (participative) leadership is characterized by collective decision-making that involves subordinate inclusiveness, transparency, and self-determination. A democratic leader makes decisions with input and supports team members through phases of an objective.

- Laissez-faire (a French expression meaning "Let them do;" also known as delegative) leadership is a near absence of management because leaders have no deliberate system of procedures that provide direction and achieve outcomes. There are few to no group-related resolutions, and subordinates are solely responsible for reaching organizational objectives, making decisions, and problem solving.[186]

As a specialist in "group dynamics," Lewin pushed the boundaries of research within the category of human relations. Today, many recognize him as the founding father of experimental social psychology, and his groundbreaking studies demonstrated "that human behavior is the product not simply of personal characteristics, instincts and other forces within us, but also of the complex, dynamic environment we inhabit."[187]

Many of Lewin's studies occurred during the Great Depression. He turned to the topic of leadership as the 1930s ended and America struggled to come back from the longest and deepest economic decline of the 20th Century. Lewin wondered what constituted an effective leader, and why sound leadership was in short supply during the era. Nevertheless, this question arises in every generation.

Solid Leadership is Uncommon and in Demand

Leaders still fail at an astounding rate, as noted by a 2013 study of 547 businesses by the American Productivity & Quality Center (APQC). The research by the benchmarking and best practices company found that 79% of organizations have ineffective leadership practices.

The study also found that organizations do not spend enough time or money on leadership development, and they often rely on selection and reward practices that encourage outdated leadership styles. Modern business challenges demand flexible leadership more than ever before, but many organizations still resist making changes to meet the need.[188]

What's worse, of the companies that do invest in leadership development, many don't succeed in creating lasting change. Writing in the *Harvard Business Review*, Michael Beer, Magnus Finnström, and Derek Schrader describe an example of the "micro-electronic products division" of a company they studied:

> Participants described the [leadership development] program as very powerful. For a whole week they engaged in numer-

ous tasks that required teamwork, and they received real-time feedback on both individual and group behavior. The program ended with a plan for taking the learning back into the organization. Pre- and post-training surveys suggested that participants' attitudes had changed.

A couple of years later, when a new general manager came in to lead the division, he requested an assessment of the costly program. As it turned out, managers thought little had changed as a result of the training, even though it had been inspiring at the time. They found it impossible to apply what they had learned about teamwork and collaboration, because of a number of managerial and organizational barriers: a lack of strategic clarity, the previous GM's top-down style, a politically charged environment, and cross-functional conflict.[189]

Another challenge is the fact that dedicated training is often isolated from the application of that training. Basically, people forget what they've learned, or at least don't have a chance to immediately use it. Three McKinsey executives assessed the reasons "Why leadership-development programs fail," including this factor:

[I]t's not easy to create opportunities that simultaneously address high-priority needs—say, accelerating a new-product launch, turning around a sales region, negotiating an external partnership, or developing a new digital-marketing strategy—and provide personal-development opportunities for the participants.[190]

These challenges are among the reasons why this book stresses:

- Providing hands-on leadership development opportunities for leaders, in the forms of specific projects with oversight.

- Creating a wider, lasting culture with shared values and a focus on Trust-Based Leadership.

- Learning the Marine Corps Leadership Traits and Principles and striving to live them every day.

- And becoming a lifelong learner who dedicates oneself to becoming a great leader, regardless of whether your employer supports you with dedicated training.

- But within this framework, there is room to adapt your *leadership style* when the scenario calls for it.

Adapting Leadership to the Situation

Since nearly half of businesses place little or no priority on leadership development, it is often up to the individual leader to evolve in a way that ensures success and a long career of accomplishing goals and objectives. This process of self-directed development should include an understanding of the three archetypal styles of leadership defined by Lewin as well as other leadership theories, such as the *transactional* and *transformational* schools of thought:

- Transactional leadership assumes an explicit contract in which obedience and productivity are exchanged for compensation. "One of the main advantages of this leadership style is that it creates clearly defined roles. People know what they are required to do and what they will be receiving in exchange for completing these tasks."

- Transformational leaders aren't merely seeking mission accomplishment for the organization, they also look to develop and professionally better their subordinates. This style has a great deal in common with the Trust-Based Leadership™ model.[191]

Armed with this education, you should begin by deciding which approach best suits your personality and the particular work environment in which you operate. Business professionals and academics continue to study and debate the merits of Lewin's three leadership styles, for example, but the main conclusion is that no definitive approach works in every setting.

Professor Jeffrey Pfeffer, who teaches at the Stanford Graduate School of Business, has written extensively on the subject. In his book, *Leadership BS: Fixing Workplaces and Careers One Truth at a Time*, Pfeffer argues that it is essential for leaders to understand what a particular situation requires and to act appropriately. "Leaders need to be true to what the situation demands and what the people around them want and need," he suggests.

In other words, the most important thing for leaders to do is to have a diverse toolbox that includes knowledge of various styles of leadership; and the wisdom to know when it is right to use each method to accomplish objectives. Pfeffer also pulls no punches about the quality of today's leadership:

> Every piece of data suggests that workplaces are in dire shape and there [are] low levels of trust in leaders. For instance, data on employee engagement from Gallup show that worldwide only about 13% of employees report being engaged with their work, and in the US, the number is barely higher at 20%. Job satisfaction has declined almost linearly since 1987 to the present. The Edelman Trust index indicates that the public at large has low trust in leaders, while other surveys show that employees do not expect their own leaders to make ethical decisions or to consistently tell them the truth about difficult situations.[192]

Lewin's Three Leadership Styles in Today's Work Environment

Critics often disparage **authoritarian leadership** because these leaders have a reputation for being distant and aloof, enacting strict orders, rules, and regulations, and using an outdated or inflexible system of punishment. It might even come as a surprise that an authoritarian leader can find any success in today's workforce dominated by independent thinkers, and especially within a trust-based organization.

These stereotypes are not always accurate, however, and in some situations, authoritarian leadership can be effective. Business magnates like Martha Stewart and the late Steve Jobs are known for using an autocratic leadership style that employees found meticulous, demanding, and mandate-driven. Both leaders achieved massive success and iconic status, though some critics believe that their legacy and success would have been greater if they would have been more flexible in their leadership roles.[193] [194]

Much of Steve Jobs' autocratic style, for example, was derived from his personality which … often wasn't particularly nice. This likely had good and bad effects, even though Jobs' acerbity was situationally applied. Robert Sutton, a Stanford professor of management science and engineering, made the case in his bluntly titled book, *The No Asshole Rule: Building a Civilized Workplace and Surviving One That Isn't*:

So many people advanced Steve Jobs as evidence that asshole CEOs build better companies that Sutton somewhat reluctantly included a chapter in his book on "The Virtues of Assholes," with Steve Jobs as Exhibit A. There is some evidence that "status displays" by aggressive bosses can motivate workers and give slackers a kick in the pants. And effective jerk bosses usually aren't assholes all the time, they're able to turn on the charm when the situation demands it, something Steve Jobs, by most accounts, was very good at doing. And it helps for companies to have skilled subordinate executives that are good at cleaning up after the Asshole-in-Chief, much like the sad-faced men carrying shovels who walk behind circus elephants.

But Sutton's book makes clear that for the most part, assholes are bad for the bottom line, to say nothing of the human toll they exact. There are plenty of very successful companies that aren't led by assholes—Google, Virgin Atlantic, Procter & Gamble and Southwest Airlines among them. Likewise, there are legions of assholes who lead companies that aren't successful, in part due to their own bad behavior.[195]

Nevertheless, an authoritarian style can work in certain situations, and may even be necessary. For example, if you happen to be leading individuals who are crucial to get a job done but simply don't have the experience or ability to think critically or independently, an authoritarian style that uses strict directives and control may be called for. And sometimes, a (metaphorical) kick in the pants is required to get certain people moving!

Conversely, **democratic leadership** draws its power from the collective voice. A democratic leader gains authority by being an accountable and active participant in all processes. Subordinates are empowered at every turn as democratic leaders distribute responsibility evenly within the team and facilitate group deliberation. Every member of the team takes personal responsibility for their work and decisions, and shows a willingness to take on the role of leader when it is appropriate and needed. Democratic leadership naturally shares many characteristics with the Trust-Based Leadership model.

The strength of the social networking platform Twitter, for example, comes from its democratic business principles, according to its founders. With Twitter, not only are the employees empowered to participate and collaborate to lead the company through ideas and suggestions, but the end user has a voice as well. Co-founder Biz Stone is fond of issuing quotes exalting the democratic business model, saying things like, "When you hand good people possibility, they do great things."[196]

And Bill Gates is a useful counterpoint to Steve Jobs, as his success involved a much more democratic leadership style:

> Bill Gates offers a more participative leadership style. He believes in the value of input from his employees for overall company success. ... He understands that in business you will have fluctuations and changes that you must adapt to in order to succeed. ... Through the process of delegation of tasks, Gates was able to develop a company that utilizes the skills of his team members to the fullest.[197]

Lastly, while **laissez-faire** is a form of leadership, there is hardly any "leading" by a central figure, per se. This model goes beyond facilitating a democratic process of reaching objectives to a style eliminating almost all ongoing management. There are few policies and centralized leadership is nearly absent. In order for this system to work, highly trained, knowledgeable, reliable, and self-directed employees are brought into a group setting and are trusted to make appropriate decisions. They are essentially leadership "franchises" working toward a common goal.

Although laissez-faire leadership is often associated with inefficiency and low production, Warren Buffet, who is considered perhaps the most successful investor of all time, uses something resembling a laissez-faire leadership style.

The CEO of Berkshire Hathaway gives full autonomy to his managers while continually refusing to put his team under a microscope. He is quoted as saying, "We tend to let our subsidiaries operate on their own without our supervising and monitoring them to any degree. Most managers use the independence we grant them magnificently, by maintaining an owner-oriented attitude." Buffet's style is known as "delegation just short of abdication."[198] [199]

Each leadership style can work in certain situations—but no one method works all of the time, with all people, and they only work when leaders use them in a deliberate way.

Companies Fail When They are Unable to Meet Objectives Due to Poor Leadership

Poor leadership leads to low engagement and productivity and other underwhelming results. It can dismantle companies quickly. Therefore, leaders must be cautious and calculating when deciding upon a leadership approach.

Even if a particular style comes naturally, a person must still evaluate whether the method is appropriate when considering the working environment, the mission of the company, and the personalities and experiences of those employed. Every person must be open to evaluation of his or her leadership skills and evolve them according to the circumstances in order to complete missions.

The authoritarian model was the most prominent style more than a century ago, but in Lewin's research, it caused the most discontent. His team discovered that excessive use of authoritarianism led to low morale and antagonism between team members. Furthermore, it has the capacity to stifle creativity and innovation and undermine employee growth, which leads to resentment and lower productivity. Therefore, leaders should know exactly when to use authoritarianism to get the best results; if used too often, it can cause more damage than reward.

Authoritarian leadership works best when there is no time for consensus. Sometimes, leaders find themselves in a precarious situation in which objectives are time-critical and must be reached with absolute precision and expedience. In situations like this, the leadership sets clear expectations and follows each phase of the operation through with tight structure and organization.

Authoritarian leadership is often required to keep team members safe in some aspects of dangerous jobs like law enforcement, industrial construction, or mining. In these cases, there is limited margin for error. Finally, it is also practical to use some form of this leadership when training staff members with little experience or novice skills, so that the subordinate can focus on learning the task.

However, in order for authoritarian leadership to be successful in any circumstance, it is important that the leader has earned the respect and trust of the subordinates who will be carrying out the tasks. This loyalty will only have been attained through past demonstrations of sound decision-making and good judgement. But even when subordinates are confident in a leader's judgement, morale must be monitored closely and addressed, if necessary, to assure success.

Lewin's research found the democratic style to be the most successful in terms of overall experience, but problems can occur when there are too many differing opinions and no clear way to make equitable decisions. This might cause members of the team to feel alienated if the final choice does not include their suggestions for meeting the objective. In addition, the consensus approach requires more time to establish objectives and the means to achieve them. Therefore, some forms of it don't necessarily work well during critical moments of crisis when time-sensitive forward movement is urgently needed. A more authoritarian leadership style may be called for in these situations.

Finally, Lewin's study showed that the absence of leadership in a laissez-faire system created an environment that sometimes lacked the motivational energy required to complete objectives, and team members were not consistent in their work. This style works best when there is no requirement for central coordination. In other words, to make laissez-faire work, the team must be flush with capable, highly trained, and self-motivated individuals that make good decisions and already work well as a team.

While many employees work harder within this leadership model in order to maintain their autonomy, commissions and bonuses can also help entice employees to move in the right direction and meet organizational goals.[200]

No Specific Leadership Style is Always "Correct"

Leadership is one of the most written about subjects out there, but there simply isn't a singular, correct definition of leadership. It's a process of trial and error to find out what works best for a person and a setting. The individual characteristics of the leader and those being led, coupled with situational specifics, should determine which style to develop and use.

Trust-Based Leadership™ fits with this idea because it is a very adaptable leadership model. A leader is trusted to use initiative and judgement to not only accomplish a mission, but to appropriately modify his or her leadership style. An effective leader will be able to utilize more than one style as warranted by each situation. Often, the given approach is based on the experience and knowledge of each individual team member, and the overall company culture.

For example, as experience blooms and employees move from rookie status to peak performers, leaders can adjust their style from authoritarian to democratic through a rational progression. Leaders must also consider that some employees come with a package of experience and knowledge that often surpasses their own. When this is the case, a good leader takes a more delegative approach that allows subordinates the autonomy to carry out tasks and make decisions rather than tightly controlling them based on title.

Always remember that it is a privilege to lead other people, and with this privilege comes high expectations. Integrity, personal core values, ethics, mission accomplishment, and genuine care and concern for your teammates should be the guiding principles with which you approach every decision, process, or action. Ego has little place in a good leader's thought process. Respect, fairness, a sense of service, and justice should be at the heart of whatever leadership style you decide to implement.

"In business, unpredictability can be a tactic, but it cannot be the strategy."

—Mike Ettore

Section III

Summary

You've learned the philosophies, techniques, art, and science of Marine Corps leadership—the elements that shape time-tested leaders in difficult environments.

I've explained how these factors build upon each other and are applicable in any environment with the Trust-Based Leadership™ model.

And this last section has explained the individual characteristics that each leader must have to succeed in a trust-based environment.

You've got all of the pieces required to become a World-Class Leader, and I encourage you to read the first three sections of this book again and consciously try to implement them in your professional and personal lives. With diligence, they will enable you to become a better leader who improves your organization.

The next section gets a little more specific by highlighting some of the things I've learned during my 40+-year leadership career. These rapid-fire lessons have directly contributed to the development and refinement of the Trust-Based Leadership™ model while improving my skills along the way. Keep in mind that this next section is one that will *always* be incomplete, as a true leader never stops learning.

I'll have undoubtedly learned some new things by the time this book is in your hands!

The Journey Begins! Parris Island – 1974.
With my father after the graduation ceremony.
One of the proudest moments of my life.

Cold weather training at the Mountain Warfare Training
Center in Bridgeport, California - 1976.

Leading Pugil Sticks Training. MCRD San Diego - 1977

SGT. T.L. MILLS   SSGT. H. DIAZ   SGT. C.F. BOWDEN   SGT. M.L. ETTORE

My first platoon as a drill instructor. The other drill instructors
were all Vietnam veterans, and I learned much from them.

College graduation-1982. I was commissioned a Second
Lieutenant of Marines earlier that day.

Staff Sergeant Mike Marshall, my platoon sergeant during combat operations in Grenada and Lebanon. A superb SNCO, he kept me out of trouble and made me look good on countless occasions.

Staff Sergeant Marshall leading our platoon in bayonet drills as we headed to Grenada aboard the USS Guam in October, 1983.

Fox Company's legendary Company Gunny, Lenny Garramone, leading a physical training session en route to Grenada. The Gunny was an impressive leader, and in many ways, he was the driving force within the unit.

Marines from Fox Company 2/8 participating in Operation Urgent
Fury – the liberation of Grenada from the grip of Communism.

With some Marines from my platoon rushing a house that a high-ranking member of the rogue People's Revolutionary Army was reportedly staying in. We received this information from an informant and had no time to plan; I issued a quick order and we stormed the house within minutes.

Upon entering the house, we discovered the person we were looking for had fled, abandoning his two young daughters, who were obviously very frightened by our sudden appearance. We spoke to them and calmed them down and quickly turned them over to Grenadian authorities for safekeeping.

Posing with a captured AK-47. I believe there were at least four
times as many weapons as citizens on Grenada. It was obvious
that the Soviet Union and Cuba had big plans to use the island as a
major base that could support military operations in the region.

Corporal Santiago Petersen and his squad resting after returning
to the soccer stadium that we'd landed in during the first day
of the operation. Several hours later, we were transported via
Marine helicopters to the western side of the island to join other
elements of 2/8 that were rushing to the aid of a Navy SEAL
unit that was pinned down in the Governor's Mansion.

In addition to the high temperatures, humidity and lack of sleep,
logistical problems and the lack of food and water resupply added
to the "Fog of War" during the operation. Marines sitting Left
to Right: Tuell, Esposito, Chavez, Joslin, Lorenz, and Harris.

Fox Company and the other elements of 2/8 were inserted onto the island of Carriacou, which is located 18 miles north of Grenada, to search for enemy soldiers and weapons stockpiles. The enemy forces did not engage us, and essentially surrendered en masse. We found huge stockpiles of small arms and military supplies.

Members of my platoon are seen loading captured weapons onto Marine helicopters. A Navy Admiral that was visiting told me that these weapons would be transported to Washington, DC, and shown to members of Congress and the media as proof that Grenada and its adjacent islands were being used by the Soviets and Cubans as military bases.

Awaiting transport back to the USS Guam, some of the newest generation of "island hopping" Marines pose for a "John Wayne" photo. Marines standing Left to Right: Harris, Unknown, Dillard, Short, and Enoch.

First Sergeant Robert Nichols
The highly-respected "old man" of Fox Company 2/8, he was a
superb leader. We all admired him and were strengthened by his
presence during combat operations in Grenada and Lebanon.

A view from the northern portion of our defensive sector in West Beirut in November, 1983. We had an observation post named "Rocky Top" on the tallest building. The small building in the center of the picture is the British Embassy.

Looking to the East from Rocky Top. Our defensive positions extended for another 500 meters past the bend in the road seen in the upper right corner of this photo.

This was my rooftop home during our stay in Beirut. The small wooden box stood about 5' high and was just large enough for a cot and a small table for tactical radios.

Rocky Top viewed from the west. The arrow indicates where the artillery shell hit the building during "that night" in February, 1984 when my Rolex Moment happened.

The point of impact of the artillery shell. The sound of this shell whistling toward us and detonating when it hit the building is something I will never forget. God's hand was surely at work that night; had the shell hit just a bit higher on the rooftop where several Marines and I were hunkered down, we'd have all been killed.

Talking with US Embassy staff members who are about to be evacuated due to the rapidly deteriorating environment in Beirut in February, 1984.

Our great platoon sergeant, SSGT Mike Marshall, in the process of "making **** happen" as he always did! Over the next three days, we helped several thousand Americans and citizens of allied nations escape the rapidly escalating violence in Beirut.

Americans and citizens of several other countries being evacuated from Beirut by Marine helicopters to US Navy ships. Once aboard ship, they were interviewed and ultimately flown to Cyprus and other nearby locations so they could continue traveling to their destination of choice.

A view from inside a Fox Company observation post at Beirut International Airport. Some of the buildings seen in the distance were abandoned and often used as firing positions by various factions. There were many intense firefights between Marines and hostile forces in this area.

With Gunnery Sergeant Lenny Garramone, one of the finest SNCOs I had the pleasure of serving with. Marine officers are trained to trust and rely on SNCOs and NCOs to execute orders and achieve desired results. Leaders like Gunny Garramone are the "force multipliers" of Marine Corps leadership; they can be trusted to accomplish any mission if provided with proper resources and support.

As the senior leader on deck, I am applying the "S in BAMCIS" while inspecting some of my Marines prior to them manning their defensive positions in West Beirut. Their squad leader had prepared them well.

With First Sergeant Robert Nichols at his retirement ceremony in 1984. He was a superb role model and mentor; and he was the epitome of the Marine Corps' Teacher-Scholar concept. I learned much from him.

My 29th birthday – 1985. We were training in a remote area in Italy, when I was suddenly greeted by a surprise party. I hadn't told anyone that it was my birthday, but there are few secrets in a Marine unit.

Talking with some of my Marines several days prior to the
assault into Kuwait during Operation Desert Storm in 1991.
I was privileged to command Weapons Company 1/8, and
to serve as the battalion's fire support coordinator.

This photo was taken on the first night of the ground war of Desert Storm. My face is swollen from the anti-nerve agent drugs we were given. Standing by me is my Company First Sergeant, Gerald Bryant - an outstanding Marine leader.

Behind us are two amtracks parked end-to-end with canvas tarps over them to create a mobile battalion command post. We sensed that this night was going to be full of action and we were not wrong. There were many heroic acts performed by our Marines and Navy Docs on this night and into the early hours of the next morning. Some close calls as well, with several Marines being wounded by Iraqi mortar rounds.

We called for a lot of artillery support during this fight. The artillery unit was positioned about 10 miles behind us and they sent death and destruction where it was needed, when it was needed. I visited with and personally thanked the members of this unit after the conflict was over. They undoubtedly saved the lives of many Marines.

The morning after the *"Reveille Engagement"* in the Kuwaiti desert. Despite having not slept in a while and looking tired in the photo, I remember that I was quite energized from the surge of adrenalin caused by the events of the past several hours.

Fought during the early morning hours of the second day of the ground war, the "Reveille Engagement" remains the biggest and fastest tank battle in United States Marine Corps history. Attached to 1/8 was Bravo Company, 4th Tank Battalion, a reserve unit from Yakima, Washington. Bravo Company was the only Marine unit equipped with M1A1 Abrams tanks, and together with our attached TOW missile teams, they destroyed or disabled 34 enemy tanks and armored vehicles within a few minutes.

LtCol Bruce Gombar, 1/8's battalion commander, looking at one of the Iraqi vehicles that we'd engaged a few hours earlier during the "Battle of the Ice Cube." Note the bloody helmet he's holding. There were several dead Iraqi soldiers in this vehicle when we first surveyed the aftermath of this engagement. It was just one of a few dozen enemy vehicles that were destroyed during the pre-dawn fight.

One of many Iraqi armored vehicles destroyed during the fight. The Marines of 1/8 performed well under fire, and our organic and attached anti-armor, heavy weapons, and tank units dominated the battlefield with incredible lethality.

Getting ready for the final push into Kuwait City.

From left to right: 1stLt Randy Newman, Captain Mike Ettore, 1stLt Doug Mason, and Major Chris Wilk.

Randy, Doug, and Chris were superb leaders and ultimately retired as highly regarded Colonels of Marines.

The original source of this photo is unknown, but it accurately depicts how we looked as we left Kuwait, making the long trip to Saudi Arabia, where we prepared for our return to America.

I remember feeling great as we headed south; a feeling of happiness, almost to the point of euphoria. I was alive and grateful for it. And, I was able to take my first shower in 104 days!

At The Basic School (TBS) with the leadership team of a Warrant
Officer Basic Company. I served on the TBS staff from 1992-1995,
and loved being around the future leaders of the Marine Corps.
I'm still in touch with many of my former students, many of whom
went on to serve as combat leaders in Iraq and Afghanistan.

From left to right: Captain D.D. Baker, Captain Stu Helgeson, Captain James
Blair, Major Mike Ettore, Captain Andre Leblanc, Captain Mike Sweitzer.

The instructors for a recent Fidelis Leadership Group training event. Everyone in this picture is a U.S. Marine. The four ladies in the front row with me were all students of mine at The Basic School - Quantico, Virginia (1992-95), when they were newly commissioned 2ndLt's.

Front Row (L-R) Nancy Broding, Wendy Arnold MD, Mike Ettore, Aisha Bakkar, Wendy Garritty

Back Row (L-R) Katy Spicer, Dennis Greene, Ed Daniel

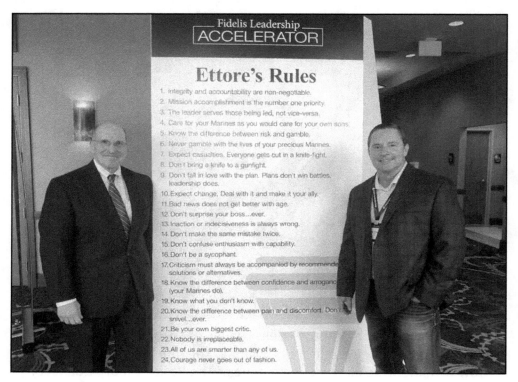

As a 2ndLt leading an infantry rifle platoon, I was fortunate to have a great platoon sergeant, Staff Sergeant Mike Marshall, and squad leaders like Tony Ochrem, Frank Spivey, and Santiago Petersen. Tony was able to attend one of my leadership seminars. I introduced him to the audience and told them that he and other leaders in the unit did much to make me look good on a daily basis.

With my grandchildren, Brooke and Cole. I truly believe that children who are encouraged to be readers often grow up to be leaders.

"A society grows great when old men plant trees whose shade they know they shall never sit in."
– Greek proverb

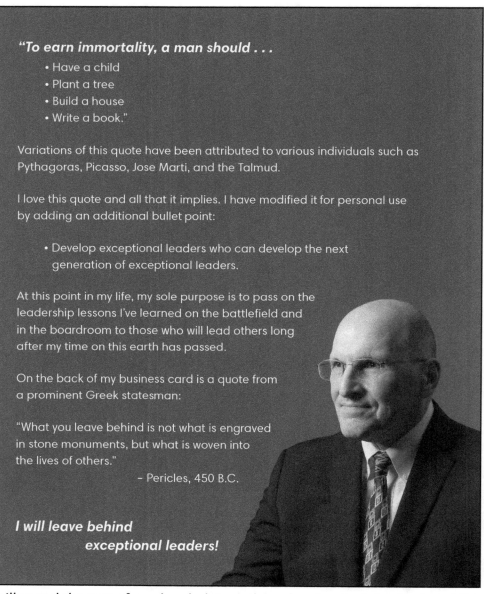

> **"To earn immortality, a man should . . .**
> - Have a child
> - Plant a tree
> - Build a house
> - Write a book."

Variations of this quote have been attributed to various individuals such as Pythagoras, Picasso, Jose Marti, and the Talmud.

I love this quote and all that it implies. I have modified it for personal use by adding an additional bullet point:

> - Develop exceptional leaders who can develop the next generation of exceptional leaders.

At this point in my life, my sole purpose is to pass on the leadership lessons I've learned on the battlefield and in the boardroom to those who will lead others long after my time on this earth has passed.

On the back of my business card is a quote from a prominent Greek statesman:

"What you leave behind is not what is engraved in stone monuments, but what is woven into the lives of others."
> – Pericles, 450 B.C.

I will leave behind exceptional leaders!

I will spend the rest of my days helping others develop their leadership skills.

Section IV:

LESSONS LEARNED

Introduction:

LESSONS LEARNED

This section contains some of the lessons learned and advice that I share with my executive coaching clients and students attending my leadership development events. I have inserted these lessons, anecdotes, and leadership maxims as they appear in numerous slide presentations, within training materials, and on various social media platforms.

I have structured this content into four main categories:

- Leadership Development

- Leadership Tactics and Techniques

- Why Leaders Succeed

- Why Leaders Fail

Sharing this information is another way for me to help others accelerate their development as leaders. I've made many mistakes as a leader, and many of them were easily avoidable had I studied the experiences and advice of other leaders more diligently. It is my hope that the knowledge and insights in this section will help others learn from my mistakes as well as my successes.

Suffice it to say that much of the content of this section was gleaned not only from my 40+ years of leadership experience, but from the experiences, wisdom, and insights of countless other leaders whom I have studied or worked with in the past.

Accelerating Leadership Development

One of the best ways a person can accelerate their leadership development is to leverage the knowledge of seasoned mentors and coaches. I always tell my executive coaching clients, "I don't claim to have the answers to all of your leadership issues, but I'm sure that I have some of them. Many of these lessons were expensive, painful, and embarrassing while I learned them!"

Exceptional leaders (and those who want to become them) continuously study the experiences of others; they adopt and effectively apply selected concepts, tactics, and techniques within their teams and operating environments. Doing this greatly accelerates a leader's development and ability to perform at levels that are *beyond his or her years and actual experience.*

Learning From the Failures of Others

While studying the successes and best practices of more-experienced leaders is obviously of great benefit, another advantage of having mentors and coaches is that they can share their errors and failures with you. This knowledge helps you avoid falling victim to some of the same pitfalls they, and most other leaders, stumbled into during their careers.

All leaders make mistakes, even those with extensive experience and a history of success—and I have found that most are *very* willing to share these lessons. And, perhaps most telling, many of these same leaders will willingly admit that it was the lessons they learned from their mistakes that caused them to make decisions that resulted in much of their subsequent success.

In my experience, the very best leaders relentlessly study the mistakes of others as much as they do their successes. And <u>they take actions to ensure they do not repeat easily avoidable ones.</u>

Just as scientific knowledge accrues with each generation and builds new insights, so does the knowledge of leadership. Every leader starting out on his or her own path will still err and learn some hard lessons. But the smarter ones will sidestep many of the knowable failures through the knowledge and experience of others.

"The roots of education are bitter, but the fruit is sweet."—Aristotle

387

Chapter 48

LEADERSHIP DEVELOPMENT

On Character

Clients often ask for my opinion on various leadership concepts, philosophies, and systems. As you might expect, they cite companies or individuals such as Baldrige, FranklinCovey, Carnegie, Blanchard, Lencioni, Maxwell, and others.

I tell them that, in my opinion, all of these systems and individuals (and countless others) are credible and can add great value to a person's development as a leader.

I also tell them that no matter which system or "thought leader" they decide to follow, their long-term success as a leader will be decided almost entirely by a single factor.

This factor is commonly referred to as "character."

There are many definitions for this word, but I am sure that everyone reading this probably understands what I mean when I state that a person's character is the biggest influence on their long-term success or failure as a leader—and this book has gone into some detail on why that's the case.

Thus, I feel that no leadership system, philosophy, or method can ever enable a person to "outrun" his or her character. Prioritize it. Develop it. Maintain it. Or you will never reach your leadership potential, regardless of which leadership school you study.

History has provided countless examples that support my assertion.

Food for thought.

"A man's character is his fate."—Heraclitus 500 A.D.

Integrity is Non-Negotiable

When teaching leadership, I obviously spend a lot of time discussing the concepts of personal character and integrity.

I emphasize that the bedrock of personal character is one's integrity, comparing this trait to the foundation of a building. If the foundation is weak and unstable, the entire building may collapse when it comes under pressure.

Likewise, without impeccable integrity, one's personal character will be fatally flawed. History shows that leaders who lack this trait are ultimately doomed to failure.

I tell my clients: "In business, everything is negotiable except your integrity."

On Being World Class

I frequently refer back to the term "World Class" and what it means in relation to leadership.

I assure my clients and students that whatever their specific situations may be in terms of their educational background, experience, the type of company they are working in, or the type of boss they are working for, they can all become good leaders if they are willing to seek knowledge and resolve to lead their people well.

I also tell them that they can go well beyond what most people would deem to be a "good leader" and become an "exceptional leader" who is respected by their department, company, and even across their entire industry.

In other words, I believe that *anyone* with the desire to do so and the commitment to make it happen can become a World-Class Leader.

Once an individual truly believes this and decides to pursue leadership excellence, he or she usually begins to acquire these skills at an exponential rate.

Even better, leadership is an art in which the artist can continue to improve throughout his or her entire life. With over forty years of leadership experience, my journey as a lifelong learner traveling along the path of leadership continues.

I'm still learning!

As Goes the Leader, So Goes the Team!

Like so many factors that are part of an exceptional team, the creation of a shared mindset of mental toughness, adaptability, and resilience starts with the leader.

In every leadership environment, culture, and scenario I have ever experienced, observed, or studied, a common denominator is that the mindset of the leader ultimately became the mindset of everyone in the organization.

Companies that possess a *"Never Quit"* approach to challenges are always led by mentally tough, adaptable, and resilient leaders who are capable of inspiring these traits in others.

When discussing this topic, I always tell my students:

"As goes the leader, so goes the team!"

Leaders of Substance > Leaders of Image

Legendary investor Warren Buffet is fond of saying, "Only when the tide goes out do you discover who's been swimming naked."

He is implying that when economic conditions are good and "the sun is shining" on the business world, almost any company is able to look good. Only when the economy goes south and challenges arise do the companies with real substance emerge, while those comprised mostly of image fall by the wayside.

We've all served with leaders who look great, sound great, and constantly tell others how great they are! Then a crisis or other serious leadership challenge emerges and suddenly "The Great One" proves incapable of delivering the substance that his previous posturing implied he possessed.

In many instances, the day is saved by the efforts of others in the organization who spent their time learning and becoming competent leaders instead of being flashy self-promoters.

Tough times do not just build a leader's character, they reveal it!

Leaders of Substance > Leaders of Image.

Advice for New Leaders

I'm often asked to provide advice to new leaders. Here's what I tell them:

(1) Lead by Example—ALWAYS!

(2) Be yourself—don't adopt a different personality as a leader. If you do this, people will likely view it as an indicator of a lack of self-confidence.

(3) Be organized. Know where the team is and where it needs to be relative to its goals and objectives.

(4) Solicit input on how to achieve the stated goals and objectives. Ensure all meetings are well-organized and result in actionable feedback, next steps, etc.

(5) Emphasize that you are there to enable your team's success by providing them with guidance, resources, and support.

(6) Let your teammates know that you respect their experience and that you are relying on their feedback and recommendations.

(7) Routinely ask the 3 Big Questions and encourage everyone to respond:

   o What should we start doing?

   o What should we stop doing?

   o What should we do differently?

(8) Effective supervision is essential to be an effective leader!

Golden Nuggets

I've been fortunate to have had many excellent mentors during my military and civilian careers. As an executive leadership coach, I'm often asked to share some of the best leadership advice that I've received over the years.

Listed below are 6 of the many "golden nuggets" that have resulted from my discussions with some wise and highly experienced leaders. They are time-tested and apply at every level of leadership!

(1) Lead by example and remember that your teammates will ultimately replicate your character and behavior.

(2) Praise in public, criticize in private.

(3) Don't give orders that cannot be enforced.

(4) Loyalty starts from the top down.

(5) Surround yourself with people who are smarter than you are, and listen to them!

(6) Execution without proper supervision typically produces poor results.

Leadership DNA

In my executive coaching practice, I often use a graphic that contains a single line of text that conveys how crucial leadership is to the success of any organization. It's a very simple mathematical formula:

Leadership > Culture > Strategy > Tactics

In today's fast-moving business world, the practice of outsourcing various services and processes has proven to be an effective way to increase productivity, enhance the customer experience, and reduce costs. An organization seeking operational excellence would be foolish to ignore this practice.

Nevertheless, I maintain my belief that the culture of any organization is merely a mirror image of the character, ethics, behavior, and standards of performance *displayed by its senior leaders*. This critical aspect of an organization's health and well-being cannot be delegated or outsourced to consultants, contractors, or other "outsiders."

Leadership is not a commodity, service, task, or process. It cannot be outsourced. It is the lifeblood—the very "DNA"—of your company. It must come from you!

Chapter 49

LEADERSHIP TACTICS AND TECHNIQUES

Leadership vs. Management

There is a longstanding debate in academia and the business world over the difference between *leadership* and *management.*

Most people use the term "manager" for those in leadership roles. In the Trust-Based Leadership™ model, <u>we refer to leaders as leaders</u> and acknowledge that they have various management responsibilities.

Here are my thoughts on this topic:

You *LEAD PEOPLE* and you *MANAGE THINGS*.

These things can be assets, resources, systems, operations, projects, focus of effort, etc.

In my experience, effective leaders of people are almost always effective managers of things. However, effective managers are not always effective leaders—because they often devote too much focus to things instead of people.

This is where those in leadership roles typically begin to underachieve or even fail; they lose sight of the fact that <u>people are not machines, systems, or projects</u> and cannot be "managed" as if they are inanimate objects incapable of thought and emotion.

I've had a fair amount of success in leadership roles, and I think this is because, through training and experience, my *"default setting"* is to focus on leading the *people* who are in charge of managing the *things* that achieve the organization's goals and objectives.

Once again, the lesson here is as obvious as it is important:

You *LEAD PEOPLE* and you *MANAGE THINGS*!

You Are the Standards!

While there is certainly a large body of knowledge surrounding the *Science and Art of Leadership*, long-term success as a leader really depends on the willingness to take the following three actions on a daily basis:

- Set the standards.

- Live the standards.

- Enforce the standards.

You cannot be an effective leader unless you are willing to do each one.

Likewise, you must also approach each of these actions with equal vigor and apply them in an unquestionably fair manner toward every member of your team, regardless of title, tenure, or past accomplishments.

And Lead by Example—Always!

Science vs. Art

I like to discuss what I refer to as the *"Science-to-Art Gap"* that many leaders unintentionally fall victim to.

In an ideal world, leaders would be educated and trained on the *Science of Leadership* before they attempt to utilize various aspects of the *Art of Leadership*.

Unfortunately, most leaders do not receive this type of training early in their careers. As a result, they typically learn some very costly lessons as they attempt *Leadership Art* that is not backed up by even the most basic elements of *Leadership Science.*

As an executive coach, I rarely see leaders fail because they aren't smart enough or lack a work ethic or other key attributes. Instead, almost all of them fail due to problems stemming from the inadequate utilization (or absence) of proven leadership concepts, principles, and fundamental techniques. In most instances, these leaders (and their teams) <u>repeatedly make easily avoidable mistakes.</u>

It doesn't have to be this way. Leadership can be learned!

As I always say, "For the untrained, leadership is a school in which the tests come before the lessons."

The 3 Big Questions

I've mentioned several times in this book that there are *"3 Big Questions"* leaders should periodically ask their subordinates. The answers to them will lead to better results as you work toward accomplishing your mission:

- What should we start doing?

- What should we stop doing?

- What should we do differently?

These 3 Big Questions can make your job as a leader much easier and result in significant gains in operational effectiveness and efficiency. The people who are doing the day-in and day-out work have a good grasp of what is working well and what isn't.

Prior to a discussion on this topic you will need to communicate to your team that you want and expect candor, openness, and honesty. Without these conditions, you will likely hear only what your team thinks you want to hear.

The gains made by asking these questions will be most effective in environments in which people at all levels are willing to "Speak Truth to Power," and it is the leader's responsibility to create and sustain such an environment. If you can get your teammates to trust you and know that you truly respect their ideas and feedback, you'll find yourself leading an organization in which everyone is continuously focused on making things better!

You Never Listen to Us!

A common (and legitimate) complaint about leaders from their teammates is, *"You never listen to us!"* Effective leaders know that it is important to seek and value feedback on a variety of issues.

That said, while leaders should always listen to what their people are saying, this doesn't mean they are obligated to always agree with them or act upon their recommendations.

Whenever I assume a leadership role, I tell my new teammates, "I promise that I will always listen to you, but I can't promise that I will always act upon your advice and recommendations. I will always have to weigh what you say against the mission and other factors associated with the situation."

I can honestly say that every time I have made this statement to teams of any size and in any environment, it has been very well-received. I often found that I was the first leader to ever explain this situation in such a manner.

People want to be heard; they want to know that their opinions and suggestions are valued and respected. And they won't expect their leaders to adopt every suggestion they come up with when they know there are almost always other complicating factors associated with the specific issues under consideration.

Having this discussion will provide clarity for your teammates, let them know you respect their opinion, and help them see things a bit more from the perspective of their leaders.

World-Class Words

I have found that the very best leaders remain aware of the fact that they exist to serve their teammates, not vice versa. One of the best ways to indicate this is to acquire the habit of using what I refer to as "World-Class Words."

As you can see below, there's nothing special about these words as they appear on the page. But when they are used routinely by leaders, special things often happen. They help create trust among leaders and those being led, improve team culture and cohesion, and drive other outcomes that have a very positive effect on any type of company, department, or team.

- I Trust You

- Please & Thank You

- I'm Sorry

- I Was Wrong

- I Don't Know

- What Do You Recommend?

- What Do You Need?

- What Can I Do to Help?

This is not an all-inclusive list, but it is a good starting point for leaders who desire to lead well and draw the very best ideas, recommendations, and actions from their teammates.

4 Words of Confidence

Leaders should constantly seek ways to add value and equip and enable their teams to be successful. One of the best ways to do this is for a leader to frequently use what I call the 4 Words of Confidence: *"How can I help?"*

Leaders who routinely ask this question—assuming they have worked hard to develop mutual trust within their teams—will receive honest and timely feedback that enables them to provide various forms of support quickly and to great effect.

When a leader asks this question in a sincere manner and teammates know that he or she is genuinely interested in helping the team accomplish their mission, the teammates will indeed provide solid recommendations or requests for help. They will feel comfortable asking for resources that provide relief for the challenges they are facing at the moment.

Leaders must be seen by others as someone willing to do whatever is necessary to set their teams up for success. Asking this question and then acting on the answers will go a long way in building mutual trust and confidence between team members and their leader.

4 Words of Development

As a leader, one of your main duties is to develop other leaders. I have found that a great way to do this is to use what I call the *"4 Words of Develop-*

ment" when interacting with my leaders. Whenever a situation presented itself that required decisions to be made, plans to be developed, and actions to be taken, I trained myself to always ask my teammates, ***"What do you recommend?"***

Doing this forces your teammates to utilize their knowledge and experience to formulate suggestions and propose options for resolving whatever issue is at hand. And, equally important, it forces the leader to actually listen to his or her subordinates instead of simply taking over the meeting and unilaterally declaring, "Here's what we're going to do!"

As I write this, I am shaking my head ruefully, knowing how often I did just that as a young leader. I think I was in my mid-30s before I learned to make this question my default setting. Unsurprisingly, some of the most significant successes that I had as a leader occurred after I adopted it as my automatic response to nearly every challenging situation my subordinate leaders brought to me.

I became known as the leader who was always going to ask, *"What do you recommend?"* and this resulted in my teammates seeking my advice or guidance only *after* they'd thought things through and had answers ready for the inevitable question.

A simple technique, for sure, but one of the most powerful that I've ever used during my 40+ years leading and developing other leaders. It is incredibly effective in developing trust, encourages your teammates to develop their critical-thinking skills, and inspires them to demonstrate initiative and a bias for action. I strongly urge you to consider making these words your default setting, too!

6 Words of Destruction

In a trust-based leadership environment, some things will inevitably go wrong while issuing mission-type orders and delegating and leveraging your subordinate leaders. Mistakes will be made, and plans won't work out as intended.

When this happens, a leader should never automatically say the 6 Words of Destruction: ***"Who told you to do that?"***

Leaders who regularly use these words when something bad happens send a very clear and chilling signal to their teammates. Despite all of their previous speeches about trust, initiative, and bias for action, immediately asking this question upon receiving bad news means leaders are essentially saying to their teammates, "I only want you to take initiative and exhibit a bias for action if everything is guaranteed to turn out well!"

When members of a team hear these words (often said in a demeaning or intolerant tone), they'll quickly realize that the leader really doesn't want them to exercise initiative and make decisions if there's a chance that something may go wrong and ultimately reflect poorly on the leader.

For sure, things will sometimes go south when you trust and empower your teammates in the Trust-Based Leadership model. When they do, I recommend that you use questions like these to find out what your subordinate leader's thought processes were while making decisions:

"Well, obviously things didn't go as planned. I'm sure you've already thought about this; why do you think things turned out like they did?"

"I know you didn't intend for things to turn out like this. Tell me why you think the situation unfolded as it did, and what would you do next time to ensure better results?"

"Relax, this is a shot down-range, we can't pull it back. Let's learn from this; what do you recommend we do or don't do to ensure that this never happens again?"

These are just a few examples of how a leader can approach key teammates when something bad happens without destroying the trust, initiative, and bias for action that he or she has spent so much effort developing within a team.

Remember, if you create a climate in which people fear being wrong or making mistakes, they will essentially turn off any form of creativity and willingness to make decisions in the absence of detailed guidance from above.

As always is the case with leadership, words matter. Use them carefully!

Master of the Small Gesture

I'd say that almost everyone reading this book at some point in their life received an unexpected compliment or "thank you" that touched them deeply, to the point they've never forgotten the gesture or the person who made it. It may have been a kind word from a parent, teacher, coach, teammate, or perhaps even from a person they didn't know—but the individual who received the gesture never forgot how it made them feel.

Doing things like this is one of the most powerful techniques a leader can use to develop mutual trust, loyalty, and camaraderie within his or her team. Sadly, I find that most leaders don't do this type of thing at all, or they don't do it as often as they could. That said, the most effective leaders almost always do these things, to the point that I call those who are exceptionally good at doing them *"Masters of the Small Gesture."*

Here are some examples of "small gestures" that are available to almost all leaders at any level of any company or team. This is by no means an all-inclusive list, but it's enough to get my point across and to cause you to reflect upon how you can utilize some of these techniques.

Small Gestures

Public Praise: Good leaders go into workspaces, department or team areas, warehouses, etc., and publicly thank a teammate for a job well done. We all like to be praised and receive compliments and, deep inside, we like it even better when we know others are watching and listening!

Handwritten Notes: This is a technique that I learned in the Marine Corps when, as a young enlisted Marine, I received handwritten notes from senior officers congratulating me for some achievement or thanking me for something I did. I still have those notes decades later and will never part with them—they mean that much to me.

I used this technique as a business leader, sending personalized, handwritten notes to teammates who deserved a pat on the back. I knew this technique was having the intended effect when my leaders started telling me that their teammates loved receiving these notes and often displayed them on their office wall or within their work-station.

Small Gifts: My leaders and I often sent flowers, gift cards, tickets to events, etc., to spouses or family members during or after a long project or initiative that required their loved one to "burn the midnight oil." These gestures went a long way in ensuring that family members knew that *I knew* their loved one was spending more time at work and away from them than usual—and that I appreciated their sacrifices and unwavering support.

Ice Cream Carts: A couple of times per year, myself and other executives would arrange for an ice cream vendor to come to the company headquarters during mid-afternoon. We'd push the ice cream carts through our respective areas and give away various treats to any of our teammates who wanted them. The message was clear to all: We (senior leaders) love and appreciate you and we want to make sure that you know it!

This technique isn't limited to ice cream carts; I've seen bagel, donut, and coffee tables set up at the entrances of office buildings a few mornings each year as people come into work, and even mobile massage vendors stationed in various locations once per quarter, or during nights and weekends when teams were working overtime. A quick Google search will yield more ideas and techniques than you could possibly ever use, but you'll likely see a few that you know would resonate with your team and could easily be used in the near term.

Now, some cynics will undoubtedly roll their eyes at the use of "small gesture" techniques like these. But as a leader, you should do anything you can to ensure that your people know how much you value and appreciate them! Do it with sincerity and they'll get the message.

Social Media: The use of social media to publish pictures, memes, and other messages thanking teammates for certain things or congratulating them for achievements, anniversaries, etc., is a very effective way of providing public praise by way of the small gesture. Smart leaders know how prevalent social media is in the lives of their teammates, and how effective a simple "Thank You" or "Congratulations!" can be in communicating with them.

As an observer of many companies from within and from afar, I see some who have mastered this low/no cost, highly effective technique, and I also see some who apparently don't have a clue regarding this tool that is at their disposable. I urge you to leverage it!

Small gestures are typically inexpensive or even "free," costing only the time it takes for a leader to do them. However, the return on investment—the goodwill that can result from doing these things in a sincere and genuine manner—is very high.

Again, my experience has been that the very best leaders are almost always *Masters of the Small Gesture!*

Chapter 50

THE TOP 10 REASONS LEADERS SUCCEED

In this chapter, I list what I believe are some of the most common reasons leaders succeed, especially over the long term. This doesn't cover every reason or all of the characteristics that make for a great leader, however.

For example, while not explicitly mentioned in this "Top 10," everything in this chapter is based upon the assumption that successful leaders possess and demonstrate impeccable character, integrity, and ethics, and that they strive to live up to the concept of Special Trust and Confidence—they should be a given if you want to succeed.

Beyond those elements, below are some of the common threads shared by good and great leaders that I've observed or experienced during my career. And suffice it to say that if you have or develop many of them, you are well on your way to becoming a high-quality leader.

1. Lead by Example

An important principle that I've emphasized throughout this book is the absolute requirement for leaders to lead by example in all that they say and do. It's a simple but critical concept that helps individuals gain the respect and trust of their teammates. If done effectively, it enables them to become the type of leader that others energetically follow.

Seasoned leaders understand that they're always leading by example because they are always being observed by their seniors, peers, and subordinates. While various individuals may use different leadership styles, they all know that their "leadership brand" is determined by how others judge their willingness to "walk the talk" and demonstrate the same attitude, self-discipline, work ethic, and sense of urgency they demand of others.

The lesson is clear: Lead by Example—Always!

2. Moral Courage

Moral courage is one of the defining characteristics of the Trust-Based Leader.

It is what enables a leader to present an opposing view on an issue when surrounded by others who have fallen victim to groupthink or perhaps even a lapse in their own moral courage. It's the driving force in situations in which a leader must choose between doing what is *correct* and what is *right*.

Leaders who follow their moral compass often feel lonely ... but they never feel lost!

3. The Leadership Epiphany

This one of the most important lessons that I can share. In my opinion, long-term and high-level success as a leader is greatly impacted by how soon one has what I call *"The Leadership Epiphany."*

This epiphany happens on the day when you finally realize and accept that:

- You don't have to be the smartest person in the room.

- You're not expected to have all of the answers.

- Saying *"I don't know"* and *"What do you recommend?"* are actually signs of strength, not weakness.

- You genuinely feel more pride and satisfaction in the success of your teammates than in your own achievements.

Obviously, the sooner one has the Leadership Epiphany, the better. Until this happens, a leader will never truly unleash the talent, experience, and fresh ideas that exist in his or her team.

Sadly, some leaders never have this epiphany. Others have it very late in their careers and regret not realizing it earlier, as they ponder what could have been.

My experience has been that the very best leaders intentionally have the Leadership Epiphany early in their careers. They become adept at leveraging the expertise, initiative, and recommendations of their talented teammates. They eagerly and relentlessly seek the advice of experienced mentors and coaches. And that's when they begin to separate themselves from their peers in terms of their ability to consistently organize, develop, and lead teams capable of producing superior results.

4. Visible and Approachable

Effective leaders are highly visible and approachable. They routinely visit their teammates to observe and interact with them, and they work hard to ensure that they are seen as a leader who is approachable and willing to listen to any concerns, suggestions, and problems.

Being a "visible leader" is very easy to do, yet so many fail to do it or don't do it effectively. It's rather simple: get out of your office and walk around your team's workspaces so you can see and talk with them. I've already mentioned this technique of *"Leadership By Walking Around"* and it is a superb way to make sure that you are seen by teammates at every level of your organization.

I'm not suggesting using this as a means of constantly checking on your teammates to see if they're working hard or not. I'm recommending it as a way of showing them that you have a genuine interest in and enjoy interacting with them.

Being *approachable* does not imply a leader's desire to be liked or to insert themselves into the personal or social lives of co-workers. It means that a leader has earned the respect and trust of his or her teammates to the point that they are willing to come to this individual with good and bad news—because they know the leader will actually listen to them.

Leaders who have earned a reputation for being approachable and responsive to the needs of others almost always outperform those who haven't. As you might imagine, one of the best ways to develop this reputation is to simply be among your teammates on a consistent basis. With this visibility (some would call it *presence*) comes the opportunity for conversations that create mutual trust and the Teacher-Scholar 360° culture discussed earlier in this book.

Being visible and approachable complement each other and, if done effectively, they greatly enhance a leader's chances for long-term success.

5. Proactive vs. Reactive

Despite using different leadership styles, the very best leaders typically adopt a proactive approach to their duties. They are forward-looking individuals capable of independent thought, and self-starters with a habit of assessing what actions need to be considered or taken in a variety of situations.

Experienced leaders are very aware of what they can control or affect and what they cannot. Rather than waste time worrying or complaining about things that are outside of their control, they focus on what they *can* impact— and they plan and execute actions that are likely to lead to favorable results.

For example, it is common knowledge that the staff noncommissioned officers (SNCOs) and noncommissioned officers (NCOs) run the daily operations of a Marine infantry platoon despite the fact that there is a commissioned officer—typically a young second lieutenant—assigned as the platoon commander. This officer is the person who has total responsibility for all that the platoon does or fails to do. Usually, however, these young officers lack the leadership experience and judgement that can only be acquired with time, and they are prone to making decisions that are less than optimal. (I'm being diplomatic here!) In some situations, these choices could even endanger the unit.

Instead of whining about having to work with young and inexperienced officers, the very best enlisted Marine leaders approach the relationship as mentors and teach *their* leader how to become a competent platoon commander. They know that an effective officer can be a huge asset to an infantry platoon and they proactively set about ensuring that *their* officer becomes one.

Being proactive is a trait that is expected of all Marines; they quickly learn that nobody is going to take them by the hand and tell them what to do. For sure, the newer and less-experienced officers will receive plenty of guidance and mentorship by their SNCOs and NCOs— but once this occurs on any given topic or task, they are expected to "figure it out and get it done" without further supervision.

I have found that all of the above applies to business leaders, too. The very best of them know that it is important to proactively control any situation which may affect them, personally or professionally. They also know that to do so, one has to be able to project and envision that which lies unseen over the horizon—and plan for it, to the extent that's possible.

In other words, the best leaders know that it is almost always better to be proactive than reactive. They know from experience that when forced to be reactive, they often are not in control of a situation. And it's never good to be powerless in fast-paced environments and tough situations.

6. They Guard Against Complacency

Physicians refer to hypertension as the "Silent Killer" because it often causes no obvious symptoms while it advances to life-threatening levels. Often, by the time this condition is discovered, an individual's health has been greatly affected. Left uncontrolled, it can result in serious issues.

The business world has its own "Silent Killers" and one of them is complacency. History is replete with examples of companies that were very successful for decades, only to suffer a "sudden death" as the result of unanticipated market conditions and disruptive influences.

Success breeds complacency when an organization is led by leaders who fail to anticipate the unanticipated. A leader must always cause his teammates to contemplate various "What if...?" scenarios that may be lurking just over the horizon of the next quarter, year, product roll-out, etc.

Many of my experiences as a combat leader are applicable to the business world, and this topic is a prime example. I tell my clients, "In combat, complacency kills people. In business, it kills companies."

7. They Choose Their Battles Wisely

I've always been competitive. As a young Marine leader, I worked to instill the same competitive spirit and *"Never Quit"* mentality among those I was privileged to lead. I wanted to win, and I wanted to be surrounded by others who wanted to win.

But over time, through experience and professional development, I realized that wise leaders recognize that there are times when even though winning a battle is possible, it is not always necessary (or desirable) to fight it relative to winning the war. And I learned that the best leaders found ways to win wars by conducting as few battles as possible.

My experience as a C-level executive proved that this concept has direct application to the business world. When mentoring business leaders, I ask them to reflect upon the following statement:

"Good leaders win battles. Great leaders know which battles are worth fighting!"

8. They Are "Developers of People"

One of the best ways a leader can acquire the ability to attract and retain talented teammates is to establish a reputation for being a "Developer of People."

High-achieving individuals with the right kind of ambition typically have a strong, relentless desire for self-improvement. They value leaders who take a vested interest in developing them and helping them maximize their potential. In many instances, these talented individuals will quit their current jobs, take a pay cut, and move thousands of miles to work with a leader who is known for mentoring and developing his or her teammates.

I dare say that most people reading this book fall into one of two categories:

(1) Those who have made a career move to work for and with a Developer of People.

(2) Those who would do so without hesitation if the opportunity presented itself.

If you desire to achieve great things, find a way to work with a Developer of People. If you want to be a great leader, you must become one! Leaders who do this are simply "talent magnets." And the individuals who gravitate to them have a huge impact on making any organization and leader succeed.

9. Thinking Without Limits

Until 1954, when Roger Bannister became the first man to run a mile in under four minutes, most track and field experts and medical professionals thought the four-minute barrier was impossible to break. They were convinced the human body couldn't physically run such a pace; they were certain that anyone attempting to run this fast would collapse under the extreme physical exertion and psychological pressure. Roger Bannister proved them wrong and set the stage for many others who also were able to "achieve (and surpass) the impossible."

Here's a brief summary of what happened after Bannister's record-breaking run:

- 46 days later, Australian Jim Landry ran 3:58

- Weeks after that, Bannister and Landry broke 4 minutes in the same race

- 30 years later, the world record has been broken 16 times

- Current record: 3:43 by Moroccan Hicham El Guerrouj

- Tens of thousands of runners have now broken 4-minute mark

- In 1997, Kenya's Daniel Komen ran TWO miles in less than 8 minutes!

The very best leaders don't blindly accept the limitations and *"can't be done"* mindsets, attitudes, biases, and taboos that may be associated with their industries, professions, companies, teams, and peer groups. Instead, they continuously engage in what I refer to as *"thinking without limits."* And they develop a culture in which they and their teammates constantly pose the question: "What if?"

10. Lifelong Learner

In every organization I've ever served in, worked with, or studied, a common and highly visible trait among the most effective leaders was their insatiable thirst for learning.

Rather than resting on their laurels and adopting an "I've got this" attitude toward their leadership roles, they instead demonstrated continuously high levels of *professional curiosity.* They relentlessly sought knowledge and advice from wherever it could be obtained and applied it to their organizations.

I often share these words of caution with clients:

"Never assume that your years of experience have automatically brought you wisdom or that your title has bestowed competence."

There's no expiration date on a leader's duty to learn!

Chapter 51

THE TOP 10 REASONS LEADERS FAIL

In this chapter, I cover what I believe are the most common reasons leaders fail. This material is not meant to serve as an all-inclusive list; there are countless additional reasons for failure. I am simply listing factors, in order of precedence, based upon my personal experiences and observations over many years.

1. Inadequate Supervision

The number one reason for leadership failures is a lack of adequate or effective supervision. We've covered the *S in BAMCIS* extensively throughout this book, and I am sure that by now you know how important I feel supervision is to being an effective leader.

In my opinion, even if all of the other elements of leadership, planning, and organizational skill are present within an organization, the results will be mediocre at best and unsatisfactory at worst without effective supervision by leaders.

In almost every instance in which I've observed substandard or unsatisfactory performance, all fingers always point back to inadequate supervision on the part of the leader.

Leaders: Ignore the *S in BAMCIS* at your peril!

2. Lack of Accountability

The number two reason for leadership failure is a lack of accountability on the part of a leader. I categorize this into two major buckets: accountability on a personal level and accountability on the professional/organizational level.

It's a given that many people, for various reasons, do not hold themselves accountable in many aspects of their personal life. And this doesn't automatically mean they are bad people or incapable of success. However, I have rarely seen leaders whose personal lives lacked accountability behave in an opposite manner in their professional lives. And this deficit inevitably bleeds over into the teams they are in charge of.

Suffice it to say that organizations that lack a culture of accountability will always experience problems stemming from the fact that there's no substance behind any policies, standards, individual and team objectives, or various other elements. When people are not held accountable, they typically do not perform well and, in most instances, their performance is actually substandard.

Like all else with leadership, <u>the concept of accountability starts at the top</u>. The lack of this trait on a personal and professional level is the main reason behind many leadership failures that I have witnessed.

3. They Stop Acting as Servant Leaders

We've talked about the concept of servant leadership quite a bit in this book. You know that it is one of the fundamental tenets of Marine Corps leadership, and something on which I have based the Trust-Based Leadership™ model. My feelings on servant leadership are clearly and succinctly stated in one of my "rules": *The leader serves those being led, not vice versa.*

I've found that leaders, especially those serving in more senior roles, can drift off course and neglect or forget the <u>service</u> aspect of servant leadership. They slowly and often subconsciously evolve from being an effective, selfless servant leader to one who feels that their role, title, and tenure grant them the right to *be served* by others.

It's my observation that leaders who believe they have earned the right to be served by their teammates—often adopting a persona and sense of entitlement akin to that of a feudal baron—are almost never successful over the long term.

I urge you to always remember that your main obligation is to serve those you've been granted the privilege of leading.

4. They Let Their Teams Get Lost

I've seen many leaders allow their teams to become "lost" and essentially wander around aimlessly or erratically as they respond to one knee-jerk directive or new priority after another. These individuals allow distractions, unforeseen circumstances, or just the everyday pressures of business and life to cloud their judgement. They "take their eye off the ball" of their team's main reason for providing a service or product that satisfies the needs of their clients or colleagues.

In many instances, leaders become distracted by "bright, shiny objects." They deliberately or subconsciously divert a lot of time and effort toward fads, pet projects, and other distractions. They allow themselves and their teams to lose focus on their mission. And in the process, they and their teammates often forget the very reason they exist, and begin to perform poorly as a result. Ultimately, leaders who allow their teams to become lost will be held accountable for the lack of results in achieving the stated mission, goals, and objectives.

Letting a team become lost is a common leadership error, despite it being an easily avoidable one. Leaders should study their team's mission statement, plan and prioritize where the effort and resources will be focused, and relentlessly supervise the execution of the plan. They must remain vigilant in avoiding anything that could serve as a distraction and cause their teams to become *"the weak link in the chain"* of their companies, divisions, or departments.

5. Lapses of Character

Character, integrity, and ethics have been heavily emphasized throughout this book. It cannot be lost on you how critical I believe impeccable personal character to be for an effective leader—much less a World-Class Leader.

In my experience, lapses of character almost always fall into five main categories:

- Ego

- Alcohol

- Sex

- Drugs

- Money

Ego

Ego should be fairly easy for all of us to understand. This is when leaders start *"believing their own press releases"* and think they have all of the answers. These leaders stop soliciting feedback or encouraging an environment in which teammates are willing to speak truth to power. These individuals essentially believe they can do no wrong, they need no advice or help, and there's literally nothing they cannot accomplish via their own talent and intelligence. Leaders of this type often bite off more than they can chew from individual and organizational perspectives. I have found that, at best, their results are adequate; at worst, they are often dismal failures that sometimes bring down their teams, departments, and even entire companies.

Alcohol

Alcohol is at the heart of many leadership failures. Its impact can range from people who suffer from alcohol dependence or abuse (which will almost always impact their performance at work), all the way down to the person who lacks self-control or exhibits poor judgement in the potentially volatile mixture of alcohol and professional events.

Most business leaders can recall at least one instance in which someone drank too much at the annual office Christmas party or other social function and said or did things that damaged their professional reputation—and perhaps stunted their chance for upward mobility within the company. All of us are taught as teenagers that alcohol impairs a person's judgement, yet I find that many leaders forget this fundamental fact and allow themselves to misuse it to the point where it causes them to fail.

Sex

Sexual activity in the workplace and anything related to sexual misconduct or harassment is obviously a huge issue these days. With the emergence of the #metoo movement, the focus on holding leaders accountable for any form of sexual misconduct has never been higher, and rightfully so, in my opinion.

Unfortunately, I have seen this type of behavior happen quite frequently in the business world and know of more than a few leaders whose careers were greatly affected or even ruined by it. My experience has been that this problem is quite common in the senior leadership ranks, where very influential and powerful leaders often lose the bearing on their moral compass and begin to behave inappropriately.

Ultimately, these individuals get discovered having an affair with a coworker, which is often a violation of company policy; or they are the subject of official complaints and accusations of sexual misconduct that are proven to be true. Sexual misconduct is one of the most common *"career derailers"* I have observed among leaders. I urge you to remember this and take steps to ensure that you will never have to worry about this issue limiting your potential as a professional leader.

Drugs

In today's society, it is common for people to experiment with illicit drugs, and many frequently use them "recreationally" much like others would drink a couple of martinis after work. In some instances, people get hooked on the prescription pain medications that were needed while recovering from serious injuries or surgeries.

Many people are unaware of the fact that drug or substance abuse is prevalent in the business world and is an underlying factor behind many leadership failures. I have personally seen this issue negatively affect the careers of everyone from young leaders in their 20s to senior leaders who are in their 50s and 60s.

The inappropriate use of drugs in the workplace, or even during non-work hours, is something that has led to many a demise. Typically, these leaders experience an inevitable decline in performance as they attempt to execute their duties while impaired. Drug use, and the negative impact it can have on a person's judgement and behavior, is another *"career derailer"* that's usually easily avoidable. I am truly saddened whenever I see the career of a leader destroyed by his or her use of illicit drugs.

Money

I think many people will be surprised to see money listed as a top reason for leadership failures, but I assure you that this occurs much more frequently than most would believe. I have personally observed people, whom I considered to be stellar leaders, derail their career due to some illegal or unethical action or poor judgement related to money—specifically, money that belongs to the companies they work for.

We've all read about, and I have witnessed, some very talented and highly compensated leaders compromise their integrity and engage in unseemly behavior regarding money. Often, the amount of money in these instances is insignificant; I know of senior executives earning 7 figures per year being fired for intentionally submitting falsified expense reports and travel claims in order to gain a few hundred dollars in added reimbursements.

Likewise, I've witnessed situations in which a leader somehow has rationalized that it was permissible for him to literally steal money from the company in one way or another. I've seen them use reasons such as *"I should have received a bigger bonus last year,"* or *"I'm worth more than I'm being paid"* to justify their abuse of reimbursement policies or, in some cases, their access to company funds and the ability to direct money to themselves.

This problem exists within the leadership ranks of many companies, often in the senior leadership ranks, because these leaders often have access to funds and approval authority for expense reimbursements that most lower-level leaders do not.

There are very few things that can negatively affect a person's emotions, judgement, and behavior more than money. Lapses of character related to financial matters have resulted in many leaders being fired and sent away with terminally damaged professional reputations that essentially cause them to be "dead in the water" within their industries and professions.

6. They Demonstrate, Encourage, or Tolerate ...

Leaders often fail because they demonstrate, encourage, or tolerate one or more of the following to happen in their organization:

- Illegal, unethical, or unacceptable behavior

- Favoritism

- Cliques

- Gossip

- Double Standards

Illegal, unethical, or unacceptable behavior

Character, integrity, and ethics have been covered extensively in previous chapters, and I don't think we need to expand too much on the topic here. Suffice it to say that, in my experience, a major reason why leaders fail is that they willingly tolerate the existence of illegal, unethical, or otherwise unacceptable behavior in their teams. Typically, it is only a matter of time before something happens that brings a high level of scrutiny on them and their units, and often, the leader is terminated for cause.

Favoritism

Favoritism (or even the perception that it exists) is a very real problem that leaders commonly fall victim to. It's human nature that we gravitate toward certain individuals in our teams more than others. While this may be a natural reaction, leaders have to guard against it. When a leader does demonstrate favoritism or allows favoritism to exist within his team, morale and performance will always suffer, sometimes to the point of individual and unit failure.

Cliques

The tolerance of the existence of cliques within a company, department, or team is one of the most destructive mistakes a leader can make—and one that may result in a leader losing his or her job. Very few things can have more of a negative impact upon team unity, morale, and productivity than the existence of cliques. Leaders often fail when, for various reasons, they do not address this issue and their teams never gel and perform as a unit. Instead, they are a maze of cliques and associated "sub-cultures" that often create a toxic workplace environment.

Gossip

Gossip should be one of the *zero-tolerance* behaviors mentioned in a previous chapter. The best organizations have cultures in which mutual respect and trust exist at every level of the chain of command. In well-led, healthy organizations, gossip, rumors, innuendo, and talking behind people's backs is simply not tolerated.

Unfortunately, many organizations do have cultures in which these and other harmful behaviors are accepted, if not actively encouraged by some leaders. I've seen more than a few leaders lose their jobs because they have tolerated or promoted an environment where gossip and "trash talking" are pervasive. Teams with this type of toxic culture never perform at exceptional levels of productivity, largely because a healthy team spirit cannot exist when these destructive behaviors are allowed to exist.

Double Standards

Leaders who tolerate or demonstrate double standards will be viewed by their teammates as hypocrites, and their character, integrity, and moral authority will be damaged to the point that these individuals become ineffective. The existence—or even the mere perception of double standards within an organization are such a potentially destructive element that leaders must fairly apply and enforce standards within their teams. They must be constantly vigilant about the existence of double standards or the *perception* of their existence.

I've seen too many leaders fail because of this perception. In most instances, these leaders weren't actually doing anything wrong; they simply were unaware that these beliefs existed and thus took no action to rectify the situation. Unfortunately, this ignorance often results in an individual being removed from a leadership role.

7. Negative Perceptions

As alluded to in the previous paragraphs, left unchecked, perceptions associated with leaders become reality from the perspective of those being led. When a leader allows certain perceptions to exist, it doesn't matter whether there is any substance to them—they will be seen as true, often presenting the risk of damaging one's professional reputation.

My experience as senior executive at Kforce is relevant. I constantly taught and held others to high standards of character and behavior, and I knew that the onus was on me to show others that I was *"walking the talk"* regarding these standards. As an older executive in his 50s and a happily married man, I knew that it was very important that I never allowed even the *slightest impression* that any inappropriate behavior was occurring between myself and any of the many women I worked with or near each day.

For example, if I wanted to take our administrative assistants (all of whom were women) out for lunch for a birthday or other special occasion, I would always ensure that we would walk out of the headquarters building as a group. The Kforce headquarters had four floors with windows facing the walkway leading to its front entrance. Anyone entering or leaving the building was visible to the many dozens of people working next to these windows.

As a seasoned leader, I knew that it was critical to maintaining proper perceptions and my professional reputation that I never be seen walking by myself into or out of the building while accompanied by a lone woman. I knew that I was always being observed and evaluated. And I needed to avoid creating perceptions that would cause some observers to jump to conclusions that something improper was happening—that I was not living up to the same standards others were held to.

Some leaders chafe at this level of scrutiny and the need to be constantly aware of how their actions or words might create negative impressions among their teammates. But I knew that this was simply part of the price one pays to serve as a leader—especially as a very senior executive who wielded a great amount of authority and influence over many other people. Sadly, I've seen leaders who've neglected to pay attention to the perceptions they were creating or allowing to exist, and in some instances, they lost their jobs partly because of these common beliefs.

The lesson here is clear: Leaders must remain vigilant about their actions and words, recognizing the potential to create damaging perceptions among those who are observing them.

8. They Make Easily Avoidable Mistakes

I see this all too frequently—leaders at all levels repeatedly making perfectly avoidable mistakes. I've been guilty of this myself (repeatedly) during my time as a leader. I know how easy it is to commit mistakes that countless others have made—and which could have been avoided, had I taken the time to study the experiences of those who preceded me in similar roles or specific business operations or situations.

I frequently tell leaders that every mistake that they have ever made or will possibly ever make has already been made hundreds, if not thousands, of times by other leaders in similar roles. And all they have to do to avoid repeating these errors is to read the books these leaders have written or listen to or read interviews they have given.

The main message I try to convey to student leaders is that they should relentlessly study their profession and associated sources of knowledge, and seek the advice of mentors and professional coaches. I have found that highly experienced leaders are typically more than willing to share their experiences with younger leaders seeking advice. Notably, they often talk more about the lessons they learned from their failures over the years than they do about their many successes.

Leaders should not remain uninformed and ignorant of valuable examples that will prevent them from making easily avoidable mistakes. In today's digital, connected world, vast amounts of knowledge, lessons learned, and wisdom are literally at your fingertips on the internet, in books, articles, interviews, and through courses and seminars.

So many leaders fail because they or their teammates make unforced errors.

Don't let this happen to you!

9. They Tolerate Intolerable Individuals

Leaders can fail when they tolerate three types of people who can become toxic elements within their organizations. I categorize these individuals as:

- Prima Donnas

- Posers

- Poisonous Personalities

Prima Donnas: These individuals are often quite competent; they may be your top salesperson, a highly accomplished engineer, or another individual whom everybody respects for their knowledge and expertise. What makes them *"prima donnas"* is the fact that they are quite often very temperamental people, with an inflated view of their importance to the team. They are prone to emotional outbursts and demanding special treatment because they are, in their minds, *"a very special person."*

There's often a very fine line between leaders appropriately recognizing their top performers with well-deserved rewards, privileges, and perquisites and the creation of a "spoiled brat" whose demands for special treatment and different standards become never-ending. These prima donnas, like their counterparts in Hollywood, professional sports, and many other professions, often throw temper tantrums when they don't get their way.

Needless to say, the presence of individuals who are prima donnas in the worst sense of the term can have a very destructive effect. Left unchecked, they can cause a team's stagnation or demise because they do not consider themselves to be a *member* of the team—instead, they have a singular focus on themselves.

Beware the prima donnas that may exist within your team!

Posers: There are posers in almost every company, department and team. All of us have observed a teammate over a period of time and thought, "He's incompetent/lazy/untrustworthy, etc." or "He doesn't produce quality work" or "She's a poor teammate and a bully toward others."

Likewise, we've all thought to ourselves, *Doesn't Bob see this?* or *Why does Bob allow her to get away with this?* Unfortunately, in too many instances like this, the boss—Bob—is oblivious to this individual's true nature. Worse, he may see the truth regarding one of his teammates but avoid conflict (which shows a lack of moral courage) and simply overlook the incompetence, poor behavior, or other lapses of character demonstrated by a poser.

Much like the destructive effect that a prima donna can have on a team, the presence of posers can be equally damaging. The fatal flaw is when everyone on the team *knows* that their leader is *aware* of the posers within the ranks but he or she takes no action to remedy the situation. This never ends well for anyone involved. This includes the leader, who will ultimately be found to be deficient in various ways; most notably perceived as lacking moral courage and the will to take care of the wellbeing of his teammates.

Poisonous Personalities: These people may exhibit some of the same traits and behavior as prima donnas and posers and, like the former two, they are sometimes some of your most competent and high-performing teammates.

When experienced in everyday life, they may be very fine, whip-smart people with pleasant personalities. You might even enjoy having a beer or two with them during a Friday afternoon happy hour.

However, when placed in the work environment—for whatever reasons—these individuals exhibit entirely different personalities, attitudes, and behaviors. They become the individual whom I refer to as *"That Person."*

We've all dealt with *"That Person"* in the past. He's the guy who causes everyone to walk on eggshells because one never knows if the *"nice guy"* came to work that day or if their *"Evil Twin"* did!

He's that person who is the perpetual cynic, naysayer, and "glass-half-empty" whiner who never wants to try a new idea—unless it's *his* idea. He's not a teammate. Far from it, he's a toxic element that nobody, regardless of their role or title, wants to deal with because he is impossible to reason with. His presence is a dark cloud that hangs over the entire team every day.

Now, these poisonous personalities are bad enough in their own right, but a leader who tolerates them sets up the organization for failure. When this happens, the leader rarely survives the aftermath because, of course, a leader is responsible for everything that happens or does not happen within an organization he or she is in charge of.

I've seen this happen many times. And sadly, typically before the poisonous personalities are outed and dealt with and the leader is fired for being weak and incompetent, most of the very best people within the team have already voted with their feet and sought new, healthier work environments in which to apply their talent and passion.

Leaders: beware the poisonous personalities that may exist within your organization. Left unchecked, they will infect your team with a disease that damages all who come in contact with them.

Rational people will start looking at what's happening and eventually it becomes clear that, "Hey, everybody *knew* this person had a poisonous personality." He or she's been tolerated for months or years and a leader knew about it but failed to act. These analysts realize "That's why half of our good employees have left." And the remaining half may lack motivation and engagement. They're just tired of it. Productivity suffers because of one individual's personality.

The main lesson regarding all three of these problematic personality types is that leaders must be fully aware of what is happening at every level of the organization. My experience is that nothing good ever happens when these people are allowed to roam free and wreak havoc within the work environment—but plenty of bad things happen. One of them is often a leader getting fired for tolerating these folks and allowing them to harm the team and its mission.

10. They Fail the Caller ID Test

A common reason why leaders are unsuccessful is because they fail what I refer to as *"The Caller ID Test."* I'm sure you're thinking, "What on earth is he talking about? I've never heard of a Caller ID Test!" Well, I'd counter that you've actually administered (and taken) this test thousands of times during your life, including while you're at work.

Everybody knows that when you make a call on your phone, your name and phone number are going to show up on the screen of the person's phone you are calling. Think about the different reactions you have depending on what name and number show up on your phone's display— and remember those feelings as you read the following example.

Let's say you're a regional sales leader in a large company that has more than 100 field offices spread across the country and its headquarters in Atlanta, Georgia. You are in charge of the company's Central Region and based in St. Louis.

When you check your email, you become aware of an issue related to the billing status of one of your region's biggest customers. They have indicated they are not happy and would like the problem to be remedied immediately. The solution to this problem is the domain of the billing department that is located in the Atlanta headquarters. Again, you're a very senior sales leader, you've dealt with the members of the billing department quite a bit over the past several years, and you pull up their phone number on your contact list and initiate the call.

It's lunchtime in Atlanta and the person who you need to speak with—literally the only person that can solve this problem for you—has just stood up with her lunch bag in hand and is about to go downstairs to the cafeteria for her break.

Just as she takes her first step outside of her cubicle, she hears her desk phone ring. She steps back and sees your name and phone number on the display.

This is *The Caller ID Test!*

Based upon your professional reputation among the members of the billing department and your past treatment of them and this particular billing clerk, what will she do, knowing that it's you on the other end of the call?

Will she put her lunch bag on the desk, sit down, and answer the phone to see how she may be of assistance?

Or will she look at your name and number and think to herself, "I'm going to go down and eat lunch with my friends and relax a bit. When my lunch hour is over, I'll come back to my desk and make a note to call him back sometime this afternoon to see what's going on. I'm sure that if he's calling me, something has gone wrong. And whether it's my fault or not, I'm going to get yelled at, threatened with being fired, and essentially be called incompetent by him. I'm in no rush to take another one of his verbal beatings."

This example is based upon an actual situation. And in that situation, the billing clerk went to lunch and called the regional manager a few hours later, which was within the established response-time standard.

The regional manager was very talented, capable, and had a history of producing solid results as a sales leader. Unfortunately, he also had a history of treating people badly, especially those operating at lower levels in the company. Because of this, he was eventually terminated from his leadership role.

He not only failed *The Caller ID Test*; he failed as a leader and was held accountable for it.

When teaching and coaching leaders, I tell them that whether they realize it or not, they are taking *The Caller ID Test* every time they make a phone call. Whether they pass this test and the person on the receiving end of the call answers it immediately, or the individual lets it go to voicemail so they can *"delay the beating"* is entirely dependent on how the leader has treated that person in the past.

I then ask these leaders to reflect upon the reactions people might have when their names and numbers show up on a caller-ID display. I tell them to think about the past several times they've called various support teams within their company and had their call answered immediately or dumped straight to voice mail. As I let some silence go by, I can almost hear the "gears turning" in their minds as they reflect upon the reception their phone calls have been receiving.

The lessons of this story are obvious: Treat people with respect and respond to their needs with vigor and a sense of urgency, and they respond in kind.

This is one test that is easy to pass, if you lead by example!

"In business, everything is negotiable except your integrity."

—Mike Ettore

"The galleries are full of critics.
They play no ball, they fight no fights.
They make no mistakes because
they attempt nothing.

Down in the arena are the doers.
They make mistakes because
they try many things.

The man who makes no mistakes lacks
boldness and the spirit of adventure.
He is the one who never tries anything.
His is the brake on the wheel of progress.

And yet it cannot be truly said
he makes no mistakes, because
his biggest mistake is the very fact
that he tries nothing, does nothing,
except criticize those who do things."

—GENERAL DAVID M. SHOUP
Commandant of the Marine Corps (1960-64)
Medal of Honor – Tarawa

Fidelis Leadership Group
— Developing World Class Leaders —

Chapter 52

HATERS, HELPERS, CRITICS, AND COWARDS

Mature, self-confident leaders understand that seeking advice and feedback on their performance from various sources is essential to their personal and professional growth. The best leaders actively cultivate cultures and environments in which teammates at all levels are willing to *Speak Truth to Power*, and provide honest, constructive criticism even though, at times, it may be difficult for the leader to listen to or accept. This cuts both ways, of course. People also must welcome and solicit honest appraisals from their leaders.

While this may seem reasonable, there's no doubt that many individuals deliberately choose to avoid seeking feedback from their leaders. In fact, the authors of a *Harvard Business Review* article assert that less than 50% of business executives ask their boss for it. I think it is safe to assume that many of these same individuals who are leaders also rarely, if ever, solicit feedback from their peers, subordinates, or anyone else.[201]

Human nature is such that most people do not enjoy being criticized, and most will avoid situations where this is possible. Wise leaders do the opposite of this; they welcome all forms of constructive criticism and recommendations, and act upon them when appropriate.

Consider the Source, However

While the lesson here is clear—leaders should actively seek feedback—it is also important to remember that not everyone is qualified to provide this, and you should always consider the source before taking action in any way. Frankly, while many people can be counted on to provide honest, well-intentioned advice to leaders, an equally large group will consistently do just the opposite and deliver unfair, petty, and often demeaning comments.

In today's highly transparent business arena, almost everything a leader does or says will inevitably be subjected to scrutiny, critique, and comment from observers at all levels of an organization; and in many instances, from those outside of it, too. And modern technology and various social media platforms often let critics make comments anonymously.

My experience has enabled me to assess providers of feedback, criticism, and various forms of support, and place them into four main categories that I call *Helpers, Haters, Critics,* and *Cowards.* I'll go into some detail on each of these buckets, and readers will likely be able to place most or all of their colleagues and professional acquaintances into one of them.

Haters

Every leader, upon reaching a certain level of success and status, will inevitably encounter what I call *Haters.* These are people who may genuinely disagree with what you are doing in your role, or they may be envious of your success and influence within an organization and among seniors, peers, and subordinates.

In many instances, these individuals have attempted to do what you are doing and failed or never even got the chance to lead. They may have aspired to serve in a role similar to yours, or perhaps even in the same position; and for various reasons, they were not selected for promotion or granted commensurate levels of authority. Simply put, they are almost always envious of you and see you and your success as a threat to their own success and self-esteem.

While it is possible and even admirable to try to win over naysayers and critics through collegiality and professionalism, and I encourage leaders to always initially err on the side of trying to do so, the reality is that there's no pleasing the true *Haters.* You'd be wise to understand this and seek to identify them in your environment sooner rather than later. Haters can be vindictive, vicious, and toxic, and while they add no value to your development as a leader, they are a negative force that can cause you harm if you allow them to.

Helpers

Leaders need various forms of support to maximize their potential and that of their teams. Seasoned and self-confident leaders recognize this, and they intentionally surround themselves with teammates, advisors, coaches, and others who can add value in various ways.

Helpers are those who are genuinely interested in helping you succeed, are quite willing to share their experience and wisdom, and typically do it without seeking reward or recognition. These individuals are found at every level in almost every organization, and they can be the difference between a leader's success and failure.

Helpers come in all shapes, sizes, and personalities, and leaders must remember this. Just because a person has a desire to help you and your team, does not always mean that he or she will do so in a way that you'd prefer. Perhaps their personalities clash with yours and others, or they lack tact when providing constructive criticism. Whatever the case may be, you should remember that these individuals are doing their best to add value in one way or another. And, if properly managed and focused, they can be of great benefit to you and your team.

Learn to recognize these individuals and thank them if they are providing assistance. If they are not actively adding value, encourage them to do so and tell them that you truly want to hear their thoughts and recommendations. Show them that you appreciate and value their experience, insights and support, and they will likely become an asset that can enhance your leadership skills and the effectiveness of your team.

Critics

I have found that there is another group of people who are capable of adding various forms of support to leaders, but they typically refrain from doing so. Instead, they tend to focus more on critiquing every aspect of a leader's decisions, actions, and those of his or her organization. I refer to this group as the *Critics*.

Smart leaders develop an ability to quickly determine whether an individual is a *Helper* or a *Critic*. Once a determination is made that a person truly falls into the category of being a *Critic*, they'll still be allowed to continue offering verbal jabs from the "peanut gallery"—but everything they say should be taken with a grain of salt.

While the *Critics* often refrain from offering genuine, actionable insights and recommendations, they can still be of service to leaders. I've found that the comments and criticisms made by even the most jaded *Critics* often contain some valuable observations, and I've benefitted from reflecting upon them.

Critics usually do not cross the line into the realm of being Haters, and they typically don't show any desire to serve as Helpers; instead, they seem to thrive on leveling a steady stream of criticism and opinions on anything and everything. I find that while most Critics don't actually harbor any ill will toward those they relentlessly criticize, they do almost always exhibit a desire to be seen as someone who is important and therefore should be listened to by all.

The approach I use when dealing with *Critics* is aligned to that old saying, "Even a broken clock is correct twice a day!" This saying was first presented to me in the context of leaders being wise enough to identify *Critics* and others who may not be willing to help, but whose remarks can frequently be "mined" for valuable nuggets of information and alternatives.

Cowards

Inevitably, every leader will have to deal with those sad individuals whom I refer to as *Cowards*. These people typically do not have your best interests in mind, nor those of your team. Instead, they seem to delight in making baseless, demeaning, and even cruel comments about you and your leadership methods and decisions, the actions of your team, and just about anything else that provides them with an opportunity to "snipe" at you.

Unfortunately, many online platforms provide *Cowards* with the ability to make their intentionally harmful and often venomous comments anonymously. Naturally, the ability to make uninhibited comments without repercussions provides these individuals with perhaps the only form of watered-down courage they will ever have. And they will gleefully spew comments that range from being merely personally insulting and nasty to outright abusive and even threatening.

In fact, such anonymous comments have, in the past, extended to my own email inbox or the comments section of online articles or blog posts in which I have been mentioned. Trust me on this: It is indeed an experience to see yourself, your team, and even your family members verbally attacked and disparaged by an anonymous coward.

Identify and Leverage—or Simply Neutralize or Ignore—Different Sources of Feedback

Wise leaders know the value of hearing the perspective and points of view of a diverse group of people. However, they also know that not everyone has their best interests in mind when offering opinions. They have learned that at least two or more of the types of individuals described in this chapter exist within their organizations and their circle of influence. The sooner these people can be assessed and put into a category, the sooner their positive or negative words and actions can be appropriately directed, adopted, applied, ignored, or neutralized.

I do think that it is possible for individuals to evolve (or devolve) from one category to another, and wise leaders should be willing to consider the possibility, for example, of a *Critic* making the shift to become a *Helper*. This does happen, and often the way a leader approaches an individual is the catalyst for this transformation.

That said, in my experience, those who are appropriately identified as *Haters* or *Cowards* typically have fundamental character flaws and biases that essentially doom them to remain in these categories. I've found that true *Haters* and *Cowards* cannot be rehabilitated and must be kept under close observation—while attempting to ignore the venom in their comments—lest their presence and actions have a negative effect on your effort to be a good leader.

Run interference on or ignore the *Haters* and *Cowards*. Leverage the *Critics* and *Helpers*, and actively thank the latter. And always keep your eyes and ears open to find the feedback that makes you a better leader.

"There is only one way to avoid criticism. Do
nothing. Be nothing. Say nothing."—Aristotle

"In combat, complacency kills people.
In business, it kills companies."

—Mike Ettore

Section V:

LEADERSHIP ARTICLES

Introduction:

LEADERSHIP ARTICLES

The articles in this section provide either high-level concepts or real-world examples in which various aspects of Trust-Based Leadership™ have been applied in the business world. Some of them are based upon my personal experiences as a retired US Marine who was able to effectively utilize these leadership concepts in business as a C-level executive. Other articles contain concepts from leadership experts that I've found valuable and informative as I've continued to learn more about leadership.

These articles will support and reinforce many of the Trust-Based Leadership philosophies covered in the previous chapters, and will enable readers to better understand how they can adopt and effectively utilize them within their unique business environments.

All of these articles have been published individually on various social media platforms, and I have left them largely in their original format.

Chapter 53

ON SELF-LEADERSHIP

An important element of applying the concept of Servant Leadership in any organization is the idea that all leaders need to first live the concept of *self-leadership.*

Self-leaders are transformational leaders who see a need, create a vision, and inspire a group. They do not work on a system of overt supervision with rewards and punishment, or deject people by inspiring excessive, unhealthy competition that kills creativity. Instead, self-leaders create a sense of positive identity for the collective group and every individual within it. They do this while inspiring commitment and encouraging each staff member to take ownership of his or her work.

Self-leadership is powerful. Self-leaders are among every company's top performers. They get more work done with fewer resources. They are valuable because they bring in customers and they keep the client relationships solid through consideration, empathy, respect, and harmony. They are also usually healthier in their personal lives, and that health has a positive influence on their work lives. They get more sleep, they have more energy, and they have a wider network of business associates and friends.

Self-leaders find success because they excel in employee relationships, and easily adapt to new challenges, shifting environments, and varying personalities. They listen to and consider staff feedback; they communicate effectively with their peers, direct reports, and senior leaders; they collaborate to accentuate their strengths and the strengths of the people they lead so that no one's weaknesses are on display.

In addition, self-leaders do not look to sabotage anyone or any situation, even when someone on their team is difficult. This is because they do not hold grudges or even entertain the idea of bitter grievances. In fact, self-leaders often have the ability to neutralize toxic people in a healthy way, so that everyone benefits.

What Constitutes Self-Leadership?

Leading yourself before you lead others might sound simple, but few people are able to hold themselves to this basic principle on a daily basis. In general, society does not nurture self-leadership. We are inhabitants of a world where pride and divisiveness have become common in the workplace as people fight for status. It has almost become second nature for individuals to be overly willful, arrogant, intolerant, and rigid in order to establish dominance within the pecking order. However, leaders with these traits are trouble, for they erode the spirit of the organization by reducing staff resolve and creating chaos.

The opposite is true of self-leaders. Self-leadership is a form of self-discipline and psychological development that relies upon humility, compassion, acceptance, and emotional intelligence when reacting to circumstances. Self-leaders manage through the example they set, and become the embodiment of the company's mission in order to create an integrity-driven culture.

Furthermore, while self-leaders are not always in leadership positions, they have a knack for bringing people together and finding creative solutions. They are problem solvers who take initiative and are not afraid to assume command when it is necessary to further production. They are empowered people who earn the respect and trust of their teammates because they make good, timely decisions when no one else is watching or leading.

Successful organizations have a symbiotic relationship between self-leading leaders and the self-leading individuals who report to those leaders. Self-leading leaders hire the right people to fit the company's needs, and then delegate tasks and some authority to them. In turn, those self-leading employees respect leaders who trust them to operate independently or lead a small team, and they relish the opportunity to make decisions and take the initiative.

A pair of studies that were published in *The Journal of Psychology: Interdisciplinary and Applied* highlight the value of self-leadership. One study of university student leaders found that "self-leadership was significantly related to higher psychological functioning (e.g., effective coping style, greater optimism and hardiness, and less ineffectiveness and interpersonal distrust) and better health status (e.g., greater perceived wellness, less perceived stress, and fewer symptoms of illness)." In the other study of corporate employees, self-leaders within organizations had "significantly greater perceptions of work satisfaction, enhanced communication, quality management, effective work relationships, and in terms of health outcomes, greater perceived wellness and less work stress." [202]

Key Aspects of Self-Leadership

Self-leadership begins with self-awareness. Cornell University, in collaboration with Green Peak Partners, examined 72 executives at public and private companies worth $50 million to $5 billion to find out what interpersonal traits were most prominent among successful executives. Self-awareness stood above the rest.

"Leadership searches give short shrift to self-awareness, which should actually be a top criterion," says Dr. Becky Winkler, principal at Green Peak. "Interestingly, a high self-awareness score was the strongest predictor of overall success."

When you self-lead, you are self-aware, and when you are self-aware, you have a near-perfect understanding of both your strengths and weaknesses. The self-aware leader understands he or she is not perfect and needs help to succeed.

"This is not altogether surprising as executives who are aware of their weaknesses are often able to hire individuals who perform well in categories in which the leaders lack acumen," said Dr. John Hausknecht, Professor of Human Resources at Cornell. "These leaders are also more able to entertain the idea that someone on their team may have an idea that is even better than their own."

The study also found that executives with "bully" traits and poor interpersonal skills often demonstrated various degrees of incompetence and lack of strategic intellect. Arrogance, impatience, stubbornness, and other expressions of low emotional intelligence correlated to inferior scores on every single performance dimension, including poor financial results. These dysfunctional executives were not sufficient self-leaders; therefore, they were unable to manage and inspire talent, and be team players.

Victor Lipman, author of *The Type B Manager*, concurs. "The qualities commonly associated with management and leadership—being authoritative, decisive, forceful, and perhaps somewhat controlling—if not moderated by a high degree of awareness as to how one comes across and is perceived by others, are also qualities that have the potential to easily alienate those on the receiving end." [203] [204]

However, solid and effective leaders must couple self-awareness with another key trait of self-leadership—self-confidence. Self-leaders do not feel threatened by talented co-workers because they find confidence in their own strengths, which avoids the manifestation of rivalry derived from envy. The self-leader chooses to encourage the talents of gifted peers instead of spending energy to control or diminish them.

Unfortunately, it is often human nature to undermine others in order to rise above the rest. Even kind and generous people fall prey to an inner drive that forces them in an unconscious way to compete at all costs to get ahead. However, this instinct creates ineffective leaders who are overcompetitive and controlling. This mix inspires a toxic work culture where employees regularly marginalize, backstab, mock, and judge their co-workers in an attempt to prop themselves up.

The self-leader chooses another avenue—the route of self-efficacy—which is another essential characteristic of self-leadership. Self-efficacy is a belief in yourself and your ability to be successful. People with a high degree of self-efficacy have control over their motivations, see their thought patterns clearly, and determine rational reactions before acting on an ultimate behavior. They also have the ability to persevere longer when faced with a crisis or challenge, which allows them to surpass obstacles—those that less-effective leaders find insurmountable—in order to reach desired goals.

A study by Albert Bandura, who coined the term and was once President of the American Psychological Association, found a positive relationship between high levels of self-efficacy and performance. Bandura writes in *Self-Efficacy: The Exercise of Control* that self-belief does not always ensure success, because people can take it to the extreme, but "self-DISBELIEF assuredly spawns failure." [205]

"Among the types of thoughts that affect action, none is more central or pervasive than people's judgements of their capabilities to deal effectively with different realities," Bandura writes in *Social Foundations of Thought and Action: A Social Cognitive Theory*. "People's beliefs about their abilities have a profound impact on those abilities."

Ability is not a fixed property because there is a huge variability in how one performs, Bandura argues. "People who have a sense of self-efficacy bounce back from failure," he writes, "They approach things in terms of how to handle them rather than worrying about what can go wrong." [206]

Becoming a Better Self-Leader

It is clear that before you can begin to lead others successfully, you need to lead yourself. But becoming a self-leader takes work. With few exceptions, it does not happen by chance. If your self-leadership skills need some polishing, there is plenty of hope. You can train your brain to self-lead because it is a highly adaptive organ, and as you practice any new skill, your mind builds bridges to it, so that you can get to your destination easier in the future. In time, the new path becomes so clear that healthy habits form.

(1) Motivation is a key element to becoming a self-leader. Figure out what truly motivates you; what you're passionate about. Material goals come and go, shiny things lose their luster quickly, but your *purpose, values, and goals* tend to stick around. Therefore, the key element to becoming a self-leader is to find internal motivations that are inspired by core values, and not by status, power, or possessions.

(2) We are instinctively drawn to the viewpoints of people and outlets that support our opinion, and because of it, we become lost in our own ideology. Consequently, we become very uncompromising in our beliefs. Notions that might be healthy for your state of being may not be a comfortable place for everyone else. We do not have to

agree with others' beliefs or ideologies, but we should not condemn people for their opinions, and we most certainly should not allow the opinions of someone else to affect us in a negative way.

(3)   It is so easy to find opinions that match our own because there is so much information readily available, but it is crucial for people seeking to be self-leaders to take some time to challenge their views by *listening*—with an open mind—to the perspective of people with opposing points of view.

(4)   Along those lines, understand that everyone has different feelings, desires, stresses, and fears. In addition, not everyone is as strong, resilient, objective, or as smart as you. You can look down on people who do not have the same competencies as you, or you can accept their deficiencies, offer them support and assistance in changing that, and hope they will accept your input. Also, remember to accept others' critiques and advice because you have weaknesses too.

(5)   Recognizing emotions as they occur allows self-leaders to be flexible and adapt to every situation. You must always accept your emotions, but you do not have to be rigid with them, so process them in a rational way before you react to them.

(6)   Complaining is futile. If you complain, it implies that you are a victim and you are choosing to remain a victim instead of productively constructing a solution to the issue. Instead of complaining, the self-leader immediately begins to look for ways to resolve the issue in a rational way and in a reasonable amount of time. A resolution might require the minds of a few people other than yourself to solve the problem, but the meetings with these people involve problem-solving, not complaining.

(7)   Self-awareness and understanding. It is very difficult to look at yourself objectively, so you must take into consid-

eration what other people say about you, especially if they say it all the time, and you hear the same criticisms from multiple sources. Are they all wrong, or are you just too stubborn to believe that you make bad choices or have some faults that you could improve? An honest self-assessment that analyzes patterns in your behavior, personality traits that you need to improve, and inadequately thought-out decisions that lead to poor outcomes and poor leadership is the best way to get started.

(8) Learning to be a self-leader takes practice and dedication to continual improvement. Revel in the process and every situation in which you own the moment in a way that shows self-leadership. If you are losing your leadership edge, your company's morale is low, or production is slipping, consider the principles of self-leadership to turn things around.

"For a man to conquer himself is the first and noblest of all victories."—Plato

Chapter 54

ON SERVANT LEADERSHIP

Many people associate the term "World-Class Leader" with individuals who possess impressive titles like "president," "ambassador," "senator," "CEO," or "general." These people are serving in positions of significance and power, so they must be the "World-Class Leaders" we are referring to, right?

Not necessarily.

In fact, the very best leaders are not always those serving in such roles, or others who constantly try to catch everyone's attention with their bravado. No, in many instances, the true leaders within an organization are the ones away from the spotlight or the executive suite, working doggedly to help their teams meet objectives, or finding ways to pitch in to accomplish a mission. They're more concerned with ensuring everyone else is empowered and enabled to perform well than worrying about whether they'll be personally recognized.

That is never more evident than in the Marine Corps, which teaches its leaders how to be servants. That may sound backwards to some of you. The common perception is that leaders aren't servants.

Actually, the very best ones are!

The Greater Good

According to Daniel Wagner, who wrote "Servant Leadership: A Vision for Inspiring the Best from Our Marines" for the *Marine Corps Gazette*, "To focus passion, conviction, and judgement in a manner that serves the greater good of our Marines is the mandate of the servant leader." [207]

Effective leaders understand that their purpose is to enable the superior performance of others. It's not to order, cajole, or browbeat others into submission, but to bring out the best in others—to make it possible for those around them to do their best work. That is servant leadership in a nutshell. It is making decisions for the good of those under your responsibility.

Instead of placing the leader at the top of an organizational pyramid, with others beneath them in seniority and rank, a servant leader places themselves at the bottom, and those whom they are responsible for above them (picture an inverted pyramid). Because, truly, leaders are there to help everyone else do their best.

Today's Marine Corps is a prime example of an organization comprised of servant leaders, but that wasn't always the case. Until General John A. Lejeune's leadership was codified in the 1921 edition of the *Marine Corps Manual*, the relationship between officers and enlisted service members was often more akin to master and servant, or superior and lackey. There was often no mutual respect—no true leadership, only a very directive-based, command-and-control environment. Enlisted men were expected to do the bidding of their superiors, no matter what the task or reason.

General Lejeune recognized the danger of this relationship and worked to correct it. Rather than positioning commissioned officers and senior enlisted leaders as being a privileged class of people who would be catered to by those of lesser rank and position, he did the opposite by teaching Marine leaders that they were solely responsible for the personal and professional development, competence, and well-being of those they were privileged to lead.

Lejeune made it clear that Marine leaders "are responsible for the physical, mental, and moral welfare" of those under their command. It's a responsibility that requires that leaders get to know the men and women they're working with—to be able to recognize their strengths and weaknesses, which skills they have mastered and which skills still need work, and what their goals and aspirations are. With that knowledge, leaders are in a position to guide and develop these individuals. [208]

Leaders Eat Last

Being responsible for the growth and development of others often requires sacrifice, whether in time, energy, or resources. In the Marine Corps, you see this in action most clearly in the field during mealtime, when the most-junior Marines line up first and the senior-enlisted Marines and officers hang back until everyone else in the unit has been served. Only after every individual under their command has been taken care of will they step up to eat. Putting the wellbeing of the junior members of the unit first means that in every situation, the leaders' needs are secondary to those of the men and women they have responsibility for.

The "leaders eat last" concept applies to every situation associated with being a Marine leader, and if you desire to be an exceptional leader, it will apply to how you treat those you are fortunate enough to lead—every single day, in all that you do!

In a recent tour of Iraq, an embedded reporter offered the Marines he was traveling with the opportunity to call home on his cell phone. Each Marine declined the opportunity and, instead, offered their comrades the chance to make a call, believing that they were more deserving of such a gift. That's a servant leader—thinking first of the needs of others.

This concept of servant leadership goes beyond basic necessities—like working conditions, compensation, and adequate resources and equipment—to supporting the mental and emotional needs of those in your care or employ. To recognize when someone needs encouragement or advice, a leader must know enough about them to be able to gauge their current mental state. That means learning everything you can about your team members, their backgrounds, their childhoods, their families, where they're from, what their current living situation is, whether they have a spouse or partner, and what they worry about at night. You need to figure out what makes them tick—what drives them, what they're aiming to achieve, and what roadblocks may get in their way.

Only then can you do all you can to make their lives better, whether that's through arranging for needed education and training, recommending them for a well-deserved promotion, negotiating time off so that they can be with family during a crisis, or simply checking in regularly to let them know they're on your mind. That's what a leader does.

Fortune magazine's annual list of the "100 Best Companies to Work For" is chock-full of companies that practice servant leadership. A review done by *Modern Servant Leader* found that 5 of the top 10 companies on 2011's list were identified as organizations that practice servant leadership. In all, the 17 servant-led companies in the top 100 had anywhere from 1,200 to 167,000 employees, and their revenues ranged in the billions.

The software company SAS topped the list that year, and is a regular on the list every year. The company's dedication to work/life balance is at such a premium that they have an entire department dedicated to it. [209]

With an unbroken chain of growth and profitability since its inception in 1976, the world's leading business analytics software vendor has 11,000 employees and its co-founder and CEO Jim Goodnight has a net worth of $10.2 billion. His wealth was created through servant leadership that begins with a mandatory employee policy of a 35-hour workweek, while other Silicon Valley companies push their employees to 80 hours or more.

"I expect parents to be with their kids on the first day of school and take time off to attend important school functions," Goodnight says. "I know they will get the job done. I trust them to do that."

Goodnight is NO fan of bureaucracy and believes that multiple management layers deter innovation, so SAS has a "flat line" leadership structure. Furthermore, when it is time to promote people, he chooses folks who put their teams first and promote the work of others before themselves. "We want our managers to be coaches, not dictators," he says. [210]

Becoming a Role Model

A servant leader also works to be the best version of themselves, to serve as a role model for others. In my experience, the best leaders in the Marine Corps and in the business world are those who live up to the high standards that have been set for them or that they have set for themselves. They demonstrate respect for others and are committed to doing their best, no matter the task. They strive to raise others up by modeling appropriate behavior and educating and instructing whenever needed. They also take constructive criticism with respect and appreciation.

Leaders model the best behavior in thought, word, and deed. Marines especially model their own behavior after their leaders, but a <u>fundamental law of leadership</u> is that the members of any organization, company, or team will inevitably mirror the character, behavior, work ethic, and sense of urgency demonstrated by its leaders.

Communication is another way that servant leaders stand out. Instead of hoarding information and keeping it to themselves, they gather facts and then share them widely with those who need it, while holding back details that are truly confidential or would distract from the task at hand.

In the Marine Corps, the goal is to share all that you know so that those under your command can make smart decisions quickly and effectively on their own. Your goal is to prep others to step into leadership roles themselves.

One good example of a role model in the business world is the outdoor clothing and gear company Patagonia, which takes servant leadership to a new level. While maintaining a servant leadership style that has "no reverence for reporting relationships or traditional hierarchies," the company also extends their servitude outside of the organization's borders to set an example for the world at large. For instance, Patagonia offers a company perk that allows employees paid leave from work for two months if they donate their time to an environmental group.

Moreover, Patagonia does not have an annual performance rating because they believe avoiding this practice changes the role of a manager from a judge to a coach and facilitator. "Our philosophy is that the manager is more of a mentor and a resource," said Dean Carter, VP of Human Resources at Patagonia. "They give you coaching and direction, they ensure the work is aligned to the highest priorities, and they allocate resources."

Patagonia encourages their staff to bring their "full selves" to work. They don't do lunch meetings because they believe that their staff should get a real break; employees can work remotely; the company offers integrated child care; and Patagonia pays "paternity" leave along with maternity leave.

"As long as you get the work done, there's a lot of flexibility in scheduling," Carter says. "People are encouraged to live the lives they want and do what they do, whether that's horseback riding, surfing, or seeing their kid's play."

In many ways, Patagonia uses strategies to "slow its growth." It creates durable products that last a long time, repairs the worn gear for their customers, encourages reselling of used clothing and equipment, and manufactures less product than is demanded to promote responsible economic growth in order to curb environmental decline. The company, which is valued at $1 billion and sees continual double-digit revenue growth, makes it very clear that their servant leadership is not a gimmick.

"We're not belting loud about a culture that we'll quickly rethink if we see a low ROI," he continues. "No, there might not be an ROI; it's just the right thing to do for our culture." [211]

The Ultimate Servant Leader?

There might not be any better example of servant leadership than that displayed by former US Defense Secretary and retired US Marine Corps General James Mattis. While his direct and aggressive leadership style is often at odds with some of the elected and appointed officials that he's served, many senior leaders call the former Gulf War, Iraq, and Afghanistan commander "bulletproof" because of his tact, ability, rational thinking, and knowledge.

Secretary Mattis entered politics with an impeccable reputation. In *One Bullet Away*, former Marine Corps Officer Nathanial Fick tells a story in his autobiography about the former general which demonstrates his servant leadership to the Marines under his command.

Fick's platoon had finished patrolling for the night in Kandahar, Afghanistan. On this particularly chilly night, Fick directed his platoon to station two men per fighting hole to provide perimeter security, so that the soldiers could take turns sleeping.

As was typical, Fick walked the line at 3 am to check on his soldiers and make sure they had the resources they needed to get them to the morning, gauge their morale, and pass on the latest information from the higher levels, so that each Marine knew what to expect over the next couple of days.

When Fick, who was a Marine lieutenant at the time, got to one of the fighting holes, he was initially frustrated to find three men in it. Why was someone not sleeping and away from his own hole? On closer inspection, he found that the third man was General Mattis, who was doing the same things as Fick—checking the line to make sure the men were well and talking to them about objectives.

"He had stopped to talk to the sergeant and the lance corporal," Fick writes. "Nobody would have criticized Mattis if he had a lieutenant like me heating up his MREs and if he stayed inside to sleep on a cot. But Mattis understood that it all comes down to personal leadership. He is the classic *fighter-leader*. He's the player-coach. He's out there with his troops. You can have all the staff meetings you want, but there's no substitute for walking around and talking to the people who do the work." [212]

The examples of Mattis's servant leadership are numerous. For instance, he took the place of a young officer who was on duty on Christmas Day, so the Marine under his command could spend it at home with his family. He did this with no fanfare, and we only know the story because another commander, General Charles C. Krulak, stopped in to check on the Marines and wish them a Merry Christmas.

"I'm a bachelor," Krulak recalls Mattis saying to him. "I thought, why should that officer miss out on the fun of having Christmas with his family, so I took the duty for him." [213]

In another example, former Marine Colonel Stanton S. Coerr recalls his first meeting with Mattis in *The Federalist*, saying, "Colonel Mattis called for me. He stood to greet me and offered to get a coffee for me. He put a hand on my shoulder; gave me, over my protestations, his own seat behind his desk; and pulled up a chair to the side. He actually took his phone off the hook, closed his office door, and spent more than an hour knee-to-knee with me." [214]

Mattis understands servant leadership because he understands that his role as a leader is to serve those under him. We understand this plainly because his behavior supports the things that he says are important. His Marines were his priority—everything else was secondary to HIS needs.

Leadership Lessons

Contrary to popular belief, being a leader does not mean you have earned the right to simply boss people around and have them do things to make your life better. Being a leader isn't about prestige or controlling others, it's about supporting your teammates in any way possible. It is about providing the leadership, guidance, and resources to enable those who work with you to do the best job possible. It's about serving your team so that they can perform at their very best.

Leadership is always about serving those you lead.

Always!

"Not for us alone are we born; our country, our friends, have a share in us." —Marcus Tullius Cicero

Chapter 55

ON ACCOUNTABILITY

The principle of accountability is a simple one to understand; it means that a person—regardless of role and tenure—is held responsible for performing as expected and delivering results on time and as promised.

It is said that the ancient Romans had a tradition: whenever one of their architects designed an arch, as the capstone was hoisted into place during its construction, the architect assumed accountability for his work in the most profound way possible: he stood under the arch. If his calculations were correct and his design viable, the arch would hold. If not...let's just say that his architectural career was over!

Like so much associated with the art of leadership, accountability starts at the top. Senior executives who refuse to hold themselves accountable for their actions will never be able to instill this trait throughout their organizations. We've all seen leaders who practice the "Do as I say, not as I do" style of leadership, which inevitably results in organizational mediocrity or even failure in some cases.

Effective leaders know that it is their responsibility to provide the strategy, policies, and processes that make up the foundation of a successful organization. However, effective leaders are also aware that the strongest foundation cannot lead an organization to success if the senior leaders aren't willing to hold themselves accountable for their own performance and adherence to the set plans and policies. Without accountability on the part of senior leaders, an organization is doomed to failure.

I recently published an article titled "Ettore's Rules," in which I described a technique that I used to convey my leadership philosophy to organizations that I've led. Not surprisingly, Rule #1 states that "Integrity and accountability are non-negotiable." While all leaders agree with the insistence on personal integrity, many of them chafe at the prospect of being held accountable for the performance and behavior of other people. They often state that "people factors" are difficult to define and measure, but I disagree entirely with this line of thinking.

Holding yourself and others accountable is quite easy if you create an environment in which everyone understands the organization's culture and core values, and in which all individual roles and tasks are clearly defined. Assuming that leaders are utilizing appropriate methods of oversight, it's quite simple: are people doing what is expected of them, as promised and on time? If so, great! If not, the leadership team must take actions that will quickly get to the heart of the matter so they can see if the lack of performance is being caused by a lack of skill or will on the part of those not performing as expected.

Accountability is a key ingredient in creating and sustaining a Culture of Execution. Most successful organizations know this, and they invest a lot of time and effort in establishing an environment in which everyone—from the most senior leaders all the way down to the most junior person on the team—is held accountable for their actions.

What are *your* thoughts on accountability as it relates to the art of leadership?

"To move the world, we must first
move ourselves."—Socrates

Chapter 56

ON HUMILITY

Humility is a trait that many do not associate with strong, effective leaders; rather, it is often associated with weakness, timidity, and indecisiveness. Experienced leaders, however, know that humility amplifies all other positive leadership traits and principles. They also understand that without humility, practically all other strengths and positive attributes become greatly diminished, often to the point where they are no longer visible to others.

Is it possible to be an effective leader without being humble? Absolutely ... but it is much more difficult and rarely sustainable. Leaders who lack humility are almost always called into question by those they work with regarding their true motives and agendas. In my opinion, the presence of humility is also a very accurate indicator of authenticity in someone who claims to be a "servant leader."

A study by the research firm Catalyst confirms this, showing that humility is one of four essential leadership factors for creating an environment in which employees from different demographic backgrounds feel included. In a survey of a large sample of workers from Australia, China, Germany, India, Mexico, and the US, it was discovered that employees responded positively when they observed selfless and altruistic behavior in their leaders.

Actions characteristic of humility include:

- Acts of humility, such as admitting mistakes and seeking criticism.

- Encouraging and empowering all members of the team to learn and develop.

- Acts of moral courage—the willingness to take personal risks to stand up for what's right, even if it is not popular.

- Holding employees accountable for results—they were more likely to report feeling included in their work teams.

The study also found that employees who perceived this type of behavior from their leaders also reported being more willing to "think outside the box" and suggest new ways of doing things to make the team function more effectively. And they were more likely to become "team players" and be willing to go beyond the call of duty, such as voluntarily picking up the slack for sick or overwhelmed teammates. [215]

Acquiring Humility

I believe that of all the virtues that are essential for successful leadership, humility is the one that elicits the most lip service—and typically the least consistency in action. True humility is a hard-won virtue and one that requires a relentless and honest self-assessment of one's true character, strengths, and weaknesses.

Such a self-assessment is often difficult, because it causes us to acknowledge our imperfections. It requires that we quickly and openly admit when we are wrong, and be able to change directions without regard for our ego or fear of "losing face" among colleagues. Humility counsels us to put others first in thought, word, and deed—it is the antithesis of the narcissistic self-promotion so common today among many senior leaders in all types of organizations.

"Researchers Bradley Owens and David Hekman have done groundbreaking research studying humble leadership–from the military to manufacturing to ministry," reported *The Washington Post*. They've found humble leaders are those who are comfortable admitting "mistakes and limitations."

A good leader is driven and consistently strives for excellence. And humility is one of the forces that pushes good leaders to improve by constantly evaluating progress, revising and updating plans when appropriate, and constantly seeking out advice, fresh perspectives, and other feedback. A humble leader "encourages subordinates to take initiative. He prefers to celebrate others' accomplishments over his own." [216]

Humility in the C-Suite

In my opinion, humility is a "must have" trait if one aspires to perform well at the executive-level. The most obvious behavior of a humble leader is that he or she willingly and publicly prioritizes the organization's success ahead of his or her self-interests.

In a recent *Journal of Management* study of 105 computer software and hardware firms, CEOs that were viewed as being humble by their colleagues "were found to have reduced pay disparity between themselves and their staff." They willingly shared their power and they hired more diverse management teams, which often results in more diverse opinions and ways to attack enterprise-level challenges and issues.

Additionally, they enabled their leaders to lead, make decisions and innovate. Not surprisingly, humble leaders historically have been associated with "less employee turnover, higher employee satisfaction, and they improve the company's overall performance." [217]

Leadership Lessons

The first step a leader must take to acquire or enhance the virtue of humility is to put his or her ego in check. Unless one can do this—and I mean *really* do it—they will fall short of their goal and, as a result, their leadership potential will never be maximized. Some ways to ensure that you are walking the path toward becoming a leader with humility are listed below:

Be Skeptical of Praise: It's not a bad thing to enjoy being praised for doing a good job, but senior leaders must be wary of all praise that they receive from others. Human nature is such that in many environments, people with personal agendas are prone to praise their leaders, inflate their egos, and do whatever else is necessary to curry favor as they look out for their self-interests. Stated another way, I offer these words of caution: "Don't fall in love with your own press releases!"

Be Concerned if You're Not Hearing "No:" This is a big one and it often leads to senior leaders believing that they can do no wrong, which of course is as dangerous as it is ludicrous! If a leader is truly humble, she's created an environment in which her teammates are willing to "Speak Truth to Power" and she'll often receive honest and critical feedback on her "great ideas." The best way for a leader to determine whether she's created such an environment is to reflect upon the question, "When's the last time someone said

'No' to me?" Think about this for a moment … and ask yourself the question!

Admit Your Mistakes and Use Them as "Teachable Moments": When leaders recognize their own imperfections, they make it okay for others to be fallible, too. People tend to relate better with leaders who share their imperfections because they appear more "human" and just like they are. These types of displays of humility help to remind team members that everyone makes mistakes, they should be willing to admit them quickly, and they must drive on to resolve errors while achieving the unit's shared objectives.

Engage in Dialogue, Not Debates: Another way to practice humility is to truly encourage your teammates to "Speak Truth to Power." Too often, leaders are insistent on changing the opinions of others and "winning" arguments. When leaders behave like this, they often become so focused on proving that "they know best" that they miss out on the opportunity to learn from their talented teammates—and this is truly a shame. Humble leaders are confident enough to suspend their own agendas and beliefs. In so doing, they not only learn things, but they often enable much better results by incorporating the suggestions of their teammates.

Reflect on Your Weaknesses: As mentioned previously, if you desire to be a leader with humility, you must become your own biggest critic in the best sense of this term. Only with constant self-assessment of your weaknesses and the things you don't seem to do well or without difficulty will you be able to develop an accurate view of yourself as a leader.

Do not allow yourself to fall into the trap of believing that since you are already serving in a senior leadership role that you "pretty much know it all." Never assume that your years of experience have automatically brought you wisdom or that your title has bestowed competence!

The best leaders are always those that demonstrate the trait of humility. Like any valuable trait or skill, acquiring it takes a lot of hard work and constant self-assessment. I encourage you to reflect upon the points conveyed in this article as you strive to learn more about yourself and maximize your leadership skills!

> *"If someone is able to show me that what I think or do is not right, I will happily change, for I seek the truth, by which no one was ever truly harmed. It is the person who continues in his self-deception and ignorance who is harmed."—Marcus Aurelius*

Chapter 57

I Had 3 Fathers

During the early days of my enlisted service, the platoon sergeant for my platoon was a Marine named Ross Carter. He was a very experienced leader of Marines and had served in combat in the Dominican Republic and in Vietnam, where he served three tours of duty and survived wounds received during each tour. He had also served as a drill instructor and exhibited all of the positive traits and characteristics of the Marines entrusted with this special duty.

Staff Sergeant Carter was very strict. In fact, he was uncompromising when it came to any Marine Corps standard, no matter how trivial. He left no doubt among the Marines in our platoon that the very least he expected of us was the very best we could do—during every minute of every hour of every day!

Because he was not a man to be trifled with, everyone in the platoon did their best to meet the high standards he set for us. SSgt. Carter was truly a bad-ass Marine, and though we all wished at times that we could have a more relaxed platoon sergeant, we also knew that if we were ever called on to go to war, we wouldn't want to be led by anyone else. It wasn't long into his tenure as our platoon sergeant that I came to the realization that if I emulated him in every way, I'd undoubtedly do well as a leader of Marines. Quite simply, I wanted to be like Staff Sergeant Carter when I grew up!

Role Model and Mentor

As a very young corporal, I lacked the experience and knowledge that many individuals had when they're placed in charge of a squad of 12 other Marines, compounded by the fact that many of my Marines were older than me. SSgt. Carter invested a lot of time to get me up to speed. He shared his wisdom and insights, providing invaluable leadership techniques and tips that I used effectively throughout my service in the Marine Corps and my subsequent business career.

Like most Marines who had never served in combat, I was very eager to hear any stories that SSgt. Carter would share with me and he did so on numerous occasions, always emphasizing the lessons embedded in each story. He had experienced a lot of infantry combat during his tours in Vietnam and, every now and then, I could tell that some of his stories were causing him to think of things that were painful. Years later, I felt some remorse over being so relentlessly inquisitive about his combat experiences. By that point, I'd matured and learned that for many combat veterans, some memories are best kept locked up in the far corners of their mind.

SSgt. Carter obviously knew that I was genuinely interested in becoming a good leader, however. He knew that I, as a young and naïve noncommissioned officer (NCO), was actually eager, if not hopeful, to one day prove myself in combat. So, he did what any good Marine leader would do: he taught me everything he knew about leadership and especially combat leadership. He would also frequently say, "Be careful what you wish for, Ettore." It would be many years until I truly understood what he was trying to tell me.

The Send-Off

One day, Staff Sergeant Carter called me into his office and told me that my request for orders to the drill field had been approved and that I was to report to drill instructor school in several weeks. I remember that I stood in front of his desk and felt happy and a bit frightened at the same time. I was getting the opportunity to become a Marine drill instructor and was certainly excited about that—but I also knew that to do so, I'd be entering an environment where I'd be competing with Marines who were much older and certainly more experienced than I was. I was about to knock on the door of "The Big Boys Club," as SSgt. Carter used to call the drill field.

Sitting in his office were two other staff noncommissioned officers (SNCOs), both of whom also had served on the drill field. They both congratulated me on my orders to DI School and offered to help me in any way before I departed the unit. Sensing that I was a bit off-balance by the news he'd just shared with me, Staff Sergeant Carter tried to lighten the mood by making a joke about my age, saying, "Hey, do you guys know that Ettore is only 20 years old? Can you believe that? Back in our day, drill instructors didn't have pimples!" They all laughed at this and so did I, knowing that they all were truly happy for me and wanted me to do well.

When the time came to depart the unit, SSgt. Carter met with me to give some last words of advice on making it through DI school. As I stood up to leave, he shook my hand and said, "Good luck, Sergeant Ettore. You're a good sergeant and a good leader. I'd be happy to go to war with you. Now go down there and make us all proud. And stay out of trouble!"

I left his office feeling good and confident. But there was also a sense of sadness. I was leaving behind someone who'd had a huge impact upon my development as both a man and Marine. I've always said that I was blessed with three fathers: Larry Ettore, my actual father and a great role model; Gary Wikander, my high school wrestling coach; and Staff Sergeant Ross Carter. I was going to miss him.

The Award Ceremony

Many years later, about a year or so after the conclusion of the Operation Desert Storm, I was informed that I was going to be awarded a medal for actions during combat operations in Kuwait. Typically, the level of this particular award called for the division commander, a two-star general, to award it to the recipient during a formal ceremony. I knew that now-*Sergeant Major* Carter was stationed on the same base and I decided that I would like to have him present the medal to me. I asked the battalion commander if he thought this was possible and he said he'd do his best to make it happen. A few days later, he told me that my request had been approved.

The awards ceremony was a fairly formal event; it included a formation of hundreds of Marines and several dozen spectators, including my wife and children. As the official presenting the award, Sergeant Major Carter would be positioned in the front of the formation, facing the assembled Marines. For the past few months, he had been using a cane to help him walk, since he was experiencing some mobility issues stemming from wounds received in Vietnam. I watched him hesitate a bit as he was about to march out to take his position. At that moment, he apparently decided that he'd ditch the cane. He handed it to a Marine standing nearby and walked, with obvious discomfort, to his designated spot on the parade ground.

An announcer read the award citation, which described the actions for which I was being recognized. Once the reading was finished, Sergeant Major Carter pinned the medal on my shirt and said some very nice things to me—the most important of which was that he was very proud of me. I told him several things; among them was that my being awarded this medal was largely due to the mentoring he had provided to me long ago, and that there were Marines standing in the formation that were alive because of some of the lessons that he'd taught me. At the end of my comments, I said, "Thank you, Sergeant Major, for everything you've done for me." I think my comments had taken him a bit by surprise and he replied, "Thank you, Sir. You've done well and I always knew that you would."

Lessons for Leaders

There are some important lessons in this story, and I want to emphasize a few of them. As a young Marine, I was very curious and wanted to learn as much as possible about my profession. This is a good quality; in fact, I think it is essential if one desires to become a world-class leader. But most importantly, I was fortunate to *have a leader who was willing to mentor me and guide my development* as a young NCO. Staff Sergeant Carter was the epitome of the teacher that General Lejeune had envisioned and encouraged all Marine leaders to become in the 1921 *Marine Corps Manual*. Ross Carter was willing to invest a lot of time in me.

Of course, simply acquiring some of Staff Sergeant Carter's knowledge and insights was, in itself, not going to make me a good leader. I had to find ways to effectively integrate what I'd learned into my own leadership style. Aside from the fact that we had different personalities, he had so much more experience and credibility than I did and a lot more rank, which obviously means a great deal in the Marine Corps! And instead of trying to completely adopt someone else's persona, mannerisms, etc.—a classic and all-too-frequent mistake made by young leaders—I did what I'd been advised to do in my previous leadership training: I remained who I was as a person while I was trying to grow as a leader instead of striving to simply become a clone of SSgt. Carter.

It should be noted that while some of the lessons I learned from Ross Carter had proven to be effective across several generations of Marines, some of them had to be modified to accommodate for new technologies, weapons systems, and very different combat environments in which I had to lead Marines. Perhaps the most important factor was that the individual Marines that I led during the latter part of my career were in some ways very different from those of my early days in the enlisted ranks. They were not any better or worse than Marines of previous eras, but they came from an American society that was different than I had been raised in, and certainly was quite a bit different than Staff Sergeant Carter's experience!

I and all other Marine leaders had to adapt to this in various ways to effectively lead Marines. At the same time, we had to ensure that our Marines were held to the timeless standards and traditions of the Corps. This has obvious parallels in today's business world, in which the leaders born during the Baby Boomer era are becoming increasingly rare and employees from Generation X, Generation Y (the Millennials), and Generation Z (the Centennials) attempt to understand each other and work effectively toward organizational goals and objectives.

Last but not least, this story reemphasizes the age-old philosophy of "don't forget where you came from." Like anyone who has achieved even a modest amount of success as a leader, I am the product of the schools, both formal and informal, that provided me with the ability to learn so much, as well as the many mentors I was fortunate to have guide me in a lifelong journey of leadership. None were more influential to me than Staff Sergeant Ross Carter. Having him present that medal to me in front of so many Marines and spectators was my small way of publicly acknowledging his patience and willingness to teach a young, inexperienced, and often hard-headed NCO. It was also a wider acknowledgment of so many superb Marines who had, in some way, helped me since the earliest days of my time in the Corps.

Everyone deserves at least one Staff Sergeant Carter to help them grow as leaders, in whatever type of organization they serve in. For those who don't yet have such a mentor, take action and find one, even if he or she is external to your team, department, or entire organization. And never forget that you have a responsibility to be *someone else's* Staff Sergeant Carter once you gain even a modest amount of experience as a leader!

"A society grows great when old men plant trees in whose shade they shall never sit." — Greek Proverb

"There are some important lessons in this story, and I want to emphasize a few of them. As a young Marine, I was very curious and wanted to learn as much as possible about my profession. This is a good quality; in fact, I think it is essential if one desires to become a world-class leader. But most importantly, I was fortunate to *have a leader who was willing to mentor me and guide my development* as a young NCO. Staff Sergeant Carter was the epitome of the teacher that General Lejeune had envisioned and encouraged all Marine leaders to become in the 1921 *Marine Corps Manual*. Ross Carter was willing to invest a lot of time in me."

—Mike Ettore

"The Marine Corps also focuses its training methodology on the warfighting skills of the individual Marine rather than on mastering the equipment he or she carries into battle. Despite the fact that modern weapons and combat systems are critical in present-day warfare, the Marine Corps has, from its inception, focused on *'equipping the man'* rather than the *'manning the equipment'* philosophy followed by many other military organizations.

This is an important concept that you must understand: <u>The Marine Corps maintains that its principal weapons system has been and always will be the individual Marine.</u>

The common responsibility and identity that are instilled in every Marine in turn drive the organization's singular focus. Every component of the Marine Corps, from recruiting to training to aviation to motor transport, shares one overall purpose: to enable infantry Marines to defeat the enemy. This philosophy has driven success spanning centuries and diverse battlefields, from Belleau Wood and Iwo Jima to Inchon, Hue City, and Fallujah."

—Mike Ettore

Fidelis Leadership Group
Developing World Class Leaders

Ettore's Rules

1. Integrity and accountability are non-negotiable.
2. Mission accomplishment is the number one priority.
3. The leader serves those being led, not vice-versa.
4. Care for your Marines as you would care for your own sons.
5. Know the difference between risk and gamble.
6. Never gamble with the lives of your precious Marines.
7. Expect casualties. Everyone gets cut in a knife-fight.
8. Don't bring a knife to a gunfight.
9. Don't fall in love with the plan. Plans don't win battles, leadership does.
10. Expect change. Deal with it and make it your ally.
11. Bad news does not get better with age.
12. Don't surprise your boss...ever.
13. Inaction or indecisiveness is always wrong.
14. Don't make the same mistake twice.
15. Don't confuse enthusiasm with capability.
16. Don't be a sycophant.
17. Criticism must always be accompanied by recommended solutions or alternatives.
18. Know the difference between confidence and arrogance (your Marines do).
19. Know what you don't know.
20. Know the difference between pain and discomfort. Don't snivel...ever.
21. Be your own biggest critic.
22. Nobody is irreplaceable.
23. All of us are smarter than any of us.
24. Courage never goes out of fashion.

Chapter 58

ETTORE'S RULES

As I publish this article, I'm actually chuckling a bit. I know that some readers, especially those with military experience, will probably roll their eyes and think something along the lines of, *This guy created his own leadership rules? You've got to be kidding me!*

For those who bristle at what might appear to be an attempt to place myself among the many leadership gurus and authors who have created and promoted their own lists of leadership rules, I want to assure you that this is not my intention.

This article is not about me. I am, however, sharing what I have experienced during my never-ending desire to clearly understand what those in leadership positions think about leadership. Please bear with me as I explain the origin and purpose of what I came to refer to as *"Ettore's Rules"* and how the concept of a formally stated leadership philosophy has direct application to leadership in any organization.

Leadership Philosophy

Throughout history, men and women have assumed leadership roles and used their authority to make decisions that affected the lives of others. Even a casual study of some of the more famous (or infamous) leaders of the earliest periods of recorded history reveals that most of these leaders had adopted and, in various ways, disseminated certain philosophies about their positions of power. Most of these leaders issued directives and statements that showed friend and foe alike what their thoughts and guiding principles were, and they typically left little room for misinterpretation.

For example, the Mongol warlord Genghis Khan was known to say to his generals, "It is not enough that I succeed, all others must fail!" I think it is safe to say his statement meets the brevity and clarity standards recommended by most communications experts!

While obviously considered harsh by today's standards, the Mongol leader's declaration enabled everyone in his army to have a clear understanding of what his mindset was regarding the conquest of their enemies. Khan's statement was essentially what is known today in the Marine Corps and other branches of the armed forces as a "command philosophy," and in the business world as a "leadership philosophy."

In both the military and business, it is customary for an incoming or newly promoted leader to express his or her philosophy regarding leadership and other important topics. Doing so helps the members of the organization to quickly get an understanding of how their new leader thinks and what his or her priorities are.

The Purpose of a Leadership Philosophy

In the military, it is a longstanding custom to have a change-of-command ceremony to recognize the outgoing leader for his or her service and achievements and to welcome the incoming leader.

In peacetime, these ceremonies can be quite elaborate, complete with military bands and mass formations of troops passing in review. During combat operations, a change-of-command is often necessitated by the fact that a unit leader has been killed or severely wounded, or in some cases, relieved of command due to the failure of the unit to accomplish its assigned missions. Naturally, these combat leadership transitions are executed in a much more serious, expeditious, and subdued manner.

In the private sector, there are often no formal ceremonies when an individual assumes a new leadership role. However, the first order of business is almost always the same in any organization—the discussion of a leadership philosophy, usually accompanied by a "philosophy statement" in the form of a letter that is sent (often via email) to all members of the team. This statement is intended to enable individuals at all levels of the organization to quickly understand the leader's thoughts, beliefs, and expectations for organizational performance.

During my service in the Marine Corps (1974-1998), lengthy command philosophy statements were not yet in vogue, and you rarely saw them being issued below the general officer or colonel level. However, all Marine leaders—enlisted and officer—did convey their leadership philosophy and expectations to the Marines they were responsible for.

My observations were that—due to the culture the Marine Corps and the standardized leadership training and mentoring that all Marines receive from their earliest days of service—most Marine leaders focused on the *science* of leadership when issuing their leadership philosophies. Almost all of them placed great emphasis on the Marine Corps Core Values, the Leadership Traits and Principles, and other traditional concepts, practices, and techniques associated with leading Marines.

That said, there are often huge differences among Marine leaders in the application of the *art* of leadership, and these differences are also present among leaders in any non-military organization or institution—but that's a topic best discussed in a future article.

Ettore's Rules

After giving my leadership philosophy orally several times during my early years of service as an officer, I realized that, in some instances, I had forgotten to mention something that was important. You only get one crack at giving your leadership philosophy for the first time. And obviously, it's best if you don't omit any key elements when initially speaking to your Marines. To remedy this, I created a list of statements and quotes that I felt effectively captured my outlook on leadership and which, when stated orally or in writing, would enable my Marines to quickly get a grasp on my philosophy and approach to being their leader.

I used this "cheat sheet" when speaking to units or groups of Marines, or when an incoming Marine met with me for the traditional "welcome aboard" meeting. At some point, some of the leaders within my units, enlisted and officer alike, began to ask me for a copy of this document so they could better emphasize my leadership philosophy and intent within their respective units. I am also quite sure that some of them, as I had done, "borrowed" some of the material for their own leadership philosophies; after all, I had always made it clear to them that everything on the document had been taken from various sources and that none of it was my own original thought.

Over time, I put the title of "Ettore's Rules" on this document and, as the years passed, the list grew longer and I occasionally reworded and reprioritized some of the content. I always made sure that my Marines knew this material was not my original work for two reasons: First, to of course be honest with my men; and second, to reinforce the practice of Marine leaders being willing to adopt and utilize time-tested knowledge, concepts, tactics, and techniques rather than wasting time trying to "reinvent the wheel," especially during situations in which time is a scarce commodity.

I urge you to read "Ettore's Rules." After doing so, ask yourself if you were able to quickly get a solid understanding of my main views on leadership and what I expected of all Marines in my units. I hope that you can say "yes" to this question but if not, let me know and I'll consider revising the list for additional impact and clarity!

I do think it is appropriate for me to address what you will probably notice when reading the rules: they were written in a completely male-oriented manner. They also contain some aggressive statements, some of which literally or figuratively imply violence, while others may imply what some would consider an "insensitive" approach to leading people.

The truth is that I was never in command of an operational unit that had females assigned to it (women were not assigned to infantry units during my era); thus, I was addressing only male Marines during the vast majority of my service.

Regarding the allusions to violence and what some may view as a bit of a "hard-ass" approach to leadership, I don't have much to say about this other than the fact that the Marine Corps exists to fight and win in combat. I was training and leading Marines who were expected to—and in some instances, did—kill enemy combatants who were trying their best to do the same to them. Thus, while I make no apologies for the tone and tenor of this document, I do want to explain the context in which it was created and utilized.

The following are "Ettore's Rules" in their final form when I retired from the Marine Corps in 1998:

Ettore's Rules

(1) Integrity and accountability are non-negotiable.

(2) Mission accomplishment is the number one priority.

(3) The leader serves those being led, not vice-versa.

(4) Care for your Marines as you would care for your own sons.

(5) Know the difference between risk and gamble.

(6) Never gamble with the lives of your precious Marines.

(7) Expect casualties. Everyone gets cut in a knife-fight.

(8) Don't bring a knife to a gunfight.

(9) Don't fall in love with the plan. Plans don't win battles, leadership does.

(10) Expect change. Deal with it and make it your ally.

(11) Bad news does not get better with age.

(12) Don't surprise your boss ... ever.

(13) Inaction or indecisiveness is always wrong.

(14) Don't make the same mistake twice.

(15) Don't confuse enthusiasm with capability.

(16) Don't be a sycophant.

(17) Criticism must always be accompanied by recommended solutions or alternatives.

(18) Know the difference between confidence and arrogance (your Marines do).

(19) Know what you don't know.

(20) Know the difference between pain and discomfort. Don't snivel … ever.

(21) Be your own biggest critic.

(22) Nobody is irreplaceable.

(23) All of us are smarter than any of us.

(24) Courage never goes out of fashion.

Leadership Lessons

In recent years, leadership philosophies have increasingly become somewhat of a spectacle, with some military and business leaders issuing verbose declarations that can take quite a long time to read or listen to. If you've ever watched C-Span and seen a member of Congress reading a lengthy statement so that it is included in the Federal Register, often after normal business hours and in front of an empty or nearly empty senate chamber, you'll know what I'm talking about!

Simply stated, *an effective leadership philosophy should be simply stated!*

If you focus on substance instead of your image when you craft your leadership philosophy, I think you'll find it rather easy to produce a brief and accurate portrayal of what is in your heart and mind regarding your role as a leader. Remember, when it comes to formalizing a leadership philosophy that you're going to share with others, take care to ensure that brevity prevails; and that your most important thoughts, beliefs, and expectations are easy for all to understand, remember, and act upon.

In subsequent articles, I will describe in detail about how well "Ettore's Rules" were received and utilized by some of the leaders I ultimately served with in the corporate arena. For now, I think this article makes it obvious that I believe strongly in the power and utility of a well-crafted leadership philosophy being shared by leaders at every level of an organization with their teammates.

If done effectively, these statements can capture a leader's beliefs, priorities, and expectations of the individuals and teams he or she is now responsible for. I strongly urge all leaders—even those who aren't currently in leadership roles but hope to be one day—to craft a personal leadership philosophy.

Let me know your thoughts on the 24 Rules—based on your experience, would you make any changes to the list?

"The Spartans do not ask how many the enemy are,
but where they are."
—Agis II

"Every organization has 'untitled experts'— the business world's equivalent of Marine Corps lance corporals—whose experience and expertise are often greater than that of more senior leaders and teammates. Wise leaders know this and ensure that this incredibly valuable source of intellectual capital is valued and routinely leveraged throughout all facets of business operations."

—Mike Ettore

Chapter 59

LISTEN TO YOUR LANCE CORPORALS!

It is a common practice at The Basic School (TBS) located at Marine Corps Base, Quantico, Virginia for guest-speakers to address new Marine officers and share their experiences and insights with them. One of the guest speakers who addressed my TBS class was Major General David Twomey, a combat veteran of the Korean War and Vietnam conflict. During his speech, he shared an anecdote that had a profound impact upon me and helped shape much of my core philosophy as a leader. I consider the lessons associated with this event so valuable to leaders in any type of organization that I want to share my thoughts on them, so they are not lost over time.

During his informal speech to 250 newly commissioned 2nd Lieutenants, the general mentioned that he had recently served as the Inspector General of the Marine Corps. In this role, he routinely traveled to bases and installations in and out of the United States so that he and his team could conduct various inspections designed to ensure that the Marines assigned to these commands were meeting established standards.

He told us a story of being on a Navy base in Spain to inspect the small group of Marines assigned there. While waiting in a room inside a building that was located next to a parking lot, where the personnel inspection he was about to conduct would be held, he heard the Marines outside beginning to get into formation. He said that the window was open and that he could hear the Marines clearly, though there were curtains covering the window that prevented them from seeing that anyone was inside the room. He said that he peeked around the curtain and saw a young sergeant in charge of the unit issuing last-minute guidance to his Marines.

The general said that after listening to the sergeant for only a few minutes, it was obvious that he was a skilled leader and was saying all the right things to his Marines. He also said that this individual exuded an exceptionally professional and impressive presence while addressing his Marines. Twomey went on to say that the sergeant's words of encouragement were so motivating that he found himself getting excited about the inspection!

He told us that some the sergeant's statements and motivational sayings were so effective that he promised himself that he would use them whenever he spoke in front of a group of Marines.

A Huge Impact

The general's statement had an immediate, profound, and lasting impact upon me. Here was a Marine Corps major general with well over 30 years of distinguished service telling young officers that he was willing to emulate the leadership traits of a much younger and far-less-experienced sergeant. And he was telling us this in a very matter-of-fact manner, as if it were nothing special for one Marine to learn from another—regardless of rank and experience—and when appropriate, adopt a practice or technique that could make him or her a more effective leader.

I resolved that if a Marine general could openly admit that he was willing to learn from and imitate the leadership techniques of a sergeant young enough to be his son, I should also be open-minded and willing to seek knowledge and wisdom from every possible source. By adopting this attitude, I learned quite a bit from countless Marines—many of whom were younger, junior Marines—throughout my career in the Corps.

On a related note, years later, I was assigned to the TBS staff as a Tactics and Leadership instructor and department head. This enabled me the opportunity to speak to a few thousand new officers over the course of a three-year tour of duty, and I frequently told them this story. In doing so, I hoped to share with these young lieutenants what had been a profound lesson for me. But beyond that—in keeping with one of the best traditions of the Corps— I ensured that the knowledge and experience of previous generations of Marines (in this case, those of General Twomey) were preserved and passed on to current and future members of our beloved institution.

Being Taught by 19-Year-Old Experts

Upon assuming command of an infantry rifle company in 1990, I realized that I knew absolutely nothing about a machine gun that had been recently introduced to the Corps, and which some of my Marines were using as their primary weapon. To remedy this, I asked the weapons platoon commander to arrange a class for me on the weapon from a knowledgeable Marine. He replied, "Will do, sir. We'll send you one of our experts."

A few days later, at the prescribed time, I showed up at my unit's armory with a notebook, ready to learn about the weapon. As I entered, I saw the machine gun sitting on a table and two lance corporals standing close by. They introduced themselves and proceeded to teach their captain everything I needed to know to become familiar with the machine gun on a basic level. Both Marines were quite impressive, and they patiently explained various aspects of the weapon.

Toward the end of the class, they had me "field-strip" the machine gun and reassemble it several times until I could do this flawlessly and within the same time limits that new machine gunners had to meet during their initial training. While doing this, several other Marines were in the armory. It was obvious that they were surprised, and perhaps even a bit amused, at the sight of a Marine captain being put through this drill by two lance corporals whom could be heard saying, "Ten seconds over the time limit, sir. Let's try it again!"

At some point, I asked my teachers, "So, am I now as good at breaking down and reassembling this weapon as a new Marine right out of the School of Infantry?" They both replied that I was, but reminded me that to further acquaint myself with the weapon, I should get some "trigger time" with it during one of our upcoming live-fire training events.

I thanked them for taking the time to share their expertise with me and when I returned to my office, I made sure to tell the lieutenant and staff sergeant in charge of these Marines how well they'd done and asked them to relay my thanks to them. I also—as taught years earlier by one of my mentors—wrote a "Thank You" note on my personal "officer stationery" to each lance corporal.

The Tone at the Top

During the next several weeks, I received additional classes that familiarized me with various communications and encryption devices, night-vision optics, anti-tank missile systems, and other equipment that had been introduced since I last served in an infantry unit. In almost every instance, these classes were conducted by junior-enlisted Marines.

Aside from the obvious benefit of me acquiring a basic level of knowledge of the various types of equipment and weapons, the awareness among the members of the unit that their company commander was receiving instruction from junior-enlisted Marines sent a message to the members of the unit regarding my leadership philosophy. Some of these unstated but very-powerful messages included:

- Their new Captain was willing to learn from anyone (Ettore's Rule #19).

- It became obvious to all that I recognized that, in certain situations, junior-enlisted Marines were often the "untitled experts" and possessed more knowledge than the officers or staff noncommissioned officers (SNCOs) within the unit.

- My actions implied that I expected the same attitude (Ettore's Rule #23) from other leaders in the unit, including the officers and SNCOs.

- Having junior Marines teach me and other senior leaders reinforced to all members of the unit that, regardless of rank or experience, their leaders were counting on them to be competent in their specific duties.

This class and others like it, and the unspoken, yet powerful messages that resonated from them, helped to establish a culture that not only desired but demanded that all Marines be willing to *"Speak Truth to Power"* when necessary.

By getting out of my office and routinely interacting with junior Marines, I not only got to know them better, but I was able to get an unvarnished view of what was happening (or not happening) within the unit. Experienced Marine leaders can quickly learn much about a unit just by walking around, talking to

Marines, and observing them as they carry out their duties. It is imperative for commanders, despite the administrative demands of their position, to make the time to leave their office and go out among their Marines.

At this point, I hope that readers are starting to see the value in some of the concepts and techniques that I am writing about, and are reflecting on how they might integrate them into their own leadership "tool kit."

Thriving on the Corporate Battlefield

When I entered the corporate arena in 1999, I was unaware of many aspects of how a company conducted business operations. During one of the series of interviews that I went through prior to being hired into Kforce (NASDAQ:K-FRC), the executive conducting the interview used the term "back office" several times. I was so new to the business world that I didn't know what the term meant, so I asked, "What's the back office?"

I remember the executive looking a bit surprised at this question, but he patiently explained that this was a term used to refer to the "non-sales" support functions of the company, such as the human resources, finance, information technology, and marketing departments.

I was initially hired to serve in the newly created role of Director of Leadership Development, with a mandate to create a Leadership Development Program. Within several months, I assumed other responsibilities such as being in charge of developing a training department and a knowledge-management cell.

A couple of years later, I was asked to serve, in addition to my existing duties, as the Chief Information Officer and take over the company's information technology department (176 people), which had been struggling in various ways during recent times. Not long after that, a large finance-related team known as the "Order-to-Cash" group (180 people, including a team located in Manila) was added to my responsibilities, followed a few months later by the Human Resources department (25 people).

During this time, I was also tasked with creating a Program Management Office (15 people) that would oversee the planning and execution of various enterprise-level programs, projects, and initiatives. Soon after this, the Marketing department (8 people) was added to my responsibilities along with the direction to establish a Social Media function (6 people). Additionally, during this entire period of several years, I served as the executive sponsor for most of the administrative and logistical activities associated with the integration of companies that Kforce had acquired.

Now, I don't mention the above to impress you or inflate my ego; rather, to provide an adequate frame of reference regarding the rapidly expanding scope of my responsibilities. I also want to illustrate that in addition to facing the normal challenges associated with leading these teams, in some instances I was tasked with quickly taking whatever steps were required to "right a sinking ship" or create entirely new organizations that were expected to quickly produce results at the enterprise level.

Leadership Lessons

Obviously, I had no formal training or experience in any of the business or technical operations that were conducted by the various departments that I was being asked to lead or create. This was often quite interesting to observers and members of these organizations because, in some instances, I was given a publicly stated mandate to oversee the urgently needed repair or rebuilding of them.

Clearly, those who chose to assign these challenges to me—the firm's chief executive officer and president—were aware of my lack of professional knowledge and experience in those specific areas. They openly stated as much at several "all-hands" meetings attended by the members of the units being placed under my control. The CEO and president made it very clear that the main reason I was being assigned to lead these teams was to provide leadership and organizational skills, and to help these teams attain operational effectiveness and efficiency.

Now, while I do believe that I brought elevated levels of leadership and organizational skills to the table, all of these teams already had some very experienced and capable leaders within their ranks. Suffice it to say that without the loyalty, advice, and tireless efforts of these professionals, things would not have turned out as well as they usually did!

Even better, every unit that I was asked to lead at Kforce had many highly experienced, "untitled" experts at various levels, and these "lance corporals" were always willing to provide sage advice when asked what I refer to as "The 3 Big Questions:"

- What should we start doing?

- What should we stop doing?

- What should we do differently?

Together, leaders at all levels took the actions required to create a *"Culture of Execution"* within their teams, which all quickly became more capable of executing what were often very complex strategies, tactics, systems integrations, programs, and projects in the pursuit of enterprise-wide goals and objectives.

I want to ensure that credit is given where it is due: much of our success stemmed from the fact that we routinely sought the advice of our "lance corporals" and made them a key part of our decision-making and planning processes.

Listed below are some other concepts and lessons that I urge you to reflect upon:

- Leaders (and their organizations) will benefit greatly if they make it clear that they are willing to learn from anyone.

- Every organization has "untitled experts"—the business world's equivalent of Marine Corps lance corporals—whose experience and expertise are often greater than that of more senior leaders and teammates. Wise leaders know this and ensure that this incredibly valuable source of intellectual capital is valued and routinely leveraged throughout all facets of business operations.

- If senior leaders emphasize the previous two concepts by their own actions, all other leaders in the organization will adopt the same mindset and approach.

- Having the "untitled experts" and other select teammates teach or brief more senior leaders reinforces your expectations that all members of the organization should be highly competent and ready to explain various aspects of their specific roles and areas of expertise.

By doing and promoting all of the above, you will also send powerful messages that help establish a specific organizational culture—one that not only promotes *but demands* that all teammates "Speak Truth to Power" when appropriate.

Get out of your office and among your teammates as often as possible. The technique of "Leadership by Walking Around" is one that can yield countless benefits to you and the entire organization!

I can't resist the opportunity to revisit the irony of me naively asking, during the interview process prior to joining Kforce, "What's the back office?" Fast-forward several years and I was now the executive in charge of most of it, leading the teams that supported a firm with annual revenues in excess of $1 billion. Once more, I want to emphasize that I didn't do this by myself; I had many superb, loyal, and committed leaders and teammates supporting me through every step of this leadership journey. I merely leveraged them appropriately.

This should serve as a source of encouragement for those who aspire to serve in leadership roles of significant scope and responsibility. When it is all said and done, leadership skills and the ability to "make things happen" will help you achieve your career goals more than anything else, assuming your integrity and character are beyond reproach.

But ... you must be willing to listen to your lance corporals!

"The one exclusive sign of thorough knowledge
is the power of teaching."—Aristotle

Chapter 60

DO YOUR TEAMMATES MAKE THEIR BEDS?

On May 17, 2014, Admiral William H. McRaven, a Navy SEAL officer and the commander of US Special Operations Command, was the guest speaker at the graduation ceremony at The University of Texas at Austin. His commencement speech was titled "10 Life Lessons from Basic SEAL Training." During his speech, McRaven revealed a list of lessons he learned while training to become a frogman that had a profound influence on various aspects of his personal and professional life. An excerpt of his speech follows:

> "Every morning in basic SEAL training, my instructors, who at the time were all Vietnam veterans, would show up in my barracks room and the first thing they would inspect was your bed. If you did it right, the corners would be square, the covers pulled tight, the pillow centered just under the headboard and the extra blanket folded neatly at the foot of the rack—that's Navy talk for bed.

> It was a simple task—mundane at best. But every morning we were required to make our bed to perfection. It seemed a little ridiculous at the time, particularly in light of the fact that were aspiring to be real warriors, tough battle-hardened SEALs, but the wisdom of this simple act has been proven to me many times over.

If you make your bed every morning you will have accomplished the first task of the day. It will give you a small sense of pride, and it will encourage you to do another task and another and another. By the end of the day, that one task completed will have turned into many tasks completed. Making your bed will also reinforce the fact that little things in life matter. If you can't do the little things right, you will never do the big things right.

So, if you want to change the world, start off by making your bed." [218]

The admiral's speech was very well-received by everyone attending the commencement ceremony. It can be found in video or written format on various websites and I encourage you to watch or read it and reflect upon the simple, yet profound lessons contained in it.

Parris Island—June 1974

A little over 30 years prior to Admiral McRaven's now-famous speech, I was a recruit at the Marine Corps Recruit Depot at Parris Island, South Carolina. On the very first morning of training, our platoon's senior drill instructor (SDI) directed us to report to the quarterdeck—the open area at the end of the squad bay which was the large room where we lived. We did so, sprinting as fast as we could lest we be deemed to be "lacking motivation" and subjected to more of the incentive physical training that we had experienced earlier in the day!

The SDI told us to form a semicircle around a bunk bed, which are referred to as *racks* in the Marine Corps, and to sit down on the deck (the floor). It soon became obvious that he was about to teach us the proper method of making one's rack each morning. Assisted by a recruit, he proceeded to make the rack. He explained the various ways that we were to arrange and align the sheets and blanket, the exact measurements of the "hospital fold" at the head of the rack, how to create the precise corner folds of the sheets and blanket, and the precise placement of the pillow.

As he did this, I was impressed at how much attention to detail he demonstrated toward things I'd never even thought about before—proper creases in blankets, how to tuck in the corners of sheets, and even the right way to put a pillowcase on a pillow. My mother had taught me how to make my bed as a young child and I was expected to do so every morning before I left for school; but apparently in the Marine Corps, the making of one's rack had been elevated to an art form!

When the class was over, the SDI directed us to return to our racks and make them as we'd just been taught. He also said we had five minutes to complete this task and that we'd pay a heavy price if it wasn't done on time and to his satisfaction.

We ran back to our racks and began to make them up. I remember that the squad bay was a flurry of activity as sheets and blankets were being whipped through the air and placed on the racks. You could almost smell the sense of urgency in the air; we were "on the clock" and the allotted five minutes were rapidly fading away!

After a few minutes, the drill instructor yelled *"Stop...Stop...I SAID STOP!"* We all did so and stood at attention as we awaited whatever was coming next. He directed us all to look at him and then said, "Look at you! I'm disgusted by what I've just seen. You're obviously not Marines, but right now you're not even good recruits. You'll never make it through Parris Island if you think you can act like this."

The SDI let his words sink in for a very long 10 seconds or so of silence, during which we all wondered what we'd done wrong. "Look around you, what do you see?" he said. Without waiting for answers, he explained, "All of you are making your racks by yourself. You're acting like individuals, not as team-mates. This is not how Marines act when they are on a mission. The Marine Corps isn't looking for individuals, it needs Marines who are team players who understand that the way to win in combat is through teamwork and selflessness."

He let his words sink in for a few seconds and said, "You've got three minutes to get these racks squared away...*MOVE!*" As you might expect, the squad bay was immediately transformed into a flurry of two-man teams attacking their stated objective!

Long story made short: We didn't accomplish the mission within the allotted three minutes. We were taken outside to the "pit" (a 30' x 60' patch of dirt), where the SDI made us perform countless repetitions of various exercises—push-ups, leg-lifts, bends-and-thrusts, mountain-climbers, etc.—all while telling us how screwed-up we were as a platoon! After what seemed like an eternity, he yelled, *"STOP!"* and we stood at attention, sweating profusely in the blistering heat and humidity that smothers Parris Island during the summer months. I remember that this was the first time I'd ever heard a large group of winded men breathing so loudly.

The SDI told us to look at him and said, "Hopefully, you've all learned two important lessons this morning. First, when you are assigned a mission, you WILL accomplish it as directed and on time; failure is not an option. Second, the Marine Corps is a team and you're all at Parris Island trying to earn the right to be part of the team. The recruit to your left and right may serve with you in combat someday. I might be there with you, too. We are all going to have to work together to defeat the enemy and survive. If I ever again see you acting as individuals instead of as a platoon of team players, there will be hell to pay!"

We were then directed to run back into the barracks and finish making up our racks. I got with my bunky (the recruit who was assigned to the top rack; I was assigned to the lower one) and together we made up both racks, one at a time. Within a week or so, we (and the rest of the platoon) could make both racks to perfection in less than three minutes, without a word being spoken.

Leadership Lessons

Learning how to make my rack each morning as an impressionable 17-year-old recruit was as profound as any leadership lesson that I ever received in the Marine Corps. In fact, during my subsequent service as a Marine officer and later on in the private sector, I leveraged this technique by adapting it to fit specific environments or situations in which I was leading.

While serving as a C-level executive in a large, publicly traded company, as I took leadership of any team or unit, I always found ways early on to continuously emphasize the importance of everyone in the organization being *team players*. I had already personally observed that incredible things can be achieved by motivated men and women acting cohesively when they're focused on achieving well-defined goals. Thus, I knew that this was a critical factor in whether or not any business unit I was leading would simply be average or eventually become exceptional.

Now for Some Bad News

I must say that in almost every organization that I've ever assumed responsibility for, there were individuals at all levels who simply would not adopt a team-player mentality. These individuals can become exceptionally toxic if they are left unchecked. This is especially true if they are serving in leadership roles, because my experience has been that "non-team-player leaders" inevitably produce "non-team-playing organizations." Experienced leaders have all seen examples of this—that one department that always seems to be the source of non-compliance, nit-picking complaints, failure to produce deliverables on time, and other types of intentional friction.

And ... More Bad News

If you haven't yet experienced this as a leader, you certainly will at some point in time. Despite your noble intentions and best efforts, there will be individuals in your organization that will never "get with the program." It's best to acknowledge this and plan accordingly when assuming control of an organization; or if you are already leading one and desire to initiate a "course correction" regarding how your team executes its mission.

Dealing with Reality

My experience as a senior executive has shown me that when this concept is elevated to the organizational level, any leader unable (or unwilling) to get his or her team to act as team players and harness their energy and effort toward stated firm-wide goals and objectives will become a "brake on the wheel of progress" and eventually the entire organization will suffer.

Those who cannot or will not embrace a team-player philosophy will ALWAYS become a "toxic element" that endangers the development of the desired culture of the organization, and by default, the level of success it can achieve. Once it has been determined, through an appropriate amount of counseling over time, that these individuals will never be team players, they must be— regardless of tenure, title, or role—carved from the team much like a surgeon removes a malignant tumor from a patient. This may sound harsh, but experienced leaders know how damaging the presence of a single non-team player can be to the development of a team's cohesion, morale, and performance.

Finally, Some Good News!

The concept of teamwork and being a team player is one of the most endur-ing and unassailable themes in the business world. Most people really do want to be known for being great team players. Most have been taught since they were very young children that being a team player is the only way to be and that they should never intentionally do anything that would let down the team.

So, unlike some other concepts or techniques you might introduce to any or-ganization, this one typically is fully understood and well-received by almost all members of the team. In fact, I find that when addressing teams that have had a recent history of failure, friction, and divisiveness, you can sense, if not actually see, those in the audience nodding their heads in approval. They know that the team has talented individuals who can produce great results if they act as team players first and foremost.

There are many superb books and other sources of information on the team-building aspect of leadership. In addition to utilizing the knowledge and methods contained in them, I urge you to reflect upon these points:

- The most important philosophies, concepts, and lessons—ones that are critical to the creation and sustainment of an organization's cul-ture—are best delivered by the chief executive and continuously re-inforced by senior leaders. The lessons that the SDI taught my fellow recruits that day were deemed by him to be so important to our fu-ture success as Marines and the survival of the Marine Corps that he did not delegate this task. He knew, as do all seasoned and successful leaders, that <u>some messages are best delivered by the unit's senior leader.</u>

- Organizational excellence cannot be achieved unless every member of the team strives to attain what is often referred to as *"Brilliance in the Basics."*

- Leaders must ensure that their teammates know how to perform the basic tasks associated with their roles. You cannot expect them to adequately execute their tasks and duties if they are not trained ap-propriately.

- Leaders should, through their words and actions, continually emphasize the importance of teamwork and demand that their teammates embrace and demonstrate it every day. When the *"message from the top"* is that being a team player is non-negotiable, most people will respond accordingly, and amazing things will begin to happen in the organization.

- Even the most dysfunctional organizations can be quickly set upon the path to success if their people begin to work together as true team players.

- Carve out the unwilling and the unable. It's often difficult to do for a variety of reasons, but a leader must ensure that everyone on his or her team has the will and skill required to perform as needed. Please understand that I am not encouraging you to do this in an indifferent, mean-spirited, or demeaning manner; like most aspects of leadership, there are appropriate ways to terminate or otherwise remove people from your team.

Admiral McRaven's emphasis that *"If you can't do the little things right, you will never do the big things right"* is a simple yet critical lesson that all leaders should reflect upon from both a personal perspective and that of the teams they are privileged to lead.

Leaders: take the time to teach your teammates *"how to make their bed properly"* and make sure they make it every morning to exacting standards. Over time, you'll have a team capable of attaining excellence in all that they do!

"It is a common mistake in going to war to begin at the wrong end, to act first, and wait for disasters to discuss the matter." —Thucydides

"The most important philosophies, concepts, and lessons—ones that are critical to the creation and sustainment of an organization's culture—are best delivered by the chief executive and continuously reinforced by senior leaders."

—Mike Ettore

Sergeant Ettore

Marine Corps Recruit Depot, San Diego - 1977

Chapter 61

THE MARINE CORPS TRUSTED ME

The picture on the opposite page was taken in 1977 at the Marine Corps Recruit Depot in San Diego, California. I was 20 years old and the youngest drill instructor in the Marine Corps at that time.

The established policy at that time was that all drill instructors must be at least 21 years of age, though most of them were in their late 20s or early 30s. The leaders of the unit I was serving in knew I had a strong desire to serve as a drill instructor, and they approached the appropriate leaders at the Marine Corps headquarters on my behalf. The age requirement was waived, and I was soon attending Drill Instructor School.

This course was by far the most professionally executed and demanding of any school or training program that I ever attended during my career, including those attended during my subsequent service as a commissioned officer. I knew from the moment that I checked in that I was going to have to "bring my A-Game" every single day of this course if I hoped to walk across the grinder a few months later and into a squad bay full of recruits.

Aside from being an exceptional course from a curriculum standpoint, the atmosphere among the students and instructors was one that truly embodied General John A. Lejeune's 1921 directive that urged Marine leaders to promote a *Teacher-Scholar* relationship with the Marines they were entrusted to lead. Another of General Lejeune's most important and long-lasting principles, the *Special Trust and Confidence* granted to Marine leaders and the high expectations of those privileged to lead Marines, was demonstrated by the instructor staff toward the students.

Including me.

As the fresh-faced, non-hash-mark-wearing "baby" of the class, I was quickly noticed by the instructor staff and fellow students alike. To say that I was the target of a lot of good-natured jokes and comments about my inexperience is an understatement.

I can remember that during one inspection, the inspector, a veteran of the Korean and Vietnam conflicts, looked at me and asked, "Ettore, what's that smell?" I didn't know what to say, but a few seconds later he said, "Oh, I know what it is, it's the smell of mothballs. Your uniform is so new it's probably never been dry-cleaned, right?" This, of course, drew howls of laughter from the entire formation and the Gunny patted me on the shoulder as if to say, "Just kidding with you, Devil Dog!" He did make note of my Rifle Expert badge and said, "At least you can shoot."—which I took as a rare compliment!

Obviously, I graduated from the course and went on to work with my first platoon. When graduation-day ceremonies were finished, all of the drill instructors and officers in the recruit series were going to attend a party at a local "DI hang-out," a bar named "The Anchor." There was just one problem: I was still 20 and the legal drinking age was 21. I mentioned this to the Series Gunnery Sergeant, and he said, "Not a problem. Just show up. I'll let the bar's owner know." By the time I arrived, most of the other drill instructors and officers were already there and when I walked in, I noticed that many of them were "eyeballing" me; I knew that something was about to happen.

I went to the bar to be with some of my peers and the bartender asked me, "Are you Sergeant Ettore?" I replied that I was. She said, "We've been waiting for you. We have your drink all ready for you!" She then placed a glass of milk on the bar in front of me. At this point, the entire crowd erupted in laughter (some of them had already consumed more than a few beers) and once again, the joke was on me!

Now, to get serious (and to the point of this article): aside from being ribbed mercilessly about my age and lack of experience, the truth is that the Marine Corps trusted me as much as it trusted noncommissioned officers (NCOs) and staff noncommissioned officers (SNCOs) of much greater tenure and experience. All that mattered to my leaders was that I was wearing the stripes of a Marine Corps sergeant and the hard-earned, broad-brimmed "campaign cover" that is bestowed upon drill instructors. I was afforded the same level of trust and had to live up to the same high expectations associated with being a Marine drill instructor as everyone else.

Lessons For Business Leaders

After I retired from the Marine Corps in 1998 and went on to work in business and, eventually, as a leadership coach, I never forgot this lesson of trust.

I teach all of my clients, no matter what level they are serving at, about the importance of Trust-Based Leadership™. This form of leadership is exactly what its name implies; it's based on mutual trust up and down the organizational structure and across the boundaries of divisions, departments, and teams.

I've found that the *very best* leaders in Corporate America almost all practice some of the Trust-Based Leadership concepts and principles that I teach and experienced in the Marine Corps. That said, the *majority* of business leaders I encounter do not approach leadership from the perspective of trust.

Ultimately, my discussions with the "non-trusters" lead to the fact that they have been "burned" or "stabbed in the back" in the past, and this has soured them on the idea of empowering and trusting their peers and teammates. Some of these leaders muster the courage required to "trust again" but some cannot bring themselves to do it, fearing poor results or even betrayal at the hands of their colleagues. I applaud those in the former group and feel genuine sadness for the latter—knowing that without the ability to trust others, it's unlikely that they will ever attain their maximum potential and the potential of the teams they lead.

My advice for all leaders is to take some time to reflect on this issue and ask themselves:

"Do I trust and am I trusted?"

Be honest with yourself. And if you don't like the answers you're hearing in your mind, take action to remedy this situation.

Trust starts with the leader.

If you give it, you will receive it.

There are undoubtedly many young and talented "milk-drinking babies" in your organization that are waiting for an opportunity to add greater value— but are not currently being allowed to do it.

Here's the bottom line: Identify the deserving and give them the "stripes and authority" to go forth and do great things for their teams.

Trust them.

Lead them.

Teach them everything you know.

Give them room to grow and try new things.

You won't be disappointed.

Trust-Based Leadership ... it starts with you!

"Four things come back not; the spoken word, the sped arrow, time past and the neglected opportunity."—Arab Proverb

Chapter 62

I FAILED TWICE THAT DAY:
LESSONS FOR LEADERS

The Bar Fight

One of the ways a leader can exhibit moral courage is to support and, in some instances, come to the defense of one of their team members. An example from my past involves a young corporal assigned to my unit who got into trouble one night while he and some of his peers were in town enjoying a few beers. At some point during the evening, a civilian male approached him at the bar and began making insulting comments about the Marine Corps and various other things. Basically, this guy was looking for a fight and had chosen this Marine as his opponent.

The corporal, by all eye-witness accounts, tried his best to ignore the guy. As the man continued to goad the Marine with taunts of increasing severity and implications of violence, the corporal decided that it was probably best if he and his friends left the bar so they could be rid of this pest. The sight of the corporal leaving the bar was evidently a blow to the man's ego, and he decided that punching the Marine was something he had to do. And he did just that—punching the Marine squarely in the chest sending him backward into a wall. The corporal still tried to avoid a fight and told the man, "Look, I just want to leave. I don't want any trouble."

Undeterred, the man came at the Marine. As he wound up for another punch, the corporal rightfully decided that it was time to defend himself. He blocked the man's second punch with his left forearm while delivering a solid punch to his nose with his right hand; the man fell to the ground with blood gushing from his nostrils. The bar's bouncers and other staff had seen everything, and they told the Marine and his buddies to simply leave and that they'd handle things.

A couple of days later, however, the local police contacted the Marine base. This man had pressed charges against the corporal, claiming that he had been assaulted by the Marine at the bar. The police representative also conveyed that the man's nose had been broken by the corporal's punch and he had been treated for a concussion at a local hospital, likely caused by hitting his head on the floor after the hit. Obviously, the man's pride had been hurt. And knowing that the "physical option" didn't work out too well for him, he was now seeking "administrative vengeance."

Moral Cowardice

Once we had determined the facts related to this incident, we were confident that any charges made against the corporal would be dismissed. Things became more serious as the chain of command at the regimental and division level became aware of this situation, however. It quickly became obvious that for whatever reason (I suspect that the new commanding general's zero-tolerance policy toward "alcohol-related incidents" was the rationale) some senior leaders were viewing this situation as one in which the corporal had done something wrong. Incredibly, we were told that this incident was likely going to be addressed by the regimental commander.

This colonel had a reputation for being a "self-promoter." It was obvious to everyone that he was willing to do whatever was necessary to curry favor with his seniors in hopes of enhancing his chances of being selected on the upcoming brigadier general selection board.

Many of you know that the Marine Corps motto is "Semper Fidelis," which is Latin for "Always Faithful"—and that this is often shortened to "Semper Fi." This particular officer was what Marines referred to as a *"Semper I"* type: a leader who was truly always faithful ... but only to his own self-interests. It's probably pretty obvious that I did not hold this colonel in high regard. In fact, as I type this story, I can feel my teeth clenching and my body stiffening at the mere thought of him. This guy was one of the worst leaders I was exposed to during my career in the Marine Corps.

Despite my best efforts, including the strong support of my battalion commander, the corporal was indeed scheduled by the regimental commander to receive a form of military discipline known as an Article 15 hearing within 7–10 days. Clearly, this corporal was about to become the victim of a politically motivated witch-hunt, and I was determined to do everything I could to stop it. I quickly made it known that I wanted to speak with the regimental commander but received word that he was too busy. It was added that he would hear what I had to say during the disciplinary proceedings, should I desire to serve as a character witness for the corporal.

I was truly disappointed by this entire situation and the rather gutless conduct of the regimental commander and more than a few senior Marines (officer and enlisted). In my opinion, they were willing to abandon the corporal because they knew that the commanding general insisted on making examples out of anyone who dared to violate (in any way) his zero-tolerance policy toward alcohol-related incidents. I didn't know what to say to the corporal, other than that I thought he'd done nothing wrong and that I was going to do my best for him in front of the regimental commander the following week.

Tragedy Strikes

A day or so later, during the early hours of a Saturday morning, I received a call from one of my officers who informed me that one of the Marines in his platoon had experienced an unspeakable tragedy. While he and his wife were out on a "date night," their home had caught fire and their four children, along with the babysitter, had died in the blaze. Upon hearing this sad news, I hurriedly put on my uniform and went to my office on base so my staff and I could take the appropriate actions to help this Marine and his wife in their time of need.

In this situation, the chain of command performed as you'd hope it would—leaders at every level within and outside of the unit offered their assistance. I went to see the young Marine to offer my condolences and suffice it to say that he was completely distraught over what had just happened. I did my best to say whatever one can possibly say in a situation like this but being the father of two children at the time, I knew that there was nothing I could really do to stem the profound grief this young man and his wife were feeling, and would feel for the rest of their lives.

A few days later, we received notice that the funeral services for the children were taking place the following Friday at 1 pm. It is customary in such situations for members of a Marine's chain of command to attend funerals and memorial services, and I was planning on doing so along with several other members of my staff. But my executive officer took me aside and informed me that the funeral services were scheduled for the same day and time as the disciplinary proceedings being conducted for the corporal who had been in the bar fight.

The Dilemma

This was one of the worst positions that I was ever in as a leader. I knew that I was going to have to make a choice between attending the funeral services or living up to my promise to the corporal that I'd be at his hearing and do my best for him. Asking the regimental commander to reschedule the disciplinary proceedings for the corporal did not go over well with members of his staff, and it became clear that there was no possibility of that happening. Of course, there was no way I would consider doing something as inappropriate as requesting that the Marine and his wife reschedule the funeral services because I had another urgent commitment. No, both events were going to happen at the same time, and I had to decide which one I would attend.

My Decision

I chose to attend the corporal's disciplinary hearing. My rationale was that my personal endorsement while serving as a character witness for him was likely one of his only chances for escaping unjust punishment. I could send another officer or a staff noncommissioned officer, but the reality was that none of them would be able to replicate the aggressiveness and forceful support that I had planned on displaying to the regimental commander. Frankly, he was known to be a bully, and I have always had a knack for doing well when facing bullies. In this situation, I felt that certain aspects of my professional reputation, personality, and manner of speaking could prove to be the difference for the corporal—I simply had to be there for him as I had promised I would.

I asked my executive officer and first sergeant to attend the funeral services and they did, along with most of the rest of the officers and enlisted leaders from the unit. In addition to these leaders, many others from outside of the unit attended the services. It was a superb display of the Marine tradition of closing ranks around another Marine in need of support.

The Aftermath

The disciplinary hearing did not go very well for the corporal. Despite my best efforts in front of the regimental commander (who twice warned me to watch my tone of voice when speaking to him), the corporal was found guilty of some minor form of misconduct. He was fined a portion of his pay for the next month and restricted to the barracks for 15 days. Because of this stain on his official record, he was also denied the opportunity to reenlist a few months later, and the Corps lost the services of a very good Marine who'd likely have stayed in for 20 or more years. What happened to this Marine was truly an injustice, perhaps the most blatant example of abuse of power and moral cowardice by a senior officer (and a few other officers and senior-enlisted Marines) that I personally witnessed during my career in the Corps.

By all accounts, the funeral services for the children were carried out with the proper level of respect and solemnity; and the Marine and his wife thanked those in attendance for their love and support. I was gratified upon hearing this, and a few days later I called the Marine into my office to speak with him about some assistance the command was going to provide to him and his wife. I told him once again that I was sorry for his loss and that I was glad that the funeral services had turned out well.

What followed next was something I shall never forget. He looked straight at me and said, *"Well, you wouldn't know, because you weren't there!"* The look on his face said it all. I couldn't tell if he was showing more disappointment than disgust toward me, but he was clearly feeling a lot of both.

His comments pierced my heart as if I'd been shot.

I literally could not say anything for a very long ten seconds or so. Then I said, "Lance Corporal 'Jones,' I'm sorry you feel that way. I wanted to be there, but I had to attend Corporal 'Smith's' disciplinary hearing. I tried to get it rescheduled so I could be at the funeral, but it couldn't be done. I'm sorry." He again looked at me and said, "That's bullshit. You'd have been there if you really cared."

These were more words that essentially pierced the very core of my soul. This Marine, at that time anyway, truly felt that I had let him and his wife down. Even worse, he believed that I *simply didn't care enough* to be there for him and his wife when they needed me.

I knew that he was still in a state of shock after the loss of his children, and was venting at me more to blow off steam than to actually insult me. I also knew that allowing him to vent—and he was of course doing so in a disrespectful manner—wouldn't change the fact that, at this moment, this Marine despised me and nothing I could say would change his mind. Rather than continue to attempt to explain my decision to him, I told him once more that I was sorry for his loss. I then explained that the first sergeant was waiting for him in his office to discuss the possibility of him and his wife moving into base housing since their home had been destroyed. He nodded his head and left my office.

I turned around and stared out of the office window for a very long time and reflected upon what just happened. At that moment, I felt as if a part of me had died—I had let one of my Marines down! The fact that circumstances had forced me to make the choice I made did nothing to assuage my sorrow at letting one of my Marines down.

This was one of the worst days I've ever had as a leader. And it was made even worse knowing that I really did care for this Marine and had already taken action (behind the scenes and unknown to him) to bypass many of the administrative challenges of helping his family. We had worked to enable him and his wife to quickly move into a new home on the base, to get him new uniforms issued free of charge, and to get him temporarily assigned to duties that would allow him maximum time off to be with his wife during this tragic time.

I can honestly say that I felt a level of sadness as profound as the occasions when I have seen Marines lose their lives.

Reflection

There are many sayings associated with leadership and the two that come to my mind about the scenarios I just described are: *"At times, leadership can be a very lonely profession"* and President Harry Truman's well-known declaration that *"The buck stops here!"* The two situations described in this story, because they happened at the same time, presented me with leadership challenges involving moral courage, loyalty, judgement, decisiveness, and tact, to name just a few.

Many years later, I can still honestly say that I made what I thought were the best decisions based on the challenges I was facing. I chose to be where I believed my physical presence was truly needed and could potentially provide the most benefit. As much as I disliked the thought of not attending the funeral services, I knew that my executive officer and many other leaders from the unit would be there to support the Marine and his wife as they endured burying their four young children.

Failure

Nevertheless, the reality is that, when all was said and done, <u>I had failed twice on that day</u>. Despite my forceful and nearly insubordinate pleas and the recommendations of others that he be absolved of all wrong-doing, the corporal involved in the bar fight was unjustly hammered by the regimental commander. And by failing to adequately convey in advance to Lance Corporal Jones and his wife why I could not attend the funeral services, there was now a Marine who despised me and undoubtedly held me in contempt for not being what a Marine officer was supposed to be. This was tough to admit at that time because, in my mind, I'd done everything possible to handle both situations properly and with the best interests of both Marines as my sole motivation.

Lessons For Business Leaders

As painful as they were at the time, I became a better leader from these experiences. Many leadership concepts were validated, and other lessons were learned during the situations described in this story. My subsequent experience as a senior executive proved that most were applicable to serving in leadership roles in the business world. Some of these lessons are listed below and I encourage you to reflect upon them:

- As a leader, you will be confronted with challenging situations that require you to make difficult choices. Base your decisions on what's best for the institution and its people. Sometimes these clash with each other and it's difficult to do both to the degree you'd like to. Seek advice, reflect upon various options that may be available and make the best decision you can.

- Leaders are human and humans make mistakes. When something doesn't turn out as desired—despite your best intentions and motives—admit it, accept responsibility for it, and reflect upon what you might be able to do differently when faced with similar situations in the future.

- Some of your decisions will prove to be wrong, ineffective, and, in some instances, perhaps even destructive or hurtful to others. Face the aftermath head-on and be willing to admit mistakes or the fact that you caused unintended consequences.

- Be willing to apologize, even when others aren't ready to accept apologies.

- Keep your promises. If you say you're going to do something for someone—do it!

- Support your teammates—when the situation warrants it—even when it is unpopular to do so or could cause friction with your seniors.

- There will always be people in positions of authority who lack the moral courage to stand up for what's right. Sometimes they will be your boss or your boss' boss. Be aware of this and do your best to negate the impact of such individuals on your team.

Many of us have encountered natural leaders—people who instinctively do the right thing and make leading look rather effortless when compared to others or even ourselves. If you're truly one of these leaders, good for you! If not—like the majority of us—leadership is something that must be learned and continuously developed.

I hope that by reflecting upon the lessons contained in this article, you'll gain new or deeper perspective on some aspect of leadership. At a minimum, this story should help you understand that <u>if you are a leader, you will have bad days. And you must learn from them!</u>

"I will keep constant watch over myself and—most usefully—will put each day up for review. For this is what makes us evil—that none of us looks back upon our own lives. We reflect upon only that which we are about to do. And yet our plans for the future descend from the past."—Seneca

Chapter 63

WE'VE ALWAYS DONE IT THIS WAY!

During my time as an executive, I leveraged many of the lessons I learned in the Corps, both in the pursuit of operational excellence and in an effort to develop other leaders. I have found that stories and anecdotes are an effective method of conveying lessons and concepts to my teammates and leadership students. These stories will often cause even a busy, experienced executive to pause and reflect upon whether their approach is the right way to tackle an issue they might be facing. In this article, I share a story that contains lessons that can be applied to leaders at all levels in any type of organization.

Throughout its history, the Marine Corps has been well-known as an institution that sets and maintains high standards. That said, like any organization, it often falls victim to a *"that's the way we've always done it"* mentality. Thus, Marine leaders are not only charged with establishing and enforcing standards, they are also responsible for routinely "shining the light" on them to ensure that they are realistic and relevant. It is imperative, regardless how difficult it may be at times, that the standards a Marine leader is responsible for enforcing directly relate to the achievement of their objective.

As I began my military career, I served as an enlisted Marine for four years (1974-1978). When my enlistment ended, I enrolled in college with the intention of becoming a commissioned officer once I obtained my degree. In 1981, I was going through the administrative process of applying for officer candidate school (OCS) with the local Marine officer recruiter. This Marine Corps captain was aware that I was a member of my college's wrestling team and, almost immediately during our first meeting, he asked me if I had undergone any knee surgeries. I replied that I had indeed had four knee operations over the past several years. His face immediately took on a very concerned look and he said, "Mike, this is very important: do you know if the doctors used any metal wire, mesh, or anything similar during your operations?" I told him that, to the best of knowledge, they hadn't, and I asked him why this was so important.

The captain explained that Navy medical officers (The Navy handles all medical issues for the Marine Corps) had reviewed data over the past decade or so that showed that individuals who had metallic implants had experienced a very high rate of physical failure due to recurring knee problems either during OCS or after they were commissioned. Because of these issues, a policy had been instituted to automatically disqualify any applicant who had any metal or foreign material in their knee joints.

The medical policy at the time did allow applicants to have knee operations, providing the appropriate Navy medical officers determined that the individual's joints were strong, stable, and fully functional. I remember that I had to go through two special physical examinations that were solely focused on evaluating my knees. These examinations included my being asked to "duck-walk" across the room, do deep-knee bends while carrying a heavy sandbag, climb stairs, and perform other tests to see if my knees were fully functional.

While I was going through these tests, I had two friends who were also very interested in becoming Marine officers. Both were exceptional athletes (wrestlers) and were among the strongest and fittest men I have ever known. However, they had both also had knee operations, and their surgeons had used metal wire to repair their joints. As a result, they were both medically disqualified from applying to any Marine Corps commissioning programs. This was a devastating blow to these two young men, who had aspired to be Marine officers from a very early age.

At the suggestion of the Marine captain whom we were interacting with while applying to OCS, both of these men decided to see if any of the other branches of the armed forces would allow them to apply for commissioning programs. To make a long story short, one of these men became an Army Special Forces officer and the other a Navy SEAL officer, because the SEALs were smart enough to know when to disagree with Navy policy. Both went on to serve with distinction for over 20 years in the special operations community.

I'm confident you can see how a policy based on the *possibility* that these two young men *might* not make it through OCS due to their knee surgeries—or be able to perform well in their subsequent service units—was flawed. The fact that both managed to graduate from two of the most physically demanding special operations selection courses in the world and serve for over two decades in very physically demanding environments, including combat operations, clearly illustrates that flaw. In fact, neither of them ever experienced significant problems with their knees at any point during their military service.

Unfortunately, what happened to my friends routinely occurred during that era. During the course of my Marine Corps career, I personally heard of a few dozen situations like these, in which very capable individuals were arbitrarily disqualified from service in the Marine Corps based on outdated medical policies. In many cases, those same individuals went on to serve with distinction in another branch of the armed forces.

Once, while attending a training course run by another service, I met an Army officer who told me that he was rejected by the Marine Corps because he had wire mesh in one of his knees (he had been a Division I lacrosse player). This officer was exceptionally physically fit and served two tours in the 75th Ranger Regiment. Subsequently, he became a career Special Forces officer and ultimately retired from the Army as a major general. We became close friends and I'm still in contact with him. I often good-naturedly remind him that while he was good enough to become an Army general officer, he didn't meet the standards to serve as a Marine second lieutenant. Needless to say, he always delivers some terse replies to my teasing on this topic.

Sadly, the Marine Corps allowed a high number of highly qualified and talented individuals to slip away because of an outdated policy in that era. In my opinion, the senior Marine officers in charge of officer recruiting at that time had become complacent. They'd probably failed to routinely ask senior Navy medical officers if the standards for Marine commissioning programs were aligned with modern medical concepts and practices.

Lessons for Business Leaders

A fundamental principle of Marine Corps leadership is that a leader is responsible for all that his or her unit does or fails to do. In the situation described in this article, I believe the general officer in charge of Marine Corps recruiting should have ensured that the medical standards being applied to potential officer candidates were relevant and realistic.

This type of complacency (or worse) happens routinely in organizations of all types; leaders at every level are always very busy and can easily fall victim to the *"that's the way we've always done it"* mentality. An effective leader knows this and does whatever is necessary to ensure that the strategies, standards, policies, and procedures he or she is enabling and enforcing are relevant, realistic, and actually helping the organization achieve its goals and objectives.

I urge you to take some time to reflect and ask yourself, "Is anything like this happening in my organization? Are we suffering in any way due to outdated, unrealistic, or unnecessarily rigid policies or rules?"

Here are some additional questions to ponder while figuring out whether you may need to *"shine the light"* on various aspects of your company's culture and business operations:

- Do you constantly promote an environment in which your teammates can *"speak truth to power?"*

- Do you routinely ask for feedback on existing strategies, standards, policies, and procedures?

- How often do you ask your teammates the 3 Big questions?

   o What should we start doing?

   o What should we stop doing?

   o What should we do differently?

- Have you asked your teammates to offer suggestions on how to streamline and improve the existing meeting/reporting schedules and practices?

- Do you consider the best-qualified individuals for promotion to certain roles, or do you only consider those who possess certain degrees or experience? In other words, would you ever consider assigning a proven operations leader to serve in a human resources leadership role, or do you insist on considering only "HR professionals" for such roles?

- How often do you meet with peers from other companies to share best practices and thoughts on new challenges facing your industry?

- Do you read various industry-specific and general business publications to stay abreast of new technologies and concepts that may benefit your organization?

- Do you require the leaders within your organization to do all of the above on a routine basis?

It is imperative that you, as a leader, constantly strive to maintain high standards of operations within your team. It is equally important, however, that you constantly review standards and policies to ascertain whether they are relevant to the accomplishment of the company's overall objectives. Don't allow outdated or flawed policies to jeopardize the effectiveness of your efforts, or to derail you from accomplishing your mission.

"Receive without conceit; release without struggle." — *Marcus Aurelius*

Chapter 64

LET YOUR LEADERS LEAD!

I was taught early on that one of a Marine leader's most important responsibilities was the development of other leaders. I also learned, from personal experience and by observing others, that there were many ways to effectively do this. I want to share one particular technique with you because it not only conveys what I believe are some sound leadership philosophies and principles, but it's also one that can be easily replicated and utilized in almost any organization.

During peacetime operations, most Marine units operate by following a basic daily routine when they're not in the field training. Part of this routine includes what are considered normal working hours such as 7:00 am to 5:00 pm. When the work day is concluded, the members of the unit are typically free to leave the area and do whatever they wish until the start of the next day's activities.

All Marine units maintain a leadership presence after normal working hours, however, by assigning an officer or a staff noncommissioned officer (SNCO), and a noncommissioned officer (NCO) to remain in the area overnight. These individuals provide general supervision and handle any situations that may arise during off-hours. Such situations can vary from the sudden loss of proper heating or air conditioning in the barracks to a disruption in the delivery of scheduled meals in the unit's chow hall to the news that members of the unit have been injured in a car accident.

Essentially, these Marines serve as the commanding officer's representatives during this period of time and they are expected to make timely and appropriate decisions while addressing any and all situations that may occur.

The Logbook

The Marines serving in these supervisory roles all maintain an official logbook in which they make annotations of events that occur on their watch, along with any actions they have taken to address them. Most of the things that "make the logbook" are not significant and can be adequately addressed within the unit's chain of command.

However, there are situations that are more serious (the "two kinds of famous" adage applies here!) and come to the attention of leaders much higher in the command structure. These scenarios can quickly result in phone calls and emails being sent "downhill" to the unit's leaders, asking them for updates on what is being done to address the problem. Stress levels can spike rather quickly when junior leaders are told, "The colonel needs to be briefed on this as soon as possible, because the general just called him and he wants answers now!"

The Typical Approach

It is customary for Marine leaders to "check the logbook" when they come into work early each morning so they can gain awareness of anything (good or bad) that happened overnight that may require additional attention. Typically, the officers and SNCOs arrive at work very early each day and they often hear of events that "made the logbook" at the same time. Together, they set a course of action that needs to be taken to address the problem. Often, however, the unit commander is on scene and he or she naturally assesses the situation and issues the appropriate directions.

Now, this is not necessarily a bad thing. But the presence of the commander often eliminates the opportunity for subordinate leaders to exercise their own judgement and leadership in the situation at hand. This, of course, does little to develop them as leaders and to prepare them for the day when they will serve in more senior roles.

My Approach

To prevent this from happening in the units that I commanded, I deliberately arranged my daily schedule so that I would be at the base gym working out during the early morning hours while my other leaders were arriving at work at 6:00 am. I also recommended to my junior officers that they should do the same (or anything else they desired to do), as long as they did not arrive at work before the SNCOs and NCOs did, and explained why I was giving them this guidance.

Obviously, as a leader who was very focused on developing other leaders, my intention was to remove myself and my officers from this early morning routine and allow the SNCOs and NCOs to take charge of any situations that needed to be addressed. My expectations (and I shared them with all of my leaders whenever I assumed command of a unit) were that by the time I arrived at work at 7 a.m., the SNCOs and NCOs would have already assessed any existing situations and problems. They also must have taken the actions required to resolve them *or*, when appropriate, stood ready to provide their officers and me with *recommended* actions.

In other words, I refused to deny these leaders the opportunity to exercise authority and make decisions that they were all fully capable of. And it was always evident that they truly appreciated the trust I was affording them. They never let me down. I can honestly say that my SNCOs and NCOs always provided superb leadership and judgement in these situations.

While serving as an enlisted Marine, I was fortunate to serve with leaders who placed the same level of trust in me along with the high expectations that my leadership and judgement were up to the task. Thus, I knew how motivating and energizing a leadership technique like this could be, and how much learning and development could result from allowing leaders of all grades to *actually lead*.

This technique, though obviously not "rocket science," was unfortunately not common in many Marine units. Even a decentralized, trust-based organization like the Marine Corps is not immune to the "disease" of micromanagement. This was not my style, however. I suppose I could be rightfully accused of making many mistakes as a leader of Marines, but being a micromanager was not one of them. Instead, I preferred to push as much authority as possible downward through the chain of command, knowing that the short- and long-term benefits to my junior leaders and the Marine Corps as a whole were quite significant.

Trust. Delegate. Empower. Supervise.

This technique, which is based on an overarching leadership philosophy of trusting one's subordinate leaders and empowering them to learn and grow as leaders, works every bit as well in the private sector as it did in the Marine Corps. I know this to be true because I employed it during my business career with individuals at every level of leadership. And whether they were executives and vice presidents or directors, managers, or supervisors, I observed the same level of energy and motivation from leaders who truly appreciated the opportunity to lead.

If you are in a leadership role, I recommend that you first assess whether or not you are providing sound leadership and judgement that benefits *your* immediate leader. If these elements are not at the level you'd like them to be, take the steps necessary to be someone that he or she can count on to make good decisions.

Next, I urge you to take a close look at your environment and identify operations, events, and situations that offer potential opportunities for *your subordinate* leaders to exercise authority and judgement, just like my SNCOs and NCOs did. The example of me going to the gym each morning so that I was not likely to stifle their decision-making may not apply to your specific situation—but I have no doubt that anyone reading this book can easily find several situations in which they can "take a step backward" and give others more opportunity to utilize and develop their leadership skills.

Leaders who do this realize numerous benefits, including higher engagement and loyalty among employees and the development of teammates they can trust. But the main assets for a Trust-Based Leadership™ model are better-performing teams that can function in the absence of a leader. Trust-based leaders must commit to leveraging these opportunities *to leverage others*—doing so benefits you, your teammates, and the long-term success of your organization.

*"We must remember that one man is much
the same as another, and that he is best who is
trained in the severest school." — Thucydides*

Chapter 65

5 LEADERSHIP "BLIND SPOTS"

The *Merriam-Webster Dictionary* defines the term "blind spot" as follows:

Blind Spot:

- *an area where a person's view is obstructed.*

- *an area in which a person lacks understanding or impartiality.*

- *an area in which one fails to exercise judgement or discrimination.*

Blind spots can result from a variety of factors. Some leaders are overly stretched, others can become victims of time mismanagement, and yet others can simply become overly self-confident—or complacent—and feel that their leadership style is perfect as it is.

Everyone, including the most seasoned and successful leaders, can fall victim to blind spots. No matter how hard we try to be self-aware, we can all unintentionally engage in unproductive behaviors that are invisible to us, but often glaringly obvious to everyone else.

The important lesson to remember is that a leader's *learning journey* is never *done.* There is always room for improvement and growth, and leaders should never allow ego or pride to get in the way of seeking them.

Why are Blind Spots Dangerous?

When we are lacking certain skills or haven't reached a specific technical level that is needed for our role, that is an easy fix. However, blind spots are dangerous because we are completely *unaware* that they even exist! It's impossible to fix something that you don't know needs fixing.

Some of the most common blind spots that seem to surface in higher-level leaders are personal traits or aspects they don't even know about that may limit the way they act, react, behave, or believe, and therefore limit their effectiveness.

Prevalent Blind Spots in Leaders

(1) **Not Asking for Help:** Usually this is a problem because the individual who has reached a certain level of leadership starts to believe that they know best. In fact, as we've discussed in the past modules, one of the leadership traps occurs when "we don't know what we don't know." It's important, no matter what level we reach, to always remember that we don't know everything, that there are others whose vast amount of experience we can access, and that you will get farther with appropriate help than on your own.

(2) **Insensitivity:** When you are unaware of how you come across to others, the likelihood of changing is null. If you're displaying insensitive behavior toward others, whether they are peers or direct reports, you are destroying the morale of your team and of the organization. Emotional intelligence, as a manager or leader of people, is absolutely crucial.

(3) **Unwillingness to Deal with Conflict:** We all know that one of the most difficult parts of being a manager or leader is having to deal with conflict. Oftentimes, some of the decisions that some leaders make are solely based on their desire to avoid it. Worse yet is a situation where their unwillingness to handle conflict renders them incapable of making a decision!

It is very important that leaders learn *how* to deal with conflict. Although we have presented you with various lessons on how good, solid leadership practices are really the best way to prevent it, the fact is that you *will* have to deal with some form of conflict when dealing with human beings who have human emotions. It's very, very important that you are prepared for those occasions.

(4) **Ambivalence:** When you are unable to make firm, resolute decisions—regardless of the reasons why—you are ineffective as a leader. Sometimes, you may not even realize that you are being indecisive if you keep asking for information or data points on something that has been exhaustively researched; or you may not know which side of an argument to stand on; or you may just not want to commit to something simply because you are unsure of the result.

The truth is, we all face circumstances like these at some point. And, yes, the decision we make may not always pan out or have the best results. But as a *leader*, it is your job to show confidence and to stand by what you believe and know—it is your job to make decisions and to *lead.*

(5) **Conformity:** I believe this is a two-part issue.

- One part has to do with acting unethically in the work place. This can mean simply being less than truthful; or conspiring against a peer or others at work; or turning a blind eye to or even performing acts that can be considered unethical or illegal. This often happens when you work in an organization where values have been compromised—usually for a long time—and unethical behavior is the norm rather than the exception. If you are in this situation and simply go along to get along, you are no longer on the path of great or even good leadership.

- The second part of conformity as a blind spot is when you forget that striving for excellence is a constant requirement for a World-Class Leader. Some leaders—in accordance with the culture of their organization—often reward conformity and punish critical or questioning voices. This is especially true of organizations that have existed for a decade or more, because bureaucracies are often created, along with silos and competing agendas among the various leaders and their teams.

When a collective worldview becomes self-reinforcing around a set of practices, assumptions, or beliefs, there is potential for *groupthink*. Creativity and agility suffer because conformance is valued above change, and risk is discouraged. These are considered *strategy* blind spots, and they can occur among leaders in any type of organizations and at all levels. They're not restricted to values. Unfortunately, they are often spotted in hindsight, after an important opportunity is missed.

Leaders who prize openness and transparency have the best chance of spotting strategy blind spots. They encourage input at all levels, fostering a culture of trust where ideas are honestly debated and <u>teammates feel comfortable speaking truth to power</u>.

Leadership Lessons

To be a successful leader, you must become intimately aware of your weaknesses and biases, as well as other aspects of your personality that can derail you and your team. A blind spot's effects may not show up right away, so if you're not paying close attention, you may miss the warning signs. It's therefore critical for you to proactively work toward discovering them, before you feel the effects. The following actions can help you identify and overcome your blind spots:

- **Trusted Circle:** Ensure that you have at least one person (preferably more) in your inner circle whose professional capabilities and motives you are certain you can trust. This is a person who is "first among equals" in offering you feedback about your behavior and decisions; a person you can count on to "shoot straight" when you are asking for honest feedback about yourself.

- **Demand That Your Teammates "Speak Truth to Power":** Seasoned and confident leaders surround themselves with a diverse team of smart people who are willing to engage in "constructive fights" with them, when appropriate.

- **Request Solutions:** A technique that has served me well is to ask my teammates to submit their proposed solutions to problems. In these situations, I almost always have a strategy or tactic in mind on how to approach the issue, but I refrain from sharing my thoughts with the team, lest I influence their thinking. In almost every instance, the team will come up with sound courses of action to produce the desired results. Even better, they often identify related issues and challenges that I overlooked during my own assessment.

- **Think Back to Past Experiences:** A great way to identify leadership blind spots is to reflect upon past decisions and actions and the results they produced. This exercise can be done individually; however, it is often most productive when the entire leadership team participates in an environment that promotes candor and tactful (but direct and honest) feedback. Seek to determine whether one or more blind spots were present during the planning and execution of previous initiatives and projects. Solicit input on what the team can learn from mistakes or flawed decision-making and how things should be done in the future.

- **Honest Self-Assessment:** Most leaders, especially those who are seasoned and successful, possess an ample amount of self-confidence. While this trait is critical for sustained success as a leader, it can often result in an individual, after he or she establishes a history of past successes, unconsciously ceasing to conduct frequent and honest self-assessments of their strengths and weaknesses. Stated in another way, they can fall victim to "believing their own press releases," and this can result in their having one or more of the five leadership blind spots.

    It is important for leaders to remember that they must never cease to pause and reflect upon their performance, especially as they become more experienced and prone to develop biases and habits that may not always produce the best solutions to the problems facing them and their teams.

- **Consider Working With an Executive Coach:** An executive coach can help you collect feedback from your seniors, peers, and other teammates. Your coach can administer a personality test and then show you how to evaluate, interpret, and take action relative to the test results.

By discovering and resolving existing blind spots, a leader can greatly improve the effectiveness of his or her leadership. This will improve morale and it often results in increased productivity for the entire team. Don't allow blind spots to limit what you—and, ultimately your team—can achieve!

"If you seek Truth, you will not seek to gain a victory by every possible means; and when you have found Truth, you need not fear being defeated."— Epictetus

"Demand That Your Teammates *Speak Truth to Power.*

Seasoned and confident leaders surround themselves with a diverse team of smart people who are willing to engage in *constructive fights* with them, when appropriate."

—Mike Ettore

Chapter 66

HAVING TOUGH CONVERSATIONS

Leaders spend an inordinate amount of time putting out fires, particularly interpersonal ones. A leader may spend 20 percent of his or her time simply managing conflict of one degree or another.

As long as Western culture values democratic processes and individual freedom, there will be those who are encouraged to debate. This is not a bad thing because innovative ideas often spring from those who refuse to "go along just to get along." But if it's taken too far, argument can turn a workplace dysfunctional.

Conflict in the Workplace

Conflict is not necessarily something that can be suppressed in an organization, but neither should it be ignored. Left alone, conflict and interpersonal stress only get worse. Eliminating conflict is not the answer. Companies that try that approach are as doomed to failure as those who try to ignore it.

Some predict that conflict is increasing in organizations because of the pressure on people to produce more and better with less. Job insecurity, a fluctuating economy, the stress of technological advancements—along with a background of war, terrorism, and domestic political strife—provide more factors that put people on edge.

There is a strong link between the ability to resolve conflict effectively and perceived effectiveness as a leader. According to research from the Management Development Institute of Eckerd College, leaders who resolve conflict by *perspective taking, creating solutions, expressing emotions,* and *reaching out* are considered to be more effective. Executives who demonstrate these behaviors are seen as successful and more suitable for promotion.[219]

Conflict is normal and natural and can be a productive stimulant for creative processes. Managed well, it can motivate and energize individuals to stretch themselves, to be open to learning from others different from themselves, and to move beyond status quo operations.

Three Sources of Conflict

Three factors contributing to conflict in organizations are:

(1) Differences in behavior and communicating styles

(2) Differences in priorities and values

(3) Workplace conditions, including poor communication from leaders

Some personalities just seem to clash. It is important to determine why two people rub each other the wrong way. Do they have opposing behavior styles? For example, an introvert can be judged as hard to read and even untrustworthy to an extrovert who is open and expressive about everything. A time-conscious and highly organized individual can judge a more spontaneous person harshly and find that person's different priorities a source of irritation.

Understanding basic human differences can help people overcome being judgemental and help them accept differences. Training in any of several assessment tools—for example MBTI, DISC, or 360's—is a good start. Attending workshops on behavior styles is another option. An extrovert can learn to ask questions to draw out an introvert in order to gain a better understanding of their position. A highly organized person can learn to set more realistic or detailed deadlines for those who are less organized. Taking the time to understand basic differences can prevent personality clashes and conflict before these become ongoing problems.

Expectations and Assumptions

People have different needs, values, beliefs, assumptions, experience levels, expectations, and cultural frameworks. When people form expectations for the future (based on their experiences and interpretations of the past) their perceptions of reality can differ from one another, and conflict can arise.

It is necessary to explore expectations, assumptions, underlying values, and priorities. This can be done openly in group or team sessions, individually by a leader or coach, or in small groups of conflicted individuals. When there is an elevated degree of conflict, it may be wise to do this with a professional trained in interpersonal skills and mediation techniques.

Inquiring about values can help clarify issues. People don't get upset by things that don't matter to them. Behind every complaint there is an underlying value that is not being satisfied. Asking questions such as, "What's really important here?" often leads to uncovering competing values and conflicting priorities. Creating more authentic conversations by asking the right questions is the first step toward managing conflict.

Communication Skills

There are essentially three communication styles: non-assertive, assertive, and aggressive. We all have a preferential habit or style of communicating, and we are capable of switching from one to another as appropriate. The problem is that we aren't always aware of the way others may perceive us. While we may think we are being appropriately assertive, someone else who is more sensitive or who harbors resentment may perceive us as aggressive. Add to the mix the fact that we all have personal agendas and it is easy to see how communications break down and breed conflict.

Executive Sources of Conflict

Executives contribute to conflict by being ambiguous in their communications—either intentionally or unintentionally. Most people have a tendency to avoid conflict. We sometimes "talk out of both sides of our mouth" and give mixed messages. The issues will sort themselves out in the end, we hope. At worst, this communication style leads to increased conflict; at best, to an organizational climate of non-commitment.

Although it is necessary to allow people in your organization to be able to speak truth to power, it's important to understand the necessity of learning proper communication skills when dealing with conflict. When executives adopt a policy of complete candor, they may gain the benefit of new ideas; but if they continue to deal with conflict with old skills, this may backfire. The freedom to question and to challenge is crucial, but the method in which it's done is often inadequate. To overcome organizational barriers to candor and open communications, people must learn new skills in order to know how to *ask the questions behind the questions*.

This may call for a professionally trained coach or consultant, external to the organization, who is unbiased. Executives may be *standing too close to the blackboard* to see their communication errors. Working with an executive coach can help correct one of the ways that an executive may be contributing to conflict without even knowing it.

Organizational Sources of Conflict

What conditions make a workplace fertile for conflict? An organization with a rigid hierarchical structure and an authoritarian leadership culture is perfect ground for it. Usually, such places have a strong rumor mill, because open communications are not encouraged. There may be a poorly instituted reward/promotional system where unfair favoritism occurs.

Another source of conflict is limited resources. When leaders have to compete with each other for resources, their competitive agendas can limit their ability to get along with others for the benefit of the organization. They become more concerned with their own personal success or that of the business unit. As we mentioned in the Accelerator course, one of your primary duties as a leader is to provide your team with the appropriate resources to accomplish the mission.

Change itself can destabilize relations, because people struggle when they are moved out of their comfort zones. Organizations that have been involved in mergers and/or acquisitions, for example, experience more conflict. Rapidly changing environments create a ripe atmosphere for stress, anxiety, and conflict.

Four Ways to Cope with Conflict

When conflict occurs, you can react in four different ways:

(1) You can play the victim and act betrayed. You can complain to those who will listen and create alliances against the offending party. This rarely works in the business world, although most organizations have people actively engaging in such passive-aggressive behaviors rather than addressing conflict directly.

(2) You can withdraw, either by physically leaving the situation, or by emotionally and mentally disengaging. This may involve walking out of a heated meeting, moving to a new unit or team, or quitting the company. A Gallup Organization survey reports that, at any one time, as many as a fifth of an organization's employees are *actively disengaged*. Worse yet, over half are *not engaged*, but simply putting in time. [220]

(3) You can change yourself. Most people never even consider this option because it involves backing down from one's original stance. For people involved in personal battles, who are attached to core limiting beliefs, this is tantamount to failure. For others who are capable of looking at win-win possibilities, however, this option can open the door to creative solutions.

(4) You can confront each other honestly, openly and candidly. While this is the preferred option, this is the most difficult to put into practice. This is because often people are afraid of conflict and don't know how to work through issues successfully.

Keys to Managing Conflict

One of the most effective ways of facing conflict involves having realistic, open, and candid conversations. Asking the right questions to reveal underlying assumptions, expectations, and values is essential. When conflict escalates, it must be addressed as soon as possible, before it becomes chronic or pervasive. Here are six key aspects to consider when addressing conflict:

(1) Create rules of engagement. Establish procedures and rules for addressing conflict fairly.

(2) Demonstrate the importance of caring. Nothing can be re-solved without an atmosphere of trust. No one cares how much you know until they first know how much you care.

(3) Depersonalize the issues. Focus on behaviors and the problems, not on personalities.

(4) Don't triangulate or bring in political allies.

(5) Know when to let it go.

(6) Know when to bring in a professional mediator, coach, or trainer.

Ten Tips for Difficult Communications

Here are suggested "Communication Strategies for Effective Leaders" from an interview with Phil Harkins, CEO of Linkage, Inc., in his *Link & Learn News-letter*:

(1) Listen without saying a word 70% of the time. Show that you understand what the other person is saying 20% of the time, either verbally or non-verbally. 10% of the time, ask questions in a skillful way that advances the conversation.

(2) Become a people reader. Look carefully at the real mes-sage that someone is conveying by reading his or her ex-pressions.

(3) Focus not only on what someone is saying but also on what he or she is *not* saying.

(4) Check in consistently to confirm what people are thinking, feeling, and believing. Don't assume you know what they mean.

(5) Do not go into difficult conversations unprepared. First, think about where you want to end up; then, think about what's really going on; then, and only then, begin the pro-cess of designing an action plan.

(6) You get what you want in communicating by first giving

others what they need.

(7) At the end of every important conversation, review the commitments.

(8) Remember that it's imperfection that we most admire in each other. Be courageously authentic and honest.

(9) Always start with the other person's agenda.

(10) Practice the art of saying to a person when they make a point, "Tell me more."

Summary

The reality is that many of us tend to put off tough conversations because of the intensity and complexity of the emotions they may potentially arouse—both for the leaders initiating the conversation and the individual they are speaking with. Anxiety about how certain people will react, and whether you will be able to handle their reactions to a tough conversation may cause you to be reluctant to raise an issue face to face. You may even be concerned that you will not be supported by your leader(s), your Human Resources department, and/or other colleagues if you take steps to address sensitive issues.

However, by adopting the right approach, preparing yourself carefully, and developing the right counseling skills, you will be able to enhance your ability to handle tough conversations effectively and guide them to a conclusion that is best for everyone involved. Every conversation (even the tough ones!) is an opportunity to develop trust and commitment within your team. And as you know, these are two essential ingredients of the Trust-Based Leadership™ model!

"Only the dead have seen the last of war." — Plato

Chapter 67

THE PURSUIT OF RELEVANT KNOWLEDGE

Throughout this book, I continuously emphasize the importance of formal and self-directed professional education and the value of being a lifelong learner. I doubt that there are many people who would argue against the merit of any of these concepts, and I think that most individuals will also agree with the insights and recommendations that I'm about to share in this particular story.

During my time as an infantry rifle company commander, the pre-deployment training schedule listed a day/night live-fire exercise that focused on the M-60 machine gun. This meant that the unit's machine gunners would be using a firing range to train with live ammunition under a variety of scenarios during both daylight and nighttime conditions.

A few weeks prior to this event, I assigned Lt. Smith, the weapons platoon commander, to serve as the officer in charge (OIC) of this exercise. This made sense, as the machine gun section was part of his platoon. This officer was a highly motivated leader and a serious student of his profession. A voracious reader of military history, it was common to see him reading books on high-level strategy and other aspects of warfare that were more commonly associated with the level of study done by majors and lieutenant colonels. He was bright, enthusiastic, and, by all accounts, a very good Marine officer.

As the OIC of this training event, Lt. Smith had been charged with ensuring that all required administrative, logistical, technical, and safety plans were executed and that all regulations were adhered to before, during, and after the conduct of training. It is a job that requires a lot of knowledge, foresight, and attention to detail, and one that comes with a great amount of responsibility. If things go seriously wrong during a live-fire exercise and the OIC and other senior Marines are found to have been negligent in any way during the planning and execution of the event, the appropriate disciplinary actions will be quickly administered. And in most instances, their careers will essentially be over.

Training with live ammunition is a necessary but very dangerous activity. It *must* be conducted in a safe and competent manner. At worst, live-fire training can result in the death or serious injury of the Marines participating in it or perhaps even those who are operating on adjacent ranges and training areas. The OIC bears much of the responsibility for ensuring that things go right.

Now, even though Lt. Smith was the OIC of the live-fire exercise, I was, as the unit's commanding officer, still ultimately responsible for a safe and successful training evolution. To enhance my ability to effectively supervise Smith as he planned and directed the training, I obtained the appropriate field manuals and technical manuals for the M-60 machine gun and the Starlight scope, which is a night-vision device that enables the machine gunners to acquire targets in the dark. I was very comfortable with the M-60 from my previous training and experience using and directing the employment of this weapon. However, the Starlight scope that would be used was a recently released model that had been significantly modified from previous versions; essentially, it was a different scope than the one I had used.

I studied the manual closely and was pleased to learn that the scope's new features made it much more effective than its predecessors. I also discovered that several new aiming reticles had been developed for it and that there were now different versions for various weapons. This meant that the proper aiming reticle had to be mounted on the scope to ensure the best results during our live-fire training (and future real-world operations).

I met with Lt. Smith one day in his office so he could brief me on his preparation for the training. He went through his plans and it was clear that he was making great progress. I asked him questions and he answered most of them to my satisfaction. However, I noticed that Smith lacked awareness of some of the more technical aspects of machine gun employment and I provided some guidance to help him overcome this.

At some point, I pointed to the technical manual for the Starlight scope that I had brought with me to the meeting and said, "I've been reading this manual and I'm very impressed with this new version of the scope. I didn't know that new versions of the aiming reticle had been created. Tell me about them." Smith's facial expression sent a clear message—he wasn't aware of the new reticles.

I'd always emphasized to my young officers that they needed to ensure that their self-directed professional education had a proper balance. First and foremost, it should better prepare them for their current roles as platoon commanders and company executive officers. But beyond that, it should also prepare them to suddenly take charge of a full rifle company in combat (which in the current organization of the company, meant that I had been killed in action).

Lt. Smith was the most studious of all of the lieutenants in my unit and this was commendable—but it was very obvious in this instance that he had fallen short on knowing the weapon system that was about to be used in his training event. I realized that I had to provide him with guidance—and that there was no way to avoid the fact that some of it was going to touch on his lack of knowledge. I also realized that I needed to do this in a way that didn't make this officer feel as if he was inferior or that he had let me down.

I told him that, from my perspective, his planning for the live-fire event was among the best I'd ever seen. I then said that he needed to do some additional in-depth study of the weapon system and perhaps leverage his staff noncommissioned officers (SNCOs) and noncommissioned officers (NCOs) more because many of them possessed greater knowledge and experience with it than he did. Finally, I handed him the Starlight scope manual and then immediately picked up a book on high-level military strategy from his desk.

"Lt. Smith: I know that you were taught at TBS (The Basic School) and the Infantry Officer Course that professional reading is of the utmost importance. And that, even as a lieutenant, you should be able to think like a colonel regarding the conduct of warfare. All of this is true, but you have to maintain the proper perspective on this," I said. "Next week's live-fire event is all about safe and effective training with the M-60 machine gun. At no point will grand military strategy come into play during this event. But when we transition from daylight to nighttime employment of our machineguns, the knowledge and utilization of the appropriate aiming reticles on the Starlight scopes *will* be required—and it is *your* responsibility to make sure this happens. So, for the time being, I suggest that you focus entirely on the things that will make the live-fire event successful."

He took this well and I was confident that he would direct his attention and effort where they were needed. When he briefed me a few days later, I was pleased to see that his SNCO, a seasoned gunnery sergeant, and three of his most experienced NCOs were in the room and they were obviously going to deliver parts of his briefing. He was learning, and the look of confidence on his face and how he carried himself were quite telling; this officer was as ready as he could be at that moment to deliver his plan for the training event!

The brief was very well done; one of the best I'd ever observed. Every question that I asked was adequately answered by the lieutenant and his leaders. The following week, as I approached the range and met with the lieutenant, I asked him a single question: "All ready to go, Lt. Smith?"

He replied that he was and that all he needed to do was to call the Marines working at the base Range Control office and ask for permission to make the range "hot" so shooting could begin.

"Great!" I replied. "I'm going to be over here with the first sergeant, observing the exercise. Let me know if you need anything." From that point onward, the lieutenant was fully in charge and he and his leaders did a superb job. The event was one of the best most of us had ever witnessed.

This story and the lessons it contains can be applied to various situations found in all types of organizations. Leaders should strongly encourage their team members—especially their leaders—to continuously pursue knowledge that can enhance their professional capabilities. But as this specific story illustrates, leaders should also encourage teammates to keep things in the proper perspective. First and foremost, they must learn things that ensure they perform their current duties in a superior fashion.

As an executive, for example, I was able to send most of my senior leaders to graduate school so they could obtain Master of Business Administration degrees. MBAs are of course valuable in the business world, both because they enable individuals to enhance their qualifications to take on leadership roles and because they impart a well-rounded set of management skills.

Nevertheless, a lot of the curriculum was either theoretical or not directly applicable to what my Kforce leaders needed to know to do their current jobs. For example, marketing management classes and financial management principles that benefit shareholders, while certainly valuable as a component of a well-rounded business education, didn't always directly apply to getting IT projects done properly and on time.

Thus, I always counseled my senior leaders to continue to study material that would help them perform well *now*. To encourage them to "keep their eye on the ball," I always told them, "Study hard, but make sure you don't start doing dumb things while you are getting smart!"

As you establish your own culture of continuous learning, make sure that both you and your leaders maintain this perspective. Don't lose sight of the knowledge that keeps your team sharp for today's tasks and objectives.

"We are what we repeatedly do. Excellence, then, is not an act, but a habit." —Aristotle.

Chapter 68

TAKING CARE OF WHAT'S PRECIOUS

By now, I'm sure that anyone reading this book is aware of the fact that Marine leaders are trained to demonstrate a level of love and concern for the men and women they are in charge of that, in many ways, replicates that of a parent toward their children. In the following story, I will share an experience that I had as a young captain that had a profound effect on my leadership style for the rest of my Marine Corps career—and throughout my business career, too.

In the summer of 1986, I received orders directing me to report to the Marine Corps Recruit Depot at Parris Island, South Carolina. The first year of my tour at Parris Island was spent as a series officer supervising the training of new recruits. As my time as a series officer came to an end, I was offered an opportunity to transfer to Weapons Training Battalion and serve as the commanding officer of Range Company. This unit had approximately 200 Marines, most of whom were serving as marksmanship instructors and coaches for the thousands of recruits coming through the training pipeline each year.

The battalion commander was Colonel Ron Schmid, an artillery officer and Vietnam veteran. Colonel Schmid was a superb leader and I not only learned much from him, I truly enjoyed working for him. Like all Marine leaders, he took his role very seriously and there was never any doubt among the Marines in his command where his priorities were; he was always focused on ensuring that his Marines were well cared for in every way.

One day, I was standing with Colonel Schmid near one of the firing lines, observing a recruit series as it went through a course of fire. At some point, a series of recruits marched by us and he turned to me and said, "Look at them, Mike, aren't they precious?" The look on his face after he said this was much the same as I think mine was when I got my first look at my children and grandchildren after they were born. He made several other comments that conveyed how important these young men were to the continued success and survival of the Marine Corps, and how wonderful it was that generation after generation and year after year, many thousands of young Americans had the same strong desire, as we had both had, to serve America as a United States Marine.

Colonel Schmid's comments struck a chord deep within me. The range that we were standing on when he made them was very old and had been used to train recruits in rifle marksmanship since before World War II. Often, after a heavy rainstorm, I would find a spent .30-06 cartridge on the ground. This type of ammunition was used in the M-1 Garand rifle, which was the weapon most Marines used during that war.

Whenever I found one of these spent cartridges, I would look at the die markings on its base that showed the year in which it was produced. Many of them had the years during which World War II had been fought stamped on them. I always wondered if the recruit who'd fired this round in training had survived the war or if he'd been one of the many thousands of Marines who'd perished on some God-forsaken hell of an island in the South Pacific.

I spent many an hour walking around this range and others during my tour in Weapons Battalion, and I always viewed the entire area as hallowed ground. The Marine Corps is rightfully famous for the high level of competence Marines have always demonstrated with weapons, especially the service rifle. I'd often stand on the 500-yard line of one of the ranges and think about the thousands of recruits who had trained there and ultimately served in many of the most famous and deadly battles in the long history of the Corps. It was not lost upon me that as the commanding officer of the Marines charged with training all new recruits, I had the great responsibility of ensuring that the next generation of Marine marksmen was as capable and deadly as its predecessors were.

For the rest of my career, whenever I was speaking or communicating in any way about Marines, I always tried to include the word "precious" in my comments. As a member of the TBS staff, I often told new officers that they were soon going to be entrusted with the lives of America's precious Marines. I knew that many of these officers would likely serve as combat leaders one day, and I wanted to ensure they fully understood the gravity of being in charge of the lives of some of the best and brightest men and women America had to offer.

In fact, many of them did serve in combat, some with great distinction, in Iraq, Afghanistan, and other locations. I like to think that some of the lessons and insights that I conveyed to them (many of which were taught to me by veterans of WWII, Korea, and Vietnam) had helped them in some way to accomplish their assigned missions and, to the best of their ability, to preserve the lives of their precious Marines.

Even now, as an official "old-timer" and retired Marine, whenever I correspond with a Marine on active duty, I often end my letter, email, text message, or phone conversation *with "Please take care of our precious Marines."* I use *"our* precious Marines" instead of *"your* precious Marines" or *"those* precious Marines" because just as anyone who has earned the title of US Marine remains a Marine for life, a Marine who has had the honor of serving as a leader of Marines also remains one for life.

I've said repeatedly in this book, one way or another, that <u>being a leader is not something you do, it is who you are.</u> This philosophy is one that permeates the very soul of Marine leaders, and for that matter, the very best leaders in any profession or organization.

There are several traits and characteristics that I feel one must possess and demonstrate in order to become a World-Class Leader and I have addressed them throughout this book. In my opinion, none of them is more important than the genuine respect, admiration, and love from the leader toward those he or she is privileged to lead.

So, the next time you are in a position to observe the men and women you work with and perhaps are in charge of, consider viewing them as being a precious asset; one as vital to the success and well-being of your company as the thousands of new recruits entering the Marine Corps each year are to the success and survival of that great American institution.

If you do this, you too will find yourself communicating with current and former colleagues one day and closing out your conversations with a statement along the lines of, "Please take care of our precious _____."

Once again, being a leader is not something you do—*it is who you are!*

"Accept the things to which fate binds you, and love
the people with whom fate brings you together,
but do so with all your heart."— Marcus Aurelius

"There are several traits and characteristics
that I feel one must possess and demonstrate
in order to become a World-Class Leader and
I have addressed them throughout this book.
In my opinion, none of them is more important
than the genuine respect, admiration, and
love from the leader toward those he or she
is privileged to lead."

—Mike Ettore

Chapter 69

"THE VOICE"

I've kept an archive of various things I've written to my children so they can read and reflect upon them many years from now. Below is a text message sent to my youngest son in the fall of 2007, right before he was going on a timed six-mile run during a pre-season wrestling practice. He was 15 years old at the time.

> 23 October 2007
>
> Good luck on the 6 miler.
>
> Remember, when your lungs and legs are on fire and you hear that voice inside your head telling you to slow down – it takes heart and courage to ignore the pain and keep running hard.
>
> Only you will ever know what choice you made when that voice starts talking to you.
>
> You know what a champion would do.
>
> I Love You.

Sports are a great way to develop character and teach lessons that can be used throughout one's life, especially when "the voice" starts talking to young athletes! While I am sure you agree with this, you may be wondering why I am including this text in a book on leadership.

I do it because, ultimately, who we are as business leaders is largely based upon how we respond to the silent questions, deliberations, rationalizations, and temptations posed by "the voice" in our minds. There is a parallel between the inner voice heard by athletes pushing themselves to the brink of their physical and mental limits and the calls to conscience business leaders face in trying situations.

Anyone who has served in a leadership role for a significant amount of time knows that "the voice" is often present. It tempts you to take shortcuts or the path of least resistance on contentious issues; to remain silent at times when speaking up would be unpopular or inconvenient; or, in some instances, to do something "just this one time ... never again."

At various points in your leadership journey, you *will* face situations that require you to exhibit the character and moral courage required to do the *RIGHT* thing instead of the *CORRECT* thing. Often, doing so will require you to speak or act in opposition to prevailing philosophies, stated policies, or strong personalities. In these situations, the voice may warn you that speaking up or making a certain decision could disrupt the cohesion of the team, cause some teammates to reject it, and perhaps incur the wrath or disfavor of senior personnel.

In situations like this, the advice I gave my son—"...it takes heart and courage to ignore the pain and keep running hard"—applies when it's adapted to situations in which leaders know they must stand strong and be heard. They must often do this alone in environments in which groupthink has set in and opposing views or new ideas are discouraged.

Few, if any of your colleagues will ever know why you made certain decisions when various challenges arise throughout your leadership journey. But *you* will surely know what went on in your mind as you debated with *the voice*.

When you hear it, remember to make the *right* decision and not merely the "*correct*" or easy one. This decision may quickly work out well or it could cause short-term challenges or conflict—but in the long run, leaders who conquer *the voice* and stick with their principles will accomplish more than those who don't.

"Waste no more time arguing what a good man should be. Be one."
– Marcus Aurelius

Chapter 70

THE ROLEX MOMENT

When I was a young enlisted Marine, I used to see many of my officers wearing Rolex dive watches. I loved the look of them in the same way that some people favor a certain model of car or boat. I would sometimes ask my lieutenants to let me hold their watches so I could get a closer look at them. One of them once let me wear his watch for a day when I was a DI; I was "profiling" around the area that day, for sure! I promised myself that if I ever achieved my goal of becoming a commissioned officer, I'd buy one as a reward.

In 1982, shortly after becoming an officer, I bought a Rolex Submariner from the PX catalog for $550; the list price was $1,150. My take home pay in 1982 was $425 every two weeks as a prior-enlisted second lieutenant, so this was a significant purchase. I wasn't married at the time, had no mortgage or other debt, and I knew that I'd probably never again be able to justify spending that kind of money on a watch.

My First "Rolex Moment"

During my Marine career, there were several occasions in which I looked at my watch late at night, noting the time and thinking—or in this example, being convinced—that I may not be alive in the morning.

The first time this happened, my Marines and I were located in a very dangerous area of West Beirut in Lebanon. The Lebanese Civil War was one conducted largely on religious grounds. It essentially pitted Muslims against Christians, as each group and a multitude of sub-groups, militias, etc., jockeyed for power and control. Generally speaking, the city of Beirut was divided into two halves. East Beirut (Christian) and West Beirut (Muslim).

In April of 1983, the US Embassy was destroyed by a suicide bomber who drove a delivery van packed with explosives up to the building's front doors and detonated a huge, improvised bomb the van was carrying. Sixty-three people were killed and many more were seriously injured. The embassy building itself was rendered unusable and operations were relocated to a group of buildings a short distance away, with the most sensitive embassy functions being conducted inside the British embassy.

Upon arriving in Lebanon in early November after participating in operations in Grenada, I (along with my superb platoon sergeant, Staff Sergeant Mike Marshall) was tasked with leading my reinforced rifle platoon as it guarded the large area in which the various "embassy buildings" were located. My beefed-up platoon now consisted of 104 Marines, most of whom were infantrymen, along with several extra communicators, a cook, extra Navy Corpsmen, and an amphibious tractor platoon led by Staff Sergeant Allan Chase.

That Night

The situation in Beirut had become incredibly volatile and dangerous in early February 1984. The violence had reached a level that many lifelong residents of the city had never previously experienced. These people had become almost desensitized to the violence associated with years of civil war but during this period of time, they realized that things had become worse than ever before.

On February 6, 1984, a battle between rival forces occupying East and West Beirut began. Each side began lobbing artillery and mortar rounds into their opponent's sector. And they did this with a fury that I will never forget.

During the evening, the area we were located in was getting pounded by artillery and mortar fire. The sound of small arms fire was non-stop and red and green tracer rounds were zipping through the air in all directions. The larger artillery rounds started getting closer to our positions and we could hear them whistling in prior to impacting as close as 50 meters from us on all sides of our perimeter. To use the proper tactical terminology to describe our plight, our defensive positions were now *bracketed* by the incoming artillery rounds; the more experienced Marines recognized this and knew that it was only a matter of time before the high-explosive projectiles started impacting directly on our positions.

To further complicate the tactical situation, radio contact with the battalion headquarters element located about five miles away was lost. I could not inform my chain of command of the situation, and while my senior leaders were aware that the entire city was in turmoil, they were not aware of the predicament that my Marines and I were facing.

After my leaders and I had done everything we could do from a tactical standpoint, it was simply time for us to hunker down and hope that we wouldn't get hit by any of the incoming shelling. Marines are taught that "hope is not a battlefield strategy" but, at this moment, it really was all that we had going for us.

At one point, an artillery round hit the building that some of my Marines and I were on top of. The round impacted about 20 feet below our rooftop position. The entire building shook and suffice it to say that amongst the Marines on that rooftop, the "pucker factor" was very high— probably the highest it had ever been for each of us. We were very lucky; just a tad higher and that round would have killed us all.

The artillery and mortar fire seemed to be increasing in volume and I assumed it would continue for another several hours. Large portions of the neighborhoods adjacent to our positions were on fire and the sounds of explosions and small arms fire were almost non-stop.

I remember looking at my watch and it read 11:24 pm.

I thought to myself, "I won't be alive to see the sun rise in the morning."

At that moment, I wasn't simply fearful of the risk of being killed, I was *convinced* that I was going to die. It was time to pray and I did so, while trying to maintain a look of calm and confidence on my face, lest the Marines with me see how worried I was about our chances of survival.

I wasn't married at the time and my thoughts drifted toward my family, especially my parents, knowing how hard my death was going to affect them. I can still remember the sensation of having a lump in my throat and feeling as if my body weighed a ton as I laid on the deck of the roof, thinking about what my parents were about to go through.

After several minutes, I had made peace with my fate and with God, with the genuine belief that I was about to meet him. To say that I was having a "religious experience" is an understatement.

But then I felt a sudden sense of peace and calm. As I laid next to a few of my Marines, I thought to myself, "Mike, if your time has come, so be it; at least go out like a Marine leader should—leading. Go see your Marines, because they need to see you right now."

I hurried down the building's staircase in total darkness, exited the lobby onto the street, and began running from position to position in the western portion of our sector, trying to time my runs to avoid incoming shells. Thankfully, the incoming artillery barrage had slowed a bit at this point, with perhaps only a few rounds impacting every couple of minutes or so. I stopped at several positions to talk with my Marines and encourage them. I distinctly remember entering a small bunker and seeing one of my young Marines, Private First Class Justin Glymph, who looked at me and said, "Sir, these ******** are trying to kill us!"

"It sure looks like it, Glymph!" I replied. "Keep your head down; I'll see you later." I then continued to move from position to position to see and talk with my Marines.

Our best hopes were realized, and we all miraculously survived that night. When morning came, the area adjacent to our perimeter was cloaked in dense smoke from the fires that the shelling had started. Some of the streets just outside of our position had collapsed and several heavily damaged cars were strewn about, with some of them still on fire.

I've kept in touch with many of the Marines I served with during this time. Even now, after all of these years, we inevitably end up talking about *"that night"* whenever we see each other.

And throughout my Marine Corps and business careers, whenever things became stressful and I found myself being a bit aggravated or disappointed, I'd look down at my watch and remember that night and how it felt to be "scared shitless"—knowing that my fate was literally hinging on the hope that an artillery shell or bullet did not have my name on it. Doing so would always quickly ground me in useful perspective. In my mind, I'd tell myself, "This really isn't that bad. Stop whining and start leading!"

I still have my watch and wear it every day. I don't ever want to forget the lessons, emotions, and "inner conversations" associated with the several "Rolex Moments" that I was privileged to have and fortunate to survive.

The Lesson

I often share this story when speaking to various groups about leadership, usually at the very end of the training session or seminar. I emphasize to them that as they focus on their professional goals and strive to become good leaders and climb the ladder of success, they will surely face many trials and tribulations.

The lesson I share with them is that while they navigate the many challenges and obstacles along their way, they should never forget that when it's all said and done, there is nothing more important in one's life than family and friends. I encourage them to keep their priorities in the proper order and to remain focused on what's really most important.

Many of my students and clients have already experienced their own Rolex Moments, and I am sure many reading this book have, too. I've no doubt that many of their experiences make mine look rather tame by comparison. I think all would agree that it's not a matter of *if* you will experience extremely challenging moments during your life, but *when*.

When a Rolex Moment happens to you, remember to do your duty to the best of your ability and, if possible, ask for the support of the people who love you.

And, as always … Lead by Example!

*"When you arise in the morning, think of what
a precious privilege it is to be alive—to breathe,
to think, to enjoy, to love." – Marcus Aurelius*

CONCLUSION

I have done my best to provide you with a solid look into the fundamental concepts and philosophies associated with Marine Corps leadership; how Marine leaders think and how they approach various situations and tasks, and the reasons why they do it. You should realize that while Marine leaders are truly special men and women, what makes them special is not their physical strength nor specific warrior skills. It is their character and what resides in their hearts and minds—their sincere desire to serve others—that truly set them apart from many leaders.

You should close this book knowing that the traits, attitudes, skills, and winning mindset demonstrated by these exceptional leaders are attainable by anyone who desires to have them; those with the willingness to learn and develop them and, most important of all, the initiative to put these elements into action. I cannot emphasize too strongly that every aspect of Marine Corps leadership and the Trust-Based Leadership™ model mentioned in this book can be successfully adapted and utilized by business leaders at every level, in any form of corporate environment.

You already possess the talent and aptitude to achieve your leadership goals. And you have access to various individuals and resources that can help you as you continue your journey to becoming a World-Class Leader. The time for inspirational Marine Corps leadership stories and anecdotes is done—it is time for YOU to take action!

Go Forth and Lead Well!

Semper Fidelis,

Mike Ettore, US Marine

"WHAT YOU LEAVE BEHIND IS NOT
WHAT IS ENGRAVED IN STONE
MONUMENTS, BUT WHAT IS WOVEN
INTO THE LIVES OF OTHERS."

———————

PERICLES, 450 B.C.

Acknowledgments

Thank You, Kforce!

I'm not sure that I can find words to effectively convey the deep sense of gratitude I have for my Kforce teammates, but I will try!

My journey as a business leader began in 1999, when Kforce's CEO, Dave Dunkel, took a leap of faith and hired me to create a leadership development program (LDP) for the firm. Dave's sponsorship and enthusiasm helped the LDP gain traction and support from other leaders. At the same time, in the spirit of being a Trust-Based Leader, he began providing me with other opportunities to grow professionally and expand my sphere of influence within the company. I will forever be grateful for the special trust and confidence that Dave had in me, and also for his loyal support and friendship. I was truly blessed when Dave came into my life.

Although I often "didn't know what I didn't know," my first boss at Kforce, Larry Stanczak, was a superb mentor for a hard-charging Marine entering the business world. I learned much from him and cannot thank him enough for his patience as he answered my questions and, on several occasions, kept me out of trouble!

I was also blessed with the opportunity to learn from exceptionally competent colleagues such as Bill Sanders, Joe Liberatore, Steve McMahon, Kye Mitchell, Howard Sutter, Dave Kelly, Randy Marmon, Michael Blackman, Andy Thomas, and the rest of Kforce's executive team, as well as other corporate and field leaders over the years.

I can't say enough good things about colleagues such as Dustin Hicks, Don Sloan, Doug Rich, Keith Fulmer, Mike DeGore, Cathy Beaver, Sara Nichols, Eddie Davis, Tony Varano, Michael Allen, Mark Ippolito, Martin Casado, Rob Kosid, Bill Josey, Cara Barone, Jerry Gates, Amy Espinosa, Amanda Franklin, Cynthia Newlin, Dean D'Agostino, Rick Lepper, Stephanie Mohr, James Stenglein, Lee Stuiso, Virg Palumbo, Leslie Baker, Marie Greer, Marc Anderson, Dick Bramel, Rich Weede, Bonnie Baer, Beth Yovino, Paul Siem, Lisa Sanabria, Jessica Schwaller, Jason Velez, Katie Grantham, Heather Parshad, Sarah Smith, Jason Morgan and so many others who gave me their undying loyalty and support.

All of these people, *and so many more not mentioned*, took the time to teach and provide me with superb insights, recommendations, and support. Together, they certainly made me look good for many years. I hope they know that, even back then, I recognized what they were doing for the firm and me, and how much I truly appreciated their loyal support.

To say that Kforce provided my family and me with life-changing opportunities is an understatement. I will forever be indebted to my colleagues for their patience, kindness, and support.

Thank you, my Kforce friends.

I miss you and I love you!

Semper Fidelis,

Mike

Special Thanks: Kforce Technology Services

In 2001, I was unexpectedly asked to serve in the role of Kforce's Chief Information Officer (CIO). In addition to the other departments and functions I was leading, I was now responsible for the company's internal information technology department, which was titled Kforce Technology Services (KTS).

KTS was clearly a troubled organization; its reputation within the firm was quite poor at the time. A few days prior to me joining the team, a company-wide layoff had resulted in several dozen members of the department being terminated. Adding to the uncertainty and emotions associated with this event was the fact that I was now the department's third CIO in two years, and it was well-known to all that I did not have a technical background. Suffice it to say that the morale of the remaining members of the KTS team was at an all-time low.

On the morning that I assumed this new role, the 176 members of the KTS team were assembled in a conference room and I was introduced to them by Kforce's CEO, Dave Dunkel, and president, Bill Sanders. I distinctly remember the stunned look on the faces of those in the audience when Bill said, "I'd like you to meet your new CIO, Mike Ettore." Dave Dunkel took over and said, "Mike's obviously not a technician but he's a proven leader, and leadership is what KTS needs most right now." In front of me sat an already demoralized team that was shocked into stark silence by what Bill and Dave had just said. To say that the room was completely silent is an understatement.

When it was my turn to address the group, I said, "I know you're all as surprised to see me as I am to be standing in front of you right now. I obviously have no technical experience to provide but I am an experienced leader, and I think that I can be of some help to this team. All I can ask of you is to approach this with open minds and to give me a chance."

At this point, the team was dismissed and everyone left the room silently. I could only imagine what was going through their minds. I knew that it was now "Show Time" and that the burden of proving that sound leadership was the answer to many of KTS's problems was solely on my shoulders. I remember being very excited, confident, and eager to meet my new teammates and begin figuring out how I could be of help.

They Gave Me a Chance

As previously mentioned, I had asked my new teammates to have open minds and to give me a chance to prove that I could be the leader that the team needed. They did both—in spades—and everyone did whatever they could to orient me toward the nuances of an information technology team. I asked countless, ridiculously basic questions, all of which were answered by my patient and supportive teammates.

During the next two years—due to their tireless efforts—KTS did a complete turn-around, going from the worst support team in the firm to what most observers felt was the very best. I knew things had turned out well when, after a few years, I began to receive phone calls from executive recruiters trying to see if I was interested in CIO roles in companies they were representing! I was flattered but I wasn't interested. I only wanted to stay with the teammates who had given me their loyal support and patiently shaped me into a legitimate CIO capable of providing the leadership needed by an enterprise-level information technology team.

KTS's Biggest Gift

Obviously, my KTS teammates were very good to me, and I will forever be grateful for all they did to help me become the leader they needed and deserved. However, I honestly believe that the greatest gift these great people gave me *and* Kforce was the highly visible and undeniable "proof of concept" that there really is something to this thing called *leadership*.

Because they had accepted me and helped me become a successful leader in an area in which I had no formal education or experience, others at all levels of the firm took notice and realized that leadership was indeed a huge factor in a team's success or failure. This led to more of Kforce's senior leaders being willing to put other competent individuals in leadership roles in areas in which they had no formal track record. As a result, many people were promoted due to their proven leadership skills and for some individuals, these promotions provided life-changing opportunities for them and their families.

And it all happened because the great men and women in Kforce Technology Services gave me a chance to be their leader!

My Family, Friends, Mentors, and Supporters

I was fortunate to be born to loving parents: Mary Jo and Larry Ettore. I was a sick infant, born with over 100 allergies and other serious medical issues, and the bills for my medical care were very costly. My parents sacrificed many things to get me the care I needed. I distinctly remember my mother telling me, when I was 20 years old, that she and my dad had just finished paying off the medical bills incurred during the first two years of my life. It was at this point that I began to truly understand the magnitude of what they'd done for me, and how lucky my sisters and I were to have them as my parents.

My father, Larry, was a superb role model for me while I grew up. He was a great guy. A man of few words, he "said what he meant, and meant what he said" and had a very low "bullshit threshold." He once grounded me during the final month of my senior year of high school because I was supposed to be in by 9 pm. on a Friday night, but arrived ten minutes late at 9:10. I got a bit flippant with him and, by 9:15, had learned what the term "old-man strength" meant! To this day, he is the standard that I measure myself against regarding being both a man of integrity and a father.

Gary Wikander was my wrestling coach and, in many ways, a "second father" during my high school years. He spent a lot of time coaching me during the wrestling off-season, and driving me to other schools so I could get some mat time with other big kids. Starting my freshman year, he always encouraged me to keep my grades decent so I could go to college someday. I distinctly remember telling him I wasn't interested in college, but he never stopped nudging me in that direction. I'm proud to say that now, as a holder of a bachelor's and two master's degrees, Coach Wikander was the perfect role model and mentor. I have always felt indebted to him. Throughout my Marine career, he was usually the first person I'd share good news with. I never stopped seeking his approval and showing him how much I valued all of the time and effort he put into guiding me into manhood.

Master Sergeant Ken Benson was the father of my childhood friend and classmate Brian. He was the first Marine I'd ever known, and he made a lasting impression on me. He was involved in the epic battle of Fox Hill during the Korean War's pivotal fight at the Chosin Reservoir. The leadership lessons associated with this event are still taught to Marine leaders. It was always impressive to read books on this battle and see mentions of the heroism of

"PFC Kenny Benson." Like many combat veterans, he rarely spoke of his experiences and when he did, he never mentioned the significant role he played in one of the most legendary battles in Marine Corps history.

He was the major influence on my decision to join the Marine Corps after high school. I spent my entire Marine Corps career trying to uphold the standards established by Marines such as Ken Benson. On more than one occasion, when times got tough, I thought of him and his buddies fighting for their lives in -40 degree weather, and I always came to the conclusion that I'd rather die than bring dishonor to the legacy that they and other brave Marines had established. To this day, whenever I hear the term "Combat Marine", Ken Benson is the first person I think of.

Staff Sergeant Ross Carter spent a lot of time with me during my formative years as a young Marine leader, and I came to view him as my "third father." A highly experienced combat leader, he patiently shared his wisdom and insights with me, and provided invaluable leadership techniques that I used effectively throughout my service in the Marine Corps and during my subsequent business career. Every young leader deserves at least one Staff Sergeant Carter to help them develop, in whatever type of organization they serve in.

As a young lance corporal, I was fortunate to have First Lieutenant Jim Battaglini as my platoon commander. Jim was a superb leader and the epitome of what a Marine officer is supposed to be. During the time I served with him, I was promoted to the grades of corporal and sergeant. To say that he served as a role model and had a huge influence on my development as a leader of Marines is an understatement. We often hit the weight room together, and it was during our workouts that Jim started talking with me about the possibility of going to college and perhaps returning to the Corps as a commissioned officer. His encouragement led me to do this. Fifteen or so years later, when he was a lieutenant colonel and an infantry battalion commander, by then-Captain Ettore served as one of his rifle company commanders during a deployment to the Persian Gulf. I now view this as an example of what can happen when the Teacher-Scholar concept is exercised as envisioned long ago by General John A. Lejeune. Jim ultimately retired as a major general and went on to have a stellar career in the business world.

I owe much to Lieutenant Colonel Ray Smith, who commanded the 2nd Battalion, 8th Marines during combat operations in Grenada and Lebanon. In addition to serving as an exceptional role model for myself and the other leaders in the battalion, he provided me with an opportunity to serve in a leadership role in Beirut that was far greater in scope and responsibility than was typical for a young second lieutenant. To say that he afforded me an incredibly high level of special trust and confidence is an understatement, and I will always be grateful for the faith he had in me and my SNCOs and NCOs. Throughout the rest of my Marine Corps career, whenever dealing with challenging situations and dilemmas, I'd often think "What would Ray Smith do?" During a long and storied career in which he rose to the grade of major general, this renowned combat leader undoubtedly left his mark on countless Marine Corps leaders.

In addition to those already mentioned, I was fortunate to serve with and benefit from the wise counsel and mentorship of countless Marines during my time in the Corps. As a young enlisted Marine, I was blessed with the honor of serving with many veterans of World War II, Korea, and Vietnam. The lessons I learned from these combat veterans had a major impact upon my development as a leader of Marines. Later in my career, while serving as an infantry officer, I was fortunate to serve with Marines of every grade who were truly exceptional leaders and mentors. There are simply too many of them to name individually, but I want them all to know that they have my immense gratitude.

I'd also like to thank the members of a detachment from 1st Special Forces Operational Detachment-Delta, with whom I was fortunate to work in an operational setting during the early 1980s. These warriors were some of the original members of this now world-renowned counterterrorist unit, and I grew professionally by observing their professionalism, work ethic, and competence. I especially want to thank Mark G., whom I've come to view as an example of a "consummate professional soldier." I learned so much from him during our many individual and group conversations. Mark may not have realized it, but I was listening intently to everything he said when he'd share his combat experiences and leadership insights with me and the rest of the team. I used many of these lessons throughout the rest of my Marine Corps career.

I'm thankful to have known and learned much from friends such as "Shaka Zulu", BB, Tom, Tim and other "quiet professionals" who sacrificed their lives in far-off lands while serving America in ways that will forever remain known to only a few people.

Beyond the military sphere, I cannot adequately express my gratitude to Nancy Broding, Dennis Greene, Casey Compton, Doug Rich, Rudina Richter, Michelle Huynh, and my sisters, Robin and Bonnie, for providing me with kindness and support during a very challenging period of my life.

I am especially indebted to Nancy Broding and Bill Ardolino for their tireless work in helping me get this book completed and published. It was fellow Marine and close friend Nancy who spent countless hours working on the original manuscript with me, and Bill who took over during the final stages and shaped and polished it to a degree which I could not have done on my own.

Finally, I want to thank my children—Michelle, Larry, Mike II and Majda—for their enduring love, patience, sacrifices and support over the years. I love and treasure each of you!

Also by Mike Ettore

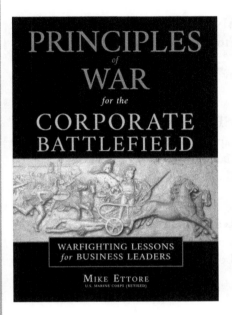

PRINCIPLES OF WAR FOR THE CORPORATE BATTLE-FIELD: Warfighting Lessons for Business Leaders

by Mike Ettore

ISBNs:
Paperback: 978-0-9898229-9-2
Hardcover: 978-1-7372881-0-7
Ebook: 978-1-7372881-1-4

Available at:
Amazon, Barnes&Noble.com, Kindle, iBooks, and many other retailers

The "missions" of the business battlefield are not dissimilar from actual military battlefields . . . establishing the desired end state, describing and assigning the necessary tasks, designing and task-organizing the unit to best support mission accomplishment, assembling and developing the team, and achieving operational unity of effort via timely and precise communications.

The risks associated with both battlefields are similar as well. It is almost inevitable that soldiers may die or become wounded in combat and their units may suffer loss. Likewise, a company may fail and place the livelihoods and welfare its employees at great risk. While this does not bring forth the physical risks associated with war, business failures are personally damaging and the negative effects are lasting.

This book contains examples of how each principle has been successfully applied in both military and business environments, and it **will enable business leaders to quickly and effectively apply The Principles of War in their own planning and operations.**

Also by Mike Ettore

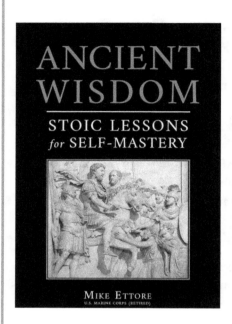

ANCIENT WISDOM:
Stoic Lessons for Self-Mastery

by Mike Ettore

ISBNs:
Paperback: 978-1-7372881-3-8
Hardcover: 978-1-7372881-2-1
Ebook: 978-1-7372881-4-5

Available at:
Amazon, Barnes&Noble.com, Kindle,
iBooks, and many other retailers

Frederick the Great, George Washington, Theodore Roosevelt, and many of today's most notable leaders, intellectuals, and high achievers learned to embrace the wisdom of the ancient Stoics as they sought to live happy, successful, and productive lives.

This book uniquely combines insights from Marcus Aurelius, Seneca, Epictetus and other Stoic philosophers with the author's interpretations, musings, and life-time of experiences and lessons learned. The result is an easy-to-read book containing timeless wisdom and empowering advice that can help readers learn how to dramatically alter and control their emotional responses to life's inevitable challenges and obstacles.

Also by Mike Ettore

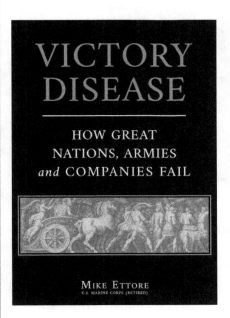

VICTORY DISEASE:
How Great Nations, Armies and
Companies Fail

by Mike Ettore

ISBNs:
Paperback: 978-1-7372881-5-2
Hardcover: 978-1-7372881-6-9
Ebook: 978-1-7372881-7-6

Available at:
Amazon, Barnes&Noble.com, Kindle,
and many other retailers

Victory Disease can infect any organization. Wise leaders recognize this and refrain from thinking, "That could never happen in our company!" The fact is, as shown throughout this book, that this disease has and will continue to infect companies, large and small, in every industry and profession in Corporate America.

Companies that successfully avoid falling victim to this affliction will be those led by humble, agile-minded leaders who ensure prudent steps are taken to recognize and mitigate its symptoms and early warning signs.

Conversely, the companies who succumb to this infectious disease will be led by executives who are so blinded by their organizations' past successes and accolades they either cannot conceive of the possibility of failure, or as previously mentioned and seen in the examples provided in this book, their hubris and overconfidence is such that they simply reject the notion that it could ever happen to them.

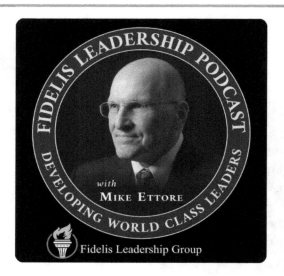

"A PLACE OF LEARNING FOR THOSE ASPIRING TO LEADERSHIP EXCELLENCE!"

The Fidelis Leadership Podcast is for those who want to become World Class Leaders. Weekly episodes convey lessons and advice from some of the world's foremost leadership experts, and discussions regarding the effective application of the Trust-Based Leadership™ model.

HTTPS://WWW.FIDELISLEADERSHIP.COM/PODCAST

Also Found on Your Favorite Podcast Platforms!

Bonus Resources

Download Your Bonus Resources!

The graphics used in this book and additional resources are available
for free in the *Bonus Resource Vault*, which you can find at:
https://fidelisleadership.com/bookbonus

Social Media – Let's Stay In Touch!

Fidelis Leadership Podcast: https://www.fidelisleadership.com/podcast

Facebook

- Fidelis: www.facebook.com/FidelisLeadershipGroup
- Mike Ettore: www.facebook.com/EttoreMike

Linkedin:

- Fidelis: www.linkedin.com/company/fidelis-leadership-group-llc
- Mike Ettore: www.linkedin.com/in/mikeettore/

Twitter: https://twitter.com/FidelisLeader

Instagram: www.instagram.com/fidelisleadership/

Fidelis Leadership Newsletter

Receive monthly emails containing valuable lessons, tactics and techniques
that can help you become a World-Class Leader! I promise that I will never
share your contact information in any way, and if you decide to stop receiving
the newsletter you can unsubscribe with one click.

Sign Up Now! https://fidelisleadership.com/

My Services

Executive Coaching

My executive coaching engagements are uniquely tailored to each individual and are designed to provide focus that can deepen an executive's self-awareness and promote personal and professional growth. The private coaching sessions provide leaders with an opportunity to engage in focused, constructive, and confidential dialogue with a skilled and objective listener. I collaborate with each leader to design a program that fosters and accelerates individual growth, while providing the coaching and facilitation to achieve desired outcomes.

Leadership Development

I help educate, train, and coach leaders so they can dramatically accelerate their personal and professional development. I work best with clients who operate in a culture of execution, accountability, and leadership by example—or those who desire to create such a culture within their organizations. I offer customized leadership training and development programs - including onsite training seminars - for leaders at every level: C-Suite and SVP-VP-Director level, high-potential individuals and others serving in mid-level and front-line leadership roles.

Speaking

I am an experienced public speaker with a strong history of delivering dynamic, interactive, and memorable presentations and keynote speeches to a wide range of organizations. Leveraging leadership lessons that were forged in the unforgiving crucible of combat and while serving as a senior executive, I inspire and energize my audiences and provide them with actionable strategies, tactics, and techniques that they can implement immediately upon returning to their teams.

CONTACT ME NOW!

info@fidelisleadership.com

813-335-3181

From the Author

Book Reviews

Thank you for reading my book. Please consider visiting the site where you purchased it and writing a brief review. Your feedback is important to me and will help others decide whether to read the book too.

New Books, Training Programs and Events

If you'd like to get notifications of my latest books, training programs and leadership events, please join my email list by visiting https://fidelisleadership.com

Bulk Purchase Discounts

If you would like to purchase 25 or more print copies of this book, we are happy to offer you a discount on the net list price of the book. Please send inquiries to: info@fidelisleadership.com

Notes and Sources

ENDNOTES

5. Servant Leadership

1   "What is Servant Leadership?" Robert K. Greenleaf Center for Servant Leadership. https://www.greenleaf.org/what-is-servant-leadership/. (Accessed June 15, 2019)

2   "Fortune's Best Companies to Work For With Servant Leadership." *Modern Servant Leader*. https://www.modernservantleader.com/servant-leadership/fortunes-best-companies-to-work-for-with-servant-leadership/ (Accessed June 15, 2019)

8. The Core Values

3   United States Marine Corps, Date signed: 12/16/96 ALMAR Number: 439/96, IMPLEMENTING INSTRUCTIONS FOR THE MARINE CORPS VALUES PROGRAM. Retrieved from: http://www.leatherneck.com/forums/showthread.php?2179-USMC-recruit-training

4   "QPME: History and Traditions of the United States Marine Corps: Ethics, Values, and Leadership Development." Marine Corps Research Library. https://grc-usmcu.libguides.com/pme/qpme/marine-corps-ethics-values-leadership-development/qualities (Accessed on Aug. 19, 2018)

5   United States Department of the Navy. *Leading Marines*. Marine Corps Warfighting Publication 6-11 (United States Government, 2002). 101-102.

6   "VALUES BASED LEADERSHIP." MCO 1500.56 Marine Corps Values Program (Dec 96). https://archive.org/stream/mipc-t3s_marines_mil/t3s.marines.mil_SRV24VYZJSHAV6BX-NOH6L63F2KYEAOWA_djvu.txt (Accessed Aug. 19, 2018)

9. Standards and Discipline

7   "Washington takes command of Continental Army in 1775." US Army Center of Military History. https://www.army.mil/article/40819/washington_takes_command_of_continental_army_in_1775 (Accessed June 24, 2019)

8   Williamson, Shelton R. "Standards and Discipline: An In-Depth Look at Where We Once Were and Where We Are Now." NCO Journal. https://www.armyupress.army.mil/Journals/NCO-Journal/Archives/2017/November/Standards-and-Discipline/ (Accessed June 16, 2019)

10. The Marine Mindset

9   Ricks, Thomas E. *Making the Corps*. Simon and Schuster, 1998. Book blurb.

10   "VALUES BASED LEADERSHIP." MCO 1500.56 Marine Corps Values Program (Dec 96). https://archive.org/stream/mipc-t3s_marines_mil/t3s.marines.mil_SRV24VYZJSHAV6BXNOH6L63F2KYEAOWA_djvu.txt (Accessed Aug. 19, 2018)

11   United States. Department of the Navy. "Leading Marines." Marine Corps Warfighting Publication No. 6-11. (United States Government, 2014) https://www.marines.mil/Portals/1/MCWP%206-11_Part1.pdf (Accessed Aug. 11, 2019)

12   Schmitt, Art F. *We Thought We Were Invincible: The True Story of Invincible Warriors*. Bloomington, IN: Author House, 2008. 209.

13   Byrne, Brian Patrick and Evers, Jishai. "Google's interview process could make you gaga." Reuters. https://www.vocativ.com/271816/the-awesome-tech-jobs-with-the-most-difficult-hiring-processes/index.html (Accessed Aug. 19, 2018)

14   Baer, Drake. "The 15 Schools With The Most Alumni At Goldman Sachs." *Business Insider*. https://www.businessinsider.com/schools-that-feed-into-goldman-sachs-2014-12 (Accessed Aug. 19, 2018)

11. Every Marine a Rifleman

15   "Recruit Training." https://www.marines.com/becoming-a-marine/enlisted/training.html (Accessed Aug. 19, 2018)

16   "TEACHABLE MOMENT: WARM AND SINCERE GREETING." *Ritz Carlton Leadership Center Blog*. http://ritzcarltonleadershipcenter.com/2016/08/teachable-moment-warm-and-sincere-greeting/ (Accessed Aug. 19, 2018)

17   "GOLD STANDARDS." Ritz Carlton Leadership Center. http://ritzcarltonleadershipcenter.com/about-us/gold-standards/ (Accessed Aug. 19, 2018)

18   Sopher, Michael. "Tips and Tech to Help Your Staff Deliver Better Service." *Rendia Blog*. https://blog.rendia.com/help-your-staff-deliver-better-service/ (Accessed Aug. 18, 2018)

19   "The top reason customers leave." *The San Francisco Business Times*. https://www.bizjournals.com/sanfrancisco/stories/1997/10/20/smallb3.html (Accessed Aug. 19, 2018)

20   Alenazi, Rebecca. "Manager Leadership Training 2018." Prezi Business. https://prezi.com/p/h8jn62_-jqrz/ (Accessed Aug. 19, 2018)

21   Gallo, Carmine. "How the Ritz-Carlton Inspired the Apple Store [video]." *Forbes*. https://www.forbes.com/sites/carminegallo/2012/04/10/how-the-ritz-carlton-inspired-the-apple-store-video/#4b135f623449 (Accessed Aug. 19, 2018)

22   "Working at Walmart: Culture." https://corporate.walmart.com/our-story/working-at-walmart#0000014f-d73a-d36d-adcf-df3b9d0a0000 (Accessed Aug. 20, 2018)

23   Martin, Emmie. "A major airline says there's something it values more than its customers, and there's a good reason why." *Business Insider*. https://www.businessinsider.com/southwest-airlines-puts-employees-first-2015-7 (Accessed Aug. 20, 2018)

24   Solomon, Micah. "What you can learn from Southwest Airlines' culture." *The Washington Post*. https://www.washingtonpost.com/business/on-small-business/what-you-can-learn-from-southwest-airlines-culture/2012/04/03/gIQAzLVVtS_story.html?noredirect=on&utm_term=.7d32e0323eea (Accessed Aug. 20, 2018)

25   Glazer, Emily. "From 'Gr-eight' to 'Gaming,' a Short History of Wells Fargo and Cross-Selling." *Moneybeat*. https://blogs.wsj.com/moneybeat/2016/09/16/from-gr-eight-to-gaming-a-short-history-of-wells-fargo-and-cross-selling/ (Accessed Aug. 20, 2018)

26   Reckard, Scott E. "Wells Fargo's pressure-cooker sales culture comes at a cost." *Los Angeles Times*. http://www.latimes.com/business/la-fi-wells-fargo-sale-pressure-20131222-story.html (Accessed Aug. 20, 2018)

27   Glazer, Emily. "From 'Gr-eight' to 'Gaming,' a Short History of Wells Fargo and Cross-Selling."

28   Olen, Helaine. "Wells Fargo Must Pay $185 Million After Opening Customer Accounts Without Asking. That's Not Enough." *Slate*. http://www.slate.com/blogs/moneybox/2016/09/08/wells_fargo_to_pay_185_million_for_account_opening_scandal_that_s_not_enough.html (Accessed Aug. 20, 2018)

29   "Wells Fargo to Pay $110 Million to Settle Fake Account Suit." Associated Press. https://www.kqed.org/news/11381780/wells-fargo-to-pay-110-million-to-settle-fake-account-suit (Accessed Aug. 20, 2018)

30   Egan, Matt. "Workers tell Wells Fargo horror stories." *CNN Money*. https://money.cnn.com/2016/09/09/investing/wells-fargo-phony-accounts-culture/ (Accessed Aug. 20, 2018)

12. Special Trust and Confidence

31   "OFFICERSHIP FOUNDATIONS B1X0856 STUDENT HANDOUT." Basic Officer Course. MARINE CORPS TRAINING COMMAND. https://www.trngcmd.marines.mil/Portals/207/Docs/TBS/B1X0856%20Officership%20Foundations.pdf?ver=2015-03-26-091435-550 (accessed Aug. 21, 2018)

32   Powers, Rod. "Marine Corps Fraternization Policies." *The Balance*. https://www.thebalancecareers.com/marine-corps-fraternization-policies-3354365 (Accessed Aug. 21, 2018)

33   Dodd, Joseph D. "The Vision of John A. Lejeune." *Marine Corps Gazette*. https://www.lejeune.marines.mil/About/About-LtGen-Lejeune/ (Accessed Aug. 21, 2018)

34   Thomas, Joseph. *Leadership Embodied: The Secrets to Success of the Most Effective Navy*. Naval Institute Press, 2014. 55.

35   "Full text of 'Marine Corps manual.'" Internet Archive. https://archive.org/stream/marinecorpsmanua00unit/marinecorpsmanua00unit_djvu.txt (Accessed Aug. 21, 2018)

36   Ulick, Jake. "Year of the scandal." *CNN Money*. https://money.cnn.com/2002/12/17/news/review_scandals/index.htm (Accessed Aug. 21, 2018)

37   "SEC Charges Adelphia and Rigas Family With Massive Financial Fraud." Securities and Exchange Commission Press Release. https://www.sec.gov/news/press/2002-110.htm (Accessed Aug. 21, 2018)

38   "Global Crossing timeline." *Los Angeles Times*. http://articles.latimes.com/2011/apr/12/business/la-fi-global-crossing-timeline-20110412 (Accessed Aug. 21, 2018)

39   Romero, Simon. "WORLDCOM'S COLLAPSE: THE OVERVIEW; WORLDCOM FILES FOR BANKRUPTCY; LARGEST US CASE." *The New York Times*. https://www.nytimes.com/2002/07/22/us/worldcom-s-collapse-the-overview-worldcom-files-for-bankruptcy-largest-us-case.html (Accessed Aug. 21, 2018)

40   Legal, Troy. "Enron Scandal: The Fall of a Wall Street Darling." *Investopedia*. https://www.investopedia.com/updates/enron-scandal-summary/ (Accessed Aug. 21, 2018)

41   O'Leary, Christopher. "Enron—What Happened?" *Encyclopaedia Britannica*. https://www.britannica.com/topic/Enron-What-Happened-1517868 (Accessed Aug. 21, 2018)

42   Legal, Troy. "Enron Scandal: The Fall of a Wall Street Darling." *Investopedia*. https://www.investopedia.com/updates/enron-scandal-summary/ (Accessed Aug. 21, 2018)

43   "The fall of Andersen." *Chicago Tribune*. http://www.chicagotribune.com/news/chi-0209010315sep01-story.html (Accessed Aug. 21, 2018)

44   Titcomb, James. "Arthur Andersen returns 12 years after Enron scandal." *The Telegraph*. https://www.telegraph.co.uk/finance/newsbysector/banksandfinance/11069713/

Arthur-Andersen-returns-12-years-after-Enron-scandal.html (Accessed Aug. 21, 2018)

45   O'Brien, Ashley. "Theranos founder Elizabeth Holmes charged with massive fraud." CNN. https://money.cnn.com/2018/03/14/technology/theranos-fraud-scandal/index.html (Accessed Aug. 21, 2018)

46   Gotten, Russell. "Volkswagen: The scandal explained." BBC News. https://www.bbc.com/news/business-34324772 (Accessed Aug. 21, 2018)

13. Teacher-Scholar 360

47   "Full text of 'Marine Corps manual.'" Internet Archive. https://archive.org/stream/marinecorpsmanua00unit/marinecorpsmanua00unit_djvu.txt (Accessed Aug. 21, 2018)

48   The Intelligence Section. "Candid Comment on The American Soldier of 1917-1918 and Kindred Topics by The Germans." General Headquarters, American Expeditionary Forces. United States Government. https://fas.org/irp/agency/army/wwi-soldiers.pdf (Accessed Aug. 22, 2018)

49   Greene, Nick. "What Germans Said About American Troops Right After WWI." *Mental Floss*. http://mentalfloss.com/article/57121/42-quotes-germans-about-american-troops-after-world-war-i (Accessed Aug. 21, 2018)

50   "Full text of 'Marine Corps manual.'" Internet Archive. https://archive.org/stream/marinecorpsmanua00unit/marinecorpsmanua00unit_djvu.txt (Accessed Aug. 21, 2018)

51   Wright, Michael. "THE MARINE CORPS FACES THE FUTURE." *The New York Times Magazine*. https://www.nytimes.com/1982/06/20/magazine/the-marine-corps-faces-the-future.html (Accessed Aug. 21, 2018)

52   Perry, Anthony. "NCOs Stand Tall Again: Marine Corps Renews Its Faith in 'Old Sarge.'" *Los Angeles Times*. http://articles.latimes.com/1987-10-04/local/me-32840_1_marine-corps/2 (Accessed Aug. 21, 2018)

53   "Annual report 2017." Randstad. https://www.randstad.com/investor-relations/results-and-reports/randstad-annual-report-archive/randstad-annual-report-2017.pdf (Accessed Aug. 21, 2018)

14. Speaking Truth to Power

54   "John F. Kelly Quotes." BrainyQuote. https://www.brainyquote.com/authors/john_f_kelly (Accessed June 16, 2019)

19. The 3 Main Responsibilities of a Leader

55   "Punitive Articles of the UCMJ." *Army Study Guide*. https://www.armystudyguide.com/content/army_board_study_guide_topics/military_justice/punitive-articles-of-the-.shtml (Accessed Aug. 24, 2018)

20. The 5 Pillars of Leadership

56   Page, Christopher L. and Miller, Scott H. "A Comparative Analysis of Leadership Skills Development in Marine Corps Training and Education Programs." Thesis. Naval Post-graduate School 2002. https://dokumen.tips/documents/a-comparative-analysis-of-leader-ship-skills-development-in-marine-.html (Accessed Aug. 23, 2018)

57   Almazan, Jose E. "A Story of Failed Accountability: Remembering LCpl Jason J. Roth-er." *Marine Corps Gazette.* https://en.wikipedia.org/wiki/Jason_Rother_incident (Accessed Aug. 23, 2018)

58   Hiltzik, Michael. "GE spent lavishly on shareholders, shortchanged pensions and still landed in a deep hole." *Los Angeles Times.* http://www.latimes.com/business/hiltzik/la-fi-hiltzik-ge-buybacks-20170616-story.html (Accessed Aug. 23, 2018)

59   Chiglinsky, Katherine, Kochkodin, Brandon, and Clough, Rick. "The $31 Billion Hole in GE's Balance Sheet That Keeps Growing." Bloomberg. https://www.bloomberg.com/news/articles/2017-06-16/ge-s-31-billion-hangover-immelt-leaves-behind-big-unfunded-tab (Accessed Aug. 23, 2018)

60   Sheetz, Michael. "Jeff Immelt's refusal to give or take bad news defined his leader-ship at GE." CNBC. https://www.cnbc.com/2018/02/21/jeff-immelts-refusal-to-give-or-take-bad-news-defined-his-leadership-at-ge.html (Accessed Aug. 23, 2018)

61   Leung, Rebecca. "Jack Welch: 'I Fell In Love'." *60 Minutes.* https://www.cbsnews.com/news/jack-welch-i-fell-in-love/ (Accessed Aug. 23, 2018)

62   "JOHN FLANNERY NAMED CHAIRMAN AND CEO OF GE." GE Press Release. http://www.genewsroom.com/press-releases/john-flannery-named-chairman-and-ceo-ge-283823 (Accessed Aug. 23, 2018)

63   Wieczner, Jen. "GE CEO Jeff Immelt's Retirement Pay May Be A Lot More Than You Think." *Fortune.* http://fortune.com/2017/06/12/ge-ceo-jeff-immelt-net-worth/ (Accessed Aug. 23, 2018)

64   Ritcey, Alicia and Melin, Anders. "GE's Immelt to Receive at Least $112 Million as CEO Steps Down." Bloomberg. https://www.bloomberg.com/news/articles/2017-06-12/ge-s-immelt-to-receive-at-least-112-million-as-ceo-steps-down (Accessed Aug. 23, 2018)

21. Leadership Traits

65   United States. Department of the Navy. "Marine Corps Values: A User's Guide for Discussion Leaders." *Marine Corps Tactical Publication No. 6-10B.* (United States Govern-ment, 2016) 15-19—15-20.

66   "Marine Corps Values: A User's Guide for Discussion Leaders." 15-19.

67   Ibid., 15-17—15-18.

68   Ibid., 15-19.

69   Ibid., 15-18.

70   Ibid., 15-20—15-21.

71   Ibid., 15-19.

72   Ibid., 15-18.

73   Ibid., 15-17.

74   Ibid., 15-21.

75   Ibid., 15-17.

76   Ibid., 15-20.

77   Ibid., 15-20.

78   Ibid., 15-18 – 15-19.

22. Leadership Principles

79   United States. Department of the Navy. "Marine Corps Values: A User's Guide for Discussion Leaders." *Marine Corps Tactical Publication No. 6-10B.* (United States Government, 2016). 15-22.

80   "Marine Corps Values: A User's Guide for Discussion Leaders." 15-22 – 15-23.

81   Ibid., 15-23.

82   Ibid., 15-24.

83   Ardolino, Bill. *Fallujah Awakens: Marines, Sheiks, and the Battle Against al Qaeda.* Annapolis: Naval Institute Press, 2013. Kindle Edition. (Kindle Locations 490-502).

84   "Marine Corps Values: A User's Guide for Discussion Leaders." 15-25.

85   Ibid., 15-25 – 15-26.

86   Ibid., 15-26 – 15-27.

87   Ibid., 15-28.

88   Ibid., 15-29.

89   Ibid., 15-30.

90   Ibid., 15-30 – 15-31.

23. Delegation

91   Gatchel, Theodore L. "Gunny, Put Up The Flagpole." *Marine Corps Gazette*.

92   Blake, Jenny. "How to Decide Which Tasks to Delegate." *Harvard Business Review*. https://hbr.org/2017/07/how-to-decide-which-tasks-to-delegate (Accessed Aug. 31, 2018)

93   Schleckser, Jim. "When to Delegate? Try the 70 Percent Rule." *Inc*. https://www.inc.com/jim-schleckser/the-70-rule-when-to-delegate.html (Accessed Sept. 1, 2018)

94   Simmons, Mark R. "The 80 Percent Rule for Delegation." *Thinking Bigger*. https://ithinkbigger.com/80-percent-rule-delegate/ (Accessed Sept. 1, 2018)

24. Supervision ("the S in BAMCIS")

95   "TACTICAL PLANNING B2B2367 STUDENT HANDOUT." UNITED STATES MARINE CORPS. THE BASIC SCHOOL. MARINE CORPS TRAINING COMMAND. 5-7. https://www.trng-cmd.marines.mil/Portals/207/Docs/TBS/B2B2367%20Tactical%20Planning.pdf   (Accessed Aug. 24, 2018)

96   "TACTICAL PLANNING B2B2367 STUDENT HANDOUT." 7.

97   "M240B MEDIUM MACHINE GUN B3M0501XQ STUDENT HANDOUT." UNITED STATES MARINE CORPS. THE BASIC SCHOOL. MARINE CORPS TRAINING COMMAND. https://www.trngcmd.marines.mil/Portals/207/Docs/TBS/B3M0501XQ%20M240B%20Medi-um%20Machine%20Gun.pdf (Accessed Aug. 24, 2018)

98   Hobbs, Stephen, Zhu, Yiran, and Chokey, Aric. "New details: How the Parkland school shooting unfolded." *Sun-Sentinel*. http://www.sun-sentinel.com/local/broward/park-land/florida-school-shooting/sfl-florida-school-shooting-timeline-20180424-htmlstory.html (Accessed Aug. 24, 2018)

99   Batchelor, Amanda. "Coral Springs police moved past deputies to enter Stoneman Douglas, reports state." Associated Press. https://www.local10.com/news/park-land-school-shooting/coral-springs-police-moved-past-deputies-to-enter-stoneman-doug-las-reports-state (Accessed Aug. 24, 2018)

100   Glover, Erika. "Broward County Sheriff Scott Israel refusing to resign telling @nbc6 ..." Twitter. https://twitter.com/ErikaGloverNBC6/status/967811615419707394/video/1 (Accessed Aug. 24, 2018)

101   Smiley, David. "Broward sheriff on shooting response: 'I can only take responsibility for what I knew about.'" *Miami Herald*. https://www.miamiherald.com/news/local/commu-nity/broward/article202057404.html (Accessed Aug. 24, 2018)

102   Bacon, John. "Scorned Parkland school cop Scot Peterson: 'It was my job, and I didn't find him'." *USA Today*. https://www.usatoday.com/story/news/nation/2018/06/04/scot-pe-terson-parkland-shooting-school-resource-officer/668353002/ (Accessed Aug. 24, 2018)

103   Burch, Audra D.S. and Blinder, Alan. "Parkland Officer Who Stayed Outside During Shooting Faces Criminal Charges. *The New York Times*. https://www.nytimes.com/2019/06/04/us/parkland-scot-peterson.html (Accessed June 22, 2019)

104   O'Matz, Megan. "Broward Sheriff Scott Israel faces 'no confidence' vote by his deputies." *Sun-Sentinel*. http://www.sun-sentinel.com/local/broward/fl-school-shooting-sheriff-confidence-vote-20180420-story.html (Accessed Aug. 24, 2018)

105   Batchelor, Amanda. "BSO deputies union puts up second billboard calling for governor to fire Israel." Associated Press. https://www.local10.com/news/parkland-school-shooting/bso-deputies-union-puts-up-second-billboard-calling-for-governor-to-fire-israel   (Accessed Aug. 24, 2018)

106   Valys, Phillip. "Who is Broward County Sheriff Scott Israel?" *Sun-Sentinel*. http://www.sun-sentinel.com/local/broward/parkland/florida-school-shooting/fl-florida-school-shooting-who-is-broward-sheriff-scott-israel-20180223-story.html (Accessed Aug. 24, 2018)

107   Huriash, Lisa J., Man, Anthony, Trischitta, Linda, and Wallman, Brittany. "Sheriff Scott Israel dumped over Parkland shooting failures; new sheriff is Gregory Tony." *South Florida Sun Sentinel*. https://www.sun-sentinel.com/local/broward/fl-ne-ron-desantis-scott-israel-decision-20190110-story.html (Accessed June 22, 2019)

108   Saunders, Forrest. "Scott Israel plans to run for Broward County Sheriff regardless of appeal's outcome." WFTS - ABC Action News. https://www.abcactionnews.com/israel-plans-to-run-for-broward-county-sheriff-regardless-of-appeals-outcome (Accessed June 22, 2019)

25. The 4 Indicators of Leadership

109   Marine Corps Institute: Fundamentals of Marine Corps Leadership (Page 3-1)

27. Trust

110   United States. Department of the Navy. *Warfighting*. *Marine Corps Doctrinal Publication No. 1*. (United States Government, 1997), 77-78.

111   "Iraqi Army." GlobalSecurity.org. https://www.globalsecurity.org/military/world/iraq/army.htm (Accessed June 29, 2019)

112   Larcker, David and Tayan, Brian. "The Management of Berkshire Hathaway." Case Studies. The Stanford School of Business. https://www.gsb.stanford.edu/faculty-research/case-studies/management-berkshire-hathaway (Accessed Aug. 18, 2018)

113   Lynch, Shana. "What Is It Like to Be Owned by Warren Buffett?" *Insights by Stanford Business*. https://www.gsb.stanford.edu/insights/what-it-be-owned-warren-buffett (Accessed Aug. 18, 2018)

28. Mission Tactics

114   United States. Department of the Navy. *Warfighting. Marine Corps Doctrinal Publication No. 1.* (United States Government, 1997), 85-86.

115   Higgins, Peter E. "Historical Applications of Maneuver Warfare in the 20th Century." Thesis, USA Command & Staff College, 1990. Retrieved from: https://www.globalsecurity.org/military/library/report/1990/HPE.htm

116   United States. Department of the Navy. *Warfighting.* 88-89.

29. Decentralized Command & Control

117   United States. Department of the Navy. *Warfighting. Marine Corps Doctrinal Publication No. 1.* (United States Government, 1997), 77-78.

118   *Warfighting.* 81

119   Keyur. "A Family of Companies – Johnson & Johnson." Assignment: Technology and Operations Management Course. Harvard Business School. https://rctom.hbs.org/submission/a-family-of-companies-johnson-johnson/ (accessed Aug. 17, 2018)

120   "Johnson & Johnson CEO William Weldon: Leadership in a Decentralized Company." *Knowledge@Wharton.* Wharton University of Pennsylvania. http://knowledge.wharton.upenn.edu/article/johnson-johnson-ceo-william-weldon-leadership-in-a-decentralized-company/ (accessed Aug. 17, 2018)

121   Conlin, Michelle. "The most decentralized company in the world." *Forbes.* https://www.forbes.com/forbes/1999/0111/6301142a.html#a81f3c78292c (accessed Aug. 17, 2018)

122   Lee, Louise. Nicholas Bloom: Decentralized Firms are More Recession-Proof. *Insights by Stanford Business.* https://www.gsb.stanford.edu/insights/nicholas-bloom-decentralized-firms-are-more-recession-proof (accessed Aug. 17, 2018)

123   Note: This is a true story, but some of the details have been changes to protect identities.

31. Simplicity

124   Carlson, Ben. "Napoleon's Corporal." *A Wealth of Common Sense.* http://awealthofcommonsense.com/2016/04/napoleons-corporal/ (Accessed Aug. 18, 2018)

125   The United States Marine Corps Officer Candidates School Training Command. "THE OPERATION ORDER – PART 1 (S.M.E.A.C.)" TACT 3020-1. https://www.usnavy.vt.edu/Marines/PLC_Junior/Fall_Semester/TACT3020_Op_Order1_Student_Outline.pdf (Accessed Aug. 18, 2018)

126   "BREVITY: MULTISERVICE BREVITY CODES." *Marine Corps Reference Publication No. 3-25B*. (United States Government, 2002). http://www.dtic.mil/dtic/tr/fulltext/u2/a404426. pdf (Accessed Aug. 8, 2018)

32. Standard Operating Procedures

127   UNITED STATES MARINE CORPS. "Marine Corps Artillery Fire Support Training Standing Operating Procedures (SOP)." JRegtO P3570.2. http://sill-www.army.mil/usmc/ documents/fire_support.pdf (Accessed Aug. 19, 2018)

128   United States. Department of the Navy. *Tactics, Techniques, and Procedures For Fire Support for the Combined Arms Commander*. Marine Corps Resource Publication No. 3-16C. (United States Government, 2002). 21

129   Farber, Betty. "8 Steps to a Successful Sales Call." *Entrepreneur*. https://www.entre-preneur.com/article/207016 (Accessed on Aug. 19, 2018)

34. Friction

130   "FMFM 1 Warfighting." https://www.marines.mil/Portals/1/Publications/MCDP %201%20Warfighting.pdf (Accessed Aug. 19, 2018)

131   United States. Department of the Navy. *Warfighting. Marine Corps Doctrinal Publication No. 1*. (United States Government, 1997), 5-6.

132   Author interview with Marine Corps Special Operator; name and identity withheld by request.

35. Detachment

133   Clausewitz, Carl von. *On War*. Princeton University Press, Princeton, 1976, 101. Via FitzSimons, Peter. "The Fog of War." Penguin.com.au. https://www.penguin.com.au/books/ victory-at-villers-bretonneux-9781742759531/article/1088-fog-war (Accessed Aug. 24, 2018)

134   Murray, Seb. "How brain science found its way into business school." *Financial Times*. https://www.ft.com/content/623f049a-1269-11e8-a765-993b2440bd73 (Accessed Aug. 24, 2018)

135   Nauert, Rick. "Stress May Impair Decision-Making." *PsychCentral*. https://psychcen-tral.com/news/2008/11/21/stress-may-impair-decision-making/3390.html (Accessed Aug. 24, 2018)

136   "Chronic Stress Linked to Mild Cognitive Impairment and Other Health Problems." *University Health News Daily*. https://universityhealthnews.com/daily/depression/chronic-stress-linked-to-mild-cognitive-impairment-and-other-health-problems/ (Accessed Aug. 24, 2018)

36. The Force Multiplier

137   Gatchel, Theodore L. "Gunny, Put Up The Flagpole." *Marine Corps Gazette*.

Introduction: The Trust-Based Leader

138   United States. Department of the Navy. *Warfighting. Marine Corps Doctrinal Publication No. 1*. (United States Government, 1997), Preface.

139   United States. Department of the Navy. *Warfighting*. 18.

37. Character

140   Henriques, Gregg. Virtue and the Four Types of Character. *Psychology Today*. https://www.psychologytoday.com/us/blog/theory-knowledge/201306/virtue-and-the-four-types-character (Accessed Sept 29, 2018)

141   Ibid.

142   Krulak, Charles C. "The Strategic Corporal: Leadership in the Three Block War." *Marines Magazine* https://apps.dtic.mil/dtic/tr/fulltext/u2/a399413.pdf (Accessed Sept. 29, 2018)

143   "String of Social Media Scandals Plagues Military." NBC News. https://www.nbcnews.com/news/military/string-social-media-scandals-plagues-military-n40501 (Accessed Sept. 29, 2018)

144   "US to probe Taliban corpses desecration." Reuters. https://www.pakistantoday.com.pk/2012/01/13/us-to-probe-taliban-corpses-desecration/ (Accessed Sept. 29, 2018)

145   "Former Iraqi detainees tell of riots, punishment in the sun, good Americans and pitiless ones." The Associated Press. http://legacy.utsandiego.com/news/world/iraq/20031101-0936-iraq-thecamps.html (Accessed Sept. 29, 2018)

146   Leung, Rebecca. "Abuse of Iraqi POWs by GIs Probed." 60 Minutes. https://www.cbsnews.com/news/abuse-of-iraqi-pows-by-gis-probed/ (Accessed Sept. 29, 2018)

147   McChrystal, Stanley. *My Share of the Task: A Memoir*. New York: Portfolio/ Penguin.

148   Siegel, Tara and Cowley, Stacy. "Equifax Breach Caused by Lone Employee's Error, Former C.E.O. Says." *The New York Times*. https://www.nytimes.com/2017/10/03/business/equifax-congress-data-breach.html (Accessed Sept. 29, 2018)

149   Surane, Jennifer and Westbrook, Jesse. "Equifax CIO Put '2 and 2 Together' Then Sold Stock, SEC Says." Bloomberg. https://www.bloomberg.com/news/articles/2018-03-14/sec-says-former-equifax-executive-engaged-in-insider-trading (Accessed Sept. 29, 2018)

150   Fleishman, Glenn. "Equifax Data Breach, One Year Later: Obvious Errors and No

Real Changes, New Report Says." *Fortune*. http://fortune.com/2018/09/07/equifax-data-breach-one-year-anniversary/ (Accessed Sept. 29, 2018)

151   Shen, Lucinda. "The 10 Biggest Business Scandals of 2017." *Fortune*. http://fortune.com/2017/12/31/biggest-corporate-scandals-misconduct-2017-pr/ (Accessed Sept. 29, 2018)

152   Egan, Matt. "I called the Wells Fargo ethics line and was fired." CNN Money. https://money.cnn.com/2016/09/21/investing/wells-fargo-fired-workers-retaliation-fake-accounts/index.html (Accessed Sept. 29, 2018)

39. Courage

153   "'I can't forgive myself': US veterans suffering alone in guilt over wartime events" The Associated Press. https://www.cbsnews.com/news/i-cant-forgive-myself-us-veterans-suffering-alone-in-guilt-over-wartime-events/ (accessed October 5, 2018)

154   Wood, David. "The Grunts: Damned If They Kill, Damned If They Don't." *The Huffington Post*. http://projects.huffingtonpost.com/moral-injury/the-grunts (Accessed October 5, 2018)

155   Burke, Jeremy. "Bill Gates says he dropped out of Harvard because he was scared of missing out on the personal computing revolution." *Business Insider*. https://www.businessinsider.com/bill-gates-on-dropping-out-of-harvard-for-the-computing-revolution-2018-2 (Accessed October 5, 2018)

156   Kirk Ladendorf. "Dell remembers his beginning while looking toward the future" *Austin American-Statesman*. November 27, 2011, pp. E1, E2.

157   Dell, Michael. "First financial statement for @Dell. The one I used to convince my parents that it was OK for me to not go back to college." 6:47 PM--17 Mar 2018. Tweet. "https://twitter.com/MichaelDell/status/975186931138080768?ref_src=twsrc%5Etfw&ref_url=https:timesofindia.indiatimes.com/business/international-business/how-dell-founder-convinced-parents-to-drop-out-of-college/articleshow/63363208.cms&tfw_site=timesofindia (Accessed Oct. 5, 2018)

158   Rozenfeld, Minica. "How DIY Electronics Startup Adafruit Industries Became a Multimillion-Dollar Company." theinstitute. http://theinstitute.ieee.org/career-and-education/startups/how-diy-electronics-startup-adafruit-industries-became-a-multimillion-dollar-company (Accessed Oct. 5, 2018)

41. Thriving In Chaos

159   Keyes, Ralph. "The Quote Verifier." *The Antioch Review*. Vol. 64, No. 2, Glorious Gardens (Spring, 2006), p. 256

160   Collins, Jim and Hansen, Morten T. *Great by Choice: Uncertainty, Chaos, and Luck-Why Some Thrive Despite Them All*. HarperBusiness, 2011.

161   Roscher, Ellie. "Keeping Faith: The Next Chapter." Personal Blog. https://ellieroscher.com/2014/09/01/keeping-faith-the-next-chapter/ (Accessed Sept. 20, 2018)

162   Magee, Tamlin. "Bitcoin and beyond: Which banks are investing in blockchain?" *Techworld*. https://www.techworld.com/picture-gallery/business/bitcoin-beyond-how-banks-are-investing-in-blockchain-technology-3625324/ (Accessed Sept. 23, 2018)

42. Resilience

163   Kearney, Mike and Ruggeri, Chris. "7 Lessons for Resilient Leaders." *The Wall Street Journal*. https://deloitte.wsj.com/cmo/2018/08/02/7-lessons-for-resilient-leaders/ (Accessed July 7,2019)

43. Team Player

164   *Collins English Dictionary*. "esprit de corps." https://www.collinsdictionary.com/us/dictionary/english/esprit-de-corps (Accessed October 10, 2018)

44. Developing Leaders

165   Wukovits, John. "Survival At Sugarloaf: US Marines in Okinawa." *Warfare History Network*. https://warfarehistorynetwork.com/daily/wwii/survival-at-sugarloaf-u-s-marines-in-okinawa/ (Accessed Oct. 24, 2018)

166   Mockenhaupt, Brian. "When Leaders Die in Battle: What It Means for the Soldiers Who Live On." *The Atlantic*. https://www.theatlantic.com/international/archive/2012/11/when-leaders-die-in-battle-what-it-means-for-the-soldiers-who-live-on/265080/ (Accessed Oct. 24, 2018)

167   "Workplace Loyalties Change, but the Value of Mentoring Doesn't." *Knowledge@Wharton*. http://knowledge.wharton.upenn.edu/article/workplace-loyalties-change-but-the-value-of-mentoring-doesnt/ (Accessed Oct. 26, 2018)

168   Ibid.

169   Eby, Lillian T., Allen, Tammy D., Evans, Sarah C., Ng, Thomas, and DuBois, David. "Does Mentoring Matter? A Multidisciplinary Meta-Analysis Comparing Mentored and Non-Mentored Individuals." *Journal of Vocational Behavior*. 2008 Apr; 72(2): 254–267.

45. Sharing Hardship

170   Wukovits, John. "Survival At Sugarloaf: US Marines in Okinawa." *Warfare History Network*. https://warfarehistorynetwork.com/daily/wwii/survival-at-sugarloaf-u-s-marines-in-okinawa/ (Accessed Oct. 24, 2018)

171   Hirschfeld Davis, Julie. "50 Years After Tet Offensive, a Marine Receives the Medal of Honor." *The New York Times*. https://www.nytimes.com/2018/10/17/us/politics/canley-medal-of-honor.html (Accessed Nov. 1, 2018)

172	Gleeson, Mat and Robinson, Ric. "Sgt. Maj. John Canley — Fearless Marine to be Awarded Medal of Honor." US Marine Corps on YouTube. https://www.youtube.com/watch?v=r-dYgU8FPUE (Accessed Nov. 1, 2018)

173	Estrada, Erik. "Medal of Honor Recipient Sgt. Maj. John Canley." US Marine Corps on Facebook. https://www.facebook.com/marines/videos/730677797272368/ (Accessed Nov. 1, 2018)

174	Arzola, Jamie. "Vietnam War Hero Sgt. Maj. John Canley to be Awarded Medal of Honor." US Marine Corps on YouTube. https://www.youtube.com/watch?v=jMZG1QKJoEQ (Accessed Nov. 1, 2018)

175	Sinek, Simon. *Leaders Eat Last: Why Some Teams Pull Together and Others Don't*. Book description via Amazon.com. https://www.amazon.com/Leaders-Eat-Last-Together-Others/dp/1543614620 (Accessed Nov. 1, 2018)

176	Schogol, Jeff. "Did Gen. Mattis pull duty on Christmas so a Marine could be with his family?" *Stars and Stripes*. https://www.stripes.com/blogs-archive/the-rumor-doctor/the-rumor-doctor-1.104348/did-gen-mattis-pull-duty-on-christmas-so-a-marine-could-be-with-his-family-1.134995#.W938wS2ZPex (Accessed Nov. 1, 2018)

46. Lifelong Learner

177	United States. Department of the Navy. *Warfighting. Marine Corps Doctrinal Publication No. 1*. (United States Government, 1997), 63-64

178	"Jay Luvaas > Quotes." Goodreads. https://www.goodreads.com/author/quotes/137391.Jay_Luvaas (Accessed Oct. 13, 2018)

179	Kaplan, Fred. "Counterinsurgency by the Book." *Slate*. https://slate.com/news-and-politics/2006/07/decoding-a-new-army-manual.html (Accessed Oct. 13, 2018)

180	Fisher, Max. "The Iraq success story that propelled David Petraeus to the top." *The Washington Post*. https://www.washingtonpost.com/news/worldviews/wp/2012/11/09/the-iraq-success-story-that-propelled-david-petraeus-to-the-top/?noredirect=on&utm_term=.6e60fe62e702 (Accessed Oct. 13, 2018)

181	Packer, George. "The Lessons of Tal Afar." *The New Yorker*. https://www.newyorker.com/magazine/2006/04/10/the-lesson-of-tal-afar (Accessed Oct. 13, 2018)

182	Ardolino, Bill. *Fallujah Awakens: Marines, Sheiks, and the Battle Against al Qaeda*. Annapolis: Naval Institute Press, 2013. Kindle Edition. (Kindle Locations 1725-1736)

183	Heffernan, Margaret. "Why mergers fail." *CBS MoneyWatch*. https://www.cbsnews.com/news/why-mergers-fail/ (Accessed Oct. 13, 2018)

184	Rozario, Keith. "OpenSource Gold: The greatest Crowdsourcing story ever told."

keithrozario.com. https://www.keithrozario.com/2012/07/opensource-gold-the-greatest-crowdsourcing-story-ever-told.html (Accessed Oct. 13, 2018)

185   Wilson, Reid. "Watch the US transition from a manufacturing economy to a service economy, in one gif." *The Washington Post.* https://www.washingtonpost.com/blogs/gov-beat/wp/2014/09/03/watch-the-u-s-transition-from-a-manufacturing-economy-to-a-ser-vice-economy-in-one-gif/?utm_term=.eda083adba64 (Accessed Oct. 13, 2018)

47. Adaptability: Leadership Styles

186   Kavanagh, Earon. "Three Leadership Models: Kurt Lewin, Hershey and Blanchard, and Edwin Friedman." earonkavanagh.ca. https://www.scribd.com/document/350236677/Cio-Leader (Accessed Nov. 2, 2018)

187   Kurt Lewin: How our environment shapes our behavior. *Psychology Today.* https://www.psychologytoday.com/us/articles/200103/kurt-lewin (Accessed Nov. 1, 2018)

188   Elissa Tucker, Sue Lam, (2014) "Dynamic leadership – a leadership shortage solu-tion." *Strategic HR Review*, Vol. 13 Issue: 4/5. pp.199-204. https://doi.org/10.1108/SHR-06-2014-0035

189   Beer, Michael, Finnström, Magnus, and Schrader, Derek. "Why Leadership Training Fails—and What to Do About It." *Harvard Business Review.* https://hbr.org/2016/10/why-leadership-training-fails-and-what-to-do-about-it (Accessed Nov. 7, 2018)

190   Gurdjian, Pierre, Halbeisen, Thomas, and Lane, Kevin. "Why leadership-develop-ment programs fail." *McKinsey Quarterly.* https://www.mckinsey.com/featured-insights/leadership/why-leadership-development-programs-fail (Accessed Nov. 7, 2018)

191   Cherry, Kendra. "Leadership Styles and Frameworks You Should Know." *Verywell Mind.* https://www.verywellmind.com/leadership-styles-2795312 (Accessed Nov. 10, 2018)

192   Schawbel, Dan. "Jeffrey Pfeffer: What Most People Don't Know About Leadership." *Forbes.* https://www.forbes.com/sites/danschawbel/2015/09/15/jeffrey-pfeffer-what-most-people-dont-know-about-leadership/ (Accessed Nov. 4, 2018)

193   Eduardus. "Autocratic leadership – Martha Stewart." *Small becomes Giant.* https://smallbecomesgiant.wordpress.com/2013/04/24/autocratic-leadership-martha-stewart/ (Accessed Nov. 2, 2018)

194   Gross, Rebekah. "Style Maven Martha Stewart: The Dark Side of Her Leadership." *Penn State Liberal Arts Online.* https://sites.psu.edu/leaderfoundationsdobbs/2017/02/12/style-maven-martha-stewart-the-dark-side-of-her-leadership/ (Accessed Nov. 2, 2018)

195   McNichol, Tom. "Be a Jerk: The Worst Business Lesson From the Steve Jobs Biog-raphy." *The Atlantic.* https://www.theatlantic.com/business/archive/2011/11/be-a-jerk-the-worst-business-lesson-from-the-steve-jobs-biography/249136/ (Accessed Nov. 6, 2018)

196   "Biz Stone > Quotes." Goodreads. https://www.goodreads.com/author/quotes/251243.Biz_Stone (Accessed Nov. 8, 2018)

197   Agrawal, AJ. "Jobs or Gates: Differences in Leadership." *Inc.* https://www.inc.com/aj-agrawal/jobs-or-gates-differences-in-leadership.html (Accessed nov. 7, 2018)

198   "Laissez-Faire Leadership and Warren Buffett." *PennState LEADERSHIP PSYCH 485 blog.* https://sites.psu.edu/leadership/2013/11/10/laissez-faire-leadership-and-warren-buffett/ (Accessed Nov. 10, 2018)

199   Larcker, David and Tayan, Brian. "The Management of Berkshire Hathaway." Case Studies. The Stanford School of Business. https://www.gsb.stanford.edu/faculty-research/case-studies/management-berkshire-hathaway (Accessed Aug. 18, 2018)

200   Cherry, Kendra. "Leadership Styles and Frameworks You Should Know." *Verywell Mind.* https://www.verywellmind.com/leadership-styles-2795312 (Accessed Nov. 10, 2018)

52. Haters, Helpers, Critics, and Cowards

201   Jackman, Jay M. And Strober, Myra H. "Fear of Feedback." *Harvard Business Review.* https://hbr.org/2003/04/fear-of-feedback (Accessed July 20, 2019)

53. On Self-Leadership

202   Dolbier, Christyn L., Soderstrom, Mike, and Steinhardt, Mary A. "The Relationships Between Self-Leadership and Enhanced Psychological, Health, and Work Outcomes." *The Journal of Psychology Interdisciplinary and Applied.* https://www.researchgate.net/publication/11555115_The_Relationships_Between_Self-Leadership_and_Enhanced_Psychological_Health_and_Work_Outcomes (Accessed July 21, 2019)

203   Lipman, Victor. "All Successful Leaders Need This Quality: Self-Awareness." *Forbes.* https://www.forbes.com/sites/victorlipman/2013/11/18/all-successful-leaders-need-this-quality-self-awareness/#219ce1031f06 (Accessed July 21, 2019)

204   Lipman, Victor. "Why Are So Many Employees Disengaged?" *Forbes.* https://www.forbes.com/sites/victorlipman/2013/01/18/why-are-so-many-employees-disengaged/#2a810dca1e22 (Accessed July 21, 2019)

205   Bandura, Albert. *Self-Efficacy: The Exercise of Control.* W H Freeman & Co., 1997.

206   Bandura, Albert. *Social Foundations of Thought and Action: A Social Cognitive Theory.* Prentice Hall, 1985.

54. On Servant Leadership

207   Wagner, Daniel R. "Servant Leadership - A Vision for Inspiring the Best from our Marines." *Marine Corps Gazette* 88, no. 1 (2004): 54.

208   "Full text of 'Marine Corps manual.'" Internet Archive. https://archive.org/stream/marinecorpsmanua00unit/marinecorpsmanua00unit_djvu.txt (Accessed Aug. 21, 2018)

209   "Fortune's Best Companies to Work For With Servant Leadership." *Modern Servant Leader.* https://www.modernservantleader.com/servant-leadership/fortunes-best-companies-to-work-for-with-servant-leadership/ (Accessed June 15, 2019)

210   Brenoff, Ann. "What We Can Learn From The Man Who Runs The 'World's Happiest Company.'" *HuffPost.* https://www.huffpost.com/entry/worlds-best-company_n_4655292 (Accessed July 21, 2019)

211   Margolin, Katya. "How Patagonia's unique leadership structure enabled them to thrive." Virgin *Technology* blog. https://www.virgin.com/entrepreneur/how-patagonias-unique-leadership-structure-enabled-them-thrive (Accessed July 21, 2019)

212   Fick, Nathaniel C. *One Bullet Away: The Making of a Marine Officer.* Houghton Mifflin Harcourt, 2005.

213   Schogol, Jeff. "Did Gen. Mattis pull duty on Christmas so a Marine could be with his family?" *Stars and Stripes.* https://www.stripes.com/blogs-archive/the-rumor-doctor/the-rumor-doctor-1.104348/did-gen-mattis-pull-duty-on-christmas-so-a-marine-could-be-with-his-family-1.134995#.W938wS2ZPex (Accessed Nov. 1, 2018)

214   Coerr, Stanton S. "I Served With James Mattis. Here's What I Learned From Him." *The Federalist.* https://thefederalist.com/2016/12/02/served-james-mattis-heres-learned/ (Accessed July 21, 2019)

56. On Humility

215   Prime, Jeanine and Salib, Elizabeth. "The Best Leaders Are Humble Leaders." *Harvard Business Review.* https://hbr.org/2014/05/the-best-leaders-are-humble-leaders (Accessed July 21, 2019)

216   Merryman, Ashley. "Leaders are more powerful when they're humble, new research shows." *The Washington Post.* https://www.washingtonpost.com/news/inspired-life/wp/2016/12/08/leaders-are-more-powerful-when-theyre-humble-new-research-shows/?noredirect=on&utm_term=.1b6c9e9a8e8e (Accessed July 21, 2019)

217   Merryman, Ashley.

60. Do Your Teammates Make Their Beds?

218   "Adm. McRaven Urges Graduates to Find Courage to Change the World." *UT News.* https://news.utexas.edu/2014/05/16/mcraven-urges-graduates-to-find-courage-to-change-the-world/ (Accessed July 28, 2019)

66. Having Tough Conversations

219   Runde, Craig. "Effectiveness Study - Conflict and Your Career." *Mediate.com*. https://https://www.mediate.com/articles/rundec.cfm (Accessed July 27, 2019)

220   Harter, Jim and Agrawal, Sangeeta. "Actively Disengaged Workers and Jobless in Equally Poor Health." Gallup. https://news.gallup.com/poll/147191/actively-disen-gaged-workers-jobless-equally-poor-health.aspx (Accessed July 27, 2019)

Notes

Notes

CPSIA information can be obtained
at www.ICGtesting.com
Printed in the USA
LVHW062026190723
752909LV00008B/19